Selected Letters of
RAYMOND CHANDLER

Photo by John Engstead

Selected Letters of
RAYMOND CHANDLER

EDITED BY
Frank MacShane

Columbia University Press
New York

books by Frank MacShane

THE LIFE OF RAYMOND CHANDLER
THE LIFE OF JOHN O'HARA

Columbia University Press / New York

Letters of Raymond Chandler copyright © 1981 College Trustees Ltd; introduction, editorial matter, and selection copyright © 1981 Frank MacShane

Library of Congress Cataloging in Publication Data

Chandler, Raymond, 1888–1959.
  Selected letters of Raymond Chandler.

  Includes index.
  1. Chandler, Raymond, 1888–1959—
Correspondence.   2. Authors, American—20th
century—Correspondence.   I. MacShane, Frank.
II. Title.
PS3505.H3224Z48   1981   813'.54   [B]   81-4852
ISBN   0–231–05080–1   AACR2
11 10 9 8 7 6 5 4 3

Contents

Chronology

1888	Born in Chicago, July 23
1895	Moved to London with mother.
1900	Entered Dulwich College as day student.
1904	Graduation from Dulwich.
1905–1906	In France and Germany as student.
1907	Worked as clerk in the Admiralty, London.
1908–1911	Literary journalist in London, contributing to the *Academy* and the *Westminster Gazette*.
1912	Returned to America, settling in California.
1917	Enlisted in Canadian Army.
1918	Served in France as corporal in British Columbia Regiment.
1919	Discharged, returned to Los Angeles, entered oil business.
1924	Married Cissy Pascal.
1932	Fired from oil business for drinking.
1933	Began to write. Story "Blackmailers Don't Shoot" published in *Black Mask*.
1934–1938	Lived in Los Angeles, contributing to *Black Mask* and *Dime Detective Magazine*.
1939	Publication of *The Big Sleep* by Alfred Knopf and by Hamish Hamilton.
1940	Publication of *Farewell, My Lovely* by Alfred Knopf and by Hamish Hamilton.
1943	Collaborated on screenplay of James M. Cain's *Double Indemnity* for Paramount. Publication of *The High Window* by Alfred Knopf and by Hamish Hamilton. Contributed articles to *The Atlantic Monthly*.
1944	Publication of *The Lady in the Lake* by Alfred Knopf and by Hamish Hamilton.
1945	Wrote original screenplay *The Blue Dahlia* for Paramount.
1946	Moved to La Jolla from Los Angeles.

1947	Wrote original screenplay *Playback* for Universal.
1949	Publication of *The Little Sister* by Houghton Mifflin and by Hamish Hamilton.
1950	Publication of *The Simple Art of Murder* (early stories) by Houghton Mifflin and by Hamish Hamilton. Worked on screenplay of *Strangers on a Train* for Warner Brothers.
1952	Trip to England with Cissy.
1953	Publication of *The Long Goodbye* by Hamish Hamilton; published by Houghton Mifflin in 1954.
1954	Death of Cissy.
1955	Attempted suicide, trip to England.
1956–1957	Lived both in London and in La Jolla.
1958	Publication of *Playback* (novel) by Hamish Hamilton and by Houghton Mifflin.
1959	Died in La Jolla, March 26.

The Recipients

(The list does not include most editors of periodicals and correspondents personally unknown to Chandler.)

CLEVE ADAMS: Fellow detective writer and contributor to *Black Mask* magazine.

FREDERICK LEWIS ALLEN: Editor of *Harper's Magazine* and writer.

ALEX BARRIS: Canadian journalist and interviewer.

BERNICE BAUMGARTEN: Editor at Brandt and Brandt literary agency and wife of James Gould Cozzens. Miss Baumgarten handled booklength fiction at the agency.

JEAN BETHEL: Wife of Erle Stanley Gardner.

CARL BRANDT: Chandler's agent (1948–1952) and head of Brandt and Brandt literary agency. Brandt handled magazine publications for the agency.

PAUL BROOKS: President of Houghton Mifflin Company.

JAMES M. CAIN: American author of *Double Indemnity*, *The Postman Always Rings Twice*, and other novels.

ALAN K. CAMPBELL: Assistant Director of the Harvard Summer School.

ROBERT CAMPIGNY: French literary critic and reviewer.

EDGAR CARTER: Associate in H. N. Swanson literary agency, Hollywood.

GEORGE HARMON COXE: Fellow detective writer and contributor to *Black Mask* magazine.

FREDERICK DANNAY: With Manfred Lee, author of books published under the pseudonym of Ellery Queen.

JEAN DE LEON: Chandler's London secretary.

BERGEN EVANS: American language expert.

IAN FLEMING: English author of spy novels.

JAMES N. FOX: Dutch-born writer of adventure novels.

J. FRANCIS: Proprietor of Prince's Bookshop, Piccadilly, London.

ERLE STANLEY GARDNER: Fellow detective novelist and contributor to *Black Mask*.

DOROTHY GARDINER: Secretary of Mystery Writers of America and later co-editor of *Raymond Chandler Speaking*.

DEIRDRE GARTRELL: Young Australian correspondent whom Chandler never met.

PHILIP GASKELL: Bibliophile and librarian of King's College, Cambridge.

WILLIAM GAULT: Detective writer and novelist, author of *Bloody Bokhara*, *Ring Around Rosa*, and many other books—living in California.

MICHAEL GILBERT: English mystery writer and Chandler's solicitor in London.

HELGA GREENE: Chandler's last literary agent and later his executrix and heir.

MAURICE GUINNESS: English detective novelist, a cousin of Helga Greene.

HAMISH HAMILTON: Chandler's English publisher.

JOHN HERSEY: American novelist.

ALFRED HITCHCOCK: English film director.

H. F. HOSE: Chandler's contemporary and a master at Dulwich College.

JOHN HOUSEMAN: Hollywood producer of *The Blue Dahlia* and many other films and plays.

JAMES HOWARD: Official of Mystery Writers of America.

HOWARD HUNT: Author and diplomat, later involved in Watergate scandals under President Nixon.

JAMES KEDDIE: Sherlock Holmes enthusiast and book collector; member of the "Baker Street Irregulars."

ALFRED A. KNOPF: Chandler's first American publisher.

BLANCHE KNOPF: Wife of Alfred Knopf and his associate at the publishing house.

GENE LEVITT: Adaptor of Chandler stories to radio.

LUCIANO LUCANIA: Known as Lucky Luciano, a well-known Italian-American criminal.

ROGER MACHELL: Director of Hamish Hamilton Ltd., Chandler's English publishers.

W. SOMERSET MAUGHAM: English novelist and playwright.

FINLEY McDERMID: Production head at M.G.M. studios, Hollywood.

JUANITA MESSICK: Chandler's secretary in La Jolla for many years.

NEIL MORGAN: Columnist for San Diego *Evening Tribune*.

CHARLES MORTON: Associate Editor of *The Atlantic Monthly*.

HARDWICK MOSELEY: Sales Manager at Houghton Mifflin Company.

E. JACK NEUMAN: Writer and adaptor of Chandler's stories to television.

LUTHER NICHOLS: Book editor of the San Francisco *Examiner*.

FRANK NORMAN: English novelist and playwright. Chandler wrote the preface for his first book, *Bang to Rights*.

ERIC PARTRIDGE: English literary critic and lexicographer, author of *A Dictionary of Slang and Unconventional English* in which he frequently cited Chandler.

S. J. PERELMAN: American writer and humorist, frequent contributor to *The New Yorker*. He parodied Chandler in a story called "Farewell, My Lovely Appetizer."

J. B. PRIESTLEY: English novelist and playwright, author of *Rain Upon Godshill*, *Let the People Sing* and many other books.

LEONARD RUSSELL: English critic, literary editor of the *Sunday Times* of London.

JAMES SANDOE: Librarian at the University of Colorado, critic and reviewer of detective fiction.

WILLIAM W. SEWARD: Professor at Tift College, Forsyth, Georgia.

SOL SIEGEL: Executive at Twentieth Century-Fox studio in Hollywood.

JOSEPH SISTROM: Producer at Paramount studio, connected with various films Chandler worked on.

WILBUR SMITH: Librarian and head of Special Collections at the University of California at Los Angeles. Chandler's papers are now collected there.

RAY STARK: Hollywood agent representing clients of Carl Brandt, later a producer.

H. N. SWANSON: Hollywood literary agent, known for representing such writers as Faulkner, Fitzgerald, O'Hara and Chandler.

WILLIAM TARG: New York publisher, connected with various houses.

E. C. THIESSEN: Assistant Treasurer, *The Atlantic Monthly*.

WILLIAM TOWNEND: School friend of Chandler's from Dulwich College.

JESSICA TYNDALE: Friend of Chandler's in New York and representative of Guinness Mahon bank in America.

DALE WARREN: Publicity director of Houghton Mifflin Company.

EDWARD WEEKS: Editor of *The Atlantic Monthly*.

LEROY WRIGHT: Chandler's lawyer in San Diego.

Introduction

"I have written letters that would have made Eros hysterical and I have also written long serious letters on literary technique as well as I understand it," wrote Raymond Chandler to his publisher. Chandler was not a vain man, but he understood his capabilities. "It is true," he said, "that in letters I sometimes seem to have been more penetrating than in any other kind of writing—at times—and that as I reread some of them, I am really astonished,—astonished at the facility of expression and the range of thought I seemed to show even when I was only a struggling beginner."

In an age when the telephone has gradually killed off correspondence, Chandler, the author of such internationally famous mystery novels as *The Big Sleep*, *Farewell, My Lovely*, and *The Long Goodbye*, was one of the greatest letter writers of his time. "I don't know why the hell I write so many letters," he noted. "I guess," he answered himself, "my mind is just too active for my own good."

Chandler began his literary career in London after leaving Dulwich College in 1905. Although born in the United States, in 1888, he had been educated in England. When his American father deserted the family, his Anglo-Irish mother took him to England to stay with her relatives in London. Chandler's pre-World War I schooling equipped him with a classical education and wistful sentiments. Like his contemporary, T. S. Eliot, he wrote melancholy romantic poems and sketches about shabby houses and empty streets. Chandler contributed to a number of literary weeklies in Bloomsbury but failed to make a go of it. He therefore returned to America and settled in Los Angeles. He learned accounting and became a bookkeeper in a number of banks, dairies, and other commercial establishments. After the war, in which he served in France with the Canadian army, he returned once more to California. He eventually became employed by the Dabney Oil Syndicate and rose to become office manager and director of several of its subsidiary companies.

For the ten years he worked in the oil business, Chandler seems to have been oblivious of literature, although he knew cultured and literary people in Los Angeles. He lived with his mother, and after she died, he married Cissy Pascal, an accomplished pianist who divorced her husband in order to marry him. She was seventeen years older than Chandler was, but when he married her he didn't know she was so much older nor did she look it. In time, however, Chandler seems to have grown discontented with his life. He started to drink, and finding himself often in the company of his younger contemporaries, he began to look for women younger and more exciting than Cissy was. By 1932, the situation had reached a crisis, and he was fired from his job for alcoholism. Despite the bad times, the jolt was sufficient to make him want to take up writing again. Although he had published nothing, he listed himself as a writer in the Los Angeles phone book and began his first serious apprenticeship as a fiction writer. He lived on savings and on money provided by his friends who had faith in his capacities.

Chandler wanted to be a "serious" writer and tried to imitate Hemingway and other prominent writers of the time, but his critical mind always interfered and made him feel inadequate. Then one day he came across some pulp magazines specializing in detective fiction. He decided to try his hand at this genre and soon found it congenial. Because no one took this kind of writing seriously, he did not feel inhibited by his own or anybody else's standards. He read and imitated the work of such established writers of the "tough guy" school of American detective fiction as Erle Stanley Gardner and Dashiell Hammett. By 1933, he published his first story in *Black Mask*, the most celebrated detective magazine of the period. Over the next five or six years, he continued to write stories and novellas, gradually developing his skill and extending his range. In 1939, he published his first novel, *The Big Sleep*. Although this book did not make his reputation overnight, among detective story enthusiasts it established him as one of the most brilliant new members of the "hard-boiled" school of crime fiction.

Over the next four years, he brought out *Farewell, My Lovely*, *The High Window*, and *The Lady in the Lake*. Together, they established Chandler's literary reputation, but they did not provide him the income he had expected. Paperback sales were then not so lucrative as they have since become for popular writers. He therefore began writing screenplays for Hollywood. His appearance at Paramount and other studios coincided with the growing popularity of such gangster and crime films as *The Maltese Falcon*. His first job was to collaborate with Billy Wilder on a screen version of James M. Cain's *Double Indemnity*. The film was a success and Chandler was given other assignments. But Chandler disliked working in the studios. As an artist, he was too independent to accept willingly the interference with and alteration of his work by other writers and by directors for whom he had little respect. When he had earned enough to live on, he withdrew from Hollywood and moved with Cissy to La Jolla where he lived for most of the rest of his life.

By this time, he had become world famous as a writer, and his next books, *The Little Sister* and *The Long Goodbye*, established him not simply as an American crime writer of the first rank, but as a novelist who rendered the actualities of American life as vividly and independently as any "straight" novelist. It was a triumph of style that he was able to transform a limited type of fiction into something having universal appeal. He virtually created Los Angeles as a literary entity, and this was the great achievement of the last decade of his life.

Despite the worldly qualities of his novels and the colorful life of his central character, Philip Marlowe, Chandler was himself a retiring person. Even in Hollywood, he had been a recluse. "I suppose in some ways I was a bit of a stinker in Hollywood," he wrote. "No swimming pool, no stone marten coats for a floozie in an apartment, no charge account at Romanoff's, no parties, no ranch with riding horses, none of the trimmings at all." Chandler found social activity difficult because he needed alcohol to relax. But if he drank, he tended to lose control of himself and to drink too much. It was safer to stay at home, especially as Cissy was now in her late seventies and tiring easily.

Driven more and more to depend on his own resources, Chandler turned to letter writing as a means of communicating with the outside world. He passed the long insomniac evenings after Cissy had gone to bed writing to correspondents from all over the world. Mostly he wrote to business associates—his publishers, agents, magazine editors, or professional critics of detective fiction. Rarely did he correspond with other writers or those whose letters might have nourished him as surely his delighted others. But his correspondence meant so much to him that he said, "all of my best friends I have never met."

For Chandler, letter writing was an emotional release from his isolation. Discussing his letters with his English publisher, he noted that "some are analytical, some are a bit poetical, some sad, and a good many caustic or even funny. They reveal, I suppose, a writer's reaction to his early struggles and later his attempts to ward off the numerous people who seek to exploit him in some way. There are also love letters and letters to an unknown girl in Australia which were merely a rather kind attempt to resolve her problems after she had given me more of her heart than (as she said) she had ever given to any of her family." These letters were also an important outlet for a writer who, in order to achieve success in fiction writing, had restricted himself to detective stories. There was so much left over, crying to get out. "A real writer," Chandler wrote, "and at times I think I am one, exists on many levels of thought. Perhaps as a result of my business training I always knew that a writer had to follow a line with which the public would become familiar. He had to 'type' himself to the extent that the public would associate his name (if they remembered it) with a certain kind of writing. But that would not be enough for him in his own mind. So I suppose in my letters I more or less revealed those facets of my mind which had to be obscured or distorted in what I wrote for publication."

Chandler dictated many of his letters onto discs while sitting in his study late at night, and the next day the secretary typed them up. Taken together, they are more like a writer's notebook than ordinary correspondence. A letter might begin with a business matter, but soon Chandler would move on to more enchanting subjects—his childhood in England, the position of the writer in Hollywood, his current reading, what it takes to be a novelist, or the mores of Southern California, where he lived like an alien in his own country, half-amused, half-outraged by the world around him.

Chandler never held back in his letters. He expressed his feelings and beliefs bluntly and honestly. He was a man of passion who could also express ideas in a rational and convincing way. His letters reveal the man behind Philip Marlowe as a writer who understands art and beauty but who has no patience with the pretentiousness that is so often a part of the literary life. His prose is forceful and vigorous, the product of a classical education that gave him a sense of form and structure. His feelings arise from his sensitivity to his surroundings, and he expresses them in metaphor, using a street vocabulary that keeps all phoniness at bay.

Many writers reserve their best energies for their own novels, short stories, or poems. Others reverse the process and waste their creative powers on correspondence. The peculiar circumstances of Chandler's life placed him in between these extremes. Chandler probably would not have written more fiction had he corresponded less. He took the detective story about as far as it could go in *The Long Goodbye*. Anything else would have been a repetition. Chandler's letters are long and generous because he had much more to say and because in his loneliness he wanted to express his thoughts and feelings to whoever would write him in return.

After his wife's death in 1954, Chandler began a slow decline. The last five years of his life were marked by frantic attempts to find a solution to loneliness, and his letters are filled with details of his domestic life as he moved back and forth from California to England in search of solace. As his life fell apart through drink and illness, his letters became less interesting and more verbose. Still, he knew he had made his mark. Swinburne once wrote that to publish an author's private letters was "to commit a despicable act of felony." But in his own lifetime Chandler had enough sense of his achievement to consider this possibility himself, even though he had doubts about the value of his letters to others: "Please believe I am not asking you to publish them at all," he wrote his English publisher, "merely wondering whether they could possibly be of enough interest to be worth publishing."

Over the years since his death on March 26, 1959 Chandler's letters have been frequently quoted in books and magazines. This testimony to their lasting power helps explain why they are gathered together here. They document a sad but decent life and also the achievement of one of the finest letter writers American literature has produced over the last two hundred years.

.   .   .

The texts of the letters are reproduced as Chandler wrote them, except for a few editorial changes. Chandler was often inconsistent in punctuation, spelling, and dating his letters, and for consistency I have italicized the names of books and films. I have also corrected obvious misspellings and typographical errors, and have supplied single words that were accidentally dropped. I have also changed Chandler's use of quotation marks, which was sometimes American, sometimes British, and sometimes a combination of the two, to standard American usage. I have not standardized Chandler's spellings, however, but have preserved the British and American variants, and I have left the dates of his letters as he had written them. The correspondents, for the most part, are identified in the list of recipients (see p. ix). Brief footnotes have been supplied within the letters where necessary.

The letters reproduced in this collection fall into different categories. The first are reproduced from signed original letters or photocopies of original letters. The second category consists of carbon copies of letters dictated or written by Chandler. These do not contain any emendations that might have been made on the original letters, nor are they signed. Therefore, they have been reproduced here without signatures. A few of the letters here reproduced have been taken from transcripts made of Chandler's correspondence by Dorothy Gardiner when she was preparing a collection of Chandler's writing called *Raymond Chandler Speaking*. I have indicated these by footnotes in the text. These transcripts are less reliable than original letters, since Miss Gardiner occasionally altered the word order or made cuts, without, however, changing the substance of a given letter. There are fewer than ten letters taken from transcripts; all the other letters in this collection are reproduced from the first two categories cited—original letters or carbon copies.

Wherever possible, I have reproduced the complete letter. On occasion, however, I have deleted material, and for any of three reasons: (1) the same information may have already appeared in another letter; (2) the material excised may be of no enduring interest (generally such omitted material relates to business matters Chandler has brought up with his agent or one of his publishers); (3) the material omitted may be private and perhaps hurtful to someone still living. All substantial excisions are indicated by three dots widely spaced between paragraphs.

Occasionally there are excisions within a sentence indicated by ellipses. These generally indicate that the material omitted is private and possibly damaging to a living individual. In the few letters reproduced by Dorothy Gardiner's transcripts, there are also ellipses, but I cannot explain the reason for the cuts she made. Sometimes an individual's name is indicated by a blank line, but as with other omissions, these are rare. Every effort has been made to keep the letters as complete as possible within the limits of taste and common sense.

·   ·   ·

Chandler's letters are found in three different types of collection. The first of these are university and public libraries. The largest of these is the Chandler collection in the Department of Special Collections at the library of the University of California at Los Angeles. Chandler himself helped establish this collection, and it contains, apart from books and manuscripts, original letters and photocopies of letters to many individuals such as James Sandoe and John Houseman. Dorothy Gardiner's transcripts have also been deposited in this collection. Other university libraries contain small collections: Boston University has Chandler's correspondence with Charles Morton of the *Atlantic Monthly*; Harvard has letters from Chandler to Dale Warren, Hardwick Moseley, and others at Houghton Mifflin Company; Indiana University owns Chandler's letters to Ian Fleming and Frank Norman; the Library of Congress has a letter to James Cain from Chandler; the University of Texas owns letters between Chandler and Erle Stanley Gardner, Somerset Maugham, and J. B. Priestley; Yale owns Chandler's letters to George Harmon Coxe.

The second category consists of large private collections. The most important of these is owned by Helga Greene, Chandler's agent and literary executor. This collection is in fact made up of Chandler's own private files, and it contains original letters as well as carbon copies and drafts of letters. Other large collections are those owned by Brandt & Brandt, Chandler's agents; Hamish Hamilton Ltd., his English publishers; and Alfred Knopf Inc., his first American publishers.

Smaller collections, which make up the third category, are owned by the *Atlantic Monthly*, Jean DeLeon, William Gault, James M. Fox, Juanita Messick, Neil Morgan, Dilys Powell, Jessica Tyndale, and Leroy Wright. I am grateful to all of these individuals and institutions for their help and kindness in making this correspondence available.

In addition, I should like to thank a number of individuals who have helped me in various ways. Some have called my attention to letters or have lent me those in their possession; others have gone out of their way to be helpful in other ways. I wish to record my thanks to all of them, and in particular Hilda Bohene, Carl Brandt, William Cagle, George Harmon Coxe, Bernard Crystal, Keith Deutsch, David Farmer, Donald Gallup, Deirdre Gartrell, Philip Gaskell, Howard Gotlieb, Hamish Hamilton, John Houseman, Howard Hunt, James Keddie, William Koshland, Elfrieda Lang, Gene Levitt, Kenneth Lohf, Roger Machell, James Mink, E. Jack Neuman, Frank Norman, Austin Olney, Robert S. Powell, Kathrine Sorley Walker, Edward Weeks, Stanley Wertheim, and Brooke Whiting. I hope I have not inadvertently omitted the name of anyone whose name should be here.

Above all, I am grateful to Helga Greene for her warm and consistent help to me with this project. Without her kindness and generosity, this book would never have been made possible.

Frank MacShane

The Letters

TO THE EDITOR OF
THE FORTNIGHTLY INTRUDER[1]

June 15, 1937

Sirs:

Your essay on flower arrangement is priceless, as much so as the typography of your sheet, but to what audience in heaven's name do you address yourselves? You are precious, you write in a dead language, and in the delicate and occasionally sterile tones of the Eighteenth Century. You are of a pretty wit and a soothing yet deadly irony. Are there people who admire such fanciful tricks? I have lived in this city for some twenty-five years and now I find you, apparently also of its citizenry, dwelling with Chinese calm in a past that was even then as improbable as the novels of Richardson. Occasionally, also, as dull.

Your little paper one receives with pleasure, and yet with a certain discomfort, like a voice from an ancient chimney on a gusty October night. One hears death in it, and is tired of hearing death in so many things. You are decadent in an environment which, for all its fancy pants, is still provincial. You have the deadly smoothness of an old pistol grip.

It is only a few short years since I was told, with more emphasis than hope, that the American gentleman did not spit. Doth

---

1. A bibliophile's magazine, edited by William K. Etter, Jr. and published in Los Angeles. The text of the letter, including its omissions, is taken directly from the magazine.

[1]

he not so? I thought, then someday I shall meet him. Of course I did, but not so soon as I thought.

Who, except those by life already defeated and wasting in the twilight, has any taste for such writing as yours? I ask to know. Perhaps we are on the verge of a classic revival. God knows I am very tired of talking without moving my lips. But I'm a little afraid you are received too much with kindness, too little with understanding, that you come as a nostalgia for the Age of Culture (whatever that is, and may it rot, if it must be called by that odious word), and that you are accepted with that bewildered desperation which the Ladies of the Friday Morning Club reserved for the visiting English novelists of the tepid years before the War.

You too, Sirs, I should like to think of with gardenias in your morning coats, with grey-striped trousers of impeccable vicuna, with parted hair, and with the soft birdsong of the Oxford close in your gentle throats. But I'm afraid you wear corduroy pants and talk the flat language of the dehydrated New Englander. It is almost certain to be so. This American mind has its peculiar thinness. It acquires learning only by losing blood.

I wish you success—and can not, alas, predict it.
Sirs, Your Obedient Humble Servant,

R.C., Esqr.

TO THE EDITOR OF
THE FORTNIGHTLY INTRUDER

July 1, 1937

You do kid rather easily, don't you, pals? That I state a case against you is bosh. I pay you grave compliments and you mistake them for sneers. I call you precious, being precious myself. As to the corduroy pants, the remark was dated. It slipped out of my 1928 Anthology.

[2]

That you should have pride in your purer American heritage of language seems to me a slight thing. Latin became corrupt, but French is a sharper language than Latin ever was. The best writing in English today is done by Americans, but not in any purist tradition. They have roughed the language around as Shakespeare did and done it the violence of melodrama and the press box. They have knocked over tombs and sneered at the dead. Which is as it should be. There are too many dead men and there is too much talk about them.

But all this is beside the point, and still I lack the information for which I wrote to you the first time. It was kind of you to answer so soon, and at all. But who reads you? One knows, roughly, what sort of people read the *Post*, *Esquire*, *Terror Tales*, *New Republic*, *Mercury*, and the grand old man of Arlington Street, the *Atlantic*. But one suspects in the last case, where there is definite intention to preserve clarity of thought and expression and to exclude the sophisticated gimcracks of the cocktail mob, not only a paucity of support—which is a fact—, but a large element of snob readers whose minds are marionettes as completely as the fans of _____ or the followers of _____.

You see, I have lived here so long. I have perhaps been unfortunate, but I have not met the people who would like your kind of writing, unless someone first told them they must like to be saved.

R.C., Esq.

TO ALFRED A. KNOPF

Route 1, Box 421
Riverside, Calif
Feb. 19th. 1939

Dear Mr. Knopf:—
Please accept my thanks for your friendly letter and please believe that, whether you wrote to me or not, I should have written to thank you for the splendid send-off you are trying to give me.

[3]

Having been more or less in business a great part of my life, I have some appreciation of what this involves, even though I know nothing of the publishing business.

Mr. Conroy wrote to me twice that you had said something about my getting to work on another book and I answered him that I wanted to put it off until I had an idea what kind of reception this one would get. I have only seen four notices, but two of them seemed more occupied with the depravity and unpleasantness of the book than with anything else. In fact the notice from the *New York Times*, which a clipping agency sent me as a come-on, deflated me pretty thoroughly. I do not want to write depraved books. I was aware that this yarn had some fairly unpleasant citizens in it, but my fiction was learned in a rough school, and I probably didn't notice them much. I was more intrigued by a situation where the mystery is solved by the exposition and understanding of a single character, always well in evidence, rather than by the slow and sometimes long-winded concatenation of circumstances. That's a point which may not interest reviewers of first novels, but it interested me very much. However, there's a very good notice in today's *Los Angeles Times* and I don't feel quite such a connoisseur of moral decay as I did yesterday. They have Humphrey Bogart playing the lead, which I am in favor of also.[1] It only remains to convince Warner Brothers.

As to the next job of work for your consideration, I should like, if you approve, to try to jack it up a few more notches. It must be kept sharp, swift and racy, of course, but I think it could be a little less harsh—or do you not agree? I should like to do something which would not be automatically out for pictures and which yet would not let down whatever public I may acquire. *The Big Sleep* is very unequally written. There are scenes that are all right, but there are other scenes still much too pulpy. Insofar as I am able I want to develop an objective method—but slowly—to the point where I can carry an audience over into a genuine dramatic, even melodramatic, novel, written in a very vivid and pungent style, but not slangy or overly vernacular. I realize that this must be done cautiously and little by little, but I think it can be done. To acquire delicacy without losing power, that's the problem. But I should

1. In the film version of the novel, which was directed by Howard Hawks.

probably do a minimum of three mystery novels before I try anything else.

Thank you again and I do hope that when the returns are in, you will be not too disappointed.

Very sincerely,

Raymond Chandler

TO GEORGE HARMON COXE

Route 1 Box 421 Riverside
April 9th. 1939

Dear George:—

Thanks for your letter, and I much appreciate your remarks about it and about the detective story business in general. I had a talk with Sanders[1] while he was out here, and after that I'm surprized that anyone writes or publishes the darn things at all. He told me about Simon and Schuster's Inner Sanctum mysteries, for instance. Yet about 150 mystery books are dished out every year. I suppose if you are good enough there is a bare living in it—very bare. However I'm used to that. I don't think I'd ever make the grade with slick magazines, unless in some kind of story quite different from anything I have attempted so far. I can't read their stuff for my own amusement, and that seems to be fatal. I should never have tried to work for *Black Mask*, if I hadn't, at one time, got a kick out of reading it.[2]

Knopf seems to think that if somebody comes along who can write as well as Hammett, he should have Hammett's success.[3] Knopf

1. Sydney Sanders, Chandler's first literary agent.
2. *Black Mask*, a famous magazine of hard-boiled detective stories, edited by Joseph T. Shaw.
3. Dashiell Hammett, founder of the hard-boiled school and author of such detective novels as *The Maltese Falcon* and *The Dain Curse*.

[5]

being a publisher should know his business, but my feeling is that somebody might come along who wrote a great deal better than Hammett and still not have anything like Hammett's success. But of course these things are quite unpredictable. In my opinion *Thieves Like Us* by Edward Anderson was an infinitely better and honester book than *Of Mice and Men*.[4] Did it get anywhere? I doubt it.

Your letter doesn't sound very happy somehow. I had the idea that you would do well in Hollywood for a long time, that you had enough facility, and that you had enough character not to be impressed by the phoney side. Of course I don't know you very well. Personally I think Hollywood is poison to any writer, the graveyard of talent. I have always thought so. But perhaps I have lived too close to it.

I'm terribly sorry about Shaw.[5] He never told me anything about his affairs, always had the attitude (that rather pathetic attitude of small men trying to maintain their pride) that his failures were his own choice. He had left the *Black Mask* on a matter of policy and he had left the agency he was with because too much was going on for a man to do his own thinking. That sort of attitude, not those words. I suppose it's natural enough. It's bad enough to be kicked in the seat of the pants without having to go around and show the bruise. But as to his success or lack of it as an agent I knew absolutely nothing, except what I might deduce from the fact that he had no secretary. I think it was natural for him to think an opportunity existed for a type of agent who might be more than a marketer of merchandise. In the long run, if he could stick it out, and if he was adaptable enough, there might have been. Unfortunately he is not very adaptable and he wants to run his writers. The only kind of writers you can run are the ones who are negative, and they're hardly worth running. It's too tough a racket for people who have to be propped up from behind. Yet Shaw has, strangely enough, a great insight into writing and he can give a man a buck up when he needs it as nobody else I know can, or does. That should be worth a lot somewhere. I agree with you that he ought to have a magazine. I'd like to see him have the magazine which for years I've wondered somebody did not think worth publishing, a high class pulp detective

4. Novel by John Steinbeck.
5. See note 2.

story magazine aimed at the rather large class of people who find the pulps mostly too juvenile and who don't like the big magazines because of their fundamental dishonesty in the matter of character and motivation. He himself thought the market existed, I know, but he was doubtful about the supply of material. In that I think he was wrong, because the magazine would in a short time create its own material. Sanders told me the big magazines are getting steadily more and more starved for material, largely because of the lowering of prices and standards in the pulps. New writers do not appear to replace the ones who go to Hollywood and either stay there or learn how not to write there and never get over it. And the new writers don't appear because there's nothing in the business anymore, no encouragement to do good work, and no recognition if, in spite of all practical considerations, you insist on trying to do it. I think the effect of this will be that some of the slick magazines will become more catholic in their tastes, more receptive to stories without Boy Meets Girl motivation, even to stories with unsatisfactory endings. Probably there will be some lowering of rates to balance some loss of cheap chic advertising. But in the long run there will be better and more readable magazines. I'm hoping.

If you come out to the Coast to live, you should look at La Jolla, before you decide where to live. I think it is a much better place than Laguna in every possible way. It is dear for a small town, but it has a perfect climate both winter and summer, the finest coastline on the Pacific side of the country, no billboards or concessions or beachfront shacks, an air of cool decency and good manners that is almost startling in California. It has a few writers, not too many, no Bohemian atmosphere (but they will let you take a drink). It has fine public tennis courts and a nice gang of people who play good, but not *too* good, tennis. It has good schools, including a very fine private girls school, a hospital, and is one of the most prosperous looking places you ever laid eyes on. I'm not being paid by the Chamber of Commerce either. I simply feel that La Jolla has that intangible air of good breeding, which one imagines may still exist in New England, but which certainly does not exist any more in or around Los Angeles. In theory one may not value very much that quality. One may like a free and easy neighborhood where they smash the empty bottles on the sidewalk on Saturday night. But in practice it's very comfortable. I expect to go back there in the fall, because

[7]

whatever is the matter with me, climate seems to make very little difference, and I hate these poor man's towns. My idea of perfection would be a home in La Jolla and a very good cabin at Big Bear Lake, not too close to Pine Knot. Maybe I'll have them before my joints begin to creak very badly.

Regards and best wishes. If you write again, send me news of Nebel.[6] I've never met him, but I have always thought a lot of him.

Ray

TO ERLE STANLEY GARDNER

Route 1 Box 421
Riverside, California
May 5th 1939

Dear Erle,

.   .   .

When we were talking about the old *Action Detective* magazine I forgot to tell you that I learned to write a novelette on one of yours about a man named Rex Kane, who was an alter ego of Ed Jenkins and got mixed up with some flowery dame in a hilltop house in Hollywood who was running an anti-blackmail organization. You wouldn't remember. It's probably in your file No. 54276–84. The idea, probably not at all original to me, was so good that I tried to work it out on another tyro later on, but he couldn't see putting the effort into something he knew he couldn't sell, preferring to put the effort into nineteen things he thought he could sell and couldn't. I simply made an extremely detailed synopsis of your story and from that rewrote it and then compared what I had with yours, and then went back and rewrote it some more, and so on. It looked pretty good. Incidentally, I found out that the trickiest part of your technique was the ability to put over situations which verged on the

6. Frederick Nebel, fellow *Black Mask* writer.

[8]

implausible but which in the reading seemed quite real. I hope you understand that I mean this as a compliment. I have never come even near to doing it myself. Dumas had this quality in a very strong degree. Also Dickens. It's probably the fundamental of all rapid work, because naturally rapid work has a large measure of improvisation, and to make an improvised scene seem inevitable is quite a trick. At least I think so.

And here I am at 2.30 A.M. writing about technique, in spite of a strong conviction that the moment a man begins to talk about technique, that's proof he is fresh out of ideas.

Best wishes to you all,

Chandler

TO BLANCHE KNOPF

Box 481 Big Bear Lake Calif
August 23rd. 1939

Dear Mrs. Knopf:

The effort to keep my mind off the war has reduced me to the mental age of seven. The things by which we live are the distant flashes of insect wings in a clouded sunlight. But——

I enjoyed meeting you so much. There is a touch of the desert about everything in California, and about the minds of the people who live here. During the years when I hated the place I couldn't get away, and now that I have grown to need the harsh smell of the sage I still feel rather out of place here. But my wife is a New Yorker, and that 95 with unlimited humidity doesn't appeal much either.

If I could write another 12,000 words I should have a draft of a book finished. I know what to write, but I have momentarily mislaid the urge. However by the end of September, as you said, there should be something for you to wrinkle your very polite nose at. It's rather a mixed up mess that will run 75,000 words but I'll likely cut it at least 5000 and perhaps more. It will take me a month to shape it up. The

[9]

title, if you should happen to approve, is *The Second Murderer*.[1] Please refer to King Richard III, Act I, Scene IV.

Second Murderer: What, shall we stab him when he sleeps?

First Murderer: No; then he will say 'twas done cowardly
                    when he wakes . . .
                    How dost thou feel thyself now?

Second Murderer: 'Faith, some certain dregs of conscience are yet
                    within me.

However the joker is that the second murderer is———?

Sanders has been impressing on me the dire necessity of so contriving a detective story that it might be serialized. This is only horse sense, even though good serials seldom make good novels. I do not think this particular opus is the one he is looking for. In fact, I'm very sure of it. I'm not sure anyone is looking for it, but there's a law against burning trash up here during the fire hazard.

> Yours very truly,
>
> Raymond Chandler

TO GEORGE HARMON COXE

> Box 481
> Big Bear Lake Calif.
> October 17th. 1939

Dear George:

.   .   .

I have never made any money out of writing. I work too slowly, throw away too much, and what I write that sells is not at all the sort of thing I really want to write. I often envy these lads whose minds

---

1. Original title of Chandler's second novel, published as *Farewell, My Lovely*.

are tuned to the sort of story the slick magazines like—so that they really think it is good. I can't get around to that point of view. I sold a story to the *Post*[1] recently, but I wrote it principally because Sanders pestered me to try something for *Collier's*. I didn't think much of the story when I wrote it—I felt that it was artificial, untrue and emotionally dishonest like all slick fiction. Sanders didn't seem to think much of it either. However he sold it. I still don't know whether it is any good. When I read it in print I thought it was, but print can be so deceiving. On the other hand one of my oldest friends took the trouble to write me two pages telling me how lousy it was. I suppose you have had the same experience. Whatever you do you get smacked in the face and usually from an unprotected angle.

Is your house built and are you in it? How are you getting along? I suppose if I read the right magazines, I should know. I should like to come east very much and find somewhere to live there that is not too hot and full of mosquitos (or mosquitoes) in summer and not too damn cold in winter. Is there such a place, where a poor man can live? I'm sick of California and the kind of people it breeds. Of course I like La Jolla, but La Jolla is only a sort of escape from reality. It's not typical. Anyhow, it's not in the least a matter of how good California is or how intransigent I am. If after twenty years I still fail to like the place, it seems that the case is hopeless. My wife came from New York. She likes California except during the hot months, but I think she agrees with me that the percentage of phonies in the population is increasing. No doubt in years, or centuries to come, this will be the center of civilization, if there is any left, but the melting-pot stage bores me horribly. I like people with manners, grace, some social intuition, an education slightly above the Reader's Digest fan, people whose pride of living does not express itself in their kitchen gadgets and their automobiles. I distrust Jews, although I admit that the really nice Jew is probably the salt of the earth. I don't like people who can't sit for half an hour without a glass in their hands, although apart from that I think I should prefer an amiable drunk to Henry Ford. I like a conservative atmosphere, a sense of the past, I like everything that Americans of past generations used to go and look for in Europe, but at the same time I don't want to be bound by the rules. It all seems like asking a bit too much, now that I've written it. I like all the things about England which Margaret Halsey[2] liked and many of the things she didn't like, but that is largely because I was brought up there and English manners don't intimidate me. But I don't like Margaret Halsey, or any writer for whom a laborious and fizzled wisecrack is better than a simple truth.

.　　　.　　　.

Let's hear your news

Ray

TO GEORGE HARMON COXE

1265 Park Row
La Jolla Calif.
Dec 19th. 1939

Dear George:

Thanks for your nice meaty letter of October 30th. which I hasten to answer with my usual headlong dash for the basket. Also for the photo of your house. It must be nice to have a home. We haven't had one in so long that I look back with a touch of nostalgia to any place we have stayed in as long as six months. I don't think we shall be here long either. Too dear, too damp, too elderly, a nice place, as a visitor remarked this afternoon, for old people and their parents.

If you still have that spare copy of your last book but one I'm hoping you are still feeling generous about it. The stock in the local library is all out anyway. You're not represented. But so are not a lot of other people who should be, and so *are* represented some mighty feeble gestures at detective fiction. What do you make of a place that has one book by Hemingway, nothing by Faulkner, or Hammett,

2. Margaret Halsey, *With Malice Towards Some*, 1938.

[12]

two pieces of oh-so-irritating wise guy crap by one Kurt Steel,[1] *everything* by one J. S. Fletcher a British brother who is far far duller than even a British brother has any right to be,[2] nothing by Coxe, Nebel, Whitfield,[3] or anybody you would think of as at all representative. And my god no Gardner, yet a book called *The Bigger They Come* by A. A. Fair which copies the Gardner technique exactly and even swiped Gardner's idea of how Ed Jenkins couldn't be extradited.[4]

I had to throw my second book away, so that leaves me with nothing to show for the last six months and possibly nothing to eat for the next six. But it also leaves the world a far far better place to live in than if I had not thrown it away.

The literary colony here has undergone a few modifications since we were here last year. That is, those of the boys who are making any money are now playing their tennis at the Beach Club. The old caste system at its dirty work again. I don't think the beach club is very expensive, but a few bucks off his whisky ration plays hell with a writer's inspiration. Max Miller[5] still frequents the public courts. He is a tall angular sourpuss with motheaten hair and very surly manners and a habit of swearing under his breath at himself and out loud at his partner. He is a splendid example of the good rule, Never Meet a Writer if You Liked his Book. There is also a dick pulp writer who writes under the name of Dale something or other—I daresay I could find out. Maybe it's Dale Carnegie.[6] This one has the shoulders of a weight-lifter and is very temperamental, throwing rackets and making tragic gestures at the sky, both arms extended and a look of agony on his face. Off hand I would say he is a lead nickel, but you never know. He might be The Shadow.[7]

.   .   .

RC

1. Author of *Murder of a Dead Man* (1935) and other mystery stories.
2. Author of *Mill House Murder* (1937), *And Sudden Death* (1938), and many other mystery novels.
3. George Harmon Coxe, Frederick Nebel, and Raoul Whitfield were all members of the "tough guy" school of American detective fiction.
4. A. A. Fair was, in fact, a psudonym used by Erle Stanley Gardner.
5. Author of *I Cover the Waterfront* and a neighbor of Chandler's.
6. Ronal Kaiser, who wrote under the name of Dale Clark.
7. Hero of a popular radio series.

TO BLANCHE KNOPF

818 West Duarte Road
Monrovia
California
January 17th. 1940

Dear Mrs. Knopf:
Terribly sorry to be so dilatory in getting out some work for you. I have had bad luck, bad health and a bad disposition for a long time. I finally did get a very rough draft done but was not at all pleased with it and had to put it aside for a while, in the hope of later discovering. whether it was just plain lousy or whether it was a distorted point of view that made me think so. However I am a bit cheered up about it (in absentia) as my researches have convinced me that just plain lousy is the normal temperature of the detective story.
The troubles of advancing age drove me away from La Jolla. I actually developed a rheumatic right arm. We have not yet found a place to live but hope to soon and when there is a little peace in a world which knows no peace—all I ask is a quiet corner and deaf and dumb neighbors—I'll get at this thing again. You couldn't do anything with it now anyway, I suppose.

With respectful greetings
Most sincerely

Raymond Chandler

TO BLANCHE KNOPF

1155 Arcadia Avenue Arcadia Calif
June 14th. 1940

Dear Mrs. Knopf:
Sorry I haven't any snapshots to send you yet. I don't know how much time there is. My wife will try to take some, a very

[14]

agonizing process for both of us, since she is very particular and I am very badly behaved. Commercial photos are no good. I am reaching the age where it takes an artistic touch to make anything of me. The fellows who have this want too much money, and I doubt the importance of the cause. While I am compelled by weight of opinion, some of it expert, some frankly prejudiced, to admit being one of the handsomest men of my generation, I also have to concede that this generation is now a little seedy, and I with it.

The last time no page proofs were sent me. Your Mr. Jacobs with whom I wrangled about this and that felt it was not necessary. I guess it wasn't. I never thought it was. As the book finally appeared there were, I think, two slight typographical errors, which should be a very low average for this kind of book. I certainly don't want to read two sets of proofs, if I don't have to. Nor do I want the set of galley proofs as finally corrected which they sent me. It seems to be a custom, but I regret to say I burned them. Too heavy to carry in my hip pocket.

One thing I should like and that is a few changes in the natty biographical sketch on the jacket, if it is to be repeated. I haven't a copy of the book here, having lent my last copy to a friend who has so far failed to return it. From memory I recall three things I didn't like, one of which was my own fault, the second a misunderstanding, the third a use of the expression "checkered career" which to me has a pejorative connotation. I used the phrase "tax expert." The word expert has become something rather trying. I'd rather omit that. The third point was that your promotion man seemed to get the impression that Dulwich College was a university. It is, in fact, one of the larger English Public Schools, not ranking with Eton, Harrow, Charterhouse, or Marlborough, but certainly ranking ahead of many of those which *Life* made a fuss over in its last issue. Incidentally the editors of *Life* seem entirely unaware that a School Tie and an Old School Tie are entirely different things. But I daresay these pathetic relics of a lost world are no longer worth accuracy.

Fourth point, and one I'm sensitive on, but one which is difficult to make other Americans understand. I am not an Irish-American in the sense commonly understood. I am of Quaker descent on both sides. The Irish family my mother belonged to had not a single Catholic relative or connection, even by marriage. Furthermore the professional classes in Southern Ireland are and always have been largely non-Catholic. Those few Irish patriots who have had brains as well as spite have also been non-Catholics. I should not like to say that in Ireland Catholicism reached its all-time low of ignorance, dirt and general degredation of the priesthood, but in my boyhood it was bad enough. It does the Irish great credit that out of this flannel-mouthed mob of petty liars and drunkards there has come no real persecution of the non-Catholic elements.

Most cordially,

Raymond Chandler

TO GEORGE HARMON COXE

1155 Arcadia Avenue
Arcadia Calif.
June 27th. 1940

Dear George:

.   .   .

On your recommendation and that alone I read Agatha Christie's *And Then There Were None*, and after reading it I wrote an analysis of it, because it was blurbed as the perfect crime story, incapable of dishonesty by reason of the way it was constructed. As entertainment I liked the first half and the opening, in particular. The second half got pallid. But as an honest crime story, honest in the sense that the reader is given a square deal and the motivation and mechanisms of the murders are sound—it is bunk. The fundamental conception of the book in particular annoyed me. Here is a judge, a jurist, a man with a touch of sadism but withal a passion for exact justice, and this man condemns to death and murders a group of people on nothing but hearsay evidence. In no case did he have a shred of actual proof that any one of them had actually committed murder. In every case it was merely someone's opinion, or a possible, even probable, inference from circumstances. But proof, even absolute inner conviction, simply did not exist. Some of these people admit their crimes, but this is all *after* the murders were planned, the judgment entered, the sentence pronounced. In other words it is as complete and shameless a bamboozling of the reader as ever was perpetrated. And I won't go into the mechanism of the crimes, most of which were predicated on pure chance, and some actually impossible. They also show an abysmal ignorance of lethal drugs and their action. But I'm very glad I read the book because it finally and for all time settled a question in my mind that had at least some lingering doubt attached to it. Whether it is possible to write a strictly honest mystery of the classic type. It isn't. To get the complication you fake the clues, the timing, the play of coincidence, assume certainties where only 50 per cent chances exist at most. To get the surprise murderer you fake character, which hits me hardest of all, because I have a sense of character. If people want to play this game, it's all right by me. But for Christ's sake let's not talk about honest mysteries. They don't exist.

Time out while I take a long breath.

The title of my book is not *The Second Murderer*, and that was not the title I had in mind when I was talking to you. I used that for a while as a working title, but I didn't like it, although Mrs. Knopf did. I didn't know it had been announced under that name. When I turned the manuscript in they howled like hell about the title, which is not at all a mystery title, but they gave in. We'll see. I think the title is an asset. They think it is a liability. One of us has to be wrong. I suppose, since they are in the business, it should be I. On the other hand I have never had any great respect for the ability of editors, publishers, play and picture producers to guess what the public will like. The record is all against them. I have always tried to put myself in the shoes of the ultimate consumer, the reader, and ignore the middleman. I have assumed that there exists in the country a fairly large group of intelligent people, some formally of good education and some educated by life, who like what I like. Of course the real trouble is that you can be read by an enormous number of people who don't buy any books. My book is supposed to come out in August. The proofs were a bloody mess. I've just finished them and don't feel at all that they are a clean job yet.

All the best,

Ray

[17]

TO BLANCHE KNOPF

449 San Vicente Boulevard
Santa Monica, Oct. 9th. [1940]

Dear Mrs. Knopf:

The above address will be good for six months, I hope.

Thanks for yours of October 1st. which only just caught up with me. I am terribly sorry about the title and all that, and because the advance sales disappointed us, but you must remember that I didn't refuse to change the title, I just couldn't think of another one, you gave me no time at all, and although I said I liked the title, that should not have made you go against your business judgment.[1] Everyone I know likes the title very much, but of course they are not in the trade. And I still think '*Zounds, He Dies* was a good title.[2] If I had had some of the time the book was being prepared, I'm sure I could have come up with something that would have satisfied you. But you caught me off base and got me rattled.

Personally, and in this I am born out by one professional opinion, I think the handicap of the title will be only temporary and that if the sales do not do anything, it will really be for some other cause. For instance, the war. A woman out here who runs a string of rental libraries in and around Hollywood told a friend of mine that one of her branches had ten copies of the book out and that she hardly ever bought more than two copies of a mystery story. She said she thought this was in part due to a "very marvelous" review in the *Hollywood Citizen-News* of Sept 21st. I hope you have seen this. Evidently they jumped the gun on the publication date. Of course it would have only a local influence, but the mere fact that a critic who confessedly does not like mystery stories and thinks they are mostly tripe should take this book seriously as a piece of writing is worth an awful lot to me. Because I am not innately a hack writer.

Syd Sanders sent me a cut of your advertisement in the *New*

---

1. When Mrs. Knopf objected to *The Second Murderer*, Chandler suggested *Farewell, My Lovely*.
2. Another suggestion Chandler had made.

York Times. I don't see how you can afford it. If that doesn't start something, what's the use?

With kindest regards,

Raymond Chandler

TO ERLE STANLEY GARDNER

857 Iliff Street
Pacific Palisades, Calif.
Feb 1st. 1941

Dear Erle:

Good God, we have moved again.

Thanks very much indeed for sending me that Brentano list, but who is this guy A. A. Fair who heads the list?[1] I got the book and read it and it held one of the three or four unmistakable techniques of detective story writing. And done to the nice crisp light brown that melts in your mouth. What goes on here? I suppose you know what I mean?

Living, if you call it that, in a big apartment house in Santa Monica, brand new and all that, I longed for your ranch. I longed for some place where I could go out at night and listen and hear the grass growing. But of course it wouldn't do for us, just the two of us, even if I had the price of a piece of virgin foothill. It's better over here, quiet and a house in a nice garden. But they are just beginning to build a house across the way. I shan't mind it as much as the good neighbors bouncing on the bed springs over at the apartment house.

Awfully sorry to hear you had been sick. I know what the streps can do to a person. Sulfanilimide seems to be able to cure anything but flat brain, which is what I suffer from.

Regards to your gang,

Ray

1. Pseudonym used by Gardner.

[19]

TO BLANCHE KNOPF

12216 Shetland Lane
Los Angeles, Calif.
March 15th. 1942

Dear Mrs. Knopf:

Your letter, kind and charming as always, reaches me at a very bad time. I'm afraid the book is not going to be any good to you.[1] No action, no likable characters, no nothing. The detective does nothing. I understand that it is being typed, which seems like a waste of money, and will be submitted to you, and I'm not sure that that is a good idea, but it is out of my hands. At least I felt that you should be relieved of any necessity of being kind to me in a situation where kindness is probably not of any use. About all I can say by way of extenuation is that I tried my best and seemed to have to get the thing out of my system. I suppose I would have kept tinkering at it indefinitely otherwise.

The thing that rather gets me down is that when I write something that is tough and fast and full of mayhem and murder, I get panned for being tough and fast and full of mayhem and murder, and then when I try to tone down a bit and develop the mental and emotional side of a situation, I get panned for leaving out what I was panned for putting in the first time. The reader expects thus and thus of Chandler because he did it before, but when he did it before he was informed that it might have been much better if he hadn't.

However all this is rather vain now. From now on, if I make mistakes, as no doubt I shall, they will not be made in a futile attempt to avoid making mistakes.

Most sincerely,

Raymond Chandler

1. *The High Window*.

[20]

TO ALFRED KNOPF[1]

Idyllwild, Calif.
July 16, 1942

Dear Mr. Knopf:

.   .   .

I think the book is a very nice job indeed. I particularly like the type, which being smaller and yet very clear, keeps the page from looking crowded. The jacket also seems to be very effective. My wife does not like the photo on the back. All the photos I sent you were bad, and this is perhaps about the best, except the very first one, which no longer looks like me. I was reading in an English book the other day and noticed the remark, "the kind of squit who has his picture on the dust cover of his book," or something like that. I feel a good deal like that myself. It is the custom in this country, of course, but most writers are such horrible-looking people that their faces destroy something which perhaps wanted to like them. Perhaps I am oversensitive, but I have several times been so repelled by such faces that I have not been able to read the books without the face coming between. Especially these fat crowlike middle-aged women's faces.

.   .   .

TO BLANCHE KNOPF

Cathedral City, California
October 22nd. 1942

Dear Mrs. Knopf:

Thank you very much for writing to me about the sales of my last story, and many thanks also for your kind invitation to lunch. But alas, I'm down here in the desert 130 miles from Beverly Hills and I'm afraid I simply can't make it this time. I'm trying to bake

1. Letter reproduced from transcript.

out a sinus condition which has been weakening me for years. Don't expect any luck, but felt it had to be tried. I hope you and Mr. Knopf are well and are bearing up under the many cares of these times.

So sorry you are feeling badly about the sales of *The High Window*.[1] Last time you were out here you told me 4000 copies was the ceiling on a mystery. Either you were just saying that to comfort a broken heart or you are now repining for nothing at all. Why should it sell any more? And why should you spend so much advertising, and such very demanding advertising? I don't know anything about promotion, but when Mr. Knopf was out here he gave me the figures on what had been spent advertising *FML*, and to me they seemed very high.[2] I said: "Can you afford it?" He said: "No." But you keep on doing it. Why? *The High Window* was not the striking and original job of work that could be promoted into anything of consequence. Some people liked it better than my other efforts, some people liked it much less. But nobody went into any screaming fits either way. I'm not disappointed in the sales. I think it did well to get by at all. I am sure Sanders thinks so. I hope the next will be livelier and better and faster, because, as you know very well, it is the pace that counts, not the logic or the plausibility or the style. I have just been reading a book called *Phantom Lady*, by William Irish,[3] whoever that is. It has one of those artificial trick plots and is full of small but excessive demands on the Goddess of Chance, but it is a swell job of writing, one that gives everything to every character, every scene, and never, like so many of our overrated novelists, just flushes the highlights and then gets scared and runs. I happen to admire this kind of writing very much. I haven't seen the book advertised anywhere and such reviews as I have seen of it show a complete unawareness of the technical merits of the book. So what the hell.

But as I said I do hope the next one will be better and that one of these days I shall turn one out that will have that fresh and sudden touch that will click. Most of all perhaps, in my rather sensitive mind, I hope the day will come when I won't have to ride around on

1. Chandler's third novel.
2. *Farewell, My Lovely*.
3. Pseudonym used by Cornell Woolrich, mystery writer.

Hammett and James Cain, like an organ grinder's monkey. Hammett is all right. I give him everything. There were a lot of things he could not do, but what he did he did superbly. But James Cain— faugh! Everything he touches smells like a billygoat. He is every kind of writer I detest, a faux naif, a Proust in greasy overalls, a dirty little boy with a piece of chalk and a board fence and nobody looking. Such people are the offal of literature, not because they write about dirty things, but because they do it in a dirty way. Nothing hard and clean and cold and ventilated. A brothel with a smell of cheap scent in the front parlor and a bucket of slops at the back door. Do I, for God's sake, sound like that? Hemingway with his eternal sleeping bag got to be pretty damn tiresome, but at least Hemingway sees it all, not just the flies on the garbage can.

Heigho. I think I'll write an English detective story, one about Superientendent Jones and the two elderly sisters in the thatched cottage, something with Latin in it and music and period furniture and a gentleman's gentleman: above all one of those books where everybody goes for nice long walks.

Yours most sincerely,

Raymond Chandler

TO ALFRED A. KNOPF

Cathedral City,
Calif.
February 8th. 1943

Dear Mr. Knopf:
Thanks for yours of Jan 14th. and it was friendly, understanding and welcome, as always. Thank you also for the two-bit edition of *The Big Sleep*. I looked into it and found it both

much better and much worse than I had expected—or than I remembered. I have been so belabored with tags like tough, hardboiled, etc., that it is almost a shock to discover occasional signs of almost normal sensitivity in the writing. On the other hand I sure did run the similes into the ground.

William Irish is a man named Cornell Woolrich, an author under his own name, and one of the oldest hands there are at the pulp detective business. He is known in the trade as an idea writer, liking the tour de force, and not much of a character man. I think his stuff is very readable, but leaves no warmth behind it.

No, I don't think the sinus condition is clearing up. This place bores me. But I've just about been talked into sticking out the mountains and the desert for another year. After that to hell with the climate, let's meet a few people. We have a one-store town here, and the meat situation would make you scream. On Wednesday morning the guy opens at 7 A.M. and all the desert rats are there waiting for him to give out numbered tickets.[1] Anybody who delays long enough to wash his face is automatically classed as parasitic and gets a high number, if he gets one at all. On Thursday at 10 the inhabitants bring their bronchitis and halitosis into the store and park in front of the meat counter and the numbers are coonshouted. When we, having a very late number, kick our way up to the collapsed hunk of hamburger we are greeted with a nervous smile that suggests a deacon caught with his hand in the collection plate, and we leave bearing off enough meat for the cat. This happens once a week and that is all that happens, in the way of meat.

Of course we go to Palm Springs. If we didn't, I should not be writing this letter. I should be out in the desert trying to dig up a dead gopher. We happened on a rib roast a couple of weeks back, just walked in and said hello, and there the damn thing was. We ate for six nights running, behind drawn curtains, chewing quietly, so the neighbors wouldn't hear.

There are a bunch of great guys in Washington, high-minded and pure, but once in a while I hunger for a touch of dirty Irish politics.

1. As part of meat rationing in wartime.

I hope to get a book out fairly soon. I am trying to think up a good title for you to want me to change.

Yours sincerely,

Raymond Chandler

TO ALFRED A. KNOPF

Paramount Pictures Inc.
5451 Marathon Avenue
Hollywood, Calif.
November 13, 1943

Dear Alfred:

.   .   .

After I get through here, which should be about the end of this month, I'm going down to the desert and try to write at least the first draft of a book which presents a certain problem. I think perhaps you could help me on it. It is to be a story about a murder involving three men and two women, and practically nobody else. It is to take place in Bel-Air, and all these characters are wealthy people except the protagonist of the story. He is my problem. I should like to do a first person story about Philip Marlowe. I wouldn't have to develop him very much more than I have already because he is the sort of guy who behaves according to the company he is in. But the story is not going to be a mystery, and I hope to avoid its being tagged as a mystery novel. Is this possible if I use a character who is already established in mystery fiction?

There are probably things to be said for and against. I am strong for keeping Marlowe alive, and I feel that I may not write any more conventional mysteries. Also, the character will probably turn out to be Marlowe anyway, even if I give him another name. Would you please let me know what you think?

        Kindest regards to yourself and Blanche,

                Raymond Chandler

TO JAMES SANDOE

                Paramount Pictures Inc.
                5451 Marathon Street
                Hollywood 38, Calif.
                January 26, 1944

Dear Mr. Sandoe:

Thank you for your very kind letter of January 12th. Somewhere put away with my papers in storage I have a complete list of all the stuff I have ever had published in this country. All the earlier stories were written for *Black Mask* when Joe Shaw was editor. The Avon Book Co. is bringing out a twenty-five cent edition in the spring sometime containing five of these novelettes. If they sell them they will probably publish others. As to your being able to obtain these old pulp magazines with stuff of mine in them, I doubt it very much. A friend of mine in Kansas City has been trying to build up a collection for years and has offered as much as two dollars a copy without any success.

What you say about me and Cain is very nice. It has always irritated me to be compared with Cain. My publisher thought it was a smart idea because he had a great success with *The Postman Always Rings Twice*, but whatever I have or lack as a writer I'm not in the least like Cain. Cain is a writer of the faux naif type, which I particularly dislike.

You are certainly not without company in your wish that "something could be done about the disadvantages of the redlight segregation of detective stories from 'novels' by the reviews." Once in a long while a detective story writer is treated as a writer, but very seldom. However, I think there are a few very good reasons why this is so. For example: (a) Most detective stories are very badly written. (b) Their principal sale is to rental libraries which depend on a commercial reading service and pay no attention to reviews. (c) I believe the detective story is marketed wrong. It is absurd to expect people to pay any more for it than they would for a movie. (d) The detective or mystery story as an art form has been so thoroughly explored that the real problem for a writer now is to avoid writing a mystery story while appearing to do so. However, none of these reasons, valid or invalid as they may be, changes the essential irritation to the writer, which is the knowledge that however well and expertly he writes a mystery story, it will be treated in one paragraph while a column and a half of respectful attention will be given to any fourth-rate, ill-constructed, mock-serious account of the life of a bunch of cotton pickers in the deep south. The French are the only people I know of who think about writing as writing. The Anglo-Saxons think first of the subject matter, and second, if at all, of the quality.

Thank you again for your letter, and believe me

Yours very truly,
Ray Chandler

TO JAMES M. CAIN

1040 Havenhurst Drive
Hollywood 46
March 20th. 1944

Dear Jim:

It was very kind of you to send me an inscribed copy of your book and I'm very grateful to you. We have been down in the desert for a month, with poor luck in weather. I don't offer that as an excuse for not writing before, the fact being that I was so completely pooped after nine months at Paramount that I couldn't even make myself write a letter. Just sat and stared morosely out of the window at the sand dunes.

[27]

Very glad to hear Warners bought *Mildred Pierce*.[1] It seems I may have a chance to work on it for them, but Paramount was not too keen about loaning me. Everybody who has seen *Double Indemnity*[2] likes it (everybody that has talked to me, at least). The feeling is that it is a pretty fine picture and for once an emotionally integrated story has got on the screen in the mood in which it was written. I don't think any of the changes we made were in conflict with your basic conception. In fact, you would have had to make them yourself. I do not doubt that some of them might have been made better, but they had to be made. The emotional integration is due to the fact that the three guys who worked on the job did not at any time disagree about what they wanted to achieve, but only on how to do it.

A curious matter I'd like to call to your attention—although you have probably been all through it with yourself—is your dialogue. Nothing could be more natural and easy and to the point on paper, and yet it doesn't quite play. We tried it out by having a couple of actors do a scene right out of the book. It had a sort of remote effect that I was at a loss to understand. It came to me then that the effect of your written dialogue is only partly sound and sense. The rest of the effect is the appearance on the page. These unevenly shaped hunks of quick-moving speech hit the eye with a sort of explosive effect. You read the stuff in batches, not in individual speech and counterspeech. On the screen this is all lost, and the essential mildness of the phrasing shows up as lacking in sharpness. They tell me that is the difference between photographic dialogue and written dialogue. For the screen everything has to be sharpened and pointed and wherever possible elided. But of course you know far more about it than I do.

I hope you get as good a script of *Mildred Pierce*. You don't need one quite so sharp. Are you working on it yourself?

All the best.

Ray

1. A novel by Cain, published in 1941.
2. Chandler and Billy Wilder wrote the screenplay for the film based on *Double Indemnity*.

TO CHARLES MORTON

Paramount Pictures Inc.
5451 Marathon Street
Hollywood, Calif.
July 17, 1944

Dear Mr. Morton:

Sydney Sanders, my agent in New York, wrote to me some time ago saying that you might be interested in having me do a short article on the modern detective story for the *Atlantic*. Naturally I was both flattered and interested by the suggestion.

The last time I had an opportunity I tried to do a rough draft of such an article, only to discover that I hadn't the least idea how to go about it. The trouble seemed to be partly that I hadn't read enough detective stories to be able to indulge in the usual casual display of erudition, and partly that I really don't seem to take the mystery element in the detective story as seriously as I should. The main trouble with most detective stories, as I see it, is that the people who write them are bad writers. But this would not be a very interesting premise for an article. The detective story as I know and like it is a not too successful attempt to combine the attributes of two disparate types of minds; the mind which can produce a coolly thought-out puzzle can't, as a rule, develop the fire and dash necessary for vivid writing.

I am going to have some time off from motion picture work in the near future and I might have a fling at this article. If you have any ideas about what you would like to see me do, it would be a great pleasure to hear from you. I presume the matter of length is also important.

Yours very truly,

Raymond Chandler

[29]

TO CHARLES MORTON

6520 Drexel Avenue
Los Angeles 36, Calif.
October 12th. 1944

Dear Charles Morton:

.   .   .

Thank you for two kind letters. I am sorry somebody has to lose a paragraph or two of marble prose to make way for such thoughts as mine, and sloppily tailored at that.[1] I could have procured you innumerable copies of *The Big Sleep*, had I known. The lunch money edition, that is. Last time I was in my agent's office (not Sanders' but the glittering palace on the Strip where my other agent parks his Daimler)[2] I noticed a whole row of them taking up shelf room and no longer of any use to anybody, since the thing is now sold to Warners and Howard Hawks is even now shooting a picture from it with Bogart and a new girl he has brought out in *To Have and Have Not*.[3] Bill Faulkner and a girl named Leigh Brackett wrote the script. 'Twill do. Hawks shoots from the cuff more or less, he tells me, merely using a rough script to try out his scenes and then rewriting them on the set. I could not have worked on it, since my contract with Paramount won't allow me to work for anyone else, even when I am not working for Paramount.

The article or diatribe or whatever on screen writing is just something I should like to do, but I cannot set a date for it at all. I am roughly halfway through a Marlowe book and may not get to the other for some time. I wish I could, but I am a fellow who writes 30,000 words to turn in five, and that is a lot of work. I do most certainly agree with you that it does even a writer no harm to use his stagnant brain once in a while in thought about something or other, and I am not deterred by any financial considerations at all. But I am getting old and my cerebrum squeaks against my cerebellum and I have to write some kind of a book before they forget me. A man of

1. "The Simple Art of Murder," an article Chandler wrote for *The Atlantic Monthly*, published December 1944.
2. Chandler's Hollywood agent was H. N. Swanson.
3. Lauren Bacall, who also starred in both films.

talent would write it in a month, a man of ability without talent in two months, and a genius would not write it at all. But it will take me about three more just to get a first draft.

The other day I thought of your suggestion for an article of studied insult about the Bay City (Santa Monica) police. A couple of D.A.'s investigators got a tip about a gambling hell in Ocean Park, a sleazy adjunct to Santa Monica. They went down there and picked up a couple of Santa Monica cops on the way, telling them they were going to kick in a box, but not telling them where it was. The cops went along with the natural reluctance of good cops to enforce the law against a paying customer, and when they found out where the place was, they mumbled brokenly: "We'd ought to talk to Captain Brown about this before we do it, boys, Captain Brown ain't going to like this." The D.A.'s men urged them heartlessly forward into the chip and bone parlor, several alleged gamblers were tossed into the sneezer and the equipment seized for evidence (a truckload of it) was stored in lockers at local police headquarters. When the D.A.'s boys came back next morning to go over it everything had disappeared but a few handfuls of white poker chips. The locks had not been tampered with, and no trace could be found of the truck or the driver. The flatfeet shook their grizzled polls in bewilderment and the investigators went back to town to hand the Jury the story. Nothing will come of it. Nothing ever does. Do you wonder I love Bay City? Alas that its gambling ships are no more. The present governor of California won his office by disposing of them. Others had tried (or pretended to) for years and years. But there was always the legal argument as to whether the 12-mile limit should be measured from this place or that. Warren solved it very simply, and no doubt quite illegally.[4] He commandeered enough boats and deputies to surround the ships and keep anyone from leaving them or reaching them. Then he just stayed there until they gave up.

A real clinical study of such a town would be fascinating reading.

Sincerely,

Raymond Chandler

4. Earl Warren, Governor of California and later Chief Justice of the United States.

[31]

TO CHARLES MORTON

6520 Drexel Avenue
L.A. 36
Nov. 20th, 1944

Dear Charles:

Your letters have been weighing on me quite a bit, especially your wonderful letter about yourself. Perhaps I ought to live in Boston. The civilized intelligence is pretty rare out west. This sounds like a snobbish thing to say, but I have lived here a long time and met very few people who were not half-baked in one way or another. Hollywood is full of very clever people, some of them rather more than clever, but the hard, glossy patina of Hollywood and New York smartness depresses me. You meet the bright people who have written something successful and have arrived and are very damn conscious of the fact. You meet lively young men who are really keen on making good pictures, if it is at all possible. But you do not meet the quiet, restrained, well-bred and inconspicuously intelligent kind of mind that is fairly common in England and I imagine also in New England. At least I hope so.

One of these days I'll write you something about myself. In the meantime things are not going too well. P. Marlowe is acting up, I have had many interruptions, and also a long-drawn-out wrangle with Paramount about a contract. I wish I had one of these facile plotting brains, like Erle Gardner or somebody. I have good ideas for about four books, but the labor of shaping them into plots appals me. It would be much better if you do not expect anything from me until you get it. You don't have to like it then, but the feeling that the *Atlantic* needs encouragement from me is dreadful. I do, of course, recognize a certain duty, quite apart from any question of self-interest, to try and brighten your pages with a little arrogant nonsense here and there.

There was a time when I should have adored your kind of job, but would have been incapable of handling it. I never really had a great urge to write fiction, which is becoming more and more of a pseudo-art. (There's an article in that idea). But you guys have an obligation too. That is, to avoid pompously bad writing and the kind of dulness that comes from letting flatulent asses pontificate about things they know no more about than the next man, if as much. There is a (to me) shocking example of this in the November *Harper's*, called "Salute to the Litterateurs."[1] Consider:

> "For writers are people of peculiar sensitivity to the winds of doctrine which blow with especial violence in a time of rapid change—some more so than others, but none, except the outright hacks, completely immune."

I regard that sentence as a disgrace to English prose. It says nothing and says it ponderously, in a cliched manner, and without syntax. The "some" obviously, by the sense, refers to writers, but just as obviously by the construction refers to "winds of doctrine." (Can't we leave phrases like that to Somerset Maugham?) How outright is a hack? And how completely immune is immune. Phooey. I continue:

> "They react this way and that; they resist the currents and run with them: and while some produce works of little value in literary or any other terms, others of greater ability and substance, and therefore of greater importance, exhibit the same tendencies in writings of a high degree of excellence."

Is there anything said here that could not be said better with a simple after-dinner belch? A little later he says:

> "When the present war was in the making the most indicative scratchings on the literary seismograph were in red."

When I showed that to my little seismograph he began to indicate four letter words in a very nasty shade of brownish-purple and had to be shut up in a dark room.

"Most indicative," "literature seismograph," "run with the current," two thousand years of Christianity and this is what we get in a literary magazine. Shame on you fellows!

I had an uncle in Omaha who was a minor politician— crooked, if I am any judge of character. I've been there a time or two. As a very small boy I used to be sent to spend part of the summer at Plattsmouth. I remember the oak trees and the high wooden sidewalks beside the dirt roads and the heat and the fireflies and

1. C. Hartley Grattan, "Salute to the Litterateurs," *Harper's Magazine*, November 1944.

walking-sticks and a lot of strange insects and the gathering of wild grapes in the fall to make wine and the dead cattle and once in a while a dead man floating down the muddy river and the dandy little three-hole privy behind the house. I remember Ak-Sar-Ben and the days when they were still trying to elect Bryan.[2] I remember the rocking chairs on the edge of the sidewoak in a solid row outside the hotel and the tobacco spit all over the place. And I remember a trial run on a mail car with a machine my uncle invented to take on mail without stopping, but somebody beat him out of it and he never got a dime.

After that I went to England and was raised on Latin and Greek, like yourself. I worked for the *Westminster Gazette* and the *Daily Express* and a very snooty weekly review called the *Academy*, owned by Oscar Wilde's fag, Lord Alfred Douglas and later by a man named Cowper, who claimed to be a direct descendant of the poet.[3] I wrote some of the nastiest book reviews ever written. I reviewed Farnol's *The Broad Highway* and predicted its tremendous success.[4] I reviewed Elinor Glyn, and how.[5] I don't think education ever did me any great harm.

Yours ever

Ray

TO JAMES SANDOE

6520 Drexel Avenue
Los Angeles 36
Dec. 17th. 1944

Dear Sandoe:

Thanks for your card. I've been meaning to write you for some time, and to a lot of other people, but haven't done it. I'm not sure what you mean (in this context) by bowdlerlized. I didn't check, but I

2. Ak-Sar-Ben is Nebraska spelled backward. It was a social organization.
3. Cecil Cowper, editor of *The Academy*.
4. Jeffrey Farnol, popular English novelist.
5. Popular English novelist, born in Canada.

[34]

had a vague impression here and there that I had been ever so gently toned down. I know they had to cut, because the thing was too long, and is overlength as is. I had a very snazzy beginning which they cut out, because it didn't really have anything to do with detective stories. It was simply a general expression of contempt for what is known as significant writing. I only wrote this damn article after being hounded by Charles Morton. I had no desire to write it, particularly, and certainly it was a loss to me financially. Not that that matters; after a certain point money means nothing. I have no complaint; I could have done the cutting myself on the proof. I just didn't know how. As it is, I have enough material left over for another one. But I think most critical writing is drivel and half of it is dishonest (that is, conditioned by information about advance sales), and there is no point in my adding to it. It is a short cut to oblivion, anyway. Thinking in terms of ideas destroys the power to think in terms of emotions and sensations. I suppose, like other people, I have at times a futile urge to explain to whoever will listen why it is that the whole apparatus of intellectualism bores me. But you have to use the language of intellectualism to do it. Which is the bunk. The business of a fiction writer is to recreate the illusion of life. How he does it, if he can do it, it does not in the least help him to know.

Regards

Chandler

TO CHARLES MORTON

6520 Drexel Avenue
Los Angeles 38
Dec 18th. 1944

Dear Charles:
     Yours of Dec. 14th. received and a Merry Christmas to you and the whole idea of Christmas this year has somehow taken on the utter vile commercial falsity of Mother's Day in Peoria.

I saw Mr. De Voto's remarks about Chandler and was of a mind to write to him and ask him to stop using words like "imperatives" and ideas like "functional style" but not to stop slamming people around. But this business of writing, writing to writers, is a career in itself. You end up by having personal thoughts about everyone and speaking your own mind about nothing.

Had a letter from an old unknown friend at the U. of Colorado Library who asks me if my piece in the *Atlantic* was bowdlerized.[1] Which I answered by saying that I had not checked, but had had a vague idea that it had been toned down with an ever so gentle hand here and there, and that of course it had been cut a little, which was my fault. But this just goes to show you that when a man starts to write about the apparatus of intellectualism he begins to use something that sounds like the language of intellectualism, which is a loathsome language. I re-read the *Atlantic* article and was startled to discover that in some thirty years of odd and even living I had learned nothing whatsoever about the English language. It still has me licked. I have old essays written for the *Academy* and sketches written for the *Westminster Gazette* away back when I was an elegant young thing with an Old Alleynian[2] hatband on a very natty basket weave strawhat; they show the same childish petulance and frustrated attempt to be brilliant about nothing.

I cannot complete my piece about screenwriters and screenwriting for the simple reason that I have no honesty about it. I may wake up with a different notion, but you cannot bully me into sending you something I am so deadly unsure about. There are points like these to make, but when you make them you get in a mess. E.g., 1. There is no mature art of the screenplay, and by mature I don't mean intellectual or postgraduate or intelligentsia-little magazine writing. I mean an art which knows what it is doing and has the techniques necessary to do it. 2. An adult, that is dirty or plain-spoken art of the screen, could exist at any moment the Hays Office (Title for an Essay on same: *Dirtymindedness As a Career*) and the local censorship boards would let it, but it would be no more *mature* than *Going My Way* is. 3. There is no available body of screenplay literature, because it belongs to the studios, not to the writers, and

---

1. James Sandoe.
2. Dulwich College was founded by Edward Alleyn in 1617.

they won't show it. For instance, I tried to borrow a script of *The Maltese Falcon* from Warners; they would not lend it to me. All the writer can do is look at pictures. If he is working in a studio, he can get the scripts of that studio, but his time is not his own. He can make no leisurely study and reconstruction of the problems. 4. There is no *teaching* in the art of the screenplay because there is nothing to teach; if you do not know how pictures are made, you cannot possibly know how to write them. No outsider knows that, and no writer would be bothered, unless he was an out-of-work or manqué writer. 5. The screenplay as it exists is the result of a bitter and prolonged struggle between the writer (or writers) and the people whose aim is to exploit his talent without giving it the freedom to be a talent. 6. It is only a little over 3 years since the major (and only this very year the minor) studios were forced after prolonged and bitter struggle to agree to treat the writer with a reasonable standard of business ethics. In this struggle the writers were not really fighting the motion picture industry at all; they were fighting those powerful elements in it that had hitherto glommed off all the glory and prestige and who could only continue to do so by selling themselves to the world as the makers of pictures. This struggle is still going on, and the writers are winning it, and they are winning it in the wrong way: by becoming producers and directors, that is, by becoming showmen instead of creative artists. This will do nothing for the art of the screenplay and will actually harm those writers who are temperamentally unfitted for showmanship (and this will include always the best of them). 7. The writer is still very far from winning the right to create a screenplay without interference from his studio. Why? Because he does not know how, and it is to the interest of the producers and directors to prevent him from learning how. If even a quarter of the *highly-paid* screenwriters of Hollywood (leaving out all the people who work on program pictures) could produce a completely integrated and thoroughly photographable screenplay, with only the amount of interference and discussion necessary to protect the studio's investment in actors and freedom from libel and censorship troubles, then the producer would become a business co-ordinator and the director would become the interpreter of a completed work, instead of, as at present, the maker of the picture. They will fight to the death against it.

I have a three year contract with Paramount, for 26 weeks

[37]

work a year, at a vast sum of money (by my standards). Nothing of the above would give particular offense to the studio, but much of it would be deeply resented by many individuals and would involve me in constant arguments which would wear me out. But there is still more to be said, and it is worse yet. A system like this, prolonged over a long period of time, produces a class of kept writers without initiative, independence or fighting spirit; they exist only by conforming to Hollywood standards, but they can produce art only by defying them. Few, very few, of them are capable of earning a living as independent writers, but you will always have to have them, because you will never find enough talent in all Hollywood to make more than one tenth of its pictures even fairly good. Granted that there are too many made; they are going to be made, or the theaters will be dark. Enormous vested interests and the livelihoods of countless thousands of people are involved. Granted again that ninety per cent of Hollywood's pictures are not really worth making; I say that ninety percent of the books and plays and short stories they were made from are not worth seeing or reading, by the same standards. And you and I know those standards are not going to change in our time.

Yet a writer, like me, who has little experience in Hollywood, and presumes to discuss the writers of Hollywood, must either lie, or say that they are largely over-dressed, overpaid, servile and incompetent hacks. All progress in the art of the screenplay depends on a very few people who are in a position (and have the temperament and toughness) to fight for excellence. Hollywood loves them for it and is only too anxious to reward them by making them something else than writers. Hollywood's attitude to writers is necessarily conditioned by the mass of its writers, not by the few who have what it calls integrity. It loves the word, having so little of the quality. Yet it is not fair for me to say in print that the writers of Hollywood are what they are; they have a guild and it may be that in so large an industry they must fight as a group; it is obvious that I have done nothing to help them achieve what they have achieved, and am not likely to, except indirectly, by helping to get out a few pictures a bit above the ruck. It is not even fair to call them overpaid; because other writers as a group are shockingly underpaid; Hollywood is the only industry in the world that pays its workers the kind of money only capitalists and big executives make in other industries. If

[38]

it is something less than ideal, it is the only industry that even tries for idealism; if it makes bad art, no other makes any art, except as a by-product of money-making. If it makes money out of poor pictures, it could make more money out of good ones, and it knows it and tries to make them. There is simply not enough talent in the world to do it with, on any such scale. Its pictures cost too much and therefore must be safe and bring in big returns; but why do they cost too much? Because it pays the people who do the work, not the people who cut coupons. If it drains off all the writing talent in the world and then proceeds to destroy it by the way it treats it, then why is it able to drain off that talent? Because it knows how to pay for talent. The man who publishes my books has made more out of me than I have out of him, and he has not made it by selling the books, but by cutting himself in on radio and motion picture and reprint rights, which did not cost him a cent. Did he venture anything on the books? Of course not, not a dime. He was insured against loss by the rental libraries. He does not even know how to sell my kind of books, or how to promote them or how to get them reviewed. He just sits there and waits for something to happen, and when it happens, he rubs his hands and cuts himself a nice fat slice of it. But Hollywood pays me a large salary merely to try to write something it can perhaps use. And when I write something that pays, then it tears up my contract and writes a better one. I cannot despise an industry that does this and I cannot say the men in it are bad artists because they do not produce better art. Yet, if I am honest about art, that is the only thing I can say. It is better to say nothing, is it not? At least, for the present.

Phew! I'm exhausted. And what do I know about art anyway? Thank heaven that when I tried to write fiction I had the sense to do it in a language that was not all steamed up with rhetoric. In spite of all your kindness and understanding I am beginning to hate you. It took me twenty years to get over writing this sort of twaddle and look at me now!

Ray

P.S. I clean forgot to thank you for the proof of Nabokov's fantasy.[3] I have a novel by him somewhere. It is exquisitely composed and

3. "Time and Ebb," published in *The Atlantic Monthly*, January 1945.

very charming. I have a strange feeling that I have met the beautiful closing simile before. It sounds like T. S. Eliot. I can't place it and therefore must assume that it is false memory (paramnesis to you). The tired brain is often thus afflicted.

R

TO CHARLES MORTON

6520 Drexel Avenue
Los Angeles 36, Calif.
Jan 1st. 1945

Dear Charles:

A Happy New Year to you and the eggnog. And what horribly long letters this guy Chandler writes. Seeing the copy of it marked "excerpt" was like looking in an unexpected mirror just after falling downstairs. No, I don't keep carbons of them. I sometimes wish I did, but most of the time I am much happier not knowing. I didn't see the *New Yorker* for the day in question, but a man named McNulty whom Paramount has beguiled out here (he looks horrible already) is going to bring his copy down. He is a *New Yorker* man and has not yet bought a houndstooth sports coat.[1] I regret to say I have to go back to work tomorrow. The prospect makes me feel low enough to chin myself on the curbing. I worked all yesterday and today trying to get an article down on paper for you. You don't have to like it, because I would have written it anyway, if only to get rid of the subject. I see your point about Hollywood, and perhaps you are quite right. I guess I can get around to that after awhile.

It was very kind of you to send me Diarmuid Russell's piece, and very nice of him to write it.[2] I have known for some time that I was in a rut, but he, being an agent, should have known (as perhaps he does, privately) that the one you cash in on is not

1. John McNulty, author of *Third Avenue* (1936).
2. Son of the Irish poet A.E., and founder of Russell and Volkening, New York literary agency. He reviewed Chandler in the *New York Times Book Review*.

necessarily the one you did best; it may happen to be the one that arrives when the others have prepared the way. At any rate, sooner or later, I must do my obeisance before the trulls and pimps of Hollywood in a Marlowe story of no better or newer flavor. I have another story in mind which I hope to do before I die; it will have almost no surface toughness at all, but the go to hell attitude, which is no pose with me, is likely to appear in it all the same.

·   ·   ·

The only complaint I could make about Russell's remarks is that if you are going to take the trouble to say nice things about a man, and such very nice things, you should keep a few for the end and leave the reader with a slight taste of sugar in his mouth. I mean, I would myself have saved out a few kind words to close with, not in anyway modifying what was said in criticism, but merely arranging it a little differently. That, of course, is not at all my affair.

My doubtfully honest uncle's (by marriage only) name was Ernest Fitt, and he was a boiler inspector or something, at least in name. He is dead now. I remember him very well. He used to come home in the evening (in the Plattsmouth period) put the paper on the music rack and improvise while he read it. I have read somewhere that Harold Bauer used to play his programmes through while reading a paper, but I always thought him a dull pianist, so it didn't surprise me. My uncle had talent, but no musical education. He had a brother who was an amazing character. He had been a bank clerk or manager in a bank in Waterford, Ireland (where all my mother's people come from, but none of them were Catholics) and had embezzled money. He cleaned out the till one Saturday and, with the help of the Masons, escaped the police net to the continent of Europe. In some hotel in Germany his money was stolen, or most of it. When I knew him, long after, he was an extremely respectable old party, always immaculately dressed, and of an incredible parsimony. He once invited me to dinner and to the Ak-Sar-Ben festivities. After the dinner he leaned over and in a confidential whisper said: "We'll each pay for our own." Not a drop of Scotch blood anywhere either. Pure middle-class Protestant Irish. I have a great many Irish relatives, some poor, some not poor, and all Protestants and some of them Sinn Feiners and some entirely pro-British. The head of the family, if he is still living, is a very wealthy lawyer who hated the law, but felt obliged to carry on his father's firm. He had a housekeeper who came of a county family and did not regard my uncle (the lawyer one) as quite a gentleman because he was a solicitor. She used to say: There are only four careers for a gentleman, the Army, the Navy, the Church and the Bar. A barrister was a gentleman, but not a solicitor. This in spite of the fact that his son was a lieutenant in the Royal Navy and another of his relatives was Adjutant-General of the Royal Marines. With her he never lived down being a solicitor. An amazing people, the Anglo-Irish. They never mixed with Catholics socially. I remember playing on a cricket team with some of the local snobs and one of the players was a Catholic boy who came to the game in an elaborate chariot with grooms in livery; but he was not asked to have tea with the rest after the game. He wouldn't have accepted, of course. People over here don't understand the Irish at all. A third of the population of Eire is Protestant, and it is by far the best educated and most influential third. Almost all the great Irish rebels were Protestants, and the whole tone of their present nation is Calvinistic rather than Catholic. I grew up with a terrible contempt for Catholics, and I have trouble with it even now. My uncle's snob housekeeper wouldn't have a Catholic servant in the house, although they were probably much better than the trash she did have. What a world! The rather amusing development in my uncle's case was that he took unto himself a Jewish mistress in London, raised her son, who was an illegitimate get of a couple of Sassoons, had two illegitimate children himself, and then married her. *But he never took her to Ireland!* I could make a book about these people, but I am too much of an Irishman myself ever to tell the truth about them.

Well, Hollywood is funny too. They had a contract with me and no story for me to work on. So I cooked up an idea and went in and told it to them and they rubbed their hands and said lovely, when do we start? But when my agent enquired what they proposed to pay for the idea, they tore their clothing into shreds and heaped ashes on their heads. It tooked several weeks of bitter wrangling to get them to see the light. I don't care anything about the money, I just like to fight. I'm a tired old man, but it takes more than a motion picture studio to push me around, it seems.

All the best,

Ray

TO DALE WARREN

January 7th. 1945

Dear Warren:

I finally unearthed your kind letter from a tangled mass of correspondence dating back to the Civil War, spurred on by your letter in the *Atlantic* about my little tirade. Do not think I have not meant to write to you. My wife regards you as a somewhat rare bird, since you wrote to me twice without mentioning the fact that you were connected with a publishing firm. The *Atlantic* article has got me into a lot of trouble. Mr. P. Marlowe, a simple alcoholic vulgarian who never sleeps with his clients while on duty, is trying to go refined on me. "What the hell," he says, "do you mean by keeping me in the basement all this time. Here you are unmasked as a guy who can write English—after a fashion—so get busy and write some about me." I can imagine the result. I suppose, if I write another article in the *Atlantic,* if there is one, he will demand spats and a monocle and start collecting old pewter.

There are certain acute disadvantages in attracting attention, even the small amount that has come my way. People start telling you how you do things and then you start trying to do them that way. All I wanted when I began was to play with a fascinating new language, and trying, without anybody noticing it, to see what it would do as a means of expression which might remain on the level of unintellectual thinking and yet acquire the power to say things which are usually only said with a literary air. I didn't really care a hell of a lot what kind of story I wrote; I wrote melodrama because when I looked around me it was the only kind of writing I saw that was relatively honest and yet was not trying to put over somebody's party line. So now there are guys talking about prose and other guys telling me I have a social conscience. P. Marlowe has as much social conscience as a horse. He has a personal conscience, which is an entirely different matter. There are people who think I dwell on the ugly side of life. God help them! If they had any idea how little I have told them about it! P. Marlowe doesn't give a damn who is president; neither do I, because I know he will be a politician. There was even a bird who informed me I could write a good proletarian

[43]

novel; in my limited world there is no such animal, and if there were, I am the last mind in the world to like it, being by tradition and long study a complete snob. P. Marlowe and I do not despise the upper classes because they take baths and have money; we despise them because they are phoney. And so on. And now I see ahead of me either an acute self-consciousness about simple things which I never had any idea of explaining, or a need to explain them at length, and with fury, in the very lingo I had been trying to forget. Because that is the only lingo people who can understand explanations of the sort will accept them in.

I have a note from a friend of yours, Mary Lasswell.[1] Have to answer it, but have never read anything she wrote, which makes it embarrassing. I also have a letter from a lady in Caracas, Venezuela, who asks me if I would like to be her friend when she comes to New York. It has a faint suggestion about it of another letter I had once from a girl in Seattle who said that she was interested in music and sex, and gave me the impression that, if I was pressed for time, I need not even bother to bring my own pajamas. She probably had spots.

Raymond Chandler

TO HAMISH HAMILTON

Paramount Pictures Inc.
5451 Marathon Street
Hollywood 38, Calif.
January 11, 1945

Dear Hamish Hamilton:
    Blanche Knopf sent me a copy of your letter to her of December 5th, which was very kind of her. It points up for me how little nowadays a writer seems to have to do with his publisher. I suppose this is largely because of the agent. Once in a while I hear

1. Author of *Suds in Your Eyes*, 1943.

from Alfred or Blanche Knopf. Their letters are always friendly but there is a sort of remoteness about the whole thing. I seem to remember in the rather dim past having received one letter from you.

Another thing that strikes me is that one publisher calls the other publisher's attention to what you term "a magnificent boost in the Book Society News," and something by Desmond MacCarthy in the *Sunday Times*.[1] But nobody ever tells the writer anything about these matters. I wonder why. I have never even seen an English review of anything I wrote except once—something from the *Times*, I think.

You say also "I gather that he is a very big shot in Hollywood these days, and might resent advice, whoever the sender may be and however good his intentions." That really cuts me to the quick. I am not a big shot in Hollywood or anywhere else and have no desire to be. I am, on the contrary, extremely allergic to big shots of all types wherever found, and lose no opportunity to insult them whenever I get the chance. Furthermore, I love advice and if I very seldom take it, on the subject of writing, that is only because I have received practically none except from my agent, Sydney Sanders, and he has rather concentrated on trying to make me write stuff for what we call the slick magazines over here. That is, the big shiny paper national weeklies and monthlies which cater principally to the taste of women. I have always felt myself entirely unfitted for this kind of writing. I much prefer Hollywood, with all its disadvantages.

I should indeed like to write a more serious type of crime novel and have one firmly in mind. But as you very well know in this curious business, one has for a time at least, to follow a rather different trail. Probably by now I've gone about as far along that trail as it is worthwhile to go, but it has certainly been worthwhile to go thus far.

Why not try me with a little advice some time? I am sure I should treat yours with the greatest respect and should, in any case, like to hear from you.

Yours very sincerely,

Raymond Chandler

1. English biographer and man of letters, reviewer for *Sunday Times* of London.

TO CHARLES MORTON

Paramount Pictures Inc.
5451 Marathon Street
Hollywood 38, Calif.
Jan. 15th. 1945

Dear Charles:

.   .   .

Yes, I know damn well that Harry Fitt was one of the clan of Limerick. I didn't know that he drank, but liquor was a family vice. Those who escaped it either turned religious or went in for white duck pants, like my Uncle Gus. Harry, your father's hired hand, must have been a cousin of my uncle. He was no near relation and I hardly know him, but when I read your letter I recalled that there was a Harry Fitt, that he lived in Omaha and that he worked in a hardware store. Since I was fresh out from England at the time and a hardware store was "trade" I could hardly be expected to get on terms of anything like familiarity with him. Boy! Two stengahs, chop chop!

I am back at the grind and you might as leave write me there for a while. It makes no difference. (Perhaps you won't be writing to me any more at all). In less than two weeks I wrote an original story of 90 pages like this. All dictated and never looked at until finished. It was an experiment and for a guy subject from early childhood to plot-constipation, it was rather a revelation. Some of the stuff is good, some very much not. But I don't see why the method could not be adapted to novel writing, at least by me. Improvise the story as well as you can, in as much detail or as little as the mood seems to suggest, write dialogue or leave it out, but cover the movement, the characters and bring the thing to life. I begin to realize the great number of stories that are lost by us rather meticulous boys simply because we permit our minds to freeze on the faults rather than let them work for a while without the critical overseer sniping at everything that is not perfect. I can see where a special vice might also come out of this kind of writing; in fact two: the strange delusion that something on paper has a meaning because it is written.

[46]

(My revered HJ rather went to pieces a bit when he began to dictate.)[1]
Also, the tendency to worship production for its own sake. (Gardner suffers badly from this; but God never had any idea of making him a writer anyway. Edgar Wallace ditto. But Dumas Père might really have missed something by grinding the stuff out of the sausage machine.)

Had a nice letter from Dale Warren, but I wish people would stop writing letters about the neglected works of Raymond Chandler. I am so little neglected that I am often actually embarrassed by too much attention. Also, *The Big Sleep* and *Farewell My Murder My Sweet* have between them, in some form or other, sold almost three quarters of a million copies.[2]

All the best

Ray

TO CHARLES MORTON

Jan. 21st. 1945

Dear Charles:

. . .

I have one complaint to make, and it is an old one—the cold silence and the stalling that goes on when something comes in that is not right or is not timely. This I resent and always shall. It does not take weeks to tell a man (by pony express) that his piece is wrong when he can be told in a matter of days that it is right. Editors do not make enemies by rejecting manuscripts, but by the way they do it, by the change of atmosphere, the delay, the impersonal note that creeps in. I am a hater of power and of trading, and yet I live in a world where I have to trade brutally and exploit every item of power I may possess. But in dealing with the *Atlantic*, there is none of

1. Reference to Henry James.
2. The movie version of *Farewell, My Lovely* was called *Murder, My Sweet*.

this. I do not write for you for money or for prestige, but for love, the strange lingering love of a world wherein men may think in cool subtleties and talk in the language of almost forgotten cultures. There is little of this world; there is a pale imitation of it created by people like Barzun.[1] I like that world and I would on occasion sacrifice my sleep and my rest and quite a bit of money to enter it gracefully. That is not appreciated. It is something you cannot buy. It is something which, even when the gesture is imperfect, deserves respect. I can make $5000 in two days (sometimes), but I spend weeks trying to please the *Atlantic* for $250 or whatever it is. Do you think I want money? And as for prestige, what is it? What greater prestige can a man like me, (not too greatly gifted but understanding) have than to have taken a cheap, shoddy, and utterly lost kind of writing and have made of it something that intellectuals claw each other about? What more could I ask except the leisure and skill to write a couple of novels of the sort I want to write and to have waiting for them a public I have made myself? Certainly, the *Atlantic* cannot give that to me.

.   .   .

All the best,

Ray

TO HAMISH HAMILTON

Paramount Pictures Inc.
5451 Marathon Street
Hollywood 38, Calif.
February 26, 1945

Dear Hamish Hamilton:

1. Jacques Barzun, historian and critic of detective fiction.

[48]

.　　　.　　　.

It is nice to hear from you and to be writing to you. I suppose agents are necessary to a writer because the writer, living a more or less secluded life as a rule, cannot possibly know what is going on in the literary world, what he ought to get for his material, and on what sort of conditions he should sell it. But I think the agent's function ends there. The moment he tries to influence a writer in his work, the agent just makes a nuisance of himself. I can assure you that no agent need come between us in any but the most routine financial matters.

.　　　.　　　.

I hope to meet you some day in London. It would probably come as a shock to some of my critics to know that I went to school at Dulwich and was raised on Latin and Greek.

Kindest regards and best wishes,

Yours sincerely,

Raymond Chandler

TO CHARLES MORTON

Paramount Pictures Inc.
5451 Marathon Street
Hollywood 38, Calif.
March 19, 1945

Dear Charles:

.　　　.　　　.

A man named Inkstead[1] took some pictures of me for *Harper's Bazaar* a while ago (I never quite found out why) and one of me holding my secretary in my lap came out very well indeed. When I

1. Actually John Engstead.

[49]

get the dozen I have ordered I'll send you one. The secretary, I should perhaps add, is a black Persian cat, 14 years old, and I call her that because she has been around me ever since I began to write, usually sitting on the paper I wanted to use or the copy I wanted to revise, sometimes leaning up against the typewriter and sometimes just quietly gazing out of the window from a corner of the desk, as much as to say, "The stuff you're doing's a waste of my time, bud." Her name is Taki (it was originally Take, but we got tired of explaining that this was a Japanese word meaning bamboo and should be pronounced in two syllables), and she has a memory like no elephant ever even tried to have. She is usually politely remote, but once in a while will get an argumentative spell and talk back for ten minutes at a time. I wish I knew what she is trying to say then, but I suspect it all adds up to a very sarcastic version of "You can do better." I've been a cat lover all my life (have nothing against dogs except that they need such a lot of entertaining) and have never quite been able to understand them. Taki is a completely poised animal and always knows who likes cats, never goes near anybody that doesn't, always walks straight up to anyone, however lately arrived and completely unknown to her, who really does. She doesn't spend a great deal of time with them, however, just takes a moderate amount of petting and strolls off. She has another curious trick (which may or may not be rare) of never killing anything. She brings 'em back alive and lets you take them away from her. She has brought into the house at various times such things as a dove, a blue parakeet, and a large butterfly. The butterfly and the parakeet were entirely unharmed and carried on just as though nothing had happened. The dove gave her a little trouble, apparently not wanting to be carried around, and had a small spot of blood on its breast. But we took it to a bird man and it was all right very soon. Just a bit humiliated. Mice bore her, but she catches them if they insist and then I have to kill them. She has a sort of tired interest in gophers, and will watch a gopher hole with some attention, but gophers bite and after all who the hell wants a gopher anyway? So she just pretends she might catch one, if she felt like it.

She goes with us wherever we go journeying, remembers all the places she has been to before and is usually quite at home anywhere. One or two places have got her—I don't know why. She just wouldn't settle down in them. After a while we know enough to

[50]

take the hint. Chances are there was an axe murder there once and we're much better somewhere else. The guy might come back. Sometimes she looks at me with a rather peculiar expression (she is the only cat I know who will look you straight straight in the eye) and I have a suspicion that she is keeping a diary, because the expression seems to be saying: "Brother, you think you're pretty good most of the time, don't you? I wonder how you'd feel if I decided to publish some of the stuff *I've* been putting down at odd moments." At certain times she has a trick of holding one paw up loosely and looking at it in a speculative manner. My wife thinks she is suggesting we get her a wrist watch; she doesn't need it for any practical reason—she can tell the time better than I can—but after all you gotta have some jewelry.

I don't know why I'm writing all this. It must be I couldn't think of anything else, or—this is where it gets creepy—am I really writing it at all? Could it be that—no, it must be me. Say it's me. I'm scared.

Ray

TO ALFRED A. KNOPF

Paramount Pictures Inc.
5451 Marathon Street
Hollywood 38, Calif.
March 24, 1945

Dear Alfred:
I don't quite know how to answer your letter of March 19th. Privately and verbally, I make no secret of my age, but printing it on the jacket of a book seems to me bad psychology. I don't think it's any of the public's business, and it can very easily give a false impression. My wife is very emphatic on this point, and I have never known her to be wrong in a matter of taste.

Certainly I should agree that if a writer is of any interest to the public at all, the things about him which made him a particular sort of writer are also of interest. I should agree, in my own case, it might *possibly* be of interest that my education and social background are in almost violent contrast to my ideas about writing. I should agree that it might be of interest to know that a man who grew up in England is, in a literary sense, completely American; that a man who was at one time a classical scholar (of sorts) now chooses to write in the American vernacular. But I do not agree that my age, bathing habits, the color of my wife's eyes, or what time I get up in the morning, or, in fact, anything of a purely personal nature, is relevant. The intrusion of publicity-minded people into the private lives of writers seems to me an infinite vulgarity. It took lonely men whom I had never seen or heard of to find out that I could write with some distinction. All the blurb writers were able to see was thrill value.

A photographer for *Harper's Bazaar* made a picture of me and my cat which I think is just exactly the sort you should have for your purposes. If *Harper's Bazaar* uses it, it can't be used anywhere else. But it is one of several, and they may not use it; in which case I will send it to you.

Kindest regards to you and Blanche.

Yours,

Ray

TO JAMES SANDOE

August 18th. 1945

Dear Sandoe:

.   .   .

I have *The Small Back Room* and in fact have bought several copies.[1] Even toyed with the idea of doing a picture from it, but it got away. It would have to be made in England. I thought it a great piece of writing, disfigured a little by the relationship of the man

---

1. By Nigel Balchin.

and his girl. I don't know on what grounds of logic it rests, if any, but I find it impossible to respect a woman who lives with a man. She can sleep with him all she blame pleases and with whomever else she pleases and in whatever place she pleases, but the tawdry imitation of domesticity gets me down.

· · ·

Regards, R. C.

P.S. Am working on a screen treatment of *The Lady in the Lake* for MGM.[2] It bores me stiff. The last time I'll ever do a screenplay of a book I wrote myself. Just turning over dry bones.

TO CHARLES MORTON

Big Bear Lake, Calif.
October 13th, 1945

Dear Charles:

· · ·

As to talking about Hammett[1] In the past tense, I did myself in that essay. I hope he is not to be so spoken of. As far as I know he is alive and well, but he has gone so long without writing—unless you count a couple of screenplay jobs which, rumor says, La Hellman[2] really did for him, (I guess I needed that first comma after all)— that I wonder. He was one of the many guys who couldn't take Hollywood without trying to push God out of the high seat. I recall an incident reported to me when Hammett was occupying a suite at the Beverly-Wilshire. A party wished to make him a proposition and called late of a morning, was admitted by Hammett's house boy to a living room, and after a very long wait, an inner door

2. Chandler's fourth novel.

----

1. Detective novelist Dashiell Hammett died in 1961. His last novel, *The Thin Man*, was published in 1934.
2. Playwright Lillian Hellman, companion of Hammett for many years.

opened and the great man appeared in it, clad in an expensive lounging robe (no doubt with his initials on the pocket) with a scarf draped tastefully around his neck. He stood in silence as the man expounded. At the end he said politely: "No." He turned and withdrew, the door closed, the houseboy ushered the gent out, and the silence fell, interrupted only by the gurgling of Scotch from an inner room. If you ever saw Hammett, you will realize the dignity and pathos of this little scene. He is a very distinguished-looking guy, and I imagine he could say 'no' without perceptible trace of a Brooklyn accent. I liked him very much and he was an amazingly competent drunk, which, having a poor head for liquor, I seem always to admire. It was a great pity that he stopped writing. I've never known why. I suppose he may have come to the end of his resources in a certain style and have lacked the intellectual depth to compensate for that by trying something else. But I'm not sure. I think the man has been both overrated and underrated. Your friend Dale Warren recently read the *Falcon*,[3] for the first time too, and saw little in it. But I have read so much of this kind of writing that the gulf between Hammett and the merely tough boys seems to me vast. Old Joe Shaw may have put his finger on the trouble when he said Hammett never really cared for any of his characters.

I don't know whether this is a relaxed letter or not. I do begin to feel a little easing of the strain. This place is 7000 feet up, on the edge of a lake 20 miles long. It is no longer unspoiled nature, but it still has its points. The air is thin and dry like the desert (the Mojave is just down the hill to the east) and at this time of year it is very quiet, warm in the daytime and rather cold at night. We have had a fire before evening only once. There is nothing to do and I do it. We go out in the woods and I chop knots out of fallen trees and break up a few stumps of ironwood or mountain mahogany, a very hard reddish wood that burns like coal. I try to keep work out of my head, but can't quite do that. I had a bad time with MGM, very bad.[4] Not their fault, they were very nice to me. After the first two days I worked entirely at home, which is against their rules but they made an exception. The trouble was that I was already too fed up to do a good job on any script: that I did not like working on a story of my own, being stale on it long since; and that I assumed in the beginning

3. *The Maltese Falcon*, a novel by Hammett.
4. Chandler was working on the screenplay of his novel *The Lady in the Lake*.

that a preliminary script would be all they could expect, since they take a very long time making their pictures. I found out as I began to send it in that they were regarding it as a shooting script (subject to cutting) and didn't want any other writer on it. That put the heat on me and I began to get nervous. MGM never had a script in 13 weeks since the company was organized, and here they were talking about going into production in November. Towards the end when I realized that I was getting more mechanical every day I tried to explain to them that they were making a mistake, that this work was full of loose ends and tired attitudes, and that if they really wanted to start shooting that soon, they needed a writer with some enthusiasm. No soap. Of course these people never play straight with you. What will almost certainly happen, once they have milked me dry, will be that some executive above the producer will say, Look here, we got a lot of high-priced writers right here in the studio. For Chrissake put one on this and let him give it what he's got. The writer will then take good care, or as good care as they let him, to make enough changes to put his mark on the thing and get a credit. I don't grudge him the credit, but I do rather resent the waste of my own fading energies. On the other hand in all fairness I have to say that MGM would have kept me on the script indefinitely, had I wanted to stay. So I suppose it's all right, really.[5]

.   .   .

All the best
Ray

TO CHARLES MORTON

6520 Drexel Ave.
Los Angeles 36, Calif.
Dec. 12th. 1945

Dear Charles:

I've owed you a letter for so damn long that I suppose you

5. The script was finished by Steve Fisher and Chandler refused any credit for the film.

wonder whether I am still alive. So do I, at times. Before I delve into your two letters to see if there are any questions you wanted replies to, let me report that my blast at Hollywood was received here in frozen silence.[1] I don't think any local paper or trade-paper even mentioned it (but can't be sure); Irving Hoffman did in his column, briefly, but he doesn't function here, although his stuff appears in the *Hollywood Reporter*. In view of the subject matter, and quite regardless of the reputation of the writer, and in view of the *Atlantic*, it seems to me reasonable to think there was a suppression of the subject by request of the studio publicity heads. I could be wrong, but that is what I'm inclined to think. In various roundabout ways I heard that the piece was not received with favor. My agent was told by the Paramount story editor that it had done me a lot of harm with the producers at Paramount. Charlie Brackett, that fading wit, said: "Chandler's books are not good enough, nor his pictures bad enough, to justify that article." I wasted a little time trying to figure out what that meant. It seems to mean that the only guy who can speak his mind about Hollywood is either (a) a failure in Hollywood, or (b) a celebrity somewhere else. I would reply to Mr. Brackett that if my books had been any worse, I should not have been invited to Hollywood, and that if they had been any better, I should not have come. Of course, as you and I know, the only kind of man qualified to deal with Hollywood in any such drastic fashion is one who has enough reputation to get a hearing, has not been in Hollywood long enough to lose his sense of proportion, but has been there long enough and has accomplished enough there so that it could not be said of him he was merely knocking a racket he couldn't lick.

I noticed that (unlike the *Post*) you did not open my fan mail. Too bad you didn't raise the point so that you could have. There wasn't much, but there was a very charming letter from Beirne Lay and also one from Studs Lonigan which I have still to answer.[2] He thinks I didn't go far enough, that I should have coordinated Hollywood with the social problems of the time. That's the worst of these deep thinkers. They can't let you speak your piece, then put

1. "Writers in Hollywood," *The Atlantic Monthly*, November 1945.
2. Beirne Lay, author of *Twelve O'Clock High*; Studs Lonigan is presumably James T. Farrell.

your hat on and go home. Everything to them is just a chapter in the unfolding of the human struggle for decent expression, or like another volume from Jules Romains.[3] Of course they're right in a way, more right than Wolcott Gibbs, for example, who seems to take the view, intellectually unsound, that an art which is practised badly is simply a bad art (I wonder if he ever read *Clarissa Harlowe*) and the view, socially and factually unsound, that a man is of necessity more intelligent than his cook.[4] I liked his piece because I like the way he says things; I like but do not crave to practise the somewhat arctic style of the *New Yorker*. It has made *New Yorker* writers out of too many people who might have been their own writers. But I should somehow like to ask Wolcott whether he really believes the medium which has produced *The Last Laugh, Variety, M., Mayerling, Night Must Fall, Intolerance, The Little Foxes* (screen version), *The More the Merrier*, etc. etc. is really inferior to the medium which has produced *Dear Ruth, The Voice of the Turtle, Mrs. Tanqueray's Past, The Lion and the Mouse, Oklahoma, Dear Brutus, Getting Married*, etc. etc. And if he agrees that it is not, I should further like to ask him whether criticism has any function whatsoever in the development and self-education of an art; because if it has, all he is really saying is that he does not want to review pictures because they are bad and bore him, whereas he does want to review plays because they are good and do not bore him. That may be his privilege, but it is certainly not a critical opinion.

In case you are still planning to use this article in your anthology, I should like, if there is time, to point out a few errors. They are not very important, but we might as well get the thing right. Whom do I address? Some of them are probably actual typographical errors of a sort. There is one I should like to mention, because it is the kind of thing I never can understand. It is the 9th. line from the end of the piece. It reads: "and not examine the artistic result too critically. The." What I wrote was; "and not too critically examine the artistic result." I believe, but am not certain, that it was this last way in the original proofs, perhaps not in the revised proof. It is obvious that somebody, for no reason save that he thought he

3. Author of a long series of novels called *Men of Good Will*.
4. Gibbs was drama critic of *The New Yorker*.

[57]

was improving the style, changed the order of the words. The length is the same, therefore that could not enter into it. I confess myself completely flabbergasted by the literary attitude this expresses. Because it is the attitude that gets me, the assumption on the part of some editorial hireling that he can write better than the man who sent the stuff in, that he knows more about phrase and cadence and the placing of words, and that he actually thinks that a clause with a strong (stressed) syllable at the end, which was put there because it was strong, is improved by changing the order so that the clause ends in a weak adverbial termination. I don't mind the guy being wrong about this. That's nothing. It could even, within limits, be a matter of opinion, although I do not agree. But here is somebody who apparently decided in his own mind that Chandler was using a rhetorical word order, which he was, and that he didn't know what the hell he was doing, didn't even know he was being rhetorical, and that he, Joe Doakes with the fat red pencil, is the boy to show him how wrong he is, by changing it back to the way the editor of the Weehawken County Gazeteer would have written it in his weekly editorial about the use of steel floss to clean chicken dirt off Grade AA eggs. Christ!

While still coughing hysterically into my kidney basin I thank you for your kind remarks from the wife of the Harvard Nieman Fellow, and I am still a bit dizzy from some remarks your pal Dale Warren made about *The Maltese Falcon*, which he apparently regards as quite inferior to *The Leavenworth Case* (Read it for laughs, if you haven't). I reread the *Falcon* not long ago, and I give up. Somebody in this room has lost a straitjacket. It must be me. Frankly, I can conceive of better writing than the *Falcon*, and a more tender and warm attitude to life, and a more flowery ending; but by God, if you can show me twenty books written approximately 20 years back that have as much guts and life now, I'll eat them between slices of Edmund Wilson's head.[5] Really I'm beginning to wonder quite seriously whether anybody knows what writing is anymore, whether they haven't got the whole bloody business so completely mixed up with subject matter and significance and who's going to win the

---

5. Edmund Wilson's article "Who Cares Who Killed Roger Ackroyd?" in *The New Yorker* was unfavorable to most detective writers. Chandler was excepted.

peace and what they gave him for the screen rights and if you're not a molecular physicist, you're illiterate, and so on, that there simply isn't anybody around who can read a book and say that the guy knew how to write or didn't. Even poor old Edmund Wilson, who writes as if he had a loose upper plate (was it DeVoto who said that?) dirtied his pants in the *New Yorker* a few short weeks ago in reviewing Marquand's[6] last book. He wrote: "A novel by Sinclair Lewis, however much it may be open to objection, is at least a book by a writer—that is, a work of the imagination that imposes its atmosphere, a creation that shows the color and modelling of a particular artist's hand." Is that all a good writer has to do? Hell, I always thought it was, but hell, I didn't know Wilson knew it.

Can I do a piece for you entitled *The Insignifance of Significance*, in which I will demonstrate in my usual whorehouse style that it doesn't matter a damn what a novel is about, that the only fiction of any moment in any age is that which does magic with words, and that the subject matter is merely the springboard for the writer's imagination; that the art of fiction, if it can any longer be called that, has grown from nothing to an artificial synthesis in a mere matter of 300 years, and has now reached such a degree of mechanical perfection that the only way you can tell the novelists apart is by whether they write about miners in Butte, coolies in China, Jews in the Bronx, or stockbrokers on Long Island, or whatever it is; that all the women and most of the men write exactly the same, or at least choose one of half a dozen thoroughly standardized procedures; and that in spite of certain inevitable slight differences (very slight indeed on the long view) the whole damn business could be turned out by a machine just as well, and will be almost any day now; and that the only writers left who have *anything* to say are those who write about practically nothing and monkey around with odd ways of doing it.

I think you're all crazy. I'm going into the motion picture business. I might even get to be a producer.

Ray

---

6. *Repent in Haste*, by John P. Marquand (1893–1960).

[59]

TO HAMISH HAMILTON

6520 Drexel Ave.
Los Angeles 36 Calif.
Jan. 9, 1946

Dear Jamie:

.   .   .

I should have starved to death if I had been dependent on what Knopf
paid me. I am quite sure he did his level best, but the tradition is
all against any large sale of mysteries in their original edition. And the
publishers have cooperated in the rental library swindle over a period
of years with such infinite good humour that even I, who realise the
poisition of the author and can afford to buy mysteries, very seldom
do so, unless in cheap reprints. To say that a book which is not worth
buying unless it is worth re-reading is no answer. Practically no
fiction now being published is worth re-reading and damn little of it
worth reading at all. Yet if a novel is well reviewed in *Time* or
The New Yorker or *Newsweek*, etc. I am likely to order it sight unseen
(often to be badly fooled of course). A mystery I do not buy unless I
know what I am buying. There is something very wry about all this.
I have a book called *Mr. Bowling Buys a Newspaper* which I have
read half a dozen times and have bought right and left to give away.[1]
I think it is one of the most fascinating books written in the last
ten years and I know nobody in my limited circle who doesn't agree
with me. Yet I doubt if it sold 5000 copies over here. There is
something wrong with the book business. The publisher is probably
far the best judge of books there is, but he simply cannot put them
over. Either they sell themselves (in which case he can plunge on
advertising and build them up very fast) or they do not sell. Of course
we are all semi-literates over here and if a book is not 'significant,'
we think it is trash. And by significant we mean that it does our
thinking for us. God knows we can't do it ourselves. There is of
course a leavening of superbly intelligent people, but the average

1. By Donald Henderson

'educated' American has the all round mental equipment of a fourth form boy in an English public school. Well—enough of the griping.

I am out on strike at Paramount—a one man strike. That is to say I refuse to perform under my contract and so far they refuse to cancel it. There is much talk of money, but that is a smoke screen. Beyond a certain point money merely means complication. You have the bother and expense of handling it and protecting it and you do not have the spending of it. Fundamentally the issue is freedom. I have only a limited number of useful years left and I do not want to use any of them up destroying what talent I have. It is possible to make good pictures—within limits—but to do it you have to work with good people. They exist in Hollywood, but they are scattered and at the moment none of them is available to me at Paramount. The studio is now under the control of a man whose attitude to picture-making is that if you own 1600 theatres, all you have to do is grind out the product as quickly and economically as possible. I cannot do anything in that atmosphere except spend time and collect a salary. It's not good enough. The last picture I did there nearly killed me. The producer was in the doghouse—he has since left—and the director was a stale old hack who had been directing for thiry years without once achieving any real distinction. Obviously he never could. So here was I a mere writer and a tired one at that screaming at the front office to protect the producer and actually going on the set to direct scenes—I know nothing about directing—in order that the whole project might be saved from going down the drain. Well, it was saved. As pictures go it is pretty lively. No classic, but no dud either.[2] But at what a price! And then I had to go to MGM to work on *The Lady in the Lake*, which bored me so enormously that I practically rewrote the story in order to have something fresh to look at. I didn't finish it, and it is probably all bitched up by now (or perhaps I bitched it up), but after that one was over I had to be hit on the head with a baseball bat to make me get out of a chair.

I am now doing a Marlowe story and frankly I wish it were better. In fact, except for practical reasons I'd like to forget all about Mr. Marlowe for several years. But I have to keep him alive somehow. There are radio programs in the offing and other low ways

2. *The Blue Dahlia.*

of making money. When and if this is done I have a novel in mind which (if I can write it) ought to be a step up. There is a murder in it, but it is not a mystery. The scene should properly be laid in England, since it is that sort of story, but I can't do it. It is too long since I left. Incidentally I still regard myself as an exile and want to come back. But I suppose it will be years before that is a reasonable thing to do.

Yours most sincerely

Raymond Chandler

TO ALFRED KNOPF

6520 Drexel Ave.
Los Angeles 36, Calif.
Jan. 12th. 1946

Dear Alfred:

Good wishes to you and yours and many thanks for the Max Beerbohm book. I found it sad reading. It belongs to the age of taste, to which I once belonged. It took me back too far, to that first slim immortal volume which I still possess.[1] What a magnificent writer the old boy somehow did not become. Born half a century too late, I suppose.

I am enclosing a letter from a Jewish lady on a now familiar subject,[2] and my answer. This is the only one I have answered. Would you have the great kindness to send me a copy of my letter, in case I should want to use it again? That is, of course, if you agree with my writing it. If you do not, I should like to argue the point with you.

I no longer have a secretary since I no longer have a motion picture job. I am what is technically known as suspended. For refusing to perform under a contract which is not a proper expression of my standing in the motion picture business. I requested a

1. Max Beerbohm, *The Works of Max Beerbohm*, 1896.
2. See letter to Miss Aron, immediately following.

cancellation, but was denied that. There is no moral issue involved since the studios have destroyed the moral basis of contracts themselves. They tear them up whenever it suits them. In getting rid of a writer they use a term "adjusting the contract" which means paying him a few weeks salary under the threat of keeping his idea until his next option times comes up, with everyone knowing he has no assignment and that no producer on the lot wants him. This ought to work both ways. I have had no assistance worth mentioning in this controversy, since the Hollywood agent, however nice a fellow, is strictly a summer soldier. Syd wrote Mealand, Paramount's story editor, a very strong letter, and they were afraid to show it to Ginsberg, head of the studio.[3]

Paramount has raised the legal point that I cannot write for myself while suspended. This was all considered and thought out long ago. Their point has no validity, so far as I can determine, but they have the machinery to make trouble for me without cost to themselves, and I do not intend to spend my hard-earned (and God *was* it hard-earned) cash to defend law suits. Rather than do that I would go back and give them the two pictures I still owe.

One of the troubles is that it seems quite impossible to convince anyone that a man would turn his back on a whopping salary—whopping by the standards of normal living—for any reason but a tactical manoeuvre through which he hopes to acquire a still more whopping salary. What I want is something quite different: a freedom from datelines and unnatural pressures, and a right to find and work with those few people in Hollywood whose purpose is to make the best pictures possible within the limitations of a popular art, not merely to repeat the old and vulgar formulae. And only a little of that.

The ethics of this industry may be judged by the fact that late last night a very important independent producer called me up and asked me to do a screenplay of one of the most advertised projects of the year, do it on the quiet, secretly, with full knowledge that it would be a violation of my contract. That meant nothing to him; it never occurred to him that he was insulting me. Perhaps, in spite of my faults, I still have a sense of honor. I may quarrel, but at least I

---

3. Sydney Sanders was Chandler's agent, Richard Mealand was head of the story department, Henry Ginsberg was general manager of production.

[63]

put the point at issue down on the table in front of me. I am perfectly willing to let them examine my sleeves for hidden cards. But I don't think they really want to. They would be horrified to find them empty. They do not like to deal with honest men.

I am trying to finish up a Marlowe story. I am in a bit of a quandary about it. The practical need to keep the character alive is important for many reasons, among them the threat of a radio program which must eventually mature and which may go on for years. But I no longer have any passion for this stuff. I find myself kidding myself. I enjoy it and find it fun, but I have a suspicion that the quality that finally put these stories over was a sort of controlled half-poetical emotion. That for the story of blood and mystery I seem to have lost. Or rather I see so many other things I'd like to do. I have two novels in my head I want to write so much more. It is not that I have any ambition to become a writer of intellectual set pieces, because I know the audience I have to deal with and what they will not read is written in sand. From the beginning, from the first pulp story, it was always with me a question (first of course of how to write a story at all) of putting into the stuff something they would not shy off from, perhaps even not know was there as a conscious realization, but which would somehow distill through their minds and leave an afterglow. A man with a realistic habit of thought can no longer write for intellectuals. There are too few of them and they are too specious. Neither can he deliberately write for people he despises, or for the slick magazines (Hollywood is less degrading than that) or for money alone. There must be idealism but there must also be contempt. This kind of talk may seem a little ridiculous coming from me. It is possibly that like Max Beerbohm I was born half a century too late, and that I too belong to an age of grace. I could so easily have become everything our world has no use for. So I wrote for the *Black Mask*. What a wry joke.

No doubt I have learned a lot from Hollywood. Please do not think I completely despise it, because I don't. The best proof of that may be that every producer I have worked for I would work for again, and every one of them, in spite of my tantrums, would be glad to have me. But the overall picture, as the boys say, is of a degraded community whose idealism even is largely fake. The pretentiousness, the bogus enthusiasm, the constant drinking and drabbing, the incessant squabbling over money, the all-pervasive agent, the strutting of the big shots (and their usually utter incompetence to achieve anything they start out to do), the constant fear of losing all this fairy gold and being the nothing they have really never ceased to be, the snide tricks, the whole damn mess is out of this world. It is a great subject for a novel—probably the greatest still untouched. But how to do it with a level mind, that's the thing that baffles me. It is like one of these South American palace revolutions conducted by officers in comic opera uniforms—only when the thing is over the ragged dead men lie in rows against the wall, and you suddenly know that this is not funny, this is the Roman circus, and damn near the end of a civilization.

Ray

TO MISS ARON

6520 Drexel Ave.
Los Angeles 36, Calif.
Jan. 11, 1946

Dear Miss Aron:
I hope I address you correctly. I assume that you would have indicated, if it has been "Mrs." I thank you for your letter of November 30th and I quite agree that it deserves an answer. But I'm afraid I can't make a very good one, for the reason that I don't know what it is all about. I might say that I have received about a dozen letters on this subject, ranging from the pathological-vituperative to the courteous (of which yours is the only true example).
This book was published in 1942.[1] It has been for sale and in rental libraries for quite a long time. Apparently the outburst is due to the .25 edition. I had heard no previous whisper of complaint. I have many Jewish friends. I even have Jewish relatives. My publisher is a Jew. Are you one of those who object to that word? If so, what

1. *The High Window*.

would you like me to substitute? I am *not* being sarcastic. Also, *all* the letters have come from the east. Out here the Jews seem to be in a fair way to lose their inferiority complex. At least my doctor thinks so. He is a Jew also.

You say why don't I introduce a character as a "thin-blooded Roman Catholic or a rugged Episcopalian"? Simply, my dear, because religion has nothing to do with it. You may happen to be an orthodox Hebrew, but there are Roman Catholic Jews and Christian Scientist Jews and Jews with no religion at all, and Jews—very, very many—who are Hebrews just once a year, on the Day of Atonement. I call a character a Jew for purely intellectual reasons occasionally, since there is, except on the most exalted levels of personality a Jewish way of thought too.

The Jew is a type and I like types, that being as far as I have gone. He is of course many types, some recognizable a block away, some only on more intimate study, some hardly at all. I know there are Jewish people whom even Jews cannot pick out. I have had two secretaries who told me that, both being Jewish girls. There is a tone of voice, there is a certain eye, there is a coloring. It is not, dear lady, a matter of noses.

You are kind enough not to accuse me of anti-semitism. I am grateful for that since I am horribly tired of the whole subject. And at the same time I am terribly sorry for these tormented minds which cannot leave it alone, which worry it and keep it sore. A writer in the SRL lately said that what the Jews demand is not the right to have geniuses, but the right to have scoundrels.[2] I agree. And I demand the right to call a character named Weinstein a thief without being accused of calling all Jews thieves. That right, with certain people, I do not have.

Incidentally Dr. Carl Moss is a portrait of my publisher, Alfred Knopf. Not exact, but with the offhand respect which is all Philip Marlowe would have for anyone. And *I* am *not* Philip Marlowe.

Let me in all kindness say one final word. You are yourself not the type, but if among your friends there is an impulse to go on an anti-semitic witch hunt, let them look for their enemies not among those who call a Jew a Jew, who put Jewish characters in their books because there are many Jews in their lives and all interesting and all

2. *Saturday Review of Literature.*

[66]

different and some noble and some rather nasty—like other people—
but let them look for their enemies among the brutes (whom they
can easily recognize) and among the snobs who do not speak of Jews
at all.

You are safe and more than safe with outspoken people like
me.

Very sincerely,

Raymond Chandler

TO ERLE STANLEY GARDNER

6520 Drexel Ave.
Los Angeles 36, Calif.
Jan. 29, 1946

Dear Erle:

Most of what you write is a complete surprise to me—
including the idea that you are a lousy writer. I may later ask the
privilege of addressing the Court on that point. I don't think I ever
knew that Phil Cody had been editor of the *BM*[1] or that Hammett
and you and others had been in the book for years. I didn't know the
magazine until 1932 or 1933, although I later picked up a few older
copies. In view of the fact that I was raised on Latin and Greek and
once wrote essays and book reviews for a *very* highbrow English
weekly, the story of how I became a multiple murderer may have a
certain piquancy, but there's not time to go into it now. Nor did
I know that Cody was the real discoverer of Hammett and his first
strong encouragement. I think these things need airing. I have always
received from Shaw the definite impression (borne out by his
projected introduction to his projected anthology) that he invented the
hardboiled dick story with a ready assist from Hammett.[2] Certainly

1. *Black Mask* magazine.
2. Joseph Shaw succeeded Cody as editor of *Black Mask*.

[67]

nothing of Shaw's own fiction that I have seen has any such germs in it. It's about the deadest writing I ever saw, on a supposedly professional level. I don't know what Hammett was writing before he and Shaw had the brainwave, but it is now obvious to me and would have been earlier if I had really done any serious thinking on the subject, that it did not happen all at once. There must have been experiments and discussions and a need to get an okay from the boss. Shaw's gifts as an editor seem to me now to be exactly what you rate them. He was a warm editor and always seemed to have time to write at length and to argue with you. To some of us I think he was indeed a genuine inspiration in that, just as you say, we wrote better for him than we could have written for anybody else. The proof of that is that some writers we both know have never reached the standard again that they attained in the *BM* under Shaw. I also agree with you that he was blind to any kind of writing he did not think the best at the moment. I don't believe Cornell Woolrich or Cleve Adams ever made the *BM* under his editorship, although both were probably far better men than some of his regulars. Norbert Davis also, who took his murders rather lightly when allowed, made the *BM* only two or three times.[3] He said Shaw was too fussy for him and took the whole thing too seriously. I'm quite sure Shaw would never have published a story I once wrote kidding the pants off the tough dick story, but Ken White did.[4]

·   ·   ·

I now address the Court, by permission, on the subject of one Gardner, an alleged writer of mysteries. As I speak I have two solid rows of Gardners in front of me, and am still trying to shop around to complete the collection. I probably know as much about the essential qualities of good writing as anybody now discussing it. I do not discuss these things professionally for the simple reason that I do not consider it worthwhile. I am not interested in pleasing the intellectuals by writing literary criticism, because literary criticism as an art has in these days too narrow a scope and too limited a public,

3. Adams and Davis belonged to the hard-boiled school of detective novelists.
4. "Pearls Are a Nuisance," originally published in *Dime Detective Magazine*, edited by White.

just as has poetry. I do not believe it is a writer's function to talk to a dead generation of leisured people who once had time to relish the niceties of critical thought. The critics of today are tired Bostonians like Van Wyck Brooks or smart-alecks like Fadiman or honest men confused by the futility of their job, like Edmund Wilson. The reading public is intellectually adolescent at best, and it is obvious that what is called "significant literature" will only be sold to this public by exactly the same methods as are used to sell it toothpaste, cathartics and automobiles. It is equally obvious that since this public has been taught to read by brute force it will, in between its bouts with the latest "significant" bestseller, want to read books that are fun and excitement. So like all half-educated publics in all ages it turns with relief to the man who tells a story and nothing else. To say that what this man writes is not literature is just like saying that a book can't be any good if it makes you want to read it. When a book, any sort of book, reaches a certain intensity of artistic performance, it becomes literature. That intensity may be a matter of style, situation, character, emotional tone, or idea, or half a dozen other things. It may also be a perfection of control over the movement of a story similar to the control a great pitcher has over the ball. That is to me what you have more than anything else and more than anyone else. Dumas Père had it. Dickens, allowing for his Victorian muddle, had it; begging your pardon I don't think Edgar Wallace approached it. His stories died all along the line and had to be revived. Yours don't. Every page throws the hook for the next. I call this a kind of genius. I regard myself as a pretty exacting reader; detective stories as such don't mean a thing to me. But it must be obvious that if I have half a dozen unread books beside my chair and one of them is a Perry Mason, and I reach for the Perry Mason and let the others wait, that book must have quality.

Strangely enough I didn't always feel this way, and I think for the same reason Shaw didn't. I was so steeped in the rugged stuff that I didn't realize how stupid it can be unless it is superbly well done. Today I could no more read a book by Coxe or Adams than I could eat a kangaroo. I think also that I do agree you didn't do your best work for *BM*. In fact you've only been doing it at the peak the last four or five years. It's pretty obvious to me why that is too. You never were a *Black Mask* writer in Shaw's meaning of the term. You never really were tough. You owed nothing to Hammett or Hemingway. Your books have no brutality or sadism, very little sex, and the blood doesn't count. What counts, at least for me, is a supremely skilful combination of the mental quality of the detective story and the movement of the mystery-adventure story. I read the Doug Selby stories and like them and try to guess where the hell Madison City is (the nearest I can come is Riverside, and that isn't quite right) but there is something missing. I liked the A. A. Fair stories, especially the first ones, but they have in the end the same defect the Nero Wolfe stories have: an eccentric character wears out its welcome. The character that lasts is an ordinary guy with some extraordinary qualities. Perry Mason is the perfect detective because he has the intellectual approach of the juridical mind and at the same time the restless quality of the adventurer who won't stay put. I think he is just about perfect. So let's not have any more of that phooey about "as literature my stuff still stinks." Who says so— William Dean Howells?

As to me, I am not busy and I am not successful in any important way. I don't get written what I want to write and I get balled up in what I do write. I made a lot of money last year, but the government took half of it and expenses took half of the rest. I'm not poor, but neither am I in anything like your condition, or ever will be. My wife has been under the weather with the flu for ten days, but she wants to come down to your place as much as I do. I'm working at home because I refused to report to Paramount and took a suspension. They refused to tear up my contract. A writer has no real chance in pictures unless he is willing to become a producer, and that is too tough for me. The last picture I worked on was just one long row.[5] The producer was fine, but he was on the way out. The director has been thirty years in Hollywood without ever doing a first class job, or, I should add in fairness, a very bad one. But it was my picture, I wrote it from the ground up, and I hoped for a little more finesse than I got. However, they say it's good, and good original screenplays are almost as rare in Hollywood as virgins.

Ray

5. *The Blue Dahlia.*

TO WILLIAM W. SEWARD

6520 Drexel Drive
Los Angeles, California
Mar 27 1946

Dear Professor Seward:

Some time ago, at your request, I sent you one of my books. I am wondering if you ever received it. It seems rather curious that you should not have acknowledged it, if it arrived.

I don't exactly know why I am writing this note. It is not a matter of great consequence either way. I suppose I find the incident rather shocking.

Yours very truly,

Raymond Chandler

TO BLANCHE KNOPF

6520 Drexel Ave.
Los Angeles 36, Calif.
Mar 27 1946

Dear Blanche:

Thanks for your note, and it's always a pleasure to hear from you. I got pretty well into a Marlowe story but ran into a bad spell of flu and have been dragging myself around ever since. Also I am in trouble with Paramount and may have to go back and finish a couple of jobs for them. Short of an action to cancel the contract, there seems no other way to deal with the situation. And even an equity action takes time and money and is uncertain. I have developed a peculiar phobia about contracts, seem unable to function as a free man when tied up in any way. All very silly, no doubt, but there it is. The mere fact that sometime I must go to a studio to do a job of work seems to prevent my doing anything valid for myself. Hollywood is a trying place in many ways, but at least they pay you for your work.

I don't understand this reprint situation at all. There is a body of opinion that seems to regard the royalities the Pocket Book people are paying as something like outright theft. I do not understand why a publisher should collect three times as much *in royalities* on a writer's books as the publisher pays the writer out in royalities on the original edition. I have a feeling that a situation has developed which needs airing. Why is it not explained? Is it right that a sale of a million copies of a two-bit reprint should bring the man who created the material sold a matter of $7500? This needs an answer. I do not think it *is* right. I think the author on *all* reprints should have a minimum royalty of ten percent of the retail price. Anything less has me wondering what goes on. No wonder writers accept the conditions of Hollywood and say to hell with bookwriting. Leave it to the women. It's all mechanics and promotion anyway. As I told my friend Morton of the *Atlantic* not long ago, the technique of marketable fiction has become almost entirely epicene. It won't be long now until somebody invents a machine to write novels. How often do I pick up a book and say, "This was written by an individual unlike any other individual, a unique person."? Practically never.

But don't take me too seriously. I am becoming a pretty sour kind of citizen. Even Hemingway has let me down. I've been rereading a lot of his stuff. I would have said here is one guy who writes like himself, and I would have been right, but not the way I meant it. Ninety per cent of it is the godddamndest self-imitation. He never really wrote but one story. All the rest is the same thing in different pants—or without different pants. And his eternal preoccupation with what goes on between the sheets becomes rather nauseating in the end. One reaches a time of life when limericks written on the walls of comfort stations are not just obscene, they are horribly dull. This man has only one subject and he makes that ridiculous. I suppose the man's epitaph, if he had the choosing of it, would be: Here Lies A Man Who Was Bloody Good in Bed. Too Bad He's Alone Here. But the point is I begin to doubt whether he ever

was. You don't have to work so hard at things you are really good
at—or do you?

> I thank you.
> Ray

TO ERLE STANLEY GARDNER

> 6520 Drexel Ave.
> Los Angeles 36 Calif.
> April 4th. 1946

Dear Erle:

Thanks for your kind message. I don't think either my wife or
myself could hike or ride. She had an operation on her foot about
a year ago and it's still weak. We don't know how to ride. I am a
complete nervous wreck and theoretically could walk a few miles, but
probably not your kind of walking. Haven't the equipment anyhow.
What we hoped to do was just to get down to your place around
noon and spend a few hours with you. We have some business in
Riverside and were thinking of stopping over at the Mission Inn and
then driving to Temecula in the morning.

However, my war with Paramount has flared up again and I
am stuck here at any rate until next week, and then may have to go to
Santa Barbara. So we'll just have to let it ride for the time being. I
have been trying for six months to get my contract with Paramount
torn up. Have refused to go to work, they hurled threats, I responded
with a dignified silence (at times). We are now making an armistice to
be followed by a peace treaty. The great difficulty in dealing with
a studio is that the men you deal with are in their turn responsible to
a New York hierarchy which had no part in making pictures, but
only in exhibiting and promoting them. To them a picture is just as
much a manufactured product as a can of beans. They cannot allow

[73]

for the personal equation because they don't meet it. I believe I and my lawyer and agent have won a remarkable victory in fact, which can still by the studio's legal department be made to look like a practical victory for the company. And that of course is what they must have for face-saving purposes.

I was very eager to discuss the reprint situation with you. I understood that you did not agree with the position of Rex Stout's committee on reprint royalties, but I don't think I have heard why. I personally think that the royalty *to the author* on any reprint should not be less than 10 per cent of the retail price. It seems like pure theft that Pocket Books should shell out a measly fifteen grand on a million sale and that the publisher should get half of that. I may be all wet on this, but surely the publishers are getting an excessive share of the returns from markets which did not even exist when they made their contracts and which they have done almost nothing to create. Of course I admit you never get what you should. Nobody but the middleman ever does. In Hollywood it is now recognized that the screenplay cost should approximate ten per cent of the picture cost, but if a single writer does the whole job, he cannot get anything like that without going into a percentage deal. I am not talking about sales of screen rights, but of the cost of making the screenplay itself, the shooting script. The big money still goes to the wrong people. Nevertheless Hollywood does pay the writer pretty well if he is any good. The book trade pays him abominably unless he writes best sellers, and that means best sellers in the original edition. You and I may never write a best seller, even a moderate best seller, in that sense, and yet there is a better continuing sale for our kind of stuff than for any other kind. I think we are getting gyped on the reprints. A man whose book sells a quarter or half a million copies in any kind of edition ought to get a very substantial income out of it. We don't. You beat the racket by having so many books around. I can't beat it that way because I am a slow writer. Of course you don't beat it really. You simply make a lot of money, but that doesn't mean you shouldn't make five times as much for the same out put.

I refused to write an introduction for Shaw's anthology. Don't know whether he is hurt about it or not.

Ray

[74]

TO HAMISH HAMILTON

Dear Jamie:

.　　　.　　　.

When and if you see *The Big Sleep* (the first half of it anyhow), you will realize what can be done with this sort of story by a director with the gift of atmosphere and the requisite touch of hidden sadism. Bogart, of course, is also so much better than any other tough-guy actor that he makes bums of the Ladds and the Powells. As we say here, Bogart can be tough without a gun. Also he has a sense of humor that contains that grating undertone of contempt. Ladd is hard, bitter and occasionally charming, but he is after all a small boy's idea of a tough guy, Bogart is the genuine article. Like Edward G. Robinson when he was younger all he has to do to dominate a scene is to enter it. *The Big Sleep* has had an unfortunate history. The girl who played the nymphy sister[1] was so good she shattered Miss Bacall completely. So they cut the picture in such a way that all her best scenes were left out except one. The result made nonsense and Howard Hawks threatened to sue to restrain Warners from releasing the picture. After long argument, as I hear it, he went back and did a lot of re-shooting. I have not seen the result of this. The picture has not even been trade-shown. But if Hawks got his way, the picture will be the best of its kind. Since I had nothing to do with it, I say this with some faint regret. Well, that's not exactly true because Hawks time after time got dissatisfied with his script and would go back to the book and shoot scenes straight out of it. There was also a wonderful scene he and I planned together in talk. At the end of the picture Bogart and Carmen were caught in Geiger's house by the Eddie Mars and his lifetakers. That is Bogart (Marlowe) was trapped there and the girl came along and they let her go in. Bogart knew she was a murderess and he also knew that the first person out of that door would walk into a hail of machine gun bullets. The girl didn't know this. Marlowe also knew that if he sent the girl out to be killed, the gang would take it on the lam, thus saving his own life for the time being. He didn't feel like

1. Martha Vickers.

[75]

playing God or saving his skin by letting Carmen leave. Neither did he feel like playing Sir Philip Sidney to save a worthless life. So he put it up to God by tossing a coin. Before he tossed the coin he prayed out loud, in a sort of way. The gist of his prayer was that he, Marlowe, had done the best he knew how and through no fault of his own was put in a position of making a decision God had no right to force him to make. He wanted that decision made by the authority who allowed all this mess to happen. If the coin came down heads, he would let the girl go. He tossed and it came down heads. The girl thought this was some kind of a game to hold her there for the police. She started to leave. At the last moment, as she had her hand on the doorknob, Marlowe weakened and started for her to stop her. She laughed in his face and pulled a gun on him. Then she opened the door an inch or two and you could see she was going to shoot and was thoroughly delighted with the situation. At that moment a burst of machine gun fire walked across the panel of the door and tore her to pieces. The gunmen outside had heard a siren in the distance and panicked and thrown a casual burst through the door just for a visiting card—without expecting to hit anyone. I don't know what happened to this scene. Perhaps the boys wouldn't write it or couldn't. Perhaps Mr. Bogart wouldn't play it. You never know in Hollywood. All I know is it would have been a hair-raising thing if well done. I think I'll try it myself sometime.

.   .   .

All the best,

Ray

TO CHARLES MORTON

Paramount Pictures
5451 Marathon Street
Hollywood 38, Calif.
June 14, 1946

Dear Charles:

What Wolcott Gibbs has to say about it [*The Hucksters* by Frederic Wakeman] in *The New Yorker* doesn't mean a thing to me. The fact that Gibbs (together with other *New Yorker* critical minds) is gifted with a talent for derogatory criticism, doesn't necessarily make him a good critic. I remember, long ago, when I was doing book-reviews in London, that my first impulse always was to find something smart and nasty to say because that sort of writing is so much easier. In spite of its superficial sophistication, the whole attitude of the *New Yorker* seems to me to have that same touch of under-graduate sarcasm. I find this sort of thing rather juvenile. In fact, heretical as it may seem, I'm beginning to find the *New Yorker* a very dull periodical.

Kindest regards,

Ray

TO H. N. SWANSON

Sunday August 4th [1946]

Dear Swanie:

Thanks for yours of July 31st. I imagine everyone ought to meet Samuel Goldwyn this side of paradise, I've heard he feels so good when he stops. But since the whole thing is predicated on my working for him and I ain't gonna, is it worth while? I don't know. I don't know anything, except that the standard method of working with writers is not for me. I think it works for 80% of the writers in Hollywood, that through it the studios somehow get pictures they would never get and ought never to get, if they relied on the writers having any judgment of what is a picture. I don't think the system works for those writers who, whatever their faults, cannot work effectively unless they can somehow preserve the illusion that they are doing their own writing according to their own sense of what is right. If Paramount had had the sense to let me write my own idea of a rough screenplay on *Mrs. Duff*, without the interference of a producer's ideas, ambition, and eagerness to dominate a project to his own advantage, they would have got something in a comparatively short time which would have shown them at a glance where the picture was.[1] It wouldn't have to be perfect, or even right. It would have been a screen treatment in screenplay form (with probably a lot of usable scenes) of the story as it interested me to write it. But no, they simply cannot realize that what they want from me is what I write in my own way; they think they can get that and at the same time control almost every move I make and every idea I have. It just can't be done. What I have to give them is not craftmanship but a certain quality. If they want that quality, they can't get it anywhere else. If they bring in the Steve Fishers to polish my work, they get something entirely different, so why bother with me at all?[2] I suppose you would regard Dudley Nichols as a great screenplay writer, and I shouldn't deny it. But what is there in his work that is Nichols? Is there anything in the *Bells of Saint Mary, Scarlet Street* and *Stagecoach* that belongs to one man and one man only? If there is, I can't see it. Perhaps to someone more expert in the business, it would be apparent. To me all three of these pictures, and any others of his you care to mention that I have seen, could have been written by different writers. As far as any individual style is concerned, they are completely anonymous. That is not the kind of work I want to do in pictures. If that is the only kind of work—or something much inferior, technically—I am allowed to do, then I have nothing to contribute. For this reason I will not work for dominating people like Selznick or Goldwyn. If you deprive me of the right to do my own kind of writing, there is almost nothing left.

We are going to La Jolla tomorrow for a few days.

What's holding me up on the book is that in the disgusted (and disgusting) state of mind I am in I wouldn't dare look at it.

Love

Ray

P.S. La Valencia Hotel, Glencoe 52175 (San Diego) in case of emergency. An emergency would to my mind be a lot of money for nothing.

R.

1. Chandler worked on the screenplay of *The Innocent Mrs. Duff*, a novel by Elisabeth Sanxay Holding.
2. Fisher completed the screenplay of *The Lady in the Lake*.

TO DALE WARREN

6005 Camino de la Costa
La Jolla, California
October Second 1946

Dear Dale Warren:

.　　　　.　　　　.

I suppose you read a bookseller out here was convicted of selling indecency in Edmund Wilson's *Memoirs of Hecate County*. Very discouraging. The book is indecent enough, of course, and in exactly the most offensive way—without passion, like a phallus made of dough. Now they are bootlegging the damn thing at $25 a copy. It isn't worth the original asking price. Being, like all those who have worked in Hollywood, somewhat of a connoisseur of the damp fart, I place Mr. Wilson high on the list. His careful and pedestrian and sometimes rather intelligent book reviews misguide one into thinking there is something in his head besides mucilage. There isn't.

Having started both the above paragraphs with I—I was taught not to as a schoolboy—let me add that I (we) have moved to La Jolla permanently, or as permanently as anything can be nowadays. If I do any more work for Hollywood, which I probably shall, I can do nine tenths of it here anyway. That is, if I can find a secretary. We live close beside the sounding sea—it's just across the street and down a low cliff—but the Pacific is usually very sedate. We have a much better home than an out-of-work pulp writer has any right to expect.

The story I am working on seems to me to lack some of the nobler qualities. In addition to which I find it dull. I wonder could I be washed up for good. It's possible. Better men than I have gone to grease in Hollywood.

.　　　　.　　　　.

Sincerely,

Raymond Chandler

[79]

TO HAMISH HAMILTON

Dear Jamie:

Your letter of September 30th. makes me rather uneasy. "A new Philip Marlowe story by Raymond Chandler, tentatively called *The Little Sister*, and dealing with some rather queer characters in Hollywood, not to mention an innocent little girl from Kansas, who may or may not be quite as innocent as she looks." That's about all I could tell you at the moment.

I have what you people called "a thing" about discussing or writing about anything I haven't licked. I'm never sure I shall lick it. I might blow up completely about page 250 (which means the silly little triple-spaced half pages I type on) and shelve the whole project.

Three years in Hollywood leaves its mark. My kind of writing takes a certain quality of high spirits and impudence. I'm a tired character, a battered pulp writer, an out of work hack. Also, as a mental hazard I might mention that although it seems to me almost mandatory as a business move that I should do a Marlowe story, I have a couple of other notions I'd much rather be trying to work out.

My title may not be very good. It's just the best I can think of without straining. I have peculiar ideas about titles. They should never be obviously provocative, nor say anything about murder. They should be rather indirect and neutral, but the form of words should be a little unusual. I haven't achieved this here. However, as some big publisher once remarked, a good title is the title of a successful book. Offhand, nobody would have thought *The Thin Man* a great title. *The Maltese Falcon* is, because it has rhyme and rhythm and makes the mind ask questions.

As to publishers, I wonder if they know anything about titles. Knopf made me change the title of *The High Window*, but I see Twentieth Century-Fox has restored the original title. Knopf objected strenuously to *Farewell, My Lovely*, and this, according to my Hollywood friends (who are a pretty good judge of these things) is one of the great titles of pure magic that rarely come along. Knopf still feels, I think, that the title hurt the sales of the book. Perhaps he is right. But Pocketbooks didn't find it any disadvantage.

Oh yes, the book will run in length, I hope, not more than 70,000 words, perhaps less.

I never really solved my agent problem. I still feel much about the same about agents as a class: that they are often a nuisance and sometimes do very stupid things. But living down here in La Jolla, and not being able to face a regular secretary around the house, I don't see how I could function without an agent. The thing about agents that really annoys me is not that they make mistakes, but that they never admit them.

All the best,

Ray

TO WILLIAM TARG[1]

6005 Camino de la Costa
La Jolla, California
Nov. 14th. 1946

Dear Mr. Targ:

Thanks for yours of Nov. 12th. which I am sending to my Hollywood agent, Mr. H. N. Swanson, 8523 Sunset Boulevard, Hollywood 46, Calif. What New York representation he will arrange I do not know yet.

The terms on this deal I will leave to him. What I am concerned with is what goes into the book, and whether a somewhat intellectual article such as the *Atlantic* piece is an appropriate introduction to a collection of what are after all just old pulp novelettes. Frankly, I just don't know about the last point. The article rather takes the position, which I still think valid, that the old

1. Targ, then of World Publishing Company, had proposed an anthology of Chandler's *Black Mask* stories using Chandler's *Atlantic* article, "The Simple Art of Murder," as a preface.

fashioned body-in-the-library detection novel is a good deal of bunk
a) because it can never be about anything real and b) because it
doesn't stand up under its own rules. Then I say that the only thing
that's any good is the realistic detective or mystery novel. And *then* I
proceed to hand the public a bunch of stories which, whatever their
merits or demerits, were certainly not what I was building up to in
the essay. I could have written them much better even then, but the
point is I wasn't allowed to. And I can't alibi on that score.

I can't avoid the thought that the use of the essay as a preface
to my own early writings makes me look kind of silly. I presume you
have considered that. I presume you have an argument against it.

As to the actual selection of the stories, since they have already
been republished in both .49 and .25 editions, I suppose a larger
book on the same reprint price scale is not going to do any harm. I
know you want a fairly long book to justify your price. But there are
a few of these stories I'd just as soon see go out of circulation, for
various reasons. I'd like to discuss these reasons with my agent too.
I'll be seeing him next week.

Sincerely yours,

Raymond Chandler

TO H. N. SWANSON

6005 Camino de la Costa
La Jolla, California
December 20, 1946

Dear Swanie:

This is to thank you very, very much for your Christmas gift
of the little radio.

From the shape of it, I gather that it was to be placed on a
bookshelf. I have therefore placed it between Roget's *Thesaurus* and

[82]

Bartlett's *Quotations*, and the cretinous dialogue of "When a Girl Marries" coming out from between these two books certainly gives me a laugh.

My wife said (paraphrased slightly), "Why the hell should Swanson keep on giving you presents when you don't do a damned thing for him except cause him a lot of worry, and especially when you give him nothing in return?"

I am therefore going to look for a pair of twelve-hundred-year old Ming vases to present to you on your next birthday, and I hope they will be large enough to be used as receptacles for your discarded clients.

Kindest regards and best wishes to you and yours,

TO MRS. ROBERT J. HOGAN[1]

December 27, 1946

Dear Mrs. Hogan:

.   .   .

My experience with trying to help people to write has been limited but extremely intensive. I have done everything from giving would-be writers money to live on to plotting and rewriting their stories for them, and so far I have found it to be all waste. The people whom God or nature intended to be writers find their own answers, and those who have to ask are impossible to help. They are merely people who want to be writers.

.   .   .

Yours very truly,

Raymond Chandler

1. A New Jersey teacher who had written asking for advice to give to the young.

TO CHARLES MORTON

6005 Camino de la Costa
La Jolla, California
·Sunday Jan. 5th. 1947

Dear Charles:

.   .   .

Have just finished reading *Command Decision*, not in the *Atlantic*, the book.[1] I suppose some was omitted. I found it absolutely (or almost) unputdownable and at the same time as complete a waste of time in a sense as one of Gardner's Perry Mason stories, which I also find unputdownable. *B.F.'s Daughter* is the same, but has a little more penetration into character.[2] Books like this start me pondering without getting very far on just what literature is turning into. I wrote you once in a mood of rough sarcasm that the techniques of fiction had become so highly standardized that one of these days a machine would write novels. What bothers me about this book, *Command Decision*, and others like it is that it has everything in the way of skill and perception and wit and honesty a good novel ought to have. It has a subject, something I never had yet; it has a sharp immediate sense of life as it is right now. I'd be hard put to it to say just what it does *not* have, but that thing, whatever it is, is more important than what it does have. I'm absolutely sure of that, although I don't expect to sell anyone else on the idea. Your Mr. Weeks, who is a much more intelligent man than I am, thinks Marquand is a serious writer.[3] I do not. I think he is a quick and clever journalist. I think he will be utterly forgotten five years after he dies, by all but a few. Is it that these books are written very quickly, in a kind of heat? No answer; so was a lot of literature that has lasted a long time. The time of composition has nothing to do with it; some minds distill much faster than others. Is it that the writers of these books are using completely borrowed techniques and consequently do not convey the feeling that they have created, but

1. William Wister Haines, *Command Decision*, 1947.
2. By John P. Marquand.
3. Edward Weeks, editor of *The Atlantic Monthly*.

rather that they have reported? Closer, but still not quite the answer. Undoubtedly we are getting a lot of adept reportage which masquerades as fiction and will go on getting it, but essentially I believe that what is lacking is an emotional quality. Even when they deal with death, and they often do, they are not tragic. I suppose that is to be expected. An age which is incapable of poetry is incapable of any kind of literature except that cleverness of a decadence. The boys can say anything, their scenes are almost tiresomely neat, they have all the facts and all the answers, but they are little men who have forgotten how to pray. As the world grows smaller, so the minds of men grow smaller, more compact, and more empty. These are the machine-minders of literature.

Ray

TO EDWARD WEEKS

6005 Camino de la Costa
La, Jolla, California
Jan. 18th, 1947

Dear Mr. Weeks:

I'm afraid you've thrown me for a loss. I thought "Juju Worship in Hollywood" was a perfectly good title.[1] I don't see why it has to be linked up with crime and mystery. But you're the Boss. When I wrote about writers this did not occur to you. I've thought of various titles such as *Bank Night in Hollywood, Sutter's Last Stand, The Golden Peepshow, All it Needs is Elephants, The Hot Shot Handicap, Where Vaudeville Went it Died*, and rot like that. But nothing that smacks you in the kisser. By the way, would you convey my compliments to the purist who reads your proofs and tell him or her that I write in a sort of broken-down patois which is something like the way a Swiss

1. Article on Hollywood Academy Awards. Published as "Oscar Night in Hollywood," *Atlantic Monthly*, March 1948.

[85]

waiter talks, and that when I split an infinitive, God damn it, I split it so it will stay split, and when I interrupt the velvety smoothness of my more or less literate syntax with a few sudden words of barroom vernacular, this is done with the eyes wide open and the mind relaxed but attentive. The method may not be perfect, but it is all I have. I think your proofreader is kindly attempting to steady me on my feet, but much as I appreciate the solicitude, I am really able to steer a fairly clear course, provided I get both sidewalks and the street between.

If I think of anything, I'll wire you.

Kindest regards,

TO MRS. ROBERT HOGAN

March 8th. 1947

Dear Mrs. Hogan:
Thank you for your elegant letter. It was charming of you to write at such length. I'm pleased to find someone else than myself who writes long letters. A few notes on your questionnaire. I might say that my first piece of writing was a poem. I had extensive experience writing for daily papers and weekly reviews in England when quite young, but although I made as much at it as most people, I still did not make a decent living. So went into business when I came to this country. Started writing pulp during the depression as my highly paid executive job went by the board. Particular medium I picked was due to a belief on my part that (a) some of the pulps at that time had very honest and forthright stuff in them; (b) that the literary standard was flexible and there was a chance to get "paid while learning"; (c) that although the average story in the *Black Mask* was not too good, there was a possibility of writing them very much better without hurting their chances of being read.

I have never written but one story for a slick magazine. It was sold to the *Post* and they liked it and wanted more about the same character. But in spite of my agent's advice (later objurgation and finally almost fury) I had a conviction that the superficial neatness of slick writing was only natural when it was feminine, and that if I got good at it (which as I look back seems easy, but did not seem so then), I would eventually be damn sorry. Mine was of course a losing game, on the surface. I wrote pulp stories with as much care as slick stories. It was very poor pay for the work I put into them. I obeyed the formula because I honestly liked it, but I was always trying to stretch it, trying to get in bits of peripheral writing which were not necessary but which I felt would have a subconscious effect even on the semi-literate readers; I felt somehow that the thing to get in this kind of story was a kind of richness of texture, and that you couldn't get it in a slick story. Or at least I couldn't. In the end I did get it, and it is quite clear now that when men of the quality of, say Charles Morton of the *Atlantic* say they think any one of my novelettes is better than anything Hammett ever wrote, they are not talking about the quality of mystery or violence or plot, but about this richness of texture. I myself don't like the stories any more and am a bit apprehensive about their being published in a collected edition. But I do like what I was trying to do in them.

One of my peculiarities and difficulties as a writer is that I won't discard anything. I have heard this is unprofessional and that it is a weakness of the amateur not to be able to tell when his stuff is not coming off. I can tell that all right, as to the matter in hand, but I can't overlook the fact that I had a reason, a feeling, for starting to write it, and I'll be damned if I won't lick it. I have lost months of time because of this stubbornness. However, after working in Hollywood, where the analysis of plot and motivation is carried on daily with an utter ruthlessness, I realize that it was always a plot difficulty that held me up. I simply would not plot far enough ahead. I'd write something I liked and then I would have a hell of a time making it fit in to the structure. This resulted in some rather starting oddities of construction, about which I care nothing, being fundamentally rather uninterested in plot.

Another of my oddities (and this one I believe in absolutely) is that you never quite know where your story is until you have written the first draft of it. So I always regard the first draft as raw material. What seems to be alive in it is what belongs in the story. Even if

[87]

the neatness has to be lost, I will still keep whatever has that effect of getting up on its own feet and marching. A good story cannot be devised; it has to be distilled. In the long run, however little you talk or even think about it, the most durable thing in writing is style, and style is the most valuable investment a writer can make with his time. It pays off slowly, your agent will sneer at it, your publisher will misunderstand it, and it will take people you never heard of to convince them by slow degrees that the writer who puts his individual mark on the way he writes will always pay off. He can't do it by trying, because the kind of style I am thinking about is a projection of personality and you have to have a personality before you can project it. But granted that you have one, you can only project it on paper by thinking of something else. This is ironical in a way; it is the reason, I suppose, why in a generation of "made" writers I still say you can't make a writer. Preoccupation with style will not produce it. No amount of editing and polishing will have any appreciable effect on the flavor of how a man writes. It is the product of the quality of his emotion and perception; it is the ability to transfer these to paper which makes him a writer, in contrast to the great number of people who have just as good emotions and just as keen perceptions, but cannot come within a googol of miles of putting them on paper. I know several made writers. Hollywood, of course, is full of them; their stuff often has an immediate impact of competence and sophistication, but it is hollow underneath, and you never go back to it. I don't, anyway.

If anyone asked me to give advice to beginning writers, I should probably say quite sincerely that I don't know enough to give advice of a general nature. You are largely preoccupied with the problem of showing people how to make their material marketable. You probably, or certainly, know a lot more about that than I do. Anyhow, I've never had any luck helping anyone to do it. Such wisdom as I may have acquired through my own struggles is only useful for the long pull, since it rather goes to the belief that too much preoccupation with the mechanics of writing is a sure sign of a weak talent or none at all.

Sincerely,

Raymond Chandler

[88]

TO JAMES SANDOE

6005 Camino de la Costa
La Jolla, California
March 8th. 1947

Dear Sandoe:

Thanks for yours of 19th. Feb. Have had the flu and am just crawling out. Haven't sent *Blondes' Requiem* yet, but hope to Monday. No, I shouldn't take any action.[1] I am only one of several plagiarized writers and there is probably no measurable damage. I tried to get my publisher to write the publisher of *BR* telling him the facts, just in case he had a chance to put out a pocket book edition. Seems as if his lawyer was afraid to go even that far. I think he is wrong.

I dispute your point about *Pin to see Peepshow* connecting up with Hamlet, etc.[2] I think *Hamlet*, *Macbeth*, the great Greek tragedies, *Anna Karenina* and Dostoievsky etc. are quite another matter, not so much because they are better, as because they are not nervous-making in the same sense. There is a great difference (to me at least) between a tragic ending and a miserably unhappy ending. You cannot write tragedy on the level of the suburban novel; you just get misery without the purging of high emotions. And naturally the quality of the emotions is a matter of projection, how it is done, what the total effect of style is. It is not a matter of dealing with heroic-sized people.

I have not seen *Lady in the Lake*. It is only fair, I think. *The Brashear Doubloon*[3] is definitely bad: poor acting, poor direction, wretched scripting. It should have made the best picture of all of them. I messed up the story, but the story was there. I see where in his anthology Haycraft can't understand why you picked *The High Window* over *Farewell My Lovely*.[4] I felt in sympathy with you. *The High Window*, with its faults, was more than a tough stylized mystery.

No, I am not working on a story of murder without detection.

---

1. By Raymond Marshall, pseudonym for Rene Raymond, who also wrote under the name of James Hadley Chase. Chandler's publisher successfully pressed charges against this author for plagiarism of works by Chandler, Dashiell Hammett, and Jonathan Latimer.
2. F. Tennyson Jesse, *A Pin to See the Peepshow*, 1934.
3. Film version of *The High Window*.
4. Howard Haycraft, *Art of the Mystery Story*.

I have such a story in mind, but have not got down to it yet. I am working, or was, on another Marlowe, because for business or professional reasons I think the guy is too valuable to let die out. But I find myself spoofing more and more. My next job, however, is to do a job for Universal on one of the most unusual deals ever made in Hollywood, or so I am told.[5] They pay me a large sum of money and a percentage of the picture to write them a screenplay, and they only get the picture rights. The unusual feature, which may not seem striking to you but I can assure you it is, is that they do *not* employ me, but merely agree to buy the motion picture rights to something I write in my own way and without any supervision. Of course I can't control what they do to it in production. I tried to get that, but it was a little too rich for their blood. It is like a studio buying the rights to a screenplay a writer has turned out on his own time, with the difference that they gamble before I write a word.

.   .   .

I am a damn fool not to be writing novels. I'm still getting about $15,000 a year out of those I did write. If I turned out a really good one in the near future, I'd probably get a lot out of it. Curiously enough my best public, relatively, is in England where my publisher, in spite of the terrible shortage of paper, is re-issuing all my books. And over there the topflight critics, like Desmond MacCarthy and Elizabeth Bowen review them. MacCarthy panned me, said the toughness was largely bluff (which is true), but in view of the fact that he does only one article a week for the *Observer* or *Sunday Times*, I forget which, and devoted it all to one of mine, I am less concerned with his strictures than with what he did with his space.

Kindest regards,

RC

5. To write original screenplay of *Playback*.

TO B. D. ZEVIN[1]

6005 Camino de la Costa
La Jolla, California
March 9th. 1947

Dear Mr. Zevin:

My only excuse for not writing to you before is that I have had a bad case of the flu, much more prolonged than usual, and am only now beginning to get sassy again.

Thank you very much indeed for the Sandburg book. These poems are curious reading now. When they were first published, apparently they were blunt and brutal as hell. Now they seem, if anything, restrained. They have a lot of Whitmanesque blether about man-child and woman-child etc. which seems curiously strained, like a pulp writer trying to achieve force by the use of harsh words instead of harsh things. The "he latchkeyed his way into the room" sort of style. Once in a while I find it in my old stories, but I don't think I put it there. Editors took a lot of liberties with me in those days. I have had a couple of letters from Sandburg, very nice ones and very kind. They are written in this same hopped-up lingo, which I suppose is natural to him by now, but I think originally it was just heavy breathing.

Regards and best wishes,

Raymond Chandler

1. Of World Publishing Company.

TO THE EDITORS, HARPER'S MAGAZINE[1]

To the Editors:

It was kind of unfortunate that DeVoto's blast against professorial writing pretensions ["The Easy Chair," March 1947] should appear in the same number with Eric Bentley's elegant "Broadway and Its Intelligentsia," which is the only non-snotty piece of intelligent writing on the stage I have read for years. (I don't claim to have read them all.) Bentley is far too subtle for any point to be made in the way of generalization, but if a professor—*any* professor—can write as well as this, there is not much point in all this pseudo-elaborate differentiation between the professional and the amateur. No such difference exists, or ever did. DeVoto says that the difference "is not of degree but of kind. He (the professional) has a different nervous and muscular and psychological organization. The metabolism of his mind is different."

What kind of pretentious nonsense is this? Does DeVoto think before he writes, does he think *as* he writes, or does he let his rather muddy taste in language do his thinking for him? I suspect the last. I think he turns himself a neat bit of language and then thinks that way so he won't have to throw it away. It is, alas, a very common event with writers.

All this talk about "pros" is itself sheer amateurism. There is no such thing as professionalism in writing. Would DeVoto regard Miss Nancy Bruff and Miss Kathleen Winsor as more professional than the late Sir Walter Raleigh? Does DeVoto think he is a better writer than J. B. S. Haldane or Denis Brogan?[2] And if so, what do they have to do to get a union card—write a serial for *Collier's?*

Raymond Chandler

---

1. This letter was written in response to an article attacking the writing of English professors by Bernard DeVoto, in his column, "The Easy Chair," for March 1947. The text is reprinted from the magazine.
2. Kathleen Winsor and Nancy Bruff were popular novelists, Denis Brogan and J. B. S. Haldane professional historians whose books were widely read.

TO EDGAR CARTER[1]

March 28, 1947

. . .

By the way, do you ever read the Bible? I suppose not very often, but I had occasion to the other night and believe me it is a lesson in how not to write for the movies. The worst kind of overwriting. Whole chapters that could have been said in one paragraph. And the dialogue! I bet you Macmillan's are sore as hell they didn't get to publish it. They could have made it a best-seller easy. And as for getting it banned in Boston I don't think they'd even have to grease the Watch and Ward Committee to put the red light on it.

Regards and wet fishes,

Ray

TO JEAN BETHEL

6005 Camino de la Costa
La Jolla, California
April 20th, 1947

Dear Jean:

. . .

The really good mystery picture has not yet been made, unless by Hitchcock, and that is a rather different kind of picture. *The Maltese Falcon* came closest. The reason is that the detective in the picture always has to fall for some girl, whereas the real distinction of the detective's personality is that, as a detective, he falls for nobody. He is the avenging justice, the bringer of order out of chaos, and to make his doing this part of a trite boy-meets-girl story is to make

1. The text of this letter is taken from a transcript.

it silly. But in Hollywood you cannot make a picture which is not essentially a love story, that is to say, a story in which sex is paramount.

.   .   .

Ray

TO DALE WARREN

6005 Camino de la Costa
La Jolla, California
2 June 1947

Dear Dale:

.   .   .

The status of my work of fiction is quo. I knocked off it, much to my regret, in order to do a screen play. I am supposed to finish this screen play about October, preferably 1947. After that, I will get back to work on the fiction, if by that time I am not in a strait-jacket.

.   .   .

I have always hated the book clubs, and I have always thought that the publisher grabbed far too much of the reprint and subsidiary rights to the books he published. The fact that he will occasionally make concessions to an established writer does not alter his practice towards unestablished writers. The publisher could justify himself perhaps, but he won't give any figures out. He won't tell you what his books cost him, he won't tell you what his overhead charge is, he won't tell you anything. He won't even give you decent, understandable, prompt, reports on your own books. The moment you try to talk business with him, he takes the attitude that he is a gentleman and a scholar, and the moment you try to approach him on the level of his moral integrity, he starts to talk business.

Kindest regards,

Ray

[94]

TO ERLE STANLEY GARDNER

6005 Camino de la Costa
La Jolla, California
July 1, 1947

Dear Erle:

You didn't miss anything on last week's *Philip Marlowe* show.[1] It was thoroughly flat. Tonight, I hope, will be better.

Joe Sistrom (producer at U-I) was down over the week end and we tore the story to bits and remolded it slightly nearer to the heart's desire.[2] But I am going to have to go to Los Angeles next Monday and lay it out scene by scene, a job which may take all week. I am supposed to turn in a first draft screenplay August 1, but not a chance. My brain has been grinding along in low gear for quite a while.

I am without a secretary again. This last one was eager and willing and tried hard, but she simply had not the educational background to do the work, and being already in her forties would not be likely to learn anything. Everything she wrote had to be done over, and seldom was right even then. I sent out letters which contained gross errors of punctuation just from sheer boredom. In transcribing records she wrote stuff that was absolute nonsense, and was not aware that it was nonsense. She never came to me and said, This is what it sounds like to me, but it can't be right because it doesn't make sense. She just wrote it as she heard it and the hell with the sense. I can understand a girl not being able to spell "promissory" and spelling it "promisary," if she has no dictionary available. But I can't understand her not looking it up with a Webster's Unabridged a few feet away from her desk. It wasn't exactly carelessness; her knowledge of literate English contained such vast areas of desert that she took it for granted that half of what she wrote would be meaningless to her.

All the best,

Ray

---

1. Radio adaption of Chandler's stories.
2. Screenplay of *Playback*.

TO JAMES SANDOE

6005 Camino de la Costa
La Jolla, California
August 10th 1947

Dear Sandoe:

The Partisan Review arrived. I don't know why you should take so much trouble. It is rather a good magazine of the sort. It has no Cyril Connolly or Orwell, and certainly it is far below the old *Dial*, for which I had a rather exacerbated devotion during the early twenties. These clever-clever people are a useful catharsis to the more practical minded writer who, whether he be commercial or not, has usually lived long enough not to take any set of opinions too seriously. As a very young man, when Shaw's beard was still red, I heard him lecture in London on Art for Art's Sake, which seems to have meant something then. It did not please Shaw of course; few things did unless he thought of them first. But art for propaganda's sake is even worse. And a critical magazine whose primary object is not to think intelligently but to think in such a form as to exploit a set of political ideas of whatsoever color always ends up by being critical only in the colloquial sense and intelligent only in the sense of a constant and rather labored effort to find different meanings for things than other people have found. So after a while these magazines all perish; they never achieve life, but only a distaste for other people's views of it. They have the intolerence of the very young and the anemia of closed rooms and too much midnight smoking. And God help you if you have faith in them and then meet them in person. But this last is a rather unfair jibe since it could be said of most writers. It is an awful thing to admire a man's book and then meet him, and have your entire pleasure in his work destroyed by a few egotistical attitudes, so that not only do you dislike his personality, but you can never again read anything he writes with an open mind. His nasty little ego is always leering at you from behind the words.

.   .   .

Yours, Chandler

TO JAMES SANDOE

6005 Camino de la Costa
La Jolla, California
October 2nd. 1947

Dear Jim:

.   .   .

　　The panning of *The Blue Dahlia* in *New Writing* is all right with
me. I agree with a lot of it. I have reached the happy state of being
thoroughly insensitive to adverse criticism while glowing with
pleasure at the other kind. If I were a letters-to-the-editor type guy, I
should put in a little time contesting a couple of points. E.g., it is
ludicrous to suggest that any writer in Hollywood, however
obstreperous, has a "free hand" with a script; he may have a free hand
with the first draft, but after that they start moving in on him. Also,
what happens on the set is beyond the writer's control. In this case I
threatened to walk off the picture, not yet finished, unless they
stopped the director putting in foolish dialogue out of his own head.
As to the scenes of violence, I did not write them that way at all.
Nor the massacre. The broken toe incident was an accident. The man
actually did break his toe, so the director immediately capitalized
on it.

　　The real point at issue here is whether physical violence is
worse than psychological violence. The element of burlesque is also
overlooked by this critic. But where he throws his hand in without
knowing it is in calling the cutting of the picture bad. What he really
means is that the directing was so bad that the cutting, which was
very expert, was not able to conceal it. Whenever you see a supremely
well cut picture, e.g. *Air Force*, *Murder My Sweet*, *The Big Sleep*,
you can be sure that either the director was once a cutter himself or
that a cutter was on the set and was consulted about the shots before
they were made. The best cutter in Hollywood cannot correct a
botched job of directing; he can't make scenes flow when they are
shot staccato, without reference to their movement on film together.
If the cutter wants to make a dissolve to cover an abrupt transition,
he can't do it unless he has the film to combine for the dissolve. If
every foot of film in a scene is needed for the essential action, there is

[97]

none over for a dissolve. The director has not contemplated the necessity for a dissolve (because he didn't know the scene right after the one he is doing might be left out), therefore he has not allowed film for it. Take a simple example. Two characters are discussing a letter which one of them expects. They are in an apartment, a man and a girl. The man says: He's writing to me General Delivery. The letter's probably there now. The girl says: Why don't you go down and get it? The guy says: Will you be here when I get back? The girl says: "Sure." and smiles enigmatically. The director, a bad director, holds on the enigmatic smile and holds long enough for a dissolve. He then shoots the exterior of the post office. Guy arrives in cab, pays cab, starts upstairs of post office. Close shoot of entrance doors, guy starts in, scene in lobby, guy moves across, close shot of General Delivery window, guy goes up to it and asks for letter. Clerk looks through letters and hands him one, etc. etc. Now the cutter knows that all this is bosh, dull, a holdover from the early days of the motion picture when movement itself was exciting. All you really want is the General Delivery window and the guy receiving a letter. But the director has failed to deliver this scene by dissolving on the girl's enigmatic smile and making the audience wonder what she has up her sleeve. So they have to have that wiped out by a totally unnecessary series of shots showing arrival at the post office. The director has tried to make a point of something which is not at this time a point at all, and thrown the cutting mechanism out of gear.

The point is whether a certain letter has come. A hand reaches across a counter and the guy takes the letter. That is all. But that is not what the preceding scene left you thinking about. You were thinking about what the girl would be up to while the guy went to the post office. And the poor cutter, to make his point, has to waste film to give the audience time to forget that. Not only that, but he has to make them look at dull film. Hitchcock, the only time I met him, gave me a lecture on this kind of waste. His point, which I have made above, was that Hollywood (and England too) was full of directors who had not learned to forget about the Biograph. They still thought that because a motion picture moved it interested people. In the early days of the pictures, he said, a man went to visit a woman at her home. They were old flames who had not seen each other for years. The bad director shot it this way. The man took a taxi, he was seen riding along in the taxi, there was a view of the street and the house, the taxi stopped, the man got out and paid, he looked at the front steps, went up the steps rang the bell, the maid answered, he said, Is Mrs. Gilhooley in? The maid said, I'll see, sir. What name shall I say? The man said: Finnegan. The maid said: This way please. Inside house, hallway, open door, maid stands at open door, man goes in, maid starts upstairs, man in living room looks around, sits down lights a cigarette. Maid upstairs knocks on door, female voice calls Come in, she opens door. Inside maid says Mr. Finnegan to see you, ma'am. Mrs. Gilhooley says wonderingly, Mr. Finnegan? Then slowly. All right Ellen. I'll be right down. Goes to mirror, primps, enigmatic smile, starts out, shot of her descending stairs, entering living room after a slight embarrassed pause at door. Inside living room. She enters. Finnegan stands up. They look at each other in silence. Then they smile slowly. Man, huskily: Hello, Madge. You haven't changed a bit. Mrs. Gilhooley: It's been a long time, George. A long long time. And *then* the scene begins.

Every bit of this stuff is dead film, because every point, if there is a point, can be made inside the scene itself. The rest is just camera in love with mere movement. Cliché, flat, stale, and today meaningless. Well, I don't know why I run on about this. I suppose it's a sort of wonder at realizing that in spite of all the money, all the time, all the work, all the discussion and thought, there are still hardly any people who really know much about making pictures.

As to *Chimera*, if I haven't already written you about it, I enjoyed most of it very much.[1] This fellow Barzun always amuses me; he lives in a fool's paradise.[2] He thinks the detective story is dead because the kind of detective story he idolizes is dead. What he never suspects for a moment is that it never existed. What did exist was an elaborate scheme for gulling the public into thinking it was getting something it never really did get; and after awhile the fraud was found out. The tricks became known and there was nothing behind the tricks. They were fun for a while but human ingenuity could only go so far. The piece of broken watch spring that Dr. Thorndyke picked up from behind the sofa pillow meant a lot to Dr. Thorndyke, but the rest of us didn't have laboratories.[3] It meant nothing to us. And after

1. Magazine edited by Barbara Howes.
2. Jacques Barzun, Columbia University professor and critic of detective fiction.
3. Dr. John Evelyn Thorndyke, hero of numerous mystery novels by R. Austin Freeman, 1862–1943.

a while we began to realise that the essential clue, openly planted apparently, was only a clue when fitted into a special background, and the reader was not given the background. Where the clue was not hidden behind a scientific or antiquarian screen it was messed up with so many other trivia that only a prodigious mnemonologist could hold on to it. Even the author had to keep looking back to make sure he didn't ball himself up. The real basis of the detection novel is that a problem exists which can be solved by close attention to physical clues and correct interpretation of them. My experience with reading them, and I have read as many as most people, is that the clues are only given in part. The physical clue a. has meaning only when added to the psychological clue b. And b. is always either misstated, or relies on hidden knowledge, or its importance is only revealed by a special interpretation. Otherwise the problem is transparent, and the interest, as in so many of Austin Freeman's stories, is not in the solution of the mystery, which is obvious, but in the exact reconstruction of the crime. All this type of fiction, therefore, presumes a point in time, a certain stage of knowledge, a certain freshness of routine which cannot be maintained, and a certain psychological falsity which can be manipulated only in the presence of the psychologically immature. The novel of detection little by little educates the public to its own weaknesses, which it cannot possibly remove, because they are inherent. It can flourish only until enough people know its vocabulary.

RC

TO ERLE STANLEY GARDNER

6005 Camino de la Costa
La Jolla, California
October 23rd, 1947

Dear Erle:

      ·   ·   ·

     Would you consider two objections I have to your writing, or
would you be hurt? Both small things, but they bother me. One
is where Mason says: "I don't know as I could do that." The other,
he says: "Whom shall I ask for?" My contention is a) a night school
lawyer might say the first, which is not just colloquial English but
bad English. Perry wouldn't, I'm sure, b) and the man who says the
first would not say the second, which is pedantic anyway by
colloquial standards. For all I know your secretaries do this. I don't
recall seeing the first in either of the last two books. Perhaps I am just
crazy anyway. They always bring me up short. Also, there is
carelessness in proof-checking once in a while. This sort of thing I've
noticed more than once: track is lost of the speaker in quick dialogue.
See p. 108 of *Lazy Lover*. Just below the single "Yes" halfway done.
Mason says two speeches which are printed as though Drake had said
one. "I know all about that" Mason. "Yes." Drake. "Then he must
be familiar etc." Mason. "All right, cover every etc." Also Mason.
I've caught this quite a few times in various books.

                                        Love

                                        Ray

TO CHARLES MORTON

                                        6005 Camino de la Costa
                                        La Jolla, California
                                        October 28th. 1947

Dear Charles:

            ·   ·   ·

     At the end of the week we have to go to Los Angeles and stay
quite a long time—several weeks—while I polish my screenplay.
This is a loathsome job, consisting of cutting out everything you like
and then skimping on the rest, and beating the hell out of the poor
tired lines and scenes until they have lost all meaning. I was talking to
Joe Sistrom, my producer, about it last Sunday and demanding

                              [101]

plaintively why it was so impossible for a writer to have fun writing for the screen. Making pictures is a very interesting job, in spite of having to deal with actors, but the writing part of it is sheer drudgery. I still don't know why it has to be.

I had an idea for some time back that I should like to do an article on The Moral Status of the Writer, or more frivolously, The Hell With Posterity I Want Mine Now. Not a frivolous article really. It seems to me that in all this yapping about writers selling themselves to Hollywood or the slicks or some transient propaganda idea, instead of writing sincerely from the heart about what they see around them,—the people who make this kind of complaint, and that includes practically every critic who takes himself seriously, overlook the point (I don't see how they can, but they do) that no writer ever in any age got a blank check. He always had to accept some conditions imposed from without, respect certain taboos, try to please certain people. It might have been the Church, or a rich patron, or a generally accepted standard of elegance, or the commercial wisdom of a publisher or editor, or perhaps even a set of political theories. If he did not accept them, he revolted against them. In either case they conditioned his writing. No writer ever wrote exactly what he wanted to write, because there was never anything inside himself, anything purely individual that he did want to write. It's all reaction of one sort or another.

Oh the hell with it. Ideas are poison. The more you reason, the less you create.

Ray.

TO CHARLES MORTON

6005 Camino de la Costa
La Jolla, California
January First 1948

Dear Charlie:

My first letter of the new year is to you. We are as it were old

[102]

friends and have never enjoyed the privilege of disliking each other.
My wife tells me I have a beautiful character. Have you a little liar in
your home? I am one of those people who have to be known exactly
the right amount to be liked. I am standoffish with strangers, a form
of shyness which whiskey cured when I was still able to take it in
the requisite quantities. I am terribly blunt, having been raised in that
English tradition which permits a gentleman to be almost infinitely
rude if he keeps his voice down. It depends on a complete assurance
that a punch on the nose will not be the reply. Americans have no
manners as such; they have the manners that arise from their natures,
and so when their natures are sweet they have the best manners in
the world, except those of the aristocrats, the real ones, now a dying
race, of course. I always recall in this connection an incident that
occurred to Logan Pearsall Smith. (I might even have read it in the
Atlantic.) How by devious way he secured an invitation to a country
home which had a very old library he wished to search; how the
old gentleman, his host, would wander around and occasionally peer
in at the library windows while Smith was browsing; how he never
entered the room; how Smith sat at meat with the family day after
day and none ever enquired of him what he sought in the library;
and how he departed leaving them as ignorant as when he came, a
tribute to their breeding that only a wise man could have thought of.

And then, as a comic reversal of this, I recall Train's visit to
Bewly, or Beaulieu as the blighters spell it, and how an antique fly
awaited him at the station to drive him to Beaulieu Castle, how
charmingly and indifferently he was entertained, in such a way that he
seemed to be obliging the people by being there; and how, at the
moment of his departure, the butler, having received his tip, presented
him with a bill for the rent of the fly.

And finally, from my own knowledge, the incident of the
Scotch grouse moor invitation, at the end of which the guest, not
used to such things or to the mixture of arrogance and geniality
displayed by some upper crust people, tipped the head gamekeeper
with a couple of shining golden sovereigns: tried to tip him, rather,
and the Head Gamekeeper glancing down superciliously remarked, "I
only accept paper," which in those days meant not less than a
fivepunnote. And how, when the guest, outraged, refused to tip him
at all, the H.G. refused to deliver the guest's guns; and how the titled
host, being informed of this in a polite but chilly letter from London,

replied that he never interfered in such matters; and how it took a solicitor to get the guns back to the now thoroughly-with-British-hospitality-disgusted guest. I take it you agree with me that the American gentleman would have been incapable of any one of these attitudes. Interesting stuff, just the same.

.   .   .

So blessed be your days.

Ray

TO E. C. THIESSEN

6005 Camino de la Costa
La Jolla, California
January 19, 1948

Dear Mr. Thiessen:

I am in receipt through Mr. Weeks of your check in the amount of $300 for a contribution to *The Atlantic Monthly*, not as yet definitely titled but which you call "Crime Night" for convenience. I understand that this article is to be featured in the March *Atlantic* with a cover. I do not regard the amount of your payment as adequate. For my last contribution I was paid $500. Would you be kind enough to explain to me the basis on which you arrive at these figures? Although I am of course aware that the decision is for Mr. Weeks, it seems more graceful that I should approach the subject through you.

Lest there be any misunderstanding of my motives in raising the question, let it be understood that the article is yours and that if there were any necessity for it you could give me a token payment of $10. I do not expect to make a living out of *The Atlantic Monthly* and in fact I have indirectly done a great deal of work for its benefit and my own without any remuneration whatsoever. I have thought up ideas for articles and discussed them with Mr. Morton, occasionally with the hope that if he liked them well enough he could get somebody else to do them when I was unable to do them myself. If this were an affair of friendship, I should want only such payment as would protect your proper legal rights; but if it is a business transaction, then I want the top price, as I am accustomed to getting the top price. Not everyone, I know, can write articles acceptable to the *Atlantic*; but of those who can and do, relatively few have any smash news value and any expert inner point of view on subjects of wide general interest. If the article is timely enough and good enough to excite your enthusiasm, then it should be paid for at the very highest rate your budget will permit. This is the only kind of business relationship that interests me, and business for the moment is what we are talking. I am well aware that magazine editors, like the Roman god Janus, must of necessity have two faces, one to smile benevolently on the literature contributor as writer and the other to regard more grimly the matter of his remuneration. That is part of his job, as it is also part of my job as a businessman not to let him do it too well.

Very truly yours,

Raymond Chandler

TO JAMES SANDOE

6005 Camino de la Costa
La Jolla, California
January 27, 1948

Dear Jim:

• • •

I quite agree with you about the public's capacity and adaptability to a quality of entertainment which the yucks seem to be afraid to give them. I haven't seen a good detective story in ages, have you? Yes, I'd like to read George Orwell's essay "The British People" very much. Orwell, like other clever people, probably including you and me, can be an ass on occasion. But that doesn't mean he is never interesting, perceptive, and very intelligent.

I've just read *The Iceman Cometh* and I wish somebody would tell me what is so wonderful about this guy O'Neill. Of course, I haven't seen the play. I've only read it. In fact the only play of his that I ever saw was *Strange Interlude*, and you can not only have that but, if necessary I will pay you to cart it away. An indelible characteristic of the second or third-rate talent is that it is only effective when dealing with something that borders on fantasy. When you have atmosphere you can get by without a deep perception of character. If O'Neill's purpose were not so grim and his thinking apparently so solemn, I should be inclined to say that as a dramatist he ranks beside Pinero and Henry Arthur Jones; that he is utterly artificial, and that nothing he writes has any very real context. I enjoyed *Ah, Wilderness* but it left me with no more enduring memory than, for example, *Kiss and Tell.* I am no fanatical admirer of Saroyan, but I think *The Time of Your Life* makes *The Iceman Cometh* look like a posey and laborious working over of trite materials. O'Neill is the sort of man who could spend a year in flophouses, researching flophouses, and write a play about flophouses that would be no more real than a play by a man who had never been in a flophouse, but had only read about them. If I am utterly wrong, please instruct me.

You asked my opinion about the Hollywood show in Washington. Well, I think it's pretty awful that an investigation of this sort should be conducted by a man who thinks *Abie's Irish Rose* is a novel.[1] Also, I do not think the Founding Fathers intended this sort of investigation to be conducted with microphones, flash bulbs, and moving picture cameras. Apart from that, until the Supreme Court defines the powers of Congressional committees and limits them (and our present Supreme Court is no bunch of legal masters) I cannot see where the committee exceeded its rights. If the Communist party in the United States is a legal organization, and if membership

1. Congressman J. Parnell Thomas, chairman of the Committee on Un-American Affairs of the U.S. House of Representatives, investigating Hollywood screenwriters.

in it is a matter of record available to a branch of the United States Government, then asking a man if he belongs to the Communist party or ever has belonged to it is not an invasion of his privacy. It is something like asking him if he ever was a registered Republican, which is not the same thing as asking if he voted Republican. I think the ten men who were cited had very bad legal advice. They were afraid to say they were Communists or to say that they were not Communists; therefore they tried to raise a false issue. If they had told the truth, they would have had a far better case before the courts than they have now, and they would certainly have had no worse a case as regards their bosses in Hollywood. If Jack Warner fires me because I admit to being a Communist, he's in a far more shaky legal position than if he does the same thing because, through refusing to answer the questions of the Congressional Committee, I have brought the moving picture industry into bad repute. And I guess we are all perfectly well aware, not being children, that if the Communist party is by legislative action outlawed in this country, the real practicing professional Communists will go right on doing what they are doing, only they will do it under another label and with a slightly different technique. As I understand it, there are only two grounds on which one may refuse to answer a question of a Congressional Committee. One is that to answer it would be to incriminate yourself, that is to say a truthful answer would be the confession of a crime; since membership in the Communist party is not a crime, that does not apply here. The other ground is that the question is not within the frame of the purpose for which the Committee was constituted. This is a deliberate test of the law and at least has the color of honesty. Even if a man were convicted of contempt on such refusal, it is unlikely that he would get more than a purely nominal sentence; because the courts would recognize that this man had raised a clear issue of fact and law, and had not sought to evade an issue by talking until he was thrown out of the witness chair. You call the defense forthright. What's forthright about it? It strikes me as a singularly incompetent attempt (partly unconscious, perhaps) to use the legalistic weaknesses of the democratic system in order to undermine or sabotage the functioning of that system. I don't mean that these ten men are all convinced and avowed Communists. I think about three of them are, that at least two definitely are not, and that the rest

[107]

don't know what the hell it's all about. But I ought to qualify my remarks about the boys by saying that, although I have no sympathy for them, and don't think anything very awful will happen to them, except that they will spend a lot of money on lawyers, and the worst kind of lawyers, I reserve my real contempt for the motion picture moguls who in conference decided to expel them from the industry. A business as big as the motion picture business ought to be run by men with a few guts, men with enough moral and intellectual integrity to say that while these matters are sub judice and while these men have not been declared guilty of any crime by the courts, the producers are not going to treat them as guilty. They don't have to hire them where they are not contract writers, and if they are contract writers, they can lay them off for twelve weeks a year and pay them their salary the rest of the time and not give them any work. They can do all this without public fanfare and striking poses of virtue. It might cost them a little money, but it would save them from an awful lot of real contempt. Sometimes I feel kind of sorry for the poor bastards. They are so damned scared they won't make their second or third million. In fact they are just so damned scared, period. What a wonderful thing it would have been if the Motion Pictures Producers Association had said to Mr. Thomas, "Sure, I guess we have Communists in Hollywood. We don't know who they are. How could you expect us to? We're not the F.B.I. But even if we did know, there's an Attorney General in this country. He hasn't accused these men of any crime. Congress hasn't legislated anything that would cause their present or future membership in the Communist party to be a crime, and until it does we propose to treat them just as exactly as we treat anyone else." You know what would happen if the producers had the guts to say a thing like that? They would start making good pictures, because that takes guts, too. Very much the same kind of guts.

I hope nothing in the above is annoying to you. If it is, if you are an extreme left-winger yourself, for example, we could have a lot of fun arguing about it. I've always wanted to know what made these fellows tick and if you happened to be one of them, I should get an intelligent answer.

With kindest regards,

[108]

TO JAMES KEDDIE, JR.

6005 Camino de la Costa,
La Jolla, California
March 18, 1948

Dear Mr. Keddie:

Thank you for your letter of February 14. Offhand I can't recall how Frances Wallace got the idea that I preferred reading the English type of detective stories, because said so specifically it isn't true. As a matter of fact I don't read a great many detective stories of any sort. I do think that what might be called the second-grade English detective story is better reading than an equivalent accomplishment over here. But I think the best American mystery stories are ahead of the best English stories, for the reason that they recognize and accept the inherent fallacy of the form; whereas the English practitioners prefer to disregard it and go on talking about logic and deduction as if these words actually meant something in this connection. From the English point of view the mysteries of Freeman Wills Crofts and R. Austin Freeman, both of whom you mention, are rigidly honest simply because they don't tell lies or conceal material facts or, as Agatha Christie so often does, ring in violent reversals of character in order to justify an unexpected motivation. Yet no normal reader could solve a Crofts mystery, because no normal reader has that exact a memory for insignificant details. And no normal reader could solve an Austin Freeman mystery, because, although Freeman gives you the bare facts, he does not give you the esoteric scientific interpretation of these facts, and he has no right to impute it to you as a reader. As I see it, the truly honest detective story or novel of detection (a more respectable term perhaps) is one in which the reader is given all the material for solving the mystery, where nothing significant is under-emphasized and nothing insignificant over-emphasized, and where the facts themselves carry their own interpretation and do not have to be carried into a laboratory and analyzed under microscopes to disclose their meaning. In blunt words, the English novel of detection is either transparent or it is in some sense a psychological fraud. If you know of one which isn't either I wish you'd tell me. I think it was the realization of these things that caused the development of the so-called "inverted detective story" in England, and in this country caused the emphasis to shift to character and action rather than a tabulation of clues.

As for the enjoyment of Sherlock Holmes, it appears to me at this date to rely partly on nostalgia and tradition and partly on qualities which did not originally make the principal interest of the Holmes stories. Doyle understood the uses of eccentricity, but to a person with any knowledge of the police and how they operate his policemen are utterly absurd. His scientific premises are very unreliable, and the element of mystery to a sophisticated mind frequently does not exist. Example: *The Red-Headed League.* Of course we do not have the privilege of reading Holmes fresh from the press.

With kindest regards,

Raymond Chandler

TO JOSEPH SISTROM

March 23, 1948

Dear Joe:

· · ·

I saw *Open City* again the other night.[1] You always see more the second time. I noticed, for example, that there is as much dialogue in the picture as in any of our more wordy specimens, but that this dialogue is so dynamically delivered that you don't get any impression of the action being slowed down. I am beginning to wonder whether the static quality of many pictures is not due simply to poor acting rather than overwriting or unimaginative directing. Or, if I may correct myself, I am not beginning to wonder; I am convinced.

Yours always

1. By Roberto Rossellini.

[110]

TO JOHN HERSEY

6005 Camino de la Costa
La Jolla, California
March 29, 1948

Dear John Hersey:

What a charming, old-fashioned gesture, to write a man a letter entirely in your own handwriting. I wish I could return the compliment, but my writing is of the nervous, illegible, erratic type and I am afraid you would have a lot of misery trying to read it.

I haven't seen the magazine for a long time.[1] I was very, very *mildly* irritated that I was never asked to put any money into it in the beginning; but that is probably all for the best, since I am a very poor joiner. As for writing a five or six thousand word mystery short story for you, I simply don't have the short-story mind. From time to time I get letters from people like Ellery Queen and Rex Stout and sometimes from the big magazines asking me for stories or novelettes at various prices, all of them flatteringly high (I've been offered as much as a dollar a word); but it seems to me that either you are a short-story writer or you are not. Once in a while a writer gets what might be called a compulsive idea and I suppose I have had them, although not as many as a real short-story writer would have; but I find that I throw them off without any difficulty, or else they start to grow and grow and become confused in ramifications. The only short story I ever wrote of the type you mention was published in the *Saturday Evening Post* several years ago.[2] I guess I'm just not an idea man and a good short story does really need an idea.

This is not saying that I'll never try. It might be that one of these days, when no Hollywood producer is breathing down the back of my neck, I'll write a short story and then look at it and think it fairly good and decide it obviously is not formula, nor yet neurotic enough to appeal to the polite pickpockets of the "little" magazines. But why should I try? You are a writer and you will understand. The chances are I'll never get written half of what there is in my mind

---

1. It was called *Magazine*, with each number incorporated in the title (*Magazine* 1, *Magazine* 2, etc.). It was published in New York.
2. "I'll Be Waiting."

[111]

asking to be written at this moment. Money is no longer a compelling motive, unless I could make it by writing books. If I can't, I can always make it in the Hollywood slaughterhouse, ankle-deep in blood and screaming like a Saracen. As for prestige, the magazine which can confer it no longer exists. Prestige of a sort I already have, and however much more I might chance to acquire through luck or the stupidity of the public I should always have to say to myself privately: "Yes, that's all very well, but remember you didn't write *Hiroshima* and you never could." Of course I still have ambitions—subject to change without notice. I should like to write a book of fantastic stories. Not pseudo-scientific. Realistic stories in every sense, except that each one contains an impossibility. And I should like to write a good motion picture. The problem here is not writing but of somehow creating or contriving the circumstances in which it is possible to do the work. But the short mystery story—all I can say is why?

Yours very truly,

Raymond Chandler

TO FREDERICK LEWIS ALLEN

May 7, 1948

Dear Mr. Allen:

Thanks for the kind words spoken in connection with your P. and O. notes on Eric Bentley. I did not rise to the occasion. I was afraid to try. This sort of thing can become a back-scratching routine of which the public tires very damn fast.

Just the same, I think Bentley's round-up of the plays was everything that anyone could desire. It would be invidious for me to remark (even if I knew what I was talking about) that Bentley is probably the best dramatic critic in the U.S. and, with the possible exception of Mary McCarthy, the *only* dramatic critic in the U.S.[1]

1. Eric Bentley.

[112]

The rest of the boys are just think-piece writers whose subject happens to be a play. They are interested in exploiting their own personal brand of verbal glitter. They are witty and readable and sometimes cute, but they tell you next to nothing about the dramatic art and the relationship of the play in question to that art.

It is not enough for a critic to be right, since he will occasionally be wrong. It is not enough for him to give colorable reasons. He must create a reasonable world into which his reader may enter blindfold and feel his way to the chair by the fire without barking his shins on the unexpected dust mop. The barbed phrase, the sedulously rare word, the highbrow affectation of style—these are amusing, but useless. They place nothing and reveal not the temper of the times. The great critics, of whom there are piteously few, build a home for the truth.

In his review of *The Iceman Cometh* that fading wit and tired needlepoint worker, George Jean Nathan says: "With the appearance of this long awaited work our theatre has become dramatically alive again. It makes most of the plays . . . produced during the more than twelve-year period of O'Neill's absence look comparatively like so much damp tissue paper." Cute and quite easy, and with two sentences the spuriousness of an entire career seems to stand revealed. A critic who could write that drivel about O'Neill's drivel is hors concours. It would be charitable to say he has lost contact with his brains; it would be far more accurate to say he has merely made public a truth which was privately known from the beginning: that George Jean Nathan's critical reputation is not founded on his knowing what he is talking about, since obviously he doesn't now and most probably never did, but on a certain personal dexterity with the choice and order of words.

This play, *The Iceman Cometh*, is a sort of touchstone. If that fools you, you are a knuckle-headed sucker for pretentiousness. That's all there is to say; it is quite simple, quite devastating, and there is no retrieving the position. I shall probably never read another line of Nathan. I know there is nothing there. I suspect there never was.

The current year's touchstone is *A Streetcar Named Desire*.[2] Bentley knocks it for a loop, so does McCarthy. O'Neill with a better shooting script. That's all. Zero in art, A or possibly A plus in

2. By Tennessee Williams.

[113]

adaptation to the circumstance that where there is no art, it is possible for an ingenious fellow to simulate it without losing money.

It is wrong to be harsh with the New York critics, unless one admits in the same breath that it is a condition of their existence that they should write entertainingly about something which is rarely worth writing about at all. This leads or forces them to develop a technique of pseudo-subtlety and abstruseness which, when acquired, permits them to deal with trivial things as though they were momentous. This is the basis of all successful advertising copy writing. Criticism is impossible in a world where the important thing is not to be right, or even to know the reasons for being right, but to write a column about a play—any damn play at all—which column however insignificant the ostensible subject, never lets down on the significance of the references to the subject. These people do not write about plays; they write about their neuroses. How else could they keep the ball in the air? Good critical writing is measured by the perception and evaluation of the subject; bad critical writing by the necessity of maintaining the professional standing of the critic.

I thought De Voto's piece about the drinking habits of the Great American Yahoo was quite wonderful.[3] So indirectly, and yet so devastatingly, he exposes that awful truth that where a civilization is in the process of going rotten, you will always find the symbols of this rottenness in the suburbs, in the lives and homes of supposedly rather ordinary decent people. When they begin to break up into devil worship, the disease is probably too far gone for a cure. Or would be, in any country but this.

Auden leaves me lost and groping. His piece about detective stories was brilliant in the clear cold classical manner. But why drag me in? I'm just a fellow who jacked up a few pulp novelettes into book form. How could I possibly care a button about the detective story as a form? All I'm looking for is an excuse for certain experiments in dramatic dialogue. To justify them I have to have plot and situation; but fundamentally I care almost nothing about either. All I really care about is what Errol Flynn calls "the music," the lines he has to speak. Here I am halfway through a Marlowe story and having a little fun (until I got stuck) and along comes this fellow Auden and tells me I am interested in writing serious studies of a

3. Bernard DeVoto, *Harper's* columnist.

criminal milieu. So now I look at everything I put down and say to myself, Remember, old boy, this has to be a serious study of a criminal milieu. Are you serious? No. Is this a criminal milieu? No, just average corrupt living with the melodramatic angle over-emphasized, not because I am crazy about melodrama for its own sake, but because I am realistic enough to know the rules of the game.

A long time ago whan I was writing for pulps I put into a story a line like "he got out of the car and walked across the sun-drenched sidewalk until the shadow of the awning over the entrance fell across his face like the touch of cool water." They took it out when they published the story. Their readers didn't appreciate this sort of thing: just held up the action. And I set out to prove them wrong. My theory was they just *thought* they cared nothing about anything but the action; that really, although they didn't know it, they cared very little about the action. The things they really cared about, and that I cared about, were the creation of emotion through dialogue and description; the things they remembered, that haunted them, were not for example that a man got killed, but that in the moment of his death he was trying to pick a paper clip up off the polished surface of a desk, and it kept slipping away from him, so that there was a look of strain on his face and his mouth was half open in a kind of tormented grin, and the last thing in the world he thought about was death. He didn't even hear death knock on the door. That damn little paper clip kept slipping away from his fingers and he just wouldn't push it to the edge of the desk and catch it as it fell.

With kindest regards,

TO CHARLES MORTON

6005 Camino de la Costa,
La Jolla, California
May 7, 1948

Dear Charlie:

Your magnificent piece of prose about wedding presents was read at the last meeting of the La Jolla Hermosa Writers Club. For a moment at the end there was a deathly silence, reminiscent of the silence that so discouraged Lincoln after his Gettysburg address. These hardened veterans of the rejection slip, the La Jolla writers, just sat stunned by your eloquence. Tears streamed down their worn faces and their toil-hardened hands tightened convulsively into knots of bone and sinew. Then, suddenly, with the crash of a giant comber on a reef the applause swelled up to thunder. They came to their feet as one man, although nine tenths of them were women, and screamed with enthusiasm. There were roars of Author! AUTHOR! A U T H O R ! and when the president restored order at last (by waving her hand-knitted bloomers) and it was explained that the Author was on the other side of the continent in a place called Boston (Laughter!) a resolution was passed that he be signed up for a series of lectures on *The American Home and How To Avoid It*.

Your health was then drunk in elderberry wine and a toast proposed by a recently exhumed member of the British colony, an Old Surbitonian complete with tie. There followed a rendering of several arias from *Madame Butterfly* by the Choir of Kept Women from the La Jolla Beach and Tennis Club, and the proceedings fittingly terminated by the entire company singing the Horst Wessel song in Yiddish, followed by the Palestinian National Anthem sung in Hebrew and the La Jolla Chamber of Commerce Glee Club leading the singing of the sacred Hymn to the Retail Credit Merchants Association of San Diego County. This was sung in what passes around here for English.

I think you would have been very pleased and proud and touched (for whatever you had on you—a lot of us don't eat regularly). The affair was quite orderly for La Jolla. Two stick pokings, one assault with pearl hatpin, a couple of fountain pen squirtings, and a few spitballs alone marred the perfect harmony of the occasion. There was a slight tendency to cluster at the end and one old lady was pushed a little by another old lady who told her to stick her ear trumpet in her own ear if she had to use it. For a moment it looked as if this disagreement might end in a spot of hair-pulling, but the president quickly began to read a short story of her own composition and the hall emptied in a flash.

Respectfully yours,

Raymond Chandler

[116]

TO CARL BRANDT

6005 Camino de la Costa
La Jolla, California
May 11th. 1948

Dear Mr. Brandt:

Come Michaelmas, or thereabouts, I shall be in need of a literary agent. The purpose of this is to enquire whether your office would be interested.

At the moment there is nothing much to do. I would have a radio program, if I had had the right kind of people after it at the right time. But I don't think much could be done now. I have a mystery novel half finished. The writing is of an incomparable brilliance, but something has went wrong with the story. An old trouble with me. The brain is very very tired. I have lately finished a screenplay for Universal-International, want to finish this mystery and do another novel which has a murder in it but is not a mystery. Monday I am going north for a month.

What I want to do and what I do are not always of the same family. There is, of course, the usual collection of minor troubles, such as Portuguese rights, Italian rights, Penguin book rights to a bunch of novelettes not published in England (and perhaps not worth publishing.) These are annoying things, but not lucrative. I have no ambitions as a slick writer.

My references are poor. I was eight years with Sydney Sanders who would be delighted to warn you against me, unless be deemed it undiplomatic. After leaving Sanders I tried working through my Hollywood agent, H. N. Swanson, a good fellow and a nice fellow, with whom I am on excellent terms, but not quite in the right setting except for picture work, at which I have no doubt he is excellent.

You are a stranger to me and I can't very well let my hair down, but neither should I want you to be too much in the dark. I am not a completely amiable character any more than I am a facile and prolific writer. I do most things the hard way, and I suffer a good deal over it. There may not be a lot of mileage left in me. Five years of fighting Hollywood has not left me with many reserves of energy. Whether I have had any success your Hollywood representative will be able to tell you, and if you should happen to ask him, I am hoping that for once he will (whoever he is, and I don't know) keep it to himself.

Yours very truly,

Raymond Chandler

TO CARL BRANDT

6005 Camino de la Costa,
La Jolla, California
June 1, 1948

Dear Mr. Brandt:

   Enclosed is approximately the first half of the mystery novel I was telling you about. It goes against all my principles to show it to you at this point, but I think in the circumstances you are entitled to see it if you want to. Please bear in mind that this material was all dictated to a dictaphone, an instrument which I have found very convenient for movie work, but I am not sure it is adapted to fiction writing. You will notice too many "he saids" and "she saids." Some of these were put in deliberately, so that my secretary, in transcribing the records, would know where a different speaker came on. I should probably omit a great many of these when I went over the draft. I think this batch of material runs to about 30,000 words.

   It was very pleasant meeting you and talking to you. I hope we may be friends.

Yours very truly,

Raymond Chandler

TO CARL BRANDT:

6005 Camino de la Costa
La Jolla, California
June 9, 1948

Dear Mr. Brandt:

I had a nice talk with Ray Stark last Sunday. He seems an extremely intelligent and lively young fellow and I can understand your enthusiasm for him. He seemed very frank and honest, also, even to the point of admitting that in Hollywood it is not always possible to be frank and honest, at any rate in his business.

I am sending you separately a couple of books of novelettes of mine. These were republished originally in Avon 25-cent books and then later in this World Publishing Company edition. Some time ago I raised the question with my English publisher, Hamish Hamilton, as to whether these novelettes or some of them could not be published in England, not necessarily under his imprint, but perhaps by the Penguin book people, who are bringing out some of my other books. I haven't had any reaction on them, but I know he has had two disastrous fires this year and probably has no time of anything but the most urgent matters. Do you think it would be worth while to send these on to your English representative, whoever he is? I have several more copies if you need them.

The four mystery novels which Knopf published were all handled in England by the Farquharson office for Sydney Sanders, and Innes Rose is, as I suppose you know, the successor to Farquharson, although he still uses Farquharson's name. Certain foreign translation rights have been sold, but I should have to draw up a schedule to be able to state definitely what: French, Swedish, Norwegian, Danish, Spanish, and some Italian rights I think. Innes Rose took the position that the agent in England who handled the original publication of the books was by English trade practice entitled to handle any and all publications, reprints, foreign language translations, and so on perpetually, regardless of any cessation of his agency representation. I took the position that this was a lot of bosh, that every right was a subdivision of the copyright and that he was only entitled to participate in contracts he had actually negotiated, and that his right to negotiate ceased when his agency ceased. He has conceded my point without abandoning the principle. I thought of taking this up with the Society of Authors in England, but so far have not done so. You will probably know far more about it than I do. The point is there are unsold rights, of what value I could not say. I assume you will eventually want to cover this field and see what has not been done.

When you were here we agreed in a general way that it was probably a mistake to quit a publisher without some definite reason, but I am wondering whether the mere fact that I have been ten years in some kind of an association with Knopf without ever having the slightest feeling of friendliness or warmth towards them isn't enough reason. . . . Knopf has made far more money out of his share of the reprint royalties than he has paid me on all of his own trade editions. I certainly don't owe him anything. I always thought their publicity, what there was of it, was miserable. It covered the ground all the way from irritating to down-right silly. Perhaps they sold as many of my books as the public would buy, but I've never really been convinced of it, when my English publisher, with only a third of the population to deal with, has sold just as many. I have a certain admiration for Alfred Knopf, because he has published a lot of books he couldn't possibly make any money on, and he has so far failed to publish one of those fat slabs of goosed history which almost dominate the best-seller lists these days. I have nothing positive against the house, but I think by this time I ought to have something positive in favor of it, and I haven't. It is a cold show. I have never been able to deal with people at arm's length.

With kindest regards,

Raymond Chandler

TO CHARLES MORTON

6005 Camino de la Costa
La Jolla, California
July 28, 1948

Dear Charlie:

Your realization that I live far beyond any considerations of money is all wrong. My expenses are terrible and I am not even sure I can make a living writing fiction. I am pretty sure I can't unless I write a best seller (unlikely) or sell serial rights to one of the big magazines. I simply don't want to do any more work for Hollywood. There is nothing in it but grief and exhaustion and discontent. In no real sense is it writing at all. It carries with it none of the satisfactions of writing. None of the sense of power over your medium. None of the freedom, even to fail. I may have to do some more of it, but I'd rather not. And I shall do it more and more cynically if I do have to. As a practical editor as well as a rare and pawky mind, you know that the only way I can get by is to sell some stuff to the big, shiny-paper magazines. I have to have about $50,000 a year, and yet very little of that money goes for my personal expenses. If I worked for a salary, I could get along on half of that. But I have to pay for all sorts of things which are given to you as part of your job. This house has only three bedrooms, apart from the maid's room, and two of them are given over entirely to business, except that I sleep in one of them. If I can't make this kind of an income, I have to change my whole way of life. In some ways that would not be altogether unpleasant, and certainly would be nothing like what I went through after 1930. Between you and me the writing business has grown to be a hell of a bore. There is far too much office work involved in it, far too much filing, bookkeeping, making out tax returns of various sorts, far too much concern with detail. Sometimes it seems as if the only chance one has to write is when all these other things are taken care of; and by that time the edge is off.

Yours,

Ray

TO HAMISH HAMILTON

6005 Camino de la Costa
La Jolla, California
August 10th. 1948

Dear Jamie:

•   •   •

Hardly necessary to tell you that I am typing this myself, no

[121]

longer have a secretary, just didn't have a full time job for one unless working in Hollywood. I shall probably be sorry, but can't help it. Have to retrench a bit anyhow. Things are awful over here as far as price is concerned.

The trouble with the Marlowe character is he has been written and talked about too much. He's getting self-conscious, trying to live up to his reputation among the quasi-intellectuals. The boy is bothered. He used to be able to spit and throw the ball hard and talk out of the corner of his mouth.

. . .

I am trying desperately to finish *The Little Sister*, and should have a rough draft done almost any day I can get up enough steam. The fact is, however, that there is nothing in it but style and dialogue and characters. The plot creaks like a broken shutter in an October wind.

. . .

Am reading *The Heart of the Matter*, a chapter at a time.[1] It has everything in it that makes literature except verve, wit, gusto, music and magic; a cool and elegant set-piece, embalmed by Whispering Glades. There is more life in the worst chapter Dickens or Thackeray ever wrote, and they wrote some pretty awful chapters.

All the best,

Ray

TO DALE WARREN

6005 Camino de la Costa
La Jolla, California
August 18 1948

Dear Dale:

1. By Graham Greene.

[122]

The books arrived and so very many thanks for your kindness. The short stories were removed from my sight at once and I haven't had a chance to look at them. The anthology about writing I have dipped into, but found nothing except a remark of Gertrude Atherton's about Galsworthy. Like other puzzlers over literary matters I am often stumped to understand what it is that writers like Galsworthy and Cronin and Marquand have that makes them so readable and yet in a sense so negligible. A fellow named Nevil Shute has it too. Last night I sat up to two ack emma reading *No Highway*—just couldn't put it down. And yet I know it contains no real literary art, none of that peculiar magic which makes a piece of writing, regardless of its formula or purpose, seem to be a freshly minted coin that no one has yet touched. Gertrude thinks it is technique. I do not.

The Dorothy Baker book I shall inevitably like.[1] I did my darndest when I was at Paramount to get them to buy *Trio* for me to do a screenplay on it. I told them that the Lesbian angle could be so handled that the yucks wouldn't realize it was there, that it need not even be there. It could be the story of a nice young girl's attempt to escape from the dominance of a brilliant, charming and forceful woman who was so much what she would like to be herself and couldn't be that she was held in bond to her. That settled, all the other motivations fall into place. But the fact is these Hollywood people are so filthy-minded themselves that they smell dirt even where there is none. A fellow who read the script of *The Blue Dahlia* told me: "I loved the homosexual angle." I said, "What homosexual angle?" He said between the two guys that lived in the same apartment." I said: "Oh. They shared an apartment and ate meals together. That makes them homosexuals, does it?" Whereat he looked hurt.

.   .   .

Sure, I think you are good publishers. Trouble is to decide whether there is any valid reason to change publishers. I think there ought to be a very heavy one before it is done. So I thought I would

1. *Our Gifted Son.*

just keep my trap shut about it for the time being and let the wiser mouths speak. I know what my impulse is.

All the best,

Ray

TO HAMISH HAMILTON

6005 Camino de la Costa
La Jolla, California
August 19th. 1948

Dear Jamie:

The end of Greene's book was great. It atoned for a lack I had felt before.

Yours of the 16th. crossed one of mine, so I leave the novelette question for later. The position as to *The Little Sister* is roughly that I have on paper in the rough about 85,000 words and lack two or three scenes at the end. Carl Brandt has seen half of the rough draft before I even read it over and he liked it. But I have a very, very tired mind. I can't judge the thing at all and I can't write with any regularity. I'm really exhausted with Hollywood rubbish. I do want to finish this thing so that I will have something to be published, and, although I don't expect any miracles from it, I don't want it to disappoint anyone too greatly.

The story has weaknesses. It is episodic and the emphasis shifts around from character to character and it is, as a mystery, overcomplicated, but as a story of people very simple. It has no violence in it at all; all the violence is off stage. If it has menace and suspense, they are in the writing. I think some of it is beautifully written, and my reactions to it are most unreliable. I write a scene and I read it over and think it stinks. Three days later (having done nothing in between but stew) I reread it and think it is great. So there you are. You can't bank on me. I may be all washed up.

Lately I have been trying to simplify my life so that I need not depend on Hollywood. I have no longer a business manager or a secretary. But I am not happy. I need a rest badly and I cannot rest until this is done and I sometimes think that when it is done it will be as tired as I am and it will show.

Assuming, for the moment, that the thing is any good, I feel that you may rely on receiving some kind of a script in a month. It may need more work, but it will give you a chance to see whether I am crazy or not. I guess Carl Brandt would tell you, up to a point.

I hope this is some help.

Ray

P.S. It contains the nicest whore I ever didn't meet.

TO CLEVE ADAMS

Sept 4th 1948

Dear Cleve:

It's nice to hear from you even in such queer circumstances. What is the source of your information? I may have an action for slander against someone.

I don't know Roy Huggins and have never laid eyes on him. He sent me an autographed copy of his book *Double Take* with his apologies and the dedication he says the publishers would not let him put in it. In writing to thank him I said his apologies were either unnecessary or inadequate and that I could name three or four writers who had gone as far as he had, without his frankness about it. I mentioned no names. If I had mentioned names (which, of course, I could) they would not have been the names of anyone with whom I am personally acquainted or who was writing for the pulps when I was.

I did not invent the hardboiled murder story and I have never made any secret of my opinion that Hammett deserves most or all of the credit. Everybody imitates in the beginning. What Stevenson called playing the "sedulous ape." I personally think that a deliberate attempt to lift a writer's personal tricks, his stock in trade, his

[125]

mannerisms, his approach to his material, can be carried too far—to the point where it is a kind of plagiarism, and a nasty kind because the law gives no protection. It is nasty for two main reasons. It makes the writer self-conscious about his own work; an example of this is a radio program which ran the use of extravagant similes (I think I rather invented this trick) into the ground, to the point where I am myself inhibited from writing the way I used to. The second reason is that it floods the market with bad money and that drives out the good. But none of these things can be helped. Even if I were granted the absolute power to stop such practices, I doubt that I would know where to draw the line. For one must bear in mind that they can't steal your style, if you have one. They can as a rule only steal your faults.

Since Hammett has not written for publication since 1932 I have been picked out by some people as a leading representative of the school. This is very likely due to the fact that *The Maltese Falcon* did not start the high budget mystery picture trend, although it ought to have. *Double Indemnity* and *Murder My Sweet* did, and I was associated with both of them. The result is that everybody who used to be accused of writing like Hammett may now be accused of trying to write like Chandler.

Somebody who read Huggins' book told me that it was full of scenes which were modeled in detail on scenes in my books, just moved over enough to get by. I didn't seem to notice it myself. Another party, whom I don't care to name on paper even writing to you, told me that when the script of *Double Take* was submitted, the publishers told Huggins, in effect, that it was bad enough for him to steal my approach and my method or whatever, but stealing my characters was going a little too far. I understand there was some rewriting, but cannot vouch for any of this. More power to Mr. Huggins. If he has been traveling on borrowed gas to any extent, the time will come when he will have to spew his guts into his own tank.

The law recognizes no plagiarism except that of basic plots. It is far behind the times in its concept of these things. My ideas have been plagiarized in Hollywood and I have been accused of plagiarism myself, by a guy who said *The Blue Dahlia* was lifted from an orginal of his. Luckily Paramount was in a position to show that his story never left the story department. Unconscious plagiarism is widespread and inevitable. Throughout the play *The Iceman Cometh* O'Neill uses the expression "the big sleep" as a synonym for death. He is apparently under the impression that this is a current underworld or half-world usage, whereas it is a pure invention on my part. If I am remembered long enough, I shall probably be accused of stealing the phrase from O'Neill, since he is a big shot. A fellow over in England named James Hadley Chase, the distinguished author of *No Orchids for Miss Blandish* (which is half-cent pulp writing at its worst) made a practice in one of his books of lifting verbatim or almost verbatim passages from my books and from those of Jack Latimer and Hammett. He was eventually forced to make a public apology in the English equivalent of *Publisher's Weekly*.[1] And he also had to pay the legal costs of three publishers incurred in forcing him to this apology. My American publisher's attorney would not even risk writing a letter to Chase's American publisher warning him about this. They still have some business honor left in England.

If I seem to write at too great length about all this, it is because I am very interested in the subject. Yet curiously enough, when I had a radio program last year, and when the only thing I had to sell was a character, it was found impossible to get a writer who could deliver that character or to write dialogue that sounded like him. As long as this is so, why should I worry?

As for you and Ballard, I wouldn't know what the idea was at all.[2] We all grew up together, so to speak, and we all wrote the same idiom, and we have all more or less grown out of it. A lot of *Black Mask* stories sounded alike, just as a lot of Elizabethan plays sound alike. Always when a group exploits a new technique this happens. But even when we all wrote for Joe Shaw, who thought everybody had to write just like Hammett, there were subtle and obvious differences, apparent to any writer, if not to non-writers. Your stuff could never have been mistaken for mine or mine for yours.

.   .   .

Yours always,

Ray

1. *Publishers Weekly* is the trade journal of the American book industry. The British equivalent is *The Bookseller*.
2. W. T. Ballard, prolific writer of westerns and detective novels.

TO JAMES SANDOE

6005 Camino de la Costa
La Jolla, California
September 23, 1948

Dear Sandoe:

. . .

I shall order Shelley Smith's *The Woman in the Sea*. Sounds worth buying. But would very much like to see your copy of *Famous American Trials*. I did not care for *Wide Boys Never Work*,[1] but I could not tell you why, except that it belongs to the class of books I can't read because they make me nervous. They are grim and depressing without tragedy. Graham Greene's book has that quality too; very much overrated by my standards. The ending is very good, but the character of Scobie doesn't come off, largely because Greene is so utterly humorless. My reaction reminds me of a rather narrow-minded comment by an English friend on *Brief Encounter*.[2] "The point is that to people of that sort that sort of thing simply doesn't happen." He meant in England, of course. I couldn't go that far, although I am half British.

Your family sounds wonderful, including animals. Our cat is growing positively tyrannical. If she finds herself alone anywhere she emits blood curdling yells until somebody comes running. She sleeps on a table in the service porch and now demands to be lifted up and down from it. She gets warm milk about eight o'clock at night and starts yelling for it about 7.30. When she gets it she drinks a little, goes off and sits under a chair, then comes and yells all over again for someone to stand beside her while she has another go at the milk. When we have company she looks them over and decides almost instantly if she likes them. If she does she strolls over and plops down on the floor just far enough away to make it a chore to pet her. If she doesn't like them she sits in the middle of the living room, casts a contemptuous glance around, and proceeds to wash her backside.

1. By Robert Westerby.
2. By Noel Coward.

In the middle of this engaging performance she will stop dead, lift her head without any other change of position (one leg pointing straight at the ceiling) stares off into space while thinking out some abstruse problem, then resumes her rear-end-job. This work is always done in the most public manner. When she was younger she always celebrated the departure of visitors by tearing wildy through the house and ending up with a good claw on the davenport, the one that is covered with brocatelle and makes superb clawing, and it comes off in strips. But she is lazy now. Won't even play with her catnip mouse unless it is dangled in such a position that she can play with it lying down. I'm going to send you her picture. It has me in it, but you'll have to overlook that. I believe I told you how she used to catch all sorts of very breakable living things and bring them in the house quite unhurt as a rule. I'm sure she never hurt them intentionally. Cats are very interesting. They have a terrific sense of humor and, unlike dogs, cannot be embarrassed or humiliated by being laughed at. There is nothing in nature worse than seeing a cat trying to provoke a few more hopeless attempts to escape out of a half-dead mouse. My enormous respect for our cat is largely based on a complete lack in her of this diabolical sadism. When she used to catch mice—we haven't had any for years—she brought them alive and undamaged and let me take them out of her mouth. Her attitude seemed to be, "Well, here's this damn mouse. Had to catch it, but it's really your problem. Remove it at once." Periodically she goes through all the closets and cupboards on a regular mouse-inspection. Never finds any, but she realizes it's part of her job.

I sent my book off to Carl Brandt in New York yesterday. The only copy I had too.[3] A silly thing to do, but I couldn't find anyone to copy it quickly and I was beginning to chip at it too much. Never know when to let a thing alone. I begin at last to realize that I have a very unorthodox attitude to plots. Most writers think up a plot with an intriguing situation and then proceed to fit characters into it. With me a plot, if you could call it that, is an organic thing. It grows and often it overgrows. I am continually finding myself with scenes that I won't discard and that don't want to fit in. So that my plot problem invariably ends up as a desperate attempt to justify a lot of material that, for me at least, has come alive and insists on

3. *The Little Sister*, Chandler's fifth novel.

[129]

staying alive. It's probably a silly way to write, but I seem to know no other way. The mere idea of being committed in advance to a certain pattern appalls me.

The murder novel you mentioned ought to be written next, if I can write it. I'm not sure I can.

All the best,

Ray Chandler

TO CHARLES MORTON

6005 Camino de la Costa
La Jolla, California
September 27, 1948

Dear Charlie:

An evening or two ago as I was toning up my intellect with Little Orphan Annie and our cat Taki was leafing through the last issue of *Time*, she let out a whimper of acute distress and slid to the floor and went under a chair. Picking up the rag, I saw before me, looking a little askance, as well he might, none other than short, dumpy, round-headed, balding, jug-eared, carnelian-nebbed, loud-bow-tied *Atlantic*-editor Morton. Well, strike me pink, lads, is this the face that launched a thousand japes and singed the snow-capped peaks of Henry Luce? It's a nice face, a nice honest, leprechaun of a face. It could be played by Barry Fitzgerald. It has character and good humor. The tie was a little careless, as though tied by one hand, while the other attended to the customary breakfast of tomato juice laced with Worcestershire sauce and a double old-fashioned, this being the regular Number Four on the bill of fare of our local hostelry, the Casa de Mañana, (clean beds.) But somehow it wasn't what I expected.

Where was the lean hawklike profile, the casual monocle balanced in the sardonic eye, the Balkan Sobranje held in the long shapely almost bloodless fingers, the cleft and bony chin, the dry contemptuous and yet courtly smile? They just weren't there. Omaha, oh Omaha, what a spate of bourbon it took to tint that proboscis, or was it the sun on the icebergs, or the olfactory irritation of the unsolicited manuscript?[1] No use to speculate. There he is, a kind father and at times a virtuous husband, take him or leave him, give or take six points. Anyway, your piece on the fraternities was a joy. (Why did I say anyway?)

God help me I've been reading a book about the war by an English general named Fuller, who was, I believe, retired from the army while still in his prime, due to an incurable case of intelligence.[2] The book makes more sense of the war than anything I had read so far, and also of the double-cross at Versailles that we let Clemenceau put over on the Germans after they had surrendered on terms. Here is a man who has absolutely no prejudice in favor of his own countryman, who can even give Montgomery his due without gagging, who in a short brilliant chapter makes clear that MacArthur's island-hopping campaign in the South Pacific was as masterly a job of daring, imagination, and guts as the Italian campaign was a senseless and incredibly weak piece of strategic bungling. His disgust, both moral and practical and military, at so-called strategic bombing, is withering and precise. He thinks that in spite of our tactical brilliance we are a nation of military amateurs, and God knows history is proving him right. Even the English, who I am quite sure Fuller thinks incapable of all-out offensive war because there is always some muttonhead in a high place to kill a good idea or block a daring one,—even the English understood that if we did not end up in Berlin and Vienna, we had fought a war for nothing. I don't think he quite despises Eisenhower, although his temperament makes him go for men like Bradley and Patton, but it's clear he feels that Eisenhower was not a strong enough man for his job, and that at a crucial moment in September 1944 he threw away a quick victory because he couldn't stand up to either Montgomery or Bradley, but had to compromise with both. It's quite a book. The thing that stands out all through is Fuller's belief that an independent air force is a ghastly mistake, because it will insist on fighting with the most expensive, the least profitable and the most uselessly destructive weapon, the heavy

1. Morton was from Omaha, Nebraska.
2. Major General John Frederick Charles Fuller, author of *The Second World War*, 1948.

[131]

bomber, whereas its true function is ground support, interdiction of traffic and supplies, and logistics. When it was so used, usually unwillingly, the effect was immediate and startling; when it was used for saturation raids on cities like Hamburg, Berlin and Leipsig, it was militarily of small consequence and morally put us right beside the man who ran Belsen and Dachau.

Ray

TO RAY STARK

October 1948

Dear Ray:

.   .   .

The point about Marlowe to remember is that he is a first person character, whether he shows up that way in a radio script or not. A first person character is under the disadvantage that he must be a better man to the reader than he is to himself. Too many first person characters give an offensively cocky impression. That's bad. To avoid that you must not always give him the punch line or the exit line. Not even often. Let the other characters have the toppers. Leave him without a gag. Insofar as it is possible. Howard Hawks, a very wise hombre, remarked to me when he was doing *The Big Sleep* that he thought one of Marlowe's most effective tricks was just giving the other man the trick and not saying anything at all. That puts the other man on the spot. A devastating crack loses a lot of its force when it doesn't provoke any answer, when the other man just rides with the punch. Then you either have to top it yourself or give ground.

Don't have Marlowe say things merely to score off the other characters. When he comes out with a smash wisecrack it should be jerked out of him emotionally, so that he is discharging an emotion and not even thinking about laying anyone out with a sharp retort. If you use similes, try and make them both extravagant and original.

[132]

And there is a question of how the retort discourteous is delivered. The sharper the wisecrack, the less forcible should be the way it is said. There should not be any effect of gloating. All this is a question of taste. If you haven't got it, you can't get it by rules. There are a lot of clever people in Hollywood who overreach themselves because they don't know where to stop. It's bad enough in pictures, but on the radio it is worse, because the voice is everything and you can't have an expression on the face that offsets the words. You can't really throw away a line as if it was something that tasted bad when you said it.

Oh well, I'm not so smart either.

Yours,

Ray

TO H. N. SWANSON

6005 Camino de la Costa
October 15, 1948

Dear Swanie,

That was a very nice and very clever letter. Who the hell told you my name was Joe Ugly. I've been the most successful real-name-hider in the business. The Uglies (It should probably be Uglys in this case) are a small but persistent clan of hobnail-boot wearers well known and little liked for kissing their women to death of a Saturday night in small noisome alleys off the Mile End Road. Many a time as a kid sleeping in my old man's extra pair of hunting breeks have I seen Inspector Sir Marmaduke Fitzboodle (of the East Riding Fitzboodles) ease himself into the old man's pot of porter and ask a few searching questions about all that blood on the floor in the corner of the room. Once, I mind, they thought of digging up the floor, which was solid fish and chips twenty feet thick, but the old man just laughed and wiped his nose on the Inspector's knitted muffler. The Uglies never bothered about cops, except once in a

[133]

while to kick one in a thick fog. Ah well, it's a long time since I put the boot to an underprivileged child.

Yes, I finished the book, if that'a a fair name for this ill-written and ill-constructed 75,000 words of nose thumbing.[1] What may happen to it I dunno. It's a mite fruity for the carriage trade and a little too literate for the Democrats, besides having only six murders in it. But I have not ripened into manhood. My five years in the salt mines left me a typical case of arrested development, and the more I stay away from the picture business, the better I like it. I suppose you know Joe Sistrom has left Universal and Paramount's top price for a property is five grand. Any moment now Henry the Gin will finalize a deal to a remake of The King of Kings, with Alan Ladd as Christ, Cecil B. de Mille as God, and Betty Hutton as the Virgin Mary. But I bet Bill Bendix steals the picture as Mary Magdalene. I will eat lunch with you only if my gun jams.

Ray

TO JAMES SANDOE

Camino de la Costa
La Jolla, California
October 17, 1948

Dear Sandoe:

.   .   .

There is no top-drawer critical writing about the murder or mystery novel, factually based or otherwise. A book like Pritchett's *The Living Novel* would be very interesting, possibly not too remunerative in dollars, but well worthwhile from the prestige point of view.[1] Neither in this country nor in England has there been any critical recognition that far more art goes into these books at their best than into any number of fat volumes of goosed history or social-

1. *The Little Sister.*

1. V. S. Pritchett, *The Living Novel*, 1946.

significance rubbish. The psychological foundation for the immense popularity with all sorts of people of the novel about murder or crime or mystery hasn't been scratched. A few superficial and a few frivolous attempts, but nothing careful and cool and leisurely. There is a lot more to this subject than most people realize, even those who are interested in it. The subject has usually been treated lightly because it seems to have been taken for granted, quite wrongly, that because murder novels are easy reading they are also light reading. They are no easier reading than *Hamlet, Lear* or *Macbeth*. They border on tragedy and never quite become tragic. Their form imposes a certain clarity of outline which is only found in the most accomplished "straight" novels. And incidentally—quite incidentally, of course, a very large proportion of the surviving literature of the world has been concerned with violent death in some form. And if you have to have significance (the demand for which is the inevitable mark of a half-baked culture), it is just possible that the tensions in a novel of murder are the simplest and yet most complete pattern of the tensions in which we live in this generation.

RC

TO CARL BRANDT

6005 Camino de la Costa
La Jolla, California
November 12, 1948

Dear Carl:

.   .   .

We had lovely weather all the way to San Francisco and back. It rained the night we stayed at Carmel but was fine again in the morning. Carmel, which I suppose you know, is a very cute place, but has a slightly unreal look as though it had been constructed on MGM's back lot. It has been compared to La Jolla and does resemble it in the lack of billboards and other ugly things, but the resemblance stops there. I really think it is more attractive than La Jolla, and has

[135]

the advantage of not being near a large city. La Jolla is full of tired old men and tired old money; Carmel seems a more middle-class sort of place. If you ever go to Santa Barbara, stop at the Biltmore in Montecito. There is *really* a hotel. San Francisco I liked, but its hotels stink. The Fairmont has a magnificent lobby and that's all. The Mark [Hopkins] has a beautiful grill room (and the sky lounge, of course) but its food is exorbitant, its lobby has no trace of style, and the place is full of chisel-eyed characters who look as if they were afraid they might not smile at a producer. Next time we'll try the Clift, which we visited many times when Clift was alive, but not since. I regret to confess that I left the addresses home which Bernice sent me, but I probably should not have called them anyhow because we spent all our time shopping or trying to shop.[1] The thing I love about S.F. is its go to hell attitude. The narrow streets are lined with NO PARKING AT ANY TIME signs and also lined with parked automobiles which look as if they had been there all day. For the first time in my life I saw a lady traffic cop, a real cop too, complete with nickel star and whistle. I saw one other cop. He was driving around with a piece of chalk on the end of a long stick and about once a block he took a swipe at some rear tire, just to keep his hand in. The taxi drivers are wonderful too. They obey no laws but those of gravity and we even had one who passes street cars on the left, an offense for which you would probably get ninety days in Los Angeles. In case you should ever think I am too cynical about the police, it just isn't possible to be. A committee of Superior Court judges in L.A. has been going into the habeas corpus business which seemed to them to be flourishing too richly and taking up too much court time. The chairman just let loose with a statement in which he announced that he was fed up with the racket of arresting bookies or supposed bookies, then springing them on habeas corpus writs, at a cost of $500 in bail and anywhere from $200 to $500 legal fees. He said that the Vice squad boys seem to have perfected a system whereby they pull in supposed bookies and the moment the boys are booked along comes a lawyer and a bondsmen with a writ; when the case is called the cops have lost the evidence. Judge Ambrose said quite clearly and audibly that the Los Angeles police have developed a very slippery clutch on evidence. Five or six of these operations per night could be quite

1. Bernice Baumgarten, of Brandt and Brandt agency.

lucrative over a period of time. The courts have to hear arguments on all these writs and they take up time. Anybody who is not a damn fool must know that this shakedown is all worked out in advance and is a substitute for the former method of having a "juicer" call around at the gambling houses for the rake-off. It has the advantage of looking legal too. The point is, of course, that each of these arrests and releases implies a crooked judge, a crooked lawyer, a crooked bondsman, and some crooked cops. No honest judge would set bail so high that the bond would cost $500. Last night a couple of the boys didn't get writs. They had to stay in jail, and were they sore! The judge got cold feet. The thing that gets me in our lovely civilization is the complete indifference with which the public greets these disclosures. We just don't expect anybody to be honest. A few weeks ago, for example, the *Times* caught a photo of an imcomplete forward pass on the goal line. It was incomplete because the end or back who was the receiver had his right arm locked tight between the left arm and body of the defending back. The whole dirty foul was as clear as daylight in the photo. THE PHOTO WAS PUBLISHED WITHOUT COMMENT as a photo of the play; there was simply no reaction to the foul at all. Well for Chrissake, if we teach the boys to be crooked in college, what can you expect? And they *are* taught to be crooked, coldly, deliberately and with malice.

.   .   .

All my best,

Ray

TO HAMISH HAMILTON

6005 Camino de la Costa
La Jolla, California
November 20, 1948

Dear Jamie:

.   .   .

My punctuation is unorthodox at times, but I don't make any

mistakes of ignorance. They are deliberate violations of standard practice. It's nice of Priestley to want to read my stuff.[1] Bless him! I remember his saying of it, "They don't write like that at Dulwich."[2] That may be, but if I hadn't grown up on Latin and Greek, I doubt if I would know so well how to draw the very subtle line between what I call a vernacular style and what I should call an illiterate or faux naif style, There's a hell of a lot of difference, to my mind.

.   .   .

Yours,
Ray

TO CARL BRANDT

6005 Camino de la Costa
La Jolla, California
November 26, 1948.

Dear Carl:

.   .   .

I worked at MGM once in that cold storage plant they call the Thalberg Building, fourth floor. Had a nice producer, George Haight, a fine fellow. About that time some potato-brain, probably Mannix.[1] had decided that writers would do more work, if they had no couches to lie on. So there was no couch in my office. Never a man to be stopped by trifles, I got a streamer rug out of the car and spread it on the floor and lay down on that. Haight coming in for a courtesy call rushed to the phone and yelled down to the story editor (I forget the name and never even met the man) that I was a horizontal writer and for Chrissake send up a couch. However, the cold storage atmosphere got me too quick, and the coteries at the writers table in the commissary. I said I would work at home. They said Mannix had issued orders no writers to work at home. I said a man as big as Mannix ought to be allowed the privilege of changing his mind.

1. J. B. Priestley.
2. Chandler's English school.

---

1. Edgar J. Mannix, Thalberg's assistant, who later became General Manager of MGM Studios.

So I worked at home, and only went over there three or four times to talk to Haight. I've only worked at three studios and Paramount was the only one I liked. They do somehow maintain the country club atmosphere there to an extent. At the writers table at Paramount I heard some of the best wit I've ever heard in my life. Some of the boys are at their best when not writing. I remember Harry Tugend's wonderful crack about _____, when Tugend was trying to be a producer and hating it. He said: "You know this is a lousy job. You got to sit and talk to that birdbrain seriously about whether or no this part is going to be good for her _____ career and at the same time you got to keep from being raped." Whereat a rather innocent young man piped up: "You mean to say she's a nymphomaniac?" Harry frowned off into the distance and sighed and said slowly, "Well, I gues she would be, if they could get her quieted down a little." The other was a contribution from a man named Seton Miller, a lousy writer but a very good brain in other ways. "Somebody was discussing the picture that introduced Miss Lauren Bacall to immortality, *To Have and Have Not*, and the singing she did in it. An innocent said, "I guess they probably dubbed that song in." Whereat Seton Miller screamed: "For Jesus Christ sake, you damn idiot, do you think somebody actually went out and *looked* for a voice like that?"

.   .   .

All the best,
Ray

TO CARL BRANDT

6005 Camino de la Costa
La Jolla, California
December 5, 1948

Dear Carl:

.   .   .

As for Dore Schary, I'm sure he is an able man and a nice fellow, but like a great many intellectual Jews he is hipped on significance.[1] He believes in pictures that carry a message. I regard that

1. Motion picture producer and playwright.

[139]

as a facet of Hollywood's adult infantilism. I regard the whole matter of social significance in pictures as a bore. *Gentleman's Agreement* lasted twenty minutes with me before I walked out on it. I thought it one of the worst pictures I had ever tried to sit through, an insult to my intelligence, because its so-called message was pitched on a level I can only call grammar school. As a European by education, though not by birth, I share the European feeling that Hollywood's attempts to propound social and political ideas, claptrap about democracy and such, is an indication of a half-baked culture. "From the cinema one does not learn about politics; from films one can only learn about people."

Ray

TO JAMES SANDOE

6005 Camino de la Costa
La Jolla, California
December 6, 1948

Dear Sandoe:

.　　　.　　　.

I knew a banker once from Aberdeen, Washington, who served two or three years in federal prison for making unsecured loans from the bank's funds to the ranchers on whom the bank's business was built. He was a perfectly honest man, he didn't make a cent out of what he did. It was during the depression and the ranchers had to have money or go broke. If they went broke, the bank went broke, because its mortgage loans would become worthless. With the bank's help the ranchers might weather the depression. If they did, they would repay the loans. This bank undoubtedly broke the banking laws. He admitted it. But who was he defrauding? The stockholders of the bank? He was one himself and the others were all men of property in the neighborhood. The stock was not traded in. He was attempting by the only means he saw to keep the bank's source of income from collapsing. He was tried and convicted and the bank closed its doors. But up to that time the bank had withstood the depression, as very many other state banks had not. The chances are that it would have gone under anyway, because the whole area was directly or indirectly dependent on the lumber business, and the lumber business didn't recover until we started to rearm for World War II. But the man did his best. There is something tragically wrong with a system of justice which can and does make criminals of honest men and can only convict gangsters and racketeers when they don't pay their taxes. Of course to be fair I must also admit that there is something wrong with a financial system which insures that every corporation executive during a time of depression will risk going to jail a dozen times a month in his efforts to save his company. I personally believe, and I am not a socialist or anything of the sort, that there is a basic fallacy about our financial system. It simply implies a fundamental cheat, a dishonest profit, a non-existent value.

.   .   .

Ray

TO MIKE GIBBUD, ESQ. FROM TAKI CHANDLER, ESQ.[1]

N.D. [Christmas 1948]

Dear Mike:
This is to thank you for your card and your good wishes, which I reciprocate, although I do not reciprocate the somewhat excessive familiarity of your mode of address since we have not, so far as I recall, been formally introduced. As to your suspicions of your "old lady" (do try to get rid of these palsy-walsy mannerisms) they are probably quite unfounded and due to an inferiority complex which

1. Chandler's cat. The text of the letter is taken from a transcript.

[141]

in turn is the product of your mixed blood. But don't worry about these things. This is an age of heraldic inferiority. A bend sinister is no more a disgrace today than it was in the Middle Ages. Your father may have been a gentleman, even if your mother was no lady. Your rat tail is all the fashion now. I prefer a bushy plume, carried straight up. You are Siamese and your ancestors lived in trees. Mine lived in palaces. It has been suggested to me that I am a bit of a snob. How true! I prefer to be.

Come around sometime when your face is clean and we shall discuss the state of the world, the foolishness of humans, the prevalence of horsemeat, although we prefer the tenderloin side of a porterhouse, and our common difficulty in getting doors opened at the right time and meals served at more frequent intervals. I have got my staff up to five a day, but there is still room for improvement.

As for your parting greeting: "Happy mouse hunting," you are, I trust, a little drunk. Cats of our lineage do not hunt mice.

TO BERNICE BAUMGARTEN

6005 Camino de la Costa
La Jolla, California
December 29, 1948

Dear Bernice:

.   .   .

Of Jim's books I have *Guard of Honor, The Just and the Unjust, S.S. San Pedro.*[1] What others should I get? I mean, are there any that would be likely to disappoint me? If that is possible. I got *The Young Lions* for Christmas.[2] It looks as phony as hell in spots. And how do you do something "with careful deliberation." And, "But the girl's expression hadn't changed. She had broken off a twig from a

1. By James Gould Cozzens, Baumgarten's husband.
2. By Irwin Shaw.

[142]

bush and was absently running it along the stone fence, as though she were pondering what he had just said." The last clause and the 'absently' throw away the effect. You either describe an action and let the reader make the deduction of the inner reaction it expresses, or else you describe the inner reaction and view what she does from within. You don't do it both ways at the same time. A small thing, but it places the stuff for me. I guess I'm just being a stinker. And enjoying it.

Yours ever,

Ray

TO CARL BRANDT

January 23rd. 1949

Dear Carl:

I've mislaid your last note, but I think you said you would be in LA about the middle of Feb. I think I can pop up and see you. Just came back from there and had a talk with Stark in so far as one can have a talk with a Hollywood agent in his lair at all. Not hopeful about any English deal. Looks like I'll have to pay my own way and I'd better get busy or I won't have a reservation. Stark came up with some brain wave about me writing a Marlowe story about he goes to London and Montgomery plays him and there he was (Stark) on the phone yelling for Montgomery that he don't get anywhere near at all. Having seen how the boys suffered with M over the script of *The Saxon Charm* (which may have been their fault, of course) I'm not keen except that he is a decent fellow for an actor. (My favorite producer once remarked in a tone of muted despair, just after an interview with one: "Of course, nobody can *really like* an actor!) What gets me about going to England is the awful mess of red tape, the reservations, the deadlines, the not knowing where to go. (Certainly not the Dorchester, might as well stay at that stinkhole the Beverly Hills Hotel.)

[143]

These Hollywood people are fantastic when you have been away for a while. In their presence any calm sensible remark sounds faked. Their conversation is a mess of shopworn superlatives interrupted by four telephone calls to the sentence. Stark is a nice chap. I like him. Everybody at his bagnio is nice. He has done a fine job with the radio show. It could have been on the air five years already, if I had had him in the first place. It has a better rating they tell me than some quite expensive shows. Just the same I came away depressed. I really don't know why. Perhaps it's just Beverly Hills. It was such a nice place before the Phoenicians took it over. Now it's just a setting for an enormous confidence racket.

Ray

TO HAMISH HAMILTON

6005 Camino de la Costa
La Jolla, California
January 24th. 1949

Dear Jamie:

.   .   .

I'd want to go on one of the smaller Cunarders.[1] I'd not want to stop at the Dorchester and look at a lot of Phoenicians from Hollywood and New York. What is a good hotel where the food will keep one alive, where one can keep warm (it's going to seem awfully chilly to us after so many years of Southern California)? What clothes do I need of a special kind, if any? Do I need a dinner jacket etc? And might I use your house address for the no doubt unscrupulous purpose of telling the passport people where I am going? If so, what

1. For years Chandler had made plans to visit England, but did not go there until 1952.

[144]

is it? It seems they want to know. We live in the age of the Cads. You travel by air, but my wife won't, and I can't without her. I was thinking of having the food parcel man send me some food parcels. Much as I have read it is still a little hard for us to get a firm picture of what living is like in England. When would you suggest my coming? May or June or what?

Your remarks about red carpets, though ever so kindly meant, scare me a little. I'm strictly the background type, and my character is an unbecoming mixture of outer diffidence and inward arrogance. I don't do any of the things writers seem to do as a matter of course nowadays; I don't puff other writers' books and expect them to puff mine; I don't go to autograph parties or book marts or become a party to these cunning little interviews which are arranged by the promotion people to help their sales. In this country it is part of the racket; to me it's what makes it a racket. In England I have no doubt things are a little different. I do not come to England as a visiting author, God forbid, but as a man who loved England well when his heart was young and has never loved in the same way since, nor ever shall.

Of course I'll love the books. Brooding over the list I've been on the point of ordering a number of them. It's so very kind of you all to make so much of what to me is so simple a thing. After all what do I do? And if it were anything at all, which it is not, I have in my mind an unforgettable little story of some friends who visited Luxembourg a couple of years ago. They stayed at a very nice hotel where the food and wine were magnificent. The atmosphere was cheerful, people from all the countries of Europe, almost, were there, having their ease. At two tables were English people, only two. At one sat an elderly couple formerly well-to-do, now not so well-to-do. At the other a demobbed tank officer with his mother. On all the tables in the hotel dining room but these two were bottles of wine. This is a true story. The English could not afford wine. Those who had never surrendered drank water in order that those who had surrendered might drink wine. I think this story is wonderful. It is definitely and positively true, which makes it so much more wonderful.

Ray

[145]

TO CARL BRANDT

6005 Camino de la Costa
La Jolla, California
(February 1949)

Dear Carl:

I am trying out a new Corona so my typing will be worse than usual. For years I used a noiseless portable and then I got a standard Remington and since then have been unable to use any noiseless machine. But I must have a portable I can take away from home.

Thanks for your letter of Jan. 26. Perhaps I had better not bother anybody about advice to a traveler to England until I'm sure I'm going there. I have some very difficult personal problems to solve, or they seem difficult to me, which is the same thing. There is first the question of the house. It is a nice house, one of the nicest in La Jolla, but it seems impossible to get any competent help here. Everybody has colored people and they are no damn good to us. My wife simply will not put up with their dirt. The house is too much for her, and even if it were not too much for her in a physical sense, taking care of it, going to market, cooking and cleaning up, would prevent her from doing anything else. I guess we all slow down and tire as we get older. I know I have. I am always tired. Also, apart from that, the house is too expensive. Disregarding the investment and taxes we find that in a La Jolla everything costs too much, every service is overpriced, everybody is on the chisel. Once the place was worth it. But we don't have the same seclusion any more. It is still far better than Los Angeles or that once charming and now ruined little city of Beverly Hills. Then it is too close to the ocean. I have a lot of trouble with my sinuses. Of course we don't know where to go yet. If it were not for the smog, we would have tried San Marino, the other side of Los Angeles. The San Fernando Valley has been corrupted by the Hollywood element. They spoil everything they touch. Reversing Johnson's epitaph on Goldsmith, one might say of the movie industry, NIHIL QUOD TETIGIT NON CORRUPIT. (It touched nothing which it did not corrupt.) The trouble with the valley is its heat in summer. On the other hand we want

[146]

to get a cabin at Big Bear Lake and want it not more than a couple of hours drive away. Altogether, quite a problem.

.   .   .

I have no idea what income I can count on. I am cutting my own throat by using up my time and energies doing things that have nothing to do with writing. But I can't make any stable arrangements until I know where and how I am going to live. I don't see how any writer except a writer of best-sellers, which I am not likely to be, can exist other than in the most modest way without either Hollywood money or a steady stream of serials in the big magazines. You can't depend on radio or selling motion picture rights. They are too chancy. If I write a book a year I can probably depend on an income of $25,000, but that wouldn't pay my way here. Gosh, when I think what that income would have bought when I was a schoolboy in England. A mansion standing in large grounds, three or four servants, a full time gardener and coachman, a couple of fine horses for the victoria and the brougham, and so on. High prices and heavy taxation will destroy a society just as effectively as war. Can you recall when amid howls of fury the English income tax reached a shilling in the pound?

I've got an article on writing in Hollywood for Charlie Morton. At least I have it on records, but it isn't typed. It's too long and may be repetitious, but I had to get it off my chest. If it seems too bitter, it need not be printed. (Also, he may not like it). But I had to write it. I don't believe in handling these birds with kid gloves. It's a disgraceful thing that no reputable writer can work for Hollywood without its ending in cynicism and disgust. But even at that I'd rather work in pictures than write these slick serials, even if I could.

I have a book in mind which I have only not started because it needs a third act, or rather a better third act. It has a good idea, was originally intended to have an English setting, but I couldn't do that now. Altogether I seem to be a bit mixed up, don't I?

.   .   .

God what a long and discontented letter. Sorry,

Ray

[147]

TO BERNICE BAUMGARTEN

6005 Camino de la Costa
La Jolla, California
Feb. 13th 1949

Dear Bernice:

It is probably, in fact certainly, very inconsiderate of me to send you the enclosed in this form, but I have to get it away from me.[1] I can neither stop tinkering with it nor can I summon up the courage to throw it away. Someone is going to have to do that for me. If you approve of it, Charlie Morton has a moral option to see it and take it, if he wants it.[2]

This was something I had to get off my chest, be it ill-judged, undiplomatic and all the rest. It was something that preyed on me, but that does not mean it has to be published. I have a horror of pulling my punches for fear of offending Hollywood, for fear that that offense will hurt me in some indirect way, probably financial. If I write about it at all I will write what I think. I may be wrong but I am honest. But I do not have to write about it and I hope I shall never be betrayed into doing it again in any serious vein. Yet I did have to try to write this piece. I did have to justify to myself the conviction that the "professionalism" of the Hollywood film is killing it and that no amount of gloss, no amount of publicity build-up, no amount of Zanuckism, will save it in the long run if the imaginative basis of the film is destroyed.[3] And I have seen that happening all the time.

I am not at all sure that I approve of the fiction writer as a thinking animal. It's possible that he should do all his thinking with his solar plexus and leave the critical stuff to the boys who cannot write anything else. But there are two subjects which always seem to

---

1.   Article entitled "The Film and the Writer." It disappeared and was subsequently replaced by "A Qualified Farewell," which was published as "Farewell, My Hollywood" in *Antaeus*, Spring/Summer 1976.
2.   Editor at *The Atlantic Monthly*.
3.   Reference to Darryl Zanuck at Twentieth Century-Fox Studio.

stir me up and make me want to rant and roar. One is the assumption of such unshy pornographers as the gent who wrote about that county[1] that the mystery novel is by definition inferior writing because very many of the exhibits are inferior writing, that its particular brand of fantasy is any less vital than that of the love story or the novel of manners. They are all fantasy and scarcely anything in literature is worth a damn except what is written between the lines. The other subject is what I have written about in this piece. And I don't really care what you do with it so long as you don't let me tinker with it any more.

We are going to Riverside tommorrow Monday unless it pours rain (which it is doing at this moment) and I assume Carl will be out here by then.

Yours,

Ray

TO JAMES SANDOE

La Jolla
February 25, 1949

. . .

I know from my own knowledge that in the first world war, during the final German retreat from the Hindenburg line the machine gun crews left behind to hold up the advance as long as possible were almost always bayoneted to the last man, even though they rose out of the ground and tried to surrender. There is an element of hypocrisy in these war trials that hurts. Hanging generals and politicians and concentration camp people is fine, but when it comes to junior officers and N.C.O.'s I'm not at all easy about it. Their freedom of choice seems to me little more than freedom to prefer death to dishonor, and that's asking too much of human nature.

1. Edmund Wilson, author of *The Memoirs of Hecate County*, 1949.

TO BERNICE BAUMGARTEN

6005 Camino de la Costa
La Jolla, California
March 11th, 1949

Dear Bernice:

. . .

Every now and then I get a shock by seeing myself through other eyes. In the current number of *Partisan Review* (which incidentally has several very good things in it) a man writing about *Our Mutual Friend* says: "It is possible that the question of true-to-life did not arise, and that Dickens' contemporaries accepted his dark vision of England and London . . . as readily as we today accept Raymond Chandler's California with its brutal and neurotic crew of killers and private eyes——" etc. Another writer in an avant garde magazine referred to me as a "Cato of the Cruelties." Apart from the obvious compliment of being noticed at all by the rarified intellectuals who write for these publications—and I should understand them well, because I was one of them for many years—I cannot grasp what they do with their sense of humor. Or let me put it in a better way: Why is it that the Americans—of all people the quickest to reverse their moods—do not see the strong element of burlesque in my kind of writing? Or is it only the intellectuals who miss that? It is as though the public, most inconstant in its own emotions, expected a writer to be utterly constant in his. And as for true-to-life I don't think these cloud-dwellers can have much understanding of the kind of world they live in and the kind of world Dickens lived in. There is a strong element of fantasy in the mystery story; there is in any kind of writing that moves within an accepted formula. The mystery writer's material is melodrama, which is an exaggeration of violence and fear beyond what one normally experiences in life. (I said normally; no writer ever approximated the life of the Nazi concentration camps). The means he uses are realistic in the sense that such things happen to people like these and in places like these. But this realism is superficial; the potential of emotion is overcharged, the compression of time and event is a violation of probability, and although such things happen, they do not happen so fast and in such a tight frame of logic to so closely knit a group of people. I think there's an article in this.

Yours,

Ray

TO HAMISH HAMILTON

6005 Camino de la Costa
La Jolla, California
March 12th. 1949

Dear Jamie:

·　　　·　　　·

I regret to say I find Elizabeth Bowen's last book entirely unreadable; in places an absolute parody of Henry James.[1] When you read HJ, however tenuous the web he spins, you do at last and at least realize that he is trying to say something precise, almost too exquisitely precise. But poor dear Elizabeth is falling into the sad error of thinking that the involution of the language necessarily conceals a subtlety of thought. It doesn't; it conceals a vacuum. I used to do this sort of thing myself in my thirties, but God gave me too much sense of humor to carry on with it. I'm awfully sorry for writers. They try so hard, they are so damn vulnerable, and they look so silly when they overextend themselves. I should be grateful that I went through the arty and intellectual phase so young and grew out of it so completely that it always seems a little juvenile in others, whatever their ages. I never took myself very seriously as a writer and always knew myself to be one of those people who can do fairly well at almost anything and therefore superbly well at nothing. And considering the vast amount of talent and intelligence there is in this country, not to mention England, I'm still a bit puzzled as to why no one has come along to make me look like thirty cents. But except for an occasional tour de force like *The Big Clock* or *Mr. Bowling Buys*

1. Elizabeth Bowen's *The Heat of the Day*, 1948.

[151]

a Newspaper no one has.[2] There isn't a mystery writer on the horizon here that really has anything, or if there is, I have missed him. I thought Jack Iams might be going to amount to something, but his last book convinces me he is quite third-rate.[3] Gardner is of course tremendously saleable, but he is only by courtesy a writer at all, in a literary sense. Of course we haven't any really good fiction writers to speak of, in any field. The shoddiness of our educational system is beginning to show up in a terrible superficiality of mind. Compare the quality of the writing in the *Atlantic* and *Harper's* with the front article in the *Times Literary Supplement* and you see what has happened to us. And we don't know quality when we see it. Cozzens' *Guard of Honor* makes all the other war novels look like amateurish exercises in looking portentous, but none of the professional critics was able to evaluate it. They just don't know enough about writing.

Yours ever,

Ray

TO ALEX BARRIS

6005 Camino de la Costa
La Jolla, California
March 18, 1949

Dear Mr. Barris:

I took some snapshots of this dump a few days ago and if they are any good I'll enclose a couple. I'm not any good with a camera, although I ought to be, with a Kodak reflex and a F 3.5 lens. We lived in a rather too large one-story house on a corner across the street from the ocean. La Jolla, as you might not know, is built on a point north of San Diego, and is never either hot or cold. So we get two seasons of tourists, one in winter, one in summer. Ten years ago the town was very quiet, exclusive, expensive, and almost as dull as Victoria, B.C. on a wet Sunday afternoon in February. Now it is just

2. *The Big Clock* by Kenneth Fearing; *Mr. Bowling Buys a Newspaper* by Donald Henderson.
3. Jack Iams' *The Body Missed the Boat*, 1947.

expensive. There is a lot of shingle here and lot of low soft sandstone cliff which the ocean has wrought into very strange shapes, but very little beach, except at the north end of the town where it is much more exposed than down where we live. Our living room has a picture window which looks south across the bay to Point Loma, the most westerly part of San Diego, and at night there is a long lighted coast line almost in our laps. A radio writer came down here to see me once and he sat down in front of this window and cried because it was so beautiful. But we live here, and the hell with it.

My wife desires no publicity, is pretty drastic about it. She doesn't paint or write. She does play a Steinway grand when she gets time. About half to two thirds of the time we are between cooks, and she does not have time. She is a New Yorker and connected with the family to which Clarence Day's mother belonged. My sister-in-law's name is Vinnie (for Lavinia) which was also Clarence's mother's name. I hasten to add that I never knew any of these people myself.

As you may know I am a half-breed. My father was an American of a Pennsylvania Quaker family originally and my mother was Anglo-Irish, also of a Quaker family. She was born in Waterford where there is still, I believe, a famous Quaker school—famous to Quakers anyhow. I grew up in England and I served with the 1st Canadian Division in the first war. As a boy I spent a lot of time in Ireland and I have no romantic ideas about the Irish.

I don't know any of these radio people, so they could tell you nothing about me whatsoever. I have nothing to do with the show except to pass along any ideas I might have through my Hollywood agent. They don't have to pay the slightest attention to them. If the show is any good, all the credit beongs to the writers, actors and producers. The character of Philip Marlowe, as I see him, doesn't show up very much in this program, but neither does it in any of the pictures made about him. That's hardly surprising.

What do I do with myself from day to day? I write when I can and I don't write when I can't; always in the morning or the early part of the day. You get very gaudy ideas at night but they don't stand up. I found this out long ago. I haven't been with Paramount for a couple of years and am not under contract to any studio, thank God. I feel about Hollywood just about as I did when I wrote that piece, and I don't see why any writer should feel any different, although there could be more genial ways of expressing it. But the people who make pictures are not all idiots. They just behave as if they were.

It ought to be pretty obvious to you that I do my own typing. I'm not used to this Corona yet either. When I worked at screenplays I dictated to a secretary. A lot of screenwriters don't; it embarrasses them, but I could never do it any other way. And secretaries are about the nicest people in Hollywood. What those girls go through, what drivel they take down, what enthusiasm they engender for what lousy scripts! They are always on your side against the world and sometimes they are the only friend a writer in Hollywood has. And do they get any thanks for it? Hell, no. Most of these high-priced writers are too god damn cheap even to give their secretaries a little extra money on the side. And when the box office grosses begin to slide, it's always the secretaries that get laid off first.

When we came down here to live I got a dictaphone outfit and dictated script into that, but I never use if for fiction. I think you have to have that mechanical resistance to keep you from getting thin and prolix. Almost all the dictating writers suffer from logorrhea. When you have to use your energy to put those words down, you are more apt to make them count.

I'm always seeing little pieces by writers about how they don't ever wait for inspiration; they just sit down at their little desks every morning at eight, rain or shine, hangover and broken arm and all, and bang out their little stint. However blank their minds or dull their wits, no nonsense about inspiration from them. I offer them my admiration and take care to avoid their books. Me, I wait for inspiration, although I don't necessarily call it by that name. I believe that all writing that has any life in it is done with the solar plexus. It is hard work in the sense that it may leave you tired, even exhausted. In the sense of concious effort it is not work at all. The important thing is that there should be a space of time, say four hours a day at least, when a professional writer doesn't do anything else but write. He doesn't have to write, and if he doesn't feel like it, he shouldn't try. He can look out of the window or stand on his head or writhe on the floor. But he is not to do any other positive thing, not read, write letters, glance at magazines, or write checks. Either write or nothing. It's the same principle as keeping order in a school. If you make the pupils behave, they will learn something just to keep from being bored. I find it works. Two very simple rules. a. you don't have to write. b. you can't do anything else. The rest comes of itself.

I hate publicity, quite sincerely. I've been through the interview mill and I regard it as a waste of time. The guy I meet in those interviews masquerading under my name is usually a heel I wouldn't even know. I'm an intellectual snob who happens to have a fondness for the American vernacular, largely because I grew up on Latin and Greek. I had to learn American just like a foreign language. To learn it I had to study and analyze it. As a result, when I use slang, solecisms, colloquialisms, snide talk or any kind of off beat language, I do it deliberately. The literary use of slang is a study in itself. I've found that there are only two kinds that are any good: slang that has established itself in the language and slang that you make up yourself. Everything else is apt to be passé before it gets into print. But I'd better not get off on this subject, or I'll be writing for a week.

Yours very truly,

Raymond Chandler

P.S. You asked how I got paid for this radio program. I get a royalty for the use of the character. That's all.
RC

TO HAMISH HAMILTON

6005 Camino de la Costa
La Jolla, California
March 21st. 1949

Dear Jamie:

.   .   .

I remember several years ago when Howard Hawks was making *The Big Sleep*, the movie, he and Bogart got into an argument as to whether one of the characters was murdered or committed suicide. They sent me a wire (there's a joke about this too) asking me, and dammit I didn't know either. Of course I got hooted at. The joke was in connection with Jack Warner, the head of Warner Bros. Believe it or not he saw the wire, the wire cost the studio seventy cents, and he called Hawks up and asked him whether it was really necessary to send a telegram about a point like that.

That's one way to run a business.

Your letter just came in and I hasten to say that I was not in any worry about your possible failure to get things straight, because I know how careful English proof readers are. I do, however, remember in connection with *Farewell My Lovely* that the end of Chapter 34 a typographical error got into print, although there was clearly something wrong, since what was written made no sense. (On the other hand, of course, the printers might have assumed that it *must* make sense, even if not to them.) But a writer who deals in the vernacular and on occasion makes up his own language may find the printer making corrections of things he assumed to be errors, but which in fact were meant exactly as written. Knopf's printers once had the greatest difficulty in reconciling themselves to a sentence which read, "a guy's there and you see him and then he ain't there and you don't not see him," and which to them was clearly a double negative, but was to me a much more forcible way of saying, "don't miss him," obvious and conventional, but not alive.

.   .   .

All the best,

Ray

TO BERNICE BAUMGARTEN

6005 Camino de la Costa
La Jolla, California
March 21st. 1949

Dear Bernice:

[156]

．　　　　．　　　　．

I finished *Point of No Return*.[1] Strange that such good writing should leave me with so little feeling of having read anything of the slightest importance. Apart from the constant backtracking and jumping about in time the story irritates by its very competence. A man has no right to write that well and in the end say so little. When all is said and done who the hell cares about the Charley Grays of this world? The people who always do, say, think and wear the right thing, and yet are vaguely and weakly conscious that it is only the right thing because it pays a little more money. So life got him over a barrel and that's a tragedy. My eye, it is. So he wanted the girl, but not enough to tell her father to go jump in a tub. And if he got her what difference would it make? What has this guy Marquand got that makes him so good? Well, whatever it is he has it. He writes the perfect Victorian novel, sad but not too sad, romantic in an epicene sort of way, beautiful detailed observation and the total effect of a steel engraving with no color at all. I guess God made Boston on a wet Sunday.

If I were not so pooped out, I think I should discharge my spleen by writing a Ballade of Lament for Assistant Vice Presidents, and the refrain could be: "I think I'll wear my herringbone today."

Sometimes I wonder how Marquand ever got a reputation as a satirist. I'm inclined to suspect that John O'Hara's remark about Sinclair Lewis is much more near the truth: "It always has seemed to me that Lewis woke up to find himself called a satirist, and became one by continuing to play straight. He is King of the Corn,—and by way of being the Sweetheart of it."

Compare this book with *Guard of Honor*;[2] it's the difference between a real artist and a clever suave hack who has so much on the ball in a technical sense that you are apt to forget he really hasn't any ball to be on.

I'm going down to Palm Springs for a week to try and shake this cough.

All the best,

Ray

1. By John P. Marquand.
2. By James Gould Cozzens.

[157]

TO MRS. HOLTON[1]

6005 Camino de la Costa
La Jolla, California
March 26, 1949

Dear Mrs. Holton:

I'm sending my only copy of *LS* by air express today.[2] I guess Brandt and Brandt have a copy in their office. I certainly hope so. But Jamie Hamilton already has the book in page proofs.

No dedication. No front matter from me, unless you want to vary the usual protection clause on the back of the title page by saying that "The people and events in this book are not entirely fictional. Some of the events happened, although not in this precise time or place, and certain of the characters were suggested by real persons, both living and dead. The author regrets any resemblance to reality that may be found in the pages of his books, and he particularly regrets that he has on occasion made use of the names of real localities. He admits with shame that there actually is a place called Hollywood and a place called Los Angeles. It has streets and he has named some of them. It has a police department and he has referred to it. Los Angeles County has a District Attorney and said District Attorney has an office. To all of these matters the author has alluded. How careless of him! He should have called Los Angeles Smogville. He should have called its police department its Ministry of Corrections. Its District Attorney he might more admirably have referred to as the Master of the Rolls, and the office of this functionary might have been placed on an imaginary island somewhere off the coast of an imaginary state in an imaginary country. The characters in the story might, for additional security, have been referred to by letters of the Greek alphabet."

Yours very truly,

Raymond Chandler

1. Of Houghton Mifflin Company.
2. Chandler's fifth novel, *The Little Sister*.

TO JAMES SANDOE

Dear Sandoe:

.   .   .

My wife thought Doyle an awfully dull man.[1] I thought him the sort you would either like tremendously or writhe at. Found a two bit edition of *Hound of the Baskervilles*. God, what tripe. It looks to me as if Lincoln was wrong. You can fool all of the people all the time.

RC

TO BERNICE BAUMGARTEN

6005 Camino de la Costa
La Jolla, California
March 31, 1949

Dear Bernice:

.   .   .

Red Barrow, my lawyer pal, and incidentally a terrific admirer of the Cozzens talent, gave me the Francis Steegmuller stuff from the *N.Y. Times*, which I never see. Mr. Steegmuller is quite a guy. He not only quotes from me in quotes but without quotes. And where did I ever say that only my type of detective story is serious literature? My argument is and always has been merely that there is no such thing as serious literature, that the survivals of Puritanism in the American mind make all but the most literate people incapable of thinking of literature without reference to what they call significance, and that most of this so-called serious literature or fiction is the most transient stuff in the world; the moment its message is dated, damn quick, it is dead stuff.

1. Sir Arthur Conan Doyle.

It is one of the (few) charms of not being as young as you were that you can stick your neck out, because you don't give a damn. If a young writer knocks a reigning favorite, he can be accused of envy and malice, and it hurts him and makes him cautious. I get a lot of fun out of sticking pins in the popular balloons. The most fantastic pratfall of the moment is Elizabeth Bowen's last book, which in spots is a screaming parody of Henry James. Jamie Hamilton wrote me that the English critics are tying themselves in knots trying to be polite to it (because of course they know she is potentially a fine writer), knowing all the time that the poor girl is giving an exhibition of what happens when an over-earnest writer completely loses her sense of humor. I've felt fine ever since I went to Palm Springs. Wish I had a house there, but like everything else in California the place is overpriced.

Ray

P.S.

.　　　　　.　　　　　.

There's a lovely fight going on about the Academy. The boys were finally shamed into giving the award more or less on the basis of merit (except the musical award, which stank) and the five major companies which have been contributing to the cost of the show have withdrawn. "Look, fellows," they say without saying, "we want the Oscars to go to the best pictures all right, but we're not in business for our health. The best pictures from Hollywood, savvy." They don't care who is best as long as it's them.

Ray

TO CARL BRANDT

6005 Camino de la Costa
La Jolla, California
April 3rd. 1949

Dear Carl:

[160]

The last actual research I did was in 1945 while writing *The Blue Dahlia*, the first story incidentally which betrayed to the public the fact that the head man of the Homicide Bureau, then a very nice guy called Thad Brown (Captain), did not even have a private office. His desk was set right next to that of a female secretary and his door was always open. Outside there was a bare largish room in which the dicks lounged about and quite literally did not have enough chairs to sit down in all at once. The entrance to this was a dutch door (which we didn't use in the film) and both of these rooms together would have fitted easily into our living room. This was positively all the boys had to work with and out of. This wasn't a top notch film by any means, largely because Veronica Lake couldn't play the love scenes and too much had to be discarded, but it did show the very meager accommodations the homicide boys have to make do with. They actually built the two rooms and the hall outside to scale, and some of the shots got a cluttered effect that was right. But of course nobody sees this stuff in films. A very good cop picture I saw recently called *He Walked by Night* shows some excellent technical stuff, but the shots inside Police Headquarters are much too spacious. You got the impression of a very complex and highly efficient organization staffed by innumerable men. As a matter of fact they are a pretty dumb bunch who operate about on the mental level of plumbers.

·　　　　·　　　　·

Yours,

Ray

TO HAMISH HAMILTON

6005 Camino de la Costa
La Jolla, California
April 4 1949

Dear Jamie:

·　　　　·　　　　·

By the way, do you ever read Erle Gardner's stuff? Probably not, since you have no professional reason for doing so. I know him very well and like him. He is a terrible talker, just wears you out, but he is not a dull talker. He just talks too loud and too much. Years of yapping into a dictaphone machine have destroyed the quality of his voice, which now has all the delicate chiaroscuro of a French taxi horn. His production methods amaze me (he can write a whole book in a week or ten days easily) and once in a while he does something pretty good. But his last Perry Mason really threw me. The first chapter is largely concerned with how much of a girl's legs Perry saw as she came down the fire escape. He discusses it with the lady and afterwards frisks her for a gun. This gives occasion for a few shady leers and the sexual implications are handled by Gardner with all the aplomb of a Classical form master paraphrasing some of the more outspoken portions of the Greek drama. Gardner is well aware that an appeal to the French postcard type of aficionado is not without a certain commercial value (a matter of which he is not apt to lose sight), and he tries to get in a little leg here and there without disturbing the suburban hypocrisy of the *Ladies Home Journal*. The result has all the naughty charm—for me at any rate—of an elderly pervert surprised while masturbating in a public toilet. The poor dear is just a bloody Victorian at heart. When he lets you get a glimpse of Della Street's well filled nylons as she slides gracefully out of a car, he seems to think the frantic reader is going to rush for a bottle of triple bromides as an alternative to raping the nearest char. Me, I find the excitement less than intense. Sex cannot be dealt with in this three-cushion style. You have to face it squarely or let it alone. Anything else is a little nauseating.

.   .   .

Frankly I have no idea why Houghton Mifflin are so slow getting out the proofs of the book. Perhaps they have been entangled in the massive job of publishing Churchill. Knopf used to send proofs rather quickly with an air of being in a furious rush, air mail special delivery and all that sort of thing, and when I rushed through them in a state of urgency and mailed them back absolutely nothing would happen for months and months. I never could discover why they had been in such a hurry nor what happened when they got the proofs back. You run into the same thing in Hollywood: wild rush for conferences over some deal, then an exhausted agreement as to terms, and then a completely leisurely—in fact quite dilatory—writing of the contract. I remember once at Paramount, after a new contract had been negotiated to take the place of one I had grown to dislike, the legal department went for weeks without producing even a draft and during all that time of course I was not paid; they always hold your money up until the contract is signed. I then called the legal department and suggested politely that there was no need to write the new contract at all since they had breached the old one by not paying me any salary and there was now no agreement between us. It was fun while it lasted; their screams were audible for blocks. I always liked doing business with Jews. They are so excitable, so superficially sharp and tricky, but basically very reliable. They dramatise every business deal and act very tough and then suddenly give way in the most winning manner.

Ray

TO JAMES SANDOE

6005 Camino de la Costa
La Jolla, California
April 14th. 1949

Dear Sandoe:
Have read *The Moving Target* by John Macdonald and am a good deal impressed by it, in a peculiar way.[1] In fact I could use it as a springboard for a sermon on How Not to be a Sophisticated Writer. What you say about pastiche is of course quite true, and the materials of the plot situations are borrowed here and there. E.g. the opening set up is lifted more or less from *The Big Sleep*, mother paralyzed instead of father, money from oil, atmosphere of corrupted wealth, and the lawyer-friend villain is lifted straight out of *The Thin Man*; but I personally am a bit Elizabethan about such things, do not think

---

1. John Ross Macdonald; he later dropped the first name to avoid confusions with John D. Macdonald, another mystery writer. The text is from a transcript.

[163]

they greatly matter, since all writers must imitate to begin with, and if you attempt to cast yourself in some accepted mould, it is natural to go to the examples that have attained some notice or success.

What strikes me about the book (and I guess I should not be writing about it if I didn't feel that the author had something) is first an effect that is rather repellant. There is nothing to hitch to; here is a man who wants the public for the mystery story in its primitive violence and also wants it to be clear that he, individually, is a highly literate and sophisticated character. A car is "acned with rust" not spotted. Scribblings on toilet walls are "graffiti" (we know Italian yet, it says); one refers to "podex osculation" (medical Latin too, ain't we hell?). "The seconds piled up precariously like a tower of poker chips," etc. The simile that does not quite come off because it doesn't understand what the purpose of the simile is.

The scenes are well handled, there is a lot of experience of some kind behind this writing, and I should not be surprised to find the name was a pseudonym for a novelist of some performance in another field. The thing that interests me is whether this pretentiousness in the phrasing and choice of words makes for better writing. It does not. You could only justify it if the story itself were devised on the same level of sophistication, and you wouldn't sell a thousand copies, if it was. When you say, "spotted with rust," (or pitted, and I'd almost but not quite go for "pimpled") you convey at once a simple visual image. But when you say, "acned with rust" the attention of the reader is instantly jerked away from the thing described to the pose of the writer. This is of course a very simple example of the stylistic misuse of language, and I think that certain writers are under a compulsion to write in recherché phrases as a compensation for a lack of some kind of natural animal emotion. They feel nothing, they are literary eunuchs, and therefore they fall back on an oblique terminology to prove their distinction. It is the sort of mind that keeps avant garde magazines alive, and it is quite interesting to see an attempt to apply it to the purposes of this kind of story.

R.C.

[164]

TO ALEX BARRIS

April 16 1949

Dear Barris:

Excuse yellow paper, smeary ribbon etc. I'm doing this on a Noiseless and something is awry.

I am an American citizen by birth. Educated in England, Anglo-Irish mother. Strong pro-British feelings always and also pro-Canadian, since I served in the CEF and spent months at Victoria in Gordon Highlands of Canada long ago.[1] Don't know eastern Canada at all, only Puget Sound area. If I called Victoria dull, it was in my time dullish as an English town would be on a Sunday, everything shut up, churchy atmosphere and so on. I did not mean to call the people dull. Knew some very nice ones.

Black Mask pulp mag which in the thirties developed the hardboiled mystery technique, famous by Hammett of course, but he not only. Gardner wrote for it too, Coxe, and many who did better work then than since. My *Atlantic* article "The Simple Art of Murder" available in Pocket Books Anthology and Haycraft's *Art of Mystery Story* covers subject. Mag still exists so far as I know but sold out to Popular Publications, having lost circulation through too rigid specialization, probably.

.   .   .

Marlowe development of character used in novelettes, first named in *Big Sleep*. My views on Hammett expressed in article referred to above. He was tops. Often wonder why he quit writing after *The Thin Man*. Met him once only, very nice looking tall quiet gray-haired fearful capacity for Scotch, seemed quite unspoiled to me. (Time out for ribbon adjustment.)

.   .   .

I believe *Farewell My Lovely* would be called the best of my books, *The High Window*, the worst. But I have known people who would pick any of them as against the others. In some ways my

1. CEF is Canadian Expeditionary Force.

last, not yet published is the best.[2] But I'll never again equal *The Big Sleep* for pace nor *FML* for plot complication. I probably don't want to; the time comes when you have to choose between pace and depth of focus, between action and characters, between menace and wit. I now choose the second in each case.

Do I read my stuff when published? Yes, and at very great risk of being called an egotistical twerp, I find it damn hard to put down. Even me, that knows all about it. There must be some magic in writing after all, but I take no credit for it. It just happens, like red hair. But I find it rather humiliating to pick up a book of my own to glance at something and then find myself twenty minutes later still reading it as if someone else had written it.

The camera eye technique of *Lady in the Lake* is old stuff in Hollywood.[3] Every young writer or director has wanted to try it; it just so happened that Bob Montgomery was in a technical position where he could make them let him do it. I wrote about a sequence or part of a sequence in that manner in the first draft of the script (I refused screen credit on the final result) but it would be ridiculous for me to claim that as an inspiration to Montgomery. "Let's make the camera a character"; it's been said at every lunch table in Hollywood one time or another. I knew one fellow who wanted to make the camera the murderer; which wouldn't work without an awful lot of fraud. The camera is too honest.

Have I since "creating" Marlowe used any other central character outside screen plays? Yes, in several stories I wrote after *The Big Sleep*.

And do I think *Hamlet* was the best motion picture of 1948? Definitely not. Olivier was marvellous, Felix Aylmer was top notch, but the camera work was a pain in the neck and a lot of the acting barely acceptable. But I'm glad Hollywood was shamed into giving it [the Oscar] to a foreign picture for all that.

Yours, Chandler

2. *The Little Sister*.
3. In this film, Marlowe is the camera; everything is seen through his eyes.

TO CARL BRANDT

6005 Camino de la Costa
La Jolla, California
April 18th. 1949

Dear Carl:

It was very kind of you indeed to send me a wire about
Norbert D.[1] However, right or wrong, I am sending him a couple of
hundred dollars. Who am I to judge another man's needs or deserts?
It's a pretty miserable thing to live off in the country and watch them
all come back and be scared. He says he has sold one out of fifteen
this last year. Say it's his fault, say he got big-headed or drunk and
lazy or what have you—what difference does it make? You suffer
just as much when you're wrong. More. Write it off, call it waste,
forget it, and hope the guy won't hate you for helping him, or
rather for having to ask you to help him. I cannot draw these hairline
distinctions. I only know that two hundred bucks won't buy me
the key to heaven, but there have been times when it would have
looked like it would, and I didn't have it, and nobody was around to
give it to me. I never slept in the park but I came damn close to it.
I went five days without anything to eat but soup once, and I had just
been sick at that. It didn't kill me, but neither did it increase my
love of humanity. The best way to find out if you have any friends is
to go broke. The ones that hang on longest are your friends. I don't
mean the ones that hang on forever. There aren't any of those.

Yours,

Ray

---

1. Chandler had asked Brandt's advice about lending $200 to Norbert Davis, a former
Black Mask writer.

TO DALE WARREN

6005 Camino de la Costa
La Jolla, California
April 20 1949

Dear Dale:

.   .   .

. . . Priestley gave me a, for him, very elegant paragraph in his
new column in the *New Statesman*.[1] His original comment on first
looking into Chandler's abattoir was, "They don't write like that at
Dulwich." How true.

I can't seem to get started doing anything. Always very tough
for me to get started. The more things people say about you the
more you feel as if you were writing in an examination room, that it
didn't belong to you any more, that you had to protect critical
reputations and not let them down. Writers even as cynical as I have
to fight an impulse to live up to someone's else's idea of what they
are. Story I've been fussing with really ought to have an English
setting anyhow. Thought I could use Bel Air, but when you drag in
the whole phoney Hollywood life, and everything becomes scenery,
back projections, matt shots, miniatures, papier mache rocks, tubbed
trees, deluges of tropical rain out of which the characters come in,
having walked in it for hours, with one damp lapel and two curls out
of place. Three feet of film later the suit's pressed and the guy has
a fresh carnation in his buttonhole.

Well, it's not as bad as pinning a posthumous V.C. on the
saddle blanket of a cavalry horse, which they did in *Lives of a Bengal
Lancer*.

I see from the *Sunday Times* that your picture *He Walked by
Night* didn't get much from Dilys Powell but a remark about the
chase through the Sewers.[2] She's damn good too, and usually very
fair about American pictures. What's the matter with the films? I rack

1. J. B. Priestley, the English novelist.
2. *He Walked by Night*, a 1949 film made in imitation of *Naked City*, was directed by
Alfred Werker, produced by Brian Foy, and written by John C. Higgins and Crane Wilbur.
Dilys Powell was film critic for the *Sunday Times* of London.

my brains for an answer, and I have a queer recurring thought that its isn't anything specific, the films aren't so bad, but they're simply no longer a novelty. The medium, the things it can do, have lost the sting. We're back where silent films were when Warners bought the Vitaphone. Except for forced focus there has hardly been a real technical advance in fifteen years, and you don't realize what forced focus does unless you look at a film made in the middle thirties and note that in a medium close shot everything more than ten feet from the camera is a blur.

.   .   .

Ray

TO BERNICE BAUMGARTEN

6005 Camino de la Costa
La Jolla, California
April 21st 1949

Dear Bernice:
    Many thanks for answering me so promptly about the Mystery Guild.[1] I am dead against it and so far as I have any power I refuse to do it. . . . The economic squeeze has not got me yet although it may eventually. The money is not enough and the suggestion that these are not competitive with trade editions is to me so much baloney. I do realize that the sale of a mystery is apt to be over by, or very soon after, publication date. But it seems to me rather obvious that if my stuff has any real value, it is not as a mystery at all. Other writers do much better mysteries. Plot as such merely bores me. The people who really like my books are those who like them in spite of their being mysteries, not because of. Dorothy Sayers tried to make the jump from the mystery to the novel of manners and take the mystery along with her. She tried to move over, with all her baggage,

1. Hardwick Moseley of Houghton Mifflin had proposed that Chandler accept the offer of the Mystery Guild to select *The Little Sister* as an offering for their members. See letter to Mosley, April 23, 1949.

[169]

from the people who can plot but can't write to the people who can write and, all too often, can't plot. She didn't really make it, because the novel of manners she aimed at was in itself too slight a thing to be important. It was just the substitution of one popular trivial kind of writing for another. I am not satisfied that the thing can't be done nor that sometime, somewhere, perhaps not now nor by me, a novel cannot be written which, ostensibly a mystery and keeping the spice of mystery, will actually be a novel of character and atmosphere with on overtone of violence and fear. If people call my book just another mystery I can't help it, but by God I'm not going to do the calling myself.

·   ·   ·

I found *Men and Brethren* and *Ask Me Tomorrow* in the public library here.[2] Not obtainable to buy. I had no card and when I asked for one, the elderly white haird prim-mouthed librarian said: "Oh, you're Raymond Chandler, the writer. I read one of your books when I was in the hospital last year." "I hope it didn't make you worse," said I. "I wanted to throw it across the room, it made me so mad," she said, then grudgingly, "But I didn't. There was something about the writing."

A perfect expression of the La Jolla mentality.

Ray

TO HAMISH HAMILTON

6005 Camino de la Costa
La Jolla, California
April 22nd. 1949

Dear Jamie:
Thanks for a most delightful letter. I hope I may have a chance to insult this boor, Wilson, someday.[1] I have had at times a certain

2. Both by James Gould Cozzens, Bernice Baumgarten's husband.

---

1. Edmund Wilson.

modest success in this direction. As you (incidentally) mentioned Spender[2] I happened to be reading four excerpts from an impending autobiography, published here in *Partisan Review*, which is the nearest thing we have to an intellectual magazine not edited in some University English Course. I though it delightful writing all the way through, clear and honest and beautifully yet not ostentatiously (as Connolly is at times, I think) expressed. J. A. Spender, his uncle, was the first editor who ever showed me any kindness. I got an introduction to him from a wonderful old boy named Roland Ponsonby Blennerhasset, a barrister with a House of Lords practice, a wealthy Irish landowner (he owned some fabulous number of acres in Kerry), a member, as I understood from my Uncle in Waterford, of one of these very ancient untitled families that often make earls and marquesses appear quite parvenu. Spender bought a lot of stuff from me, verses, sketches, and unsigned things such as paragraphs lifted from foreign publications. He got me into the National Liberal Club for the run of the reading room; I was seconded by his political cartoonist, a famous man in those days, but I have forgotten his name. I never met him in the flesh. I got about three guineas a week out of all these, but it wasn't enough. I also worked for a man named Cowper who succeeded Lord Alfred Douglas in ownership of the *Academy*, and did a lot of book reviewing for him, and some essays which I still have; they are of an an intolerable preciousness of style, but already quite nasty in tone. I seldom got the best books to review, and in fact the only one of any importance I got my hands on was *The Broad Highway*, for whose author, then unknown, I am glad to say I predicted an enormous popularity.[3] Like all young nincompoops I found it very easy to be clever and snotty, very hard to praise without being ingenuous. I like this fellow Spender very much. In fact I like him better than Auden, about whom I have always had reservations. (I am also disturbed at your remark that Connolly has no conscience.) His account of the silken barbarity of Eton is wonderful, of course, and the way these fellows thought and wrote and talked, at an age when Americans can hardly spell their own names, is also most impressive. Nevertheless, there is something about the literary life that repels me; all this desperate building of

2. Stephen Spender.
3. Novel by Jeffrey Farnol.

[171]

castles on cobwebs, the long-drawn acrimonious struggle to make something important which we all know will be gone forever in a few years, the miasma of failure which is to me almost as offensive as the cheap gaudiness of popular success. I believe the really good people would be reasonably successful in any circumstances; that to be very poor and very beautiful is most probably a moral failure much more than an artistic success. Shakespeare would have done well in any generation, because he would have refused to die in a corner; he would have taken the false gods and made them over, he would have taken the current formulae and forced them into something lesser men thought them incapable of. Alive today he would undoubtedly have written and directed motion pictures, plays, and God knows what. Instead of saying "This medium is not good," he would have used it and made it good. If some people had called some of his work cheap (which some of it is), he wouldn't have cared a rap, because he would know that without some vulgarity there is no complete man. He would have hated refinement, as such, because it is always a withdrawal, a shrinking, and he was much too tough to shrink from anything.

·   ·   ·

Ray

TO HARDWICK MOSELEY

6005 Camino de la Costa
La Jolla, California
April 23, 1949

Dear Hardwick:
        Many thanks for explaining your position about the Mystery Guild so gently. Bernice wrote to me too and I believe (she could tell you better herself) that her position is that she would not take the responsibility of turning down money for a writer in these times (or in any, perhaps) but that she would possibly like a little more time to observe the effects of such enterprises as Mystery Guild.

[172]

I regret to appear intransigent in any matter whatever in dealing with a publisher. I am hot-tempered but not vicious. I am against this thing—hard against it. In most respects it is a very bad thing for a writer to get in touch with real money, but it does help with decisions of this sort. $2500 just isn't important dough to me; not worth any kind of a sacrifice, any possible danger to a reputation that, after all, has grown up against all the rules. I have before me a list from PW[1] of the Mystery Guild selections up to and including September, which means that the selections are known when the books are put out by the publishers, I cannot see but that this is all wrong for me. One of these books (May to September selections) has a certain literary pretentiousness: *The Moving Target* by John MacDonald (Very likely a pseudonym).[2] One: *Port Afrique* is entirely strange to me.[3] The others are by people we know, and we know that whatever their smoothness and accomplishment in their field, they do not matter as writers, except in a purely commercial way. To put oneself in that company is to classify oneself, and the dough aint enough. Not nearly enough. I can get money from Hollywood, if I have to. I know the racket and I can take the lumps. I am engaged and have always from the very beginning been engaged in the effort to do something with the mystery story which has never quite been done. In one way Hammett came close; in another way Sayers came close. Neither was capable of imparting emotion to the right nerves. They didn't feel it. What I have tried to do (and if I fail, someone will succeed) is not at all to get to be a good enough writer to do a "straight novel"; I could have done that long ago, just as I could have trained myself to write slick serials, if I had really worked at it. The thing is to squeeze the last drop out of the medium you have learned to use. The aim is not essentially different from the aim of Greek tragedy, but we are dealing with a public that is only semi-literate and we have to make an art of a language they can understand.

In doing this I must accept certain handicaps. No snob appeal, no uplift, no apparent social significance. Very easy to deprecate, just another hardboiled mystery, and so on. But it's a funny thing, to get anywhere you have to interest the extreme intellectuals. Our

1. *Publishers Weekly.*
2. John Ross Macdonald; it is indeed a pseudonym. The author's real name is Kenneth Millar.
3. *Port Afrique*, 1949, by B. V. Dryer.

target is not the mystery addict. He knows nothing, remembers nothing. He buys books cheap or rents them. It all goes in one ear and crosses the vacuum to the other. Circumstances compel both of us to have an eye to the dollar; but only one eye.

This $2500 would help your promotional budget. Okay, forget the promotional budget. You don't need it. You can't make me into a smash best seller, and you would be wasting money to try. Just let me percolate. I'll find my public with almost no assistance from advertising. But do as little as possible to lump me in the public mind with the smooth and shallow operators like Marsh and Stout and Christie. Very likely they write better mysteries than I do, but their words don't get up and walk. Mine do, although it is embarrassing to have to announce it.

The real estate market is floperoo here. This house is valued at around $75,000, present worth, and that's too much money for all but the carriage trade. Sure, California is slipping. And thanks ever so much for your suggestion, about which there may well be serious thought. I want to go to England awfully badly, but I dread the scramble. You can't just get up and go anywhere anymore. You have to plan until you're sick of the whole project.

Yours ever,

Ray

TO JAMES SANDOE

May 3, 1949

Dear Sandoe:

.   .   .

Houghton Mifflin seem to want to publish a trade edition collection of my old stories. I tried to argue that they had been around enough and were only pulp writing anyhow but they insist that they should be published and that "there is nothing like them anywhere." This I doubt very much.

[174]

I think I am going to have to do a little rewriting on *The Little Sister* and I dread it. In the end I was faced with the choice between a clear but boring explanation of who shot who, why and where etc., and more or less letting it hang in air on the theory that who cared anyway, it wasn't and couldn't pretend to be a proper mystery story. But the subconscious has been at work chiding me and I think I'm going to have to answer a few questions which the publisher's people (asked, for a gag) didn't seem at all clear about. As a constructionist I have a dreadful fault; I let characters run away with the scenes and then refuse to discard the scenes that don't fit. I end up usually with the bed of Procrustes. The system works if one is hitting on all twelve, but I've a few leaky sparkplugs now. But I do (since this damn letter is already impossibly egotistic) have one great advantage. I still regard myself as an amateur and insist on having some fun out of my work. I just can't take myself seriously enough to be otherwise.

TO DALE WARREN

6005 Camino de la Costa
La Jolla, California
May 5, 1949

Dear Dale:

Sales of the *Cosmopolitan* in La Jolla are not sensational, which proves that competition of articles on impotence is not serious, as the incidence of this malady is probably higher in La Jolla than in any other locality or organization except the annual get-together of us Chickamauga veterans.

I withdraw recommendation of Pat Novack.[1] Had to turn it off last time I tried to give it my business. The affectation of the writing is just too much for me. The use of similes is unrestrained and was (admittedly, by the original writer of the show) copied from me, and has now been reduced to absurdity. The character can't even take

1. Radio Show.

his hat off without saying the air striking his bald spot was as startling as a yes man saying no, or something just about that silly. Everything is like something else. You get to cringe when you feel one coming up. So ignore the whole business and tune in on the new Dick Powell show, which is swiped from Philip Marlowe which is swiped from Sam Spade which is swiped from Orson Welles's radio technique of the first person narration passing into direct dramatization. I don't know whether Welles invented it, but he certainly gets credit for adapting it to melodrama. The radio people are absolutely the most hidebound tradition-minded set in the world. They will never try anything new. I went down on my scarred knees to them to try doing a mystery show with sound effects instead of musical bridges. No soap. Their use of sound effect could be the most highly developed in the world, and should be, but they simply haven't the courage of their own craft. Norman Corwin used sound effects well, but he would insist on fouling everything up with significance. Gad, how I hate that word and all it implies.

STAY TUNED IN FOR THE DICK POWELL SHOW, STARRING (YOU GUESSED IT) DICK POWELL. THE GREATEST PRIVATE DETECTIVE OF THEM ALL (THAT SINGS TENOR).

If I wrote a non-fiction book, it would probably turn out to be the autobiography of a split personality. And speaking of Hitchcock, there is a good piece about him in the current issue of *Theatre Arts* (and hang the hanging participle.) But I don't think the man is quite fair to old Hitch. When you make a picture as good as *Shadow of a Doubt* and it flops, it takes the heart out of you. Same like *Night Must Fall* and *The Ox-Bow Incident*. . . . You mention Joan Fontaine as one of your pals. I met her once, at a lunch with John Houseman, but I know her husband, Bill Dozier, quite well. He hired me at Paramount, and gave my stoop of an agent a rooking on salary that was memorable, and remained an unhealed sore until I took Dozier for a hundred grand when he was a boss at U-I.[2] Paramount made a shocking mistake when they let him resign. At U-I it was understandable, because he was supposed to handle the contract producers while Bill Goetz handled the independent production units. These one by one folded and withdrew, leaving Goetz with nothing

2. Universal-International.

[176]

to do. Once looking out of Joe Sistrom's window on the U-I lot I happened to see the big boys strolling back from lunch in the exec dining room in a loose group. I was transfixed with a sinister delight. They looked so exactly like a bunch of topflight Chicago gangsters moving in to read the death sentence on a beaten competitor. It brought home to me in a flash the strange psychological and spiritual kinship between the operations of big money business and the rackets. Same faces, same expressions, same manners. Same way of dressing and same exaggerated leisure of movement.

.   .   .

Ray

TO HAMISH HAMILTON

6005 Camino de la Costa
La Jolla, California
May 13, 1949

Dear Jamie:

.   .   .

I don't know what's happening to the writing racket in this country. I get an offer of $1200 a year for the use of my name on the title of a new mystery magazine. *Raymond Chandler's Mystery Magazine*. I have nothing to do with the magazine, no control over the contents and no contact whatever with the editorial policy. They are not even faintly aware that the offer is an insult and that for a writer to trade on his reputation without putting something into the pot is not permissible. You can sell your work any way you please, you can subdivide it and sell it in small pieces, but your standing with the public, high or low, you do not own—you hold it in trust. I'm aware that apparently reputable people do not agree with me. I am told they take money for puffing books (I have been offered some), and they go on autographing tours as a matter of course, they talk at book fairs, they are very occasionally photographed as Men of

Distinction holding a glass of blended whiskey that I should be almost afraid to pour down the drains, for fear of corroding the metal. Woollcott took money for writing personal letters to his friends recommending a certain brand of Scotch whisky.[1] I don't want to be revoltingly old-school-tie, but it does seem to me that a line has to be drawn, and I am even willing to argue that you can rule out ethics and you would still, if you had any vision, have to draw that line as a matter of policy. But such is the brutalization of commercial ethics in this country that no one can feel anything more delicate than the velvet touch of a soft buck.

· · ·

Yours ever,

Ray

TO BERNICE BAUMGARTEN

6005 Camino de la Costa
La Jolla, California
May 15, 1949

Dear Bernice:

· · ·

I'm still boiling. If I were a commercially important writer, a big seller, which I know very well I am not, somebody's head would fall for this.[1] You just don't do this sort of thing and get away with it, because by doing it you proclaim your stupidity, carelessness or incompetence, your complete failure to understand what your job is all about. As it is, of course, all that will happen will be "A few copies got out before it was corrected," or some such soft soap which

1. Alexander Woollcott, theater critic.

1. Despite Chandler's refusal to sell *The Little Sister* to the Mystery Book Club, Houghton Mifflin announced that the book had been adopted by this book club.

[178]

I shan't believe, and which they, if they have any sense, will know I won't believe. A few copies my foot, how many booksellers do they suppose read the *Publisher's Weekly*—how many thousands of them? I've had a lot to do with publicity departments in Hollywood, and although they have intelligent individuals working for them, their total effort is bunk. They are the Great American Fake, that pseudo-religious belief that salesmanship is more important than quality and that you can sell anything if you make enough noise about it. Nothing you say need be right; it just has to be loud and incessantly repeated. When they are dealing with toothpaste or shaving lotion, articles of commerce that have absolutely no intrinsic value whatever, they are right. When they deal with books, God help us, they destroy the very basis on which the business rests. Ugh!

I'm still struggling with Charlie Morton about that Hollywood piece. I have explained to him carefully and patiently that it is now dated, and that by fall (when he says they plan publication) it will not be merely dated, it will be antique; that it is not right and so forth and so on, and that I simply do not want it published. I did not say, although it is obvious, that they have never accepted it formally, have never sent me a proof, have never given me the opportunity, which I asked and reserved, of declining publication, if I felt that the cut version misrepresented what I was trying to say.

I suppose all this makes me look like a very contentious person. I wish I could avoid that appearance. I am not really. I just don't tolerate fools gladly and I don't accept without protest the kicking around which writers get and usually take lying down. Hollywood taught me to fight and fight hard. It didn't teach me to fight clean, but I found that it respected clean fighting. The trouble is, you get so tired. The fight is never won. I was shockingly mishandled when I went to Hollywood and it took me two years of usually rather patient argument to convince Sydney Sanders, not an easy man to convince about anything, that this was so, but I don't think he ever accepted any responsibility about it in his own mind. This is a long story and I don't propose to bore you with it. Nothing like that could have happened with Carl or Ray Stark. I mention it only because in dealing with Houghton Mifflin I seem to have slipped back into a familiar atmosphere of casual and good-natured stupidity. Everybody makes mistakes and most people occasionally do stupid things, but there is a type of mistake which to me is like the red rag to the bull, a type of mistake which only happens in bad organizations. When it happens you sense that something is rotten.

Yours ever, and with apologies,

Ray

TO HAMISH HAMILTON

6005 Camino de la Costa
La Jolla, California
June 17, 1949

Dear Jamie:

.   .   .

I am very uneasy in mind. I seem to have lost ambition and have no ideas any more. I don't really want to do anything, or rather one part of me does and the other doesn't. One of the penalties of even a mild success is an indifference to it, and the effort to do something that will attract interest and praise is really something it is a pity to lose. I read these profound discussions, say in *The Partisan Review*, about art, what it is, literature what it is, and the good life and liberalism and what is the definitive position of Rilke or Kafka, and the scrap about Ezra Pound getting the Bollingen award, and it all seems so meaningless to me. Who cares? Too many good men have been dead too long for it to matter what any of these people do or don't do. What does a man work for? Money? Yes, but in a purely negative way. Without some money nothing else is possible, but once you have the money (and I don't mean a fortune, just a few thousand quid a year) you don't sit and count it and gloat over it. Everything you attain removes a reason for wanting to attain anything. Do I wish to be a great writer? Do I wish to win the Nobel Prize? Not, if it takes much hard work. What the hell, they give the Nobel Prize to too many second-raters for me to get excited about it. Besides, I'd have to go to Sweden and dress up and make a speech. Is the Nobel Prize worth all that? Hell, no. Or I read in some book like Haycraft's *Art of the Mystery Story* various so-called critical essays on the detective novel—and what second-rate stuff it all is! The whole business is on a plane of diminished values, there is a constant haste to deprecate the mystery story as literature for fear the writer of the piece should be assumed to think it important writing. This conditioned approach might well be the result of the decay of the classics, a sort of intellectual insularity which has no historical perspective. People are always suggesting to writers of my sort, "You write so well why don't you attempt a serious novel?" By which they mean something by Marquand or Betty Smith. They would probably be insulted if one suggested that the aesthetic gap, if any, between a good mystery and the best serious novel of the last ten years is hardly measurable on any scale that could measure the gap between the serious novel and any representative piece of Attic writing of the Fourth Century B.C., any ode of Pindar or Horace or Sappho, any chorus of Sophocles, and so on. You cannot have art without a public taste and you cannot have a public taste without a sense of style and quality throughout the social structure. Curiously enough this sense of style seems to have very little to do with refinement or even with humanity. It can exist in a savage and dirty age, but it cannot exist in the age of Milton Berle, Mary Margaret McBride,[1] the Book of the Month Club, the Hearst press, and the Coca-Cola machine. You can't produce art by trying, by setting up exacting standards, by talking about critical minutiae, by the Flaubert method. It is produced with great ease, in an almost offhand manner, and without self-consciousness. You can't write just because you have read all the books.

.   .   .

All the best,

Ray

1. A radio personality.

TO HAMISH HAMILTON

6005 Camino de la Costa
La Jolla, California
June 22, 1949

Dear Jamie:

.   .   .

My God, what a writer suffers with proofs. By the time he has got the damn book written he hates it. And then proofs—oh my God. In spite of this there were scenes here and there that stood up wonderfully well. To say little and convey much, to break the mood of the scene with some completely irrelevant wisecrack without entirely losing the mood—these small things for me stand in lieu of accomplishment. My theory of fiction writing (which is probably not worth serious discussion) is that the objective method has hardly been scratched, that if you know how to use it you can tell more in a paragraph than the probing writers can tell in a chapter. Last night I was reading at a hunk of pretentious twaddle called *Edge of Doom*, by one Leo Brady, by Liam O'Flaherty out of Paddy's pig. You say everything three times. You first state it as a more or less straight fact. Then you probe into the underlying subtleties and restate it as a psychic reaction. Then you express it in similes and metaphors. It's the kind of thing that is considered very subtle writing by very unsubtle people. The great Goldwyn paid a bag of sugar for this psychothriller and it was sent to me to read with the idea of doing a screenplay from it. Well, with patience and the destruction of several sanities Goldwyn will undoubtedly get himself a sort of road show *Informer* out of it. But not from this kid. According to my Hollywood agent, Ray Stark, Goldwyn really does get off a Goldwynism now and then. Talking about a script deal he pounded the desk and shouted, "I'm getting sick and tired of writers chiseling on producers in Hollywood. So here is the deal. You can either take it or like it."

I think my favorite Hollywood story is about the Warner Brothers, Jack and Harry. The day after Hal Wallis (who had been head of production at the studio) ankled and left them flat, there was deep gloom and a horrid sense of catastrophe at the executive lunch table. All the boys huddle down at the bottom of the table to get far away from Jack Warner when he came in. All but one, a pushing young producer named Jerry Wald (supposed by some to be the original of Sammy Glick in *What Makes Sammy Run*) who sits down near the head of the table. Jack and Harry Warner come in. Jack sits at the head of the table and Harry just around the corner. Jerry Wald is near and all the others as far away as possible. Jack looks at them with disgust and turns to Harry.

Jack: That sonofabitch, Wallis.

Harry: Yes, Jack.

Jack: A lousy fifty dollar a week publicity man. We built him up from nothing. We made him one of the biggest men in Hollywood. And what does he do to us? He picks up his hat and walks out and leaves us cold.

Harry: Yes, Jack.

Jack: That's gratitude for you. And take that sonofabitch Zanuck. A lousy hundred a week writer and we took him in hand and built him up and made him one of the biggest men in Hollywood. And what did he do to us? Picked up his hat and walked out on us cold.

Harry: Yes, Jack.

Jack: That's gratitude for you. Why we could take any sonofabitch we liked and build him up from nothing and make him one of the biggest men in Hollywood.

Harry: Yes, Jack.

Jack: Anybody at all. (He turns and looks at Jerry Wald) What's your name?

Wald: Jerry Wald, Mr. Warner.

Jack: (to Harry) Jerry Wald. Why, Harry, we could take this fellow here, this Jerry Wald and build him up from nothing to be one of the biggest men in Hollywood, couldn't we, Harry?

Harry: Yes, Jack, we certainly could.

Jack: And what would it get us? We build him up to be a big man,

[183]

give him power and reputation, make him one of the biggest names in Hollywood, and you know what would happen, Harry? The sonofabitch would walk out on us and leave us flat.

Harry: Yes, Jack.

Jack: So why wait for that to happen, Harry? Let's fire the sonofabitch right now.

Ray

TO DALE WARREN

6005 Camino de la Costa
La Jolla, California
July Ninth 1949

Dear Dale:

For a long time I've owed you a letter and for a long time I've found it very difficult to write letters. When my work is not moving I seem to freeze up generally. I thought Laski's book had a great idea, but she hasn't either the style or the comic invention to put it over.[1] If Waugh had written it, it would have been really something. As for *Stranger in the Land*[2] I thought it well-written in a negative anonymous sort of way, but the subject repelled me. There ought to be a good novel in homosexualism, but this isn't it. It is much more honest than *Fall of Valor*[3] (which sounded faked to me) but I don't seem to be much interested in the homo's problem in society. What I think would be interesting would be a picture of the peculiar mentality of the homosexualist, his sense of taste, his surface brilliance often, his fundamental inability to finish anything. Connolly has some good remarks on this in *Enemies of Promise*, but I forget just what he says. I can't take the homo seriously as a moral outcast.

1. Marghanita Laski's *Little Boy Lost*, 1949.
2. By Ward Thomas.
3. By Charles Reginald Jackson, author of *The Lost Weekend*.

[184]

He's no more that than the other rebels against a sanctimonious and hypocritical society. There is no more disgusting spectacle on earth than the business man at a stag smoker, and this is just the type of man who would come down hardest on the abnormal. The difficulty of writing about a homo is the utter impossibility of getting inside his head unless you are one yourself, and then you can't get inside the head of a heterosexual man. If you ever read the cross examination of Wilde by Edward Carson in the suit against Queensberry, I think you are bound to admit that here were two people shouting across oceans of misunderstanding. The mob impulse to destroy the homo is like the impulse of the wolf pack to turn on the sick wolf and tear him to pieces, or the human impulse to run away from a hopeless disease. This is probably very old and very cruel, but at the bottom of it is a kind of horror, like a woman frightened by a scorpion. All cruelty is a kind of fear. Deep inside us we must realize what fragile bonds hold us to sanity and these bonds are threatened by repulsive insects and repulsive vices. And the vices are repulsive, not in themselves, but because of their effect on us. They threaten us because our own normal vices fill us at times with the same sort of repulsion.

God, why do I write stuff like this? Who wants to hear me gabble?

.   .   .

Speaking of Miss Laski, which I am not, I happened the other night to tune in on the Town Meeting programme, the one from London, about Liberty in the Socialist State, if any, and so forth. One of the speakers was Miss Laski's uncle, Professor Laski, a guy who on the strength of his voice, accent and platform manner, without further research, I should be happy to nominate as my choice for *the man you would most like to dunk in a sewer*. The forensic irony, the playing to the gallery, the professorial pompousness and tergiversation and circumlocution, all these imposed on a gutter accent from the slums of somewhere, made up a brew I found quite nauseous. I felt sorry for Max Lerner, an earnest and honest man, though mistaken I think, to be paired up with such a shoddy mountebank. They say this guy is the brains of the British Socialist party. That's silly. People like Attlee, Herbert Morrison, Bevin, and Cripps wouldn't use him to mop up the scullery floor. The only one in the gang I can see having

[185]

any kinship with him is the rabble-rouser Nye Bevan who is a sort of leftwing Huey Long, but rather more of an emetic.[4]

.   .   .

Yours ever, RC

TO PAUL BROOKS[1]

6005 Camino de la Costa
La Jolla, California
July 19, 1949

Dear Mr. Brooks:

In answer to yours of July 12th. let me say first of all that I personally see no good reason why these stories should be reprinted, but that I am told by other people with a more objective view that they should be. And, as I told Bernice Baumgarten, I imagined "Paul Brooks was tough enough to turn them down if they were not suitable." My English publisher didn't want to publish them; felt they were early work and might damage my reputation. I told him mystery writers didn't have reputations over here and it was anything for a smooth buck. So that clears that out of the air.

You realize probably that I am going to have to revise and edit this trash. There are crudities here and there which I can no longer tolerate. The worst thing about them, the vast number of murders, I cannot change. The total in all the stories must be something fantastic—close to a hundred. There are two other stories, called "Pick-Up on Noon Street" and "No Crime in the Mountains," which are also eligible. The first of these is in print in some form, but some damn editor made me whitewash four or five niggers in it and the

---

4. Clement Attlee was then Prime Minister; Morrison, Ernest Bevin, Sir Stafford Cripps, and Aneurin Bevan were members of his cabinet. Huey Long was Governor of and later Senator from Louisiana. He was assassinated in 1935.

---

1. Brooks had wanted to publish Chandler's early stories in book form.

original version was lost by the Avon people, on whom tears and entreaties are alike lost. The second has a nazi element in it which is of no importance to the plot and I should have to write it out, which would be a pleasure anyway.

Next point is that I object to the use of the *Atlantic* article (S.A.O.M.)[2] as an introduction, for the reason that the stories by no means live up to its promise, or hope. Rather put this at the end and let me do a new piece explaining in a more personal way how a high-strung sensitive lad like me came to get so nasty. About 3 or 4,000 words, or less, if necessary.

I quite agree with your remark that under ordinary circumstances a publisher who suggests a volume of short stories to an author ought to have his head examined. Have you had this done? And do you—I am sure you do—realize that in some form or other these stories have had a very wide circulation? By this I mean that a market for them would be without any appeal of novelty. It would simply be a question of whether enough people thought it worth while to have them all in one volume.

You say some of them I will doubtless want to omit. Or in other words they stink. Which? I doubt if I'm the best judge. Well, let's be bloody frank about this. If something dates or makes you cringe, out. If it is a small thing that can be fixed, I'll try to fix it. If it is inherent in the plot, I can't. Take the story called "Blackmailers Don't Shoot," the first I ever wrote. It took me five months to write this thing, it has enough action for five stories and the whole thing is a goddam pose. "Finger Man" was the first story I felt at home with. "Smart Aleck Kill" and "BDS" are pure pastiche. When I started out to write fiction I had the great disadvantage of having absolutely no talent for it. I couldn't get characters in and out of rooms. They lost their hats and so did I. If more than two people were on scene I couldn't keep one of them alive. This failing is still with me, of course, to some extent. Give me two people snotting each other across a desk and I am happy. A crowded canvas just bewilders me. (I could say the same of some rather distinguished writers, only they don't know it and I do.) I don't know who was the original idiot who advised a writer, "Don't bother about the public. Just write what

2. "Simple Art of Murder," published in *The Atlantic Monthly*, December 1944.

[187]

you want to write." No writer ever wants to write anything. He wants to reproduce or render certain effects and in the beginning he hasn't the faintest idea how to do it.

Yours,

Raymond Chandler

TO JAMES SANDOE

6005 Camino de la Costa
La Jolla, California
August 15, 1949

Dear Sandoe:
    You seem to have had a very fruity summer. Mine has been a total loss. Don't like the radio program and wish they would drop it. It could be good, but not with such routine writing and acting. Going to Lake Arrowhead (Arrowhead Lodge) tomorrow for as long as we can stand the local fauna. When I get back I'll send you a strange little brochure which came to me in the mail from one G. Legman, New York. Evidently privately printed and containing words which even I had not seen in print. It is substantially a bitter and possibly envious attack on all kinds of murder mystery, crime books, realistic sexy writing cum murder, on the theory that since we cannot in literature deal honestly with sex, the only adequate sublimation is sadism. A few years back this guy wrote to me and asked me some questions which I did not feel like answering, and he thereupon favored me with a nasty letter in which "on internal evidence" he called me a homosexualist. However, he lams into practically everybody and makes mincemeat of Hemingway en passant. The man is, like so many such soreheads, not without talent, but everything he says leaves a nasty taste in the mouth. And this has nothing to do with what he might happen to say about me. I am

[188]

surely man of the world enough to expect a few gobs of nastiness here and there.

.   .   .

Read one rather good thriller, *Thin Edge of Violence*, by the author of *Repeat Performance*.[1] I think there is a picture in it, but Hollywood is so damn timid nowadays they would lose the picture while making it. My belief is, Hollywood will never find itself until it has the guts to tell the Catholics to go to hell.[2] I hope I am not being offensive, but I believe (and I believe they know it) that the political power of the Catholic Church is an evil thing, that it is used without scruple or fairness for only one purpose—to maintain that power, and that all the rest of the poppycock they talk is just for a smokescreen.

Yours,

RC

TO JAMES SANDOE

6005 Camino de la Costa
La Jolla, California
Sept 14 1949

Dear Sandoe:

.   .   .

Sometimes I wonder what my politics would be if I lived in England. Can't imagine myself voting for socialism now that its nasty bureaucratic soul has been revealed. If you vote Conservative, what do you vote for? You don't, you just vote against. Very much like the last election here. All very well to talk about the patriotic duty of voting and so forth, but why should it be my duty to choose either of

1. William O'Farrell.
2. Reference to the Legion of Decency, a Roman Catholic organization that acted as unofficial censor of the arts.

[189]

two candidates when I don't believe either has any business in the White House? My English friends think the Labor Party will win the next election by a small majority and that by that time the country will be in such a mess that there will be a schism in the Labor Party between the moderates like Crossman and Attlee and the wild men like Nye Bevan. I wouldn't know. Eventually, I am afraid, even in England, the scoundrels will inherit the revolution. They always have where the revolution was real and internal, not a revolt against a foreign domination. And that, to dispose of the subject, is where I can't class the Catholic Church with the Communists. The Catholic church in spite of its sins and its hypocrisy and its politicking and its fascist tendencies and its nasty unprincipled use of the boycott is capable of internal dissension and growth without liquidation of its best elements. It can tolerate heresy and it is not afraid to go abroad among the heathen. (I've got Blanshard but haven't read a word of it yet.)[1] It proselytizes constantly, but it does not shoot people in the back of the head because they are forty-eight hours behind the party line.

.   .   .

How are you coming with your classification of mystery fiction? I regret to have to admit that I am becoming less and less interested in the standard apparatus and it's possible that the things you look for don't move me any more. Granted the presence of the livelier ingredients, a good mystery gives them a purpose and meaning, but it seems to me you just don't get it all in one package. Something has to give. I'd almost be willing to go along with Barzun in his conception of what a 'tec should be, if it ever was that. But it isn't. How long since you read one in which the prime matter was a really fascinating problem and a really compelling solution? And by the way what happened to [Josephine] Tey? Didn't you promise me another?

.   .   .

Yours,

RC

1. Paul Blanshard, *American Freedom and Catholic Power*, 1949.

[190]

TO DALE WARREN

6005 Camino de la Costa
La Jolla, California
September 15, 1949

Dear Dale:

The news from here is rotten. Nervous, tired, discouraged, sick of the chauffeur-and-Cadillac atmosphere, bored to hell with the endless struggle to get help, disgusted with my lack of prescience in not seeing that this kind of life is unsuited to my temperament. Presumably my business is writing. Actually that is left to what meagre resources can survive the battle with the inessentials. Been sick too, and had a lot of trouble with my fingers coming apart. But that is going to get well with X-ray. Of course I ought to have a secretary to write letters and keep books and write checks and answer the damn telephone and kick the gardener in the fanny and so on. But somehow, although I can afford it all right, I can't seem to take myself seriously enough. To function with a secretary you have to believe that what you do is important, that your thoughts and words have an absolute validity, that your privacy is a vested interest. In short you have to be a bit of a conceited ass. In an office it's natural enough because you and the secretary are both part of the mechanism. In your own home you yourself are both the end and the means. My personality, always as sceptical of itself as of others, simply won't accept the part.

We have ideas of getting in a car and driving up to Canada pretty soon. I was thinking of doing a screenplay with my pal, John Houseman, but that's a lousy racket too. Can I write a book a year and make a living? I don't know. Depends on what you mean by a living. I suppose in some ways I was a bit of a stinker in Hollywood. I kept the money. No swimming pool, no stone marten coats for a floozie in an apartment, no charge account at Romanoff's, no parties, no ranch with riding horses, none of the trimmings at all. As a result of which I have fewer friends but a lot more money.

[191]

As to the comment you kindly quoted from me about the *LS*.[1] I disagree that this story is much the best. I think *Farewell My Lovely* is the top and that I shall never again achieve quite the same combination of ingredients. The bony structure was much more solid, the invention less forced and more fluent, and so on. Writers who get written about become self-conscious. They develop a regrettable habit of looking at themselves through the eyes of other people. They are no longer alone, they have an investment in critical praise, and they think they must protect it. This leads to a diffusion of effort. The writer watches himself as he works. He grows more subtle and he pays for it by a loss of organic dash. But since he often achieves a real success in the commercial sense just about as he reaches this stage of regrettable sophistication, he fools himself into thinking that his last book is his best. It isn't. Its success is the result of a slow accumulation. The book which is the occasion of success is more often than not by no means the cause of it.

Ray

TO JAMES SANDOE

6005 Camino de la Costa
La Jolla, California
Sept 20 1949

Dear Sandoe:

.   .   .

I have an unabridged Liddell and Scott, and in my old age I propose to return to Classical Literature—no doubt in Loeb's Library with parallel texts. I hate translations. Those into English from Greek are usually made by classical professors who, I'm sure you'll pardon me, are either pedants or pansies. Greek is a highly intricate language

1. *The Little Sister.*

with infinite shades of meaning and in translation about two thirds of it disappears. (Of course this is probably all a dream.)

.   .   .

I'm now reading Blanshard. Pretty deadly all right. As always I'd like to see a reasoned reply, but where would you get it? The Jesuits seem to have a monopoly on this sort of chore and their casuitical double talk would be disgusting if it were not so logically comical. Any time they get on dangerous ground they simply rule that its solidity is a matter of directed faith and not subject to question by the faithful. The rest are heretics who will burn in hell anyway.

I suppose I only concern myself with this because the closed mind is the worst enemy of freedom. The highbrows, fantastic as they sometimes are, seem to be about the only people we can rely on for a perpetual challenge to what passes for truth. That's why I read the *Partisan Review*. There's a lot of nonsense in it and some of the terminology used by these birds like Allen Tate nearly makes me throw my lunch. But at least they don't take things for granted. There's a beautifully written piece in the current number by William Barrett that warms my heart.

Like a lot of other people, I suppose, I have wondered persistently and even desperately why people who seem to be the kind of people I should be apt to like and admire become Catholic converts or Communists or Fellow Travelers. It is obviously neither viciousness nor stupidity. How after the Katyn Forest and the Moscow Treason Trials, the Ukraine famine, the Arctic prison camps, the utterly abominable rape of Berlin by the Mongolian divisions, any decent man can become a Communist is almost beyond understanding, *unless* it is the frame of mind that simply doesn't believe anything it doesn't like. How can the same decent man become a convert to a religious system that played ball with Franco in Spain, and still does, that never in the history of the world has refused to play ball with any scoundrel who was willing to protect and enrich the Church? Well, I guess nobody wants to hear from me about it.

.   .   .

Yours,

RC

[193]

TO HAMISH HAMILTON

6005 Camino de la Costa
La Jolla, California
October 5th. 1949

Dear Jamie:

.   .   .

I think your sales of *LS* are quite wonderful considering the sort of book it is.[1] Houghton Mifflin's advance sale was under 10,000 copies and that is not too good, since with mysteries the advance sale is apt to be a large part of the whole thing, and there is also the question of returns. One local bookseller bought 50 copies. I don't think he can sell more than half. The American reviews that I have seen or heard of are generally favorable. *Time* said I was in danger of becoming a talented hack. That's not an unpleasant fate in times like these. The *Atlantic* man reviewed the book at considerable length on the announced basis that he felt about mysteries about as Edmund Wilson did. I do not grudge reviewers their sad amusements, but there is something rather comical in a man's starting out to review a book by saying he doesn't like the kind of book it is and then proceeding to deprecate it in a nice way for not being something it never intended to be. He made one good point, though: that my "virtues . . . are merely diversions thrown in to entertain and amuse. They are embellishments; they are not intrinsic elements that transform the genre." Rather, it is a good point to the extent that it makes plain in simple language what I have suspected for a long time: that the better you write a mystery, the more clearly you demonstrate that the mystery is not really worth writing. The best mystery writers are those whose perceptiveness does not out-range their material. Christie and Gardner, for example, or your man John Dickson Carr, whose literary performance is so dull that I can't read him in spite of the ingenuity of his plots. If a man writes as well as I do (let's face it honestly) he creates a schism between the melodramatic exaggeration of his story and the way he writes about it. However,

1. *The Little Sister.*

there is the point of view that the detective character in a mystery may acquire enough substance to compensate. Nobody rereading the Sherlock Holmes stories at this time can think anything about them except that *as stories* they are pretty thin milk. But that does nothing to diminish the character of Holmes himself. He rises above them and becomes a person people want to read about even when he is being silly. Unfortunately, this just bores the author. He finds that he is becoming weary of his character just about the time the public is becoming attached to him. And the intellectual type of critic is bound to be annoyed by a book like *LS*. The fact that he is reviewing it at all implies some unusual merit or reputation, yet he doesn't really like the book. If it is well written, it shouldn't be a mystery.

·   ·   ·

Yours ever,

Ray

TO JAMES SANDOE

6005 Camino de la Costa
La Jolla, California
October 14, 1949

Dear Sandoe:

·   ·   ·

Am now reading Marquand's *So Little Time*. As I recall or seem to recall it was rather deprecated when it came out, but it seems to me full of good sharp wit and liveliness and altogether much more satisfying than *Point of No Return*, which I found boring in its total impact, although not boring as one read it. Have also started *A Sea Change* by Nigel Dennis which looks good. But I always like the wrong books anyhow. And the wrong pictures. And the wrong people. And I have a bad habit of starting a book and reading just far enough to make sure that I want to read it and look forward to

[195]

reading it and then putting it to one side while I break the ice on a couple more. In that way when I feel dull and depressed which is too often I know I have something to read late at night when I do most of it and not that horrid blank feeling of not having anybody to talk or listen to. As for mysteries that's hopeless. There don't seem to be any worth the trouble. I picked up a thing called *Arm Chair in Hell* by Henry Kane which is so godawful tough and selfconscious that it becomes a burlesque and is not funny enough for a burlesque. It would be an excellent thing right now if someone would come along with a good cool analytical mystery, the hell with suspense and witty dialogue, and let us look at the fundamentals for fresh. The whole form has lost its way, the emphasis has gone to inessential matters. Why in God's name don't those idiots of publishers stop putting photos of writers on their dust jackets? I bought a perfectly good book, . . . , was prepared to like it, had read about it, and then I take a fast gander on the guy's picture and he is obviously an absolute jerk, a really appalling creep (photogenically speaking) and I can't read the damn book. The man's probably quite all right, but to me he is that photo, that oh so unposed-posed photo with the gaudy tie pulled askew, the man sitting on the edge of his desk with his feet in his chair (always sits there, thinks better). I've been through this photograph routine, know just what it does to you. But what it does to the sensitive reader!

RC

TO JOHN HOUSEMAN[1]

[Circa October 1949]

Your article in *Vogue* was much admired here. I think it was

1. Reprinted from John Houseman, *Front and Center* (New York: Simon and Schuster, 1979), pp. 184–85. Used by permission.

beautifully written and had a lot of style. For me personally it had an effect (after-taste is a better word) of depression and it aroused my antagonism. It is artistically patronizing, intellectually dishonest and logically unsound. It is the last whimper of the Little Theatre mind in you. However, I'm all for your demand that pictures, even tough pictures, and especially tough pictures, have a moral content. (Because *The Big Sleep* had none I feel a little annoyed with you for not realizing that the book had a high moral content.) *Time* this week calls Philip Marlowe "amoral." This is pure nonsense. Assuming that his intelligence is as high as mine (it could hardly be higher), assuming his chances in life to promote his own interest are as numerous as they must be, why does he work for such pittance? For the answer to that is the whole story, the story that is always being written by indirection and yet never is written completely or even clearly. It is the struggle of all fundamentally honest men to make a decent living in a corrupt society. It is an impossible struggle; he can't win. He can be poor and bitter and take it out in wisecracks and casual amours, or he can be corrupt and amiable and rude like a Hollywood producer. Because the bitter fact is that outside of two or three technical professions which require long years of preparation, there is absolutely no way for a man of this age to acquire a decent affluence in life without to some degree corrupting himself, without accepting the cold, clear fact that success is always and everywhere a racket.

The stories I wrote were ostensibly mysteries. I did not write the stories behind those stories, because I was not a good enough writer. That does not alter the fact that Marlowe is a more honorable man than you or I. I don't mean Bogart playing Marlowe and I don't mean because I created him. I didn't create him at all; I've seen dozens like him in all essentials except the few colorful qualities he needed to be in a book. (A few even had those.) They were all poor; they will always be poor. How could they be anything else.

When you have answered that question, you can call him a zombie.

Love,

Ray

[197]

TO BERNICE BAUMGARTEN

6005 Camino de la Costa
La Jolla, California
October 15th. 1949

Dear Bernice:

.   .   .

 I cannot understand what is happening to my book, *LS*.[1]
There have been some wonderful reviews and Martindale's in Beverly
Hills my favorite booksellers write me that it is going great guns
and everybody loves it. Yet the two largest bookstores in San Diego
failed to show me a single copy. I didn't ask, being much too
diffident in that way, but I looked and couldn't find the damn thing.
I'm pretty sore about the *Newsweek* project—sore at myself really, not
at anyone else, because I let myself be taken for a ride again on that
tricky steed.[2] After getting the treatment from *Time* several years ago
I should have known better. But I was assured by the HM publicity
man that *Newsweek* was not like that. So you give them everything
they want, talking yourself silly and exhausting yourself with posing
for God knows how many pictures, get reproductions of older
pictures made for them, and in the end not only do they not give you
anything they promised, but they don't even review the book at
all. They absolutely ignore it. What hurts here is a sense of guilt
unrewarded, like the pickpocket who gets an empty wallet. When you
let yourself be persuaded into a deal like that you know in your
heart that it stinks, but you are just corrupt enough to gloss it over in
the hope that it will build up the sales. Then you get left and the
sense of humiliation is not pleasant. There is no halfway about
publicity. You either take it where and when you get it, in any form,
however vulgar, or you stick to your instincts and say, "I am not
interested in personal publicity of any kind, any time, any place, for
any purpose."

1. *The Little Sister.*
2. Chandler had been assured by the publicity department of Houghton Mifflin that
Newsweek magazine would do a cover story on him.

My fingers are well, thank God, but what a strange thing an allergy is. I am now told not to touch carbon paper or newsprint with my bare hands. So I have to read with gloves on, like a fading beauty of the stage.

Ray

TO HAMISH HAMILTON

6005 Camino de la Costa
La Jolla, California
October 17, 1949

Dear Jamie:

•   •   •

The book business is really fantastic, as ridiculous in some ways as radio. Bill Townend, an English friend and a writer, tells me that *Dinner at Antoine's* sold 148,000 copies in England in a few weeks, so he got it to read and thought it the most utter trash, and he is a very tolerant guy. I haven't read it myself. And O'Hara's book *A Rage to Live*, which I have but haven't read, is the No. 1 best seller here with a perfectly appalling press. I am sorry about this because I am a great admirer of O'Hara. But it certainly begins to look as though one of the essentials is that a book should be long and crowded. I don't know why but almost all the successful books here have been long books. And offhand I don't think I could name one which is a first class piece of writing with the exception of Thornton Wilder's *Ides of March*. Marquand's *Point of No Return*, a smash hit, is a dull book, and the same old story as before, and far inferior in wit and sharpness to *So Little Time*, which got a rather poor press, comparatively.

•   •   •

Yours,

Ray

[199]

TO BERNICE BAUMGARTEN

6005 Camino de la Costa
La Jolla California
Nov 8, 1949

Dear Bernice:

.   .   .

I should admire to have your list of mysteries for that book.[1] There is no one whose judgment I should respect more. You seem to me to achieve what the best film producers achieve even when they don't show it, the ability to be artistically intelligent and maintain a sense of what is practical and possible at the same time. I am such an extremist myself. I am at home with the avant garde magazines and with the rough tough vernacular. The company I really cannot get along with is the pseudo-literate pretentiousness of, let us say, the *Saturday Review of Literature*. That sums up everything I despise in our culture, including the out-at-elbows professors mewling maliciously at everyone who has the brains and guts to make a dime. But to be more specific to the subject in hand: I'd like to leave off "The Bronze Door" because I'd like to do a group of fantastic stories in which it would belong, if they ever got published (or written, you will add). These stories, about ten of them, longish short stories, would all be about murder in some sense, or the elimination of some annoying person, all more or less fortuitously through the happening on a magic means of doing it, all realistic in tone, with a dash of humor, and all in the nature of a spoof on some type of murder story. I am poking at one now which is a sort of reduction ad absurdam of the locked-room puzzle.

.   .   .

Yours ever,

Ray

1. *The Simple Art of Murder*, 1950.

TO HAMISH HAMILTON

6005 Camino de la Costa
La Jolla, California
November 11, 1949

Dear Jamie:

· · ·

While reviewing generally is not very reliable anywhere, I
really think that English reviewing is getting a bit absurd. There are
far, far too many novelists reviewing other novelists. There is far
too much consideration for books that are obviously going to get
nowhere, and far too little understanding of what it is in books that
make people read them. And there is a tight group of critics or
reviewers who are monotonously willing to say something nice about
almost any book at all. Your own ads show it. These names,
supposedly of influence, really can't have any because they show no
discrimination to speak of. . . . And at the other extreme is that
ridiculous publication *The Times Literary Supplement*, which is
apparently compiled from the blitherings of a group of aged dons,
whose standards of comparisons, points of reference or what have
you, seem to be stuck in the year when Jowett translated Plato. Fancy
a so-called intelligent reviewer handling Faulkner's *Intruder in the
Dust* as though it were just another thriller. You begin to wonder
whether these people have any conception of what makes writing.

· · ·

P.S. I suppose you know this, but I think it is wonderful, from
Fontemara, by Ignazio Silone:

At the head of all is God, lord of heaven.
Then comes Prince Torlonia, lord of earth.
Then comes the armed guard of Prince Torlonia.
Then come the hounds of the armed guard of Prince Torlonia.
Then nobody else.
And still nobody else.
And still again nobody else.
Then come the farmers.

[201]

TO BERNICE BAUMGARTEN

6005 Camino de la Costa
La Jolla, California
Nov 17th. 1949

Dear Bernice:

.   .   .

I have a letter inviting me to join the P.E.N. Club. I don't know what to do about it. They evidently consider the invitation a great honor, and I just don't give a damn. If they knew what a bastard I was, they probably wouldn't want me. Their board of directors contains the names of some people whom I regard as blithering idiots, but not all, and I couldn't very well say that anyhow.

Yours,

Ray

TO HAMISH HAMILTON

6005 Camino de la Costa
La Jolla, California
Dec 4, 1949

Dear Jamie:

.   .   .

Pride and Prejudice arrived and bless you. I thank you in advance for the "specially bound copy of the Little Sister"; god, what can that be? I do not think my "works" are worth special binding, my good Jamie, but the thought is damn kind. Your man Hodge is a superb editor, the rarest kind of mind.[1] These trained-seal critics, even

1. Writer and co-editor, with Robert Graves, of *The Reader Over Your Shoulder*.

the best of them, bore me at least two thirds of the time. Give a man a name of prestige and he is already a fair way to being an ass. I do not suggest that Alan Hodge lacks prestige, but he is still in that happy territory where the man's voice is more important than his name. Surely no one could write better introductions. The Betjemans (I may have spelled this wrong), the Quennels, the Mortimers, etc. are always a little intent on making a good appearance before their admiring public.[2] Hodge is concerned with the book and damn all else.

.   .   .

I expressed myself badly about playwriting. Of course Maugham is right, as he always is. It is more *difficult* to write plays, harder work, I have no doubt, although I have never even tried to write one. It is also very much more difficult to write screenplays than novels. But it does *not*, in my opinion, take the same quality of talent. It may take a more exacting use of the talent, a more beautiful job of cabinet work, a finer or more apt ear for the current jargon of a certain kind of people, but it is much more superficial all round. Take any good, but not great, play and put it in fiction form and you have a very slight matter. No richness, no vistas, no overtones, no feeling of the country beyond the hill. It is all clear and literal and immediate. The novelist, if he is any good, gives you a thousand things that he never actually says. Incidentally, if I knew Maugham, which I fear I never shall, I should ask him for an inscribed copy of *Ashenden*. I've never asked a writer for an inscribed copy and as a matter of fact I attach very little value to such things. (I wouldn't mind having the prompt copy of *Hamlet*.) And I suppose it declares my own limitations of taste to pick *Ashenden*. But I'm a bit of a connoisseur of melodramatic effects, and *Ashenden* is so far ahead of any other spy story ever written, while his novels, the best of them, and good as they are, do not outclass the field. A classic in any manner appeals to me more than the large canvas. *Carmen*, as Merimée wrote it, "Herodias," "Un Coeur Simple," *The Captain's Doll, The Spoils of Poynton, Madame Bovary, The Wings of the Dove,* and so forth and so on (*A Christmas Holiday*, by God too), these are

2. John Betjeman, the poet; Peter Quennel, the historian; Raymond Mortimer, the critic. All reviewed frequently for London papers.

all perfect.[3] Long or short, violent or still, they do something that never will be done as well again. The list, thank God, is long, and in many languages.

What a queer attitude the better minds have to mysteries. "Oh, it's just a mystery, a thriller, a 'tec. I read them in bed to put me to sleep. I read them when I am sick. I read them when I am too tired for serious reading." The deprecation is so obvious, but does anyone ever reply, "And what, my good sir, would you do if you were sick or tired or wakeful, and there *were* no mysteries?" The very people who declare they read them rapidly and forget them at once declare in the same breath that they cannot exist without them. And they know God damned well that they could exist indefinitely without the more massive classics.

Too bad you are such an old, old man of 50, or not quite. (Fiftieth year means past 49 over here.) Too bad. I have sympathy for you. It is a bad age. A man of 50 is not young, not old, not even middle-aged. His wind is gone and his dignity has not yet arrived. To the young he is already old and stodgy. To the really old he is fat and pompous and greedy. He is a mere convenience to bankers and tax collectors. Why not shoot yourself and be done with it? Think of the horrors that lie ahead. You might even get to be a whiskered bore like Shaw, a voluble cicada, an antediluvian scene-stealer.

Ray

TO HAMISH HAMILTON

6005 Camino de la Costa
La Jolla, California
Jan 5, 1950

Dear Jamie:

---

3. "Herodias," "Un Coeur Simple," and *Madame Bovary* are by Gustave Flaubert; "The Captain's Doll" by D. H. Lawrence; *The Spoils of Poynton* and *The Wings of the Dove* by Henry James; *A Christmas Holiday* by W. Somerset Maugham.

Ashenden with very handsome dedication received safely.[1] Why in hell did you spend all that money on postage? It's a ridiculous extravagance, although extremely generous. Of course I'll write to the old boy, trying not to be too deferential on the one hand nor too clubby on the other. I have a feeling that fundamentally he is a pretty sad man, pretty lonely. His description of his seventieth birthday is pretty grim. I should guess that all in all he has had a lonely life, that his declared attitude of not caring much emotionally about people is a defense mechanism, that he lacks the kind of surface warmth that attracts people, and at the same time is such a wise man that he knows that however superficial and accidental most friendships are, life is a pretty gloomy affair without them. I don't mean that he has not friends, of course; I don't know enough about him to say anything like that. I get my feeling from his writing and that is all. In a conventional sense he probably has many friends. But I don't think they build much of a fire against the darkness for him. He's a lonely old eagle. I don't suppose any writer was ever more completely the professional. He has an accurate and fearless appraisal of his own gifts, the greatest of which is not literary at all, but is rather that neat and inexorable perception of character and motive which belongs to the great judge or the great diplomat. He has no magic and very little gusto. His style, which has been greatly praised, seems to me no more than a good competent mandarin English which often only narrowly escapes dulness. He can convey the setting for emotion but very little the emotion itself. His plots are cool and deadly and his timing is absolutely flawless. As a technician he is far ahead of the good second raters like Galsworthy and Bennett and J. P. Marquand. He can never make you catch your breath or lose your head, because he never loses his. I doubt that he ever wrote a line which seemed fresh from creation, and many lesser writers have. But he still outlasts them all with ease, because he is without folly or silliness. He would have made a great Roman.

.   .   .

Ray

---

1. By W. Somerset Maugham.

TO HAMISH HAMILTON

6005 Camino de la Costa
La Jolla, California
Jan 11, 1950

Dear Jamie:

.   .   .

    I often wonder why so many English intellectuals turn to
Catholicism, just as my schoolmaster friend often used to wonder
audibly why so many otherwise intelligent and normal people went to
Cambridge. (You'd love that.) But I wonder so many things and
as I grow older I have less and less respect for the human brain and
more and more respect for human courage. Over here the Catholics
are numerous, powerful and mostly quite genial, but the hierarchy is
overwhelmingly of Irish origin and the Irish Catholics, always
excepting the Jesuits of Maynooth, are pretty crude specimens of high
Catholic thinking, compared with the French, English, Scottish,
and Italian prelates. Of course I also wonder why people turn to
religion at all. As a young man I was very high-church and very
devout. But I was cursed with an analytical mind. It still worries me.
But this is a delicate subject unless you are sure you cannot offend.
    I need your comfort and guidance about some things over
there. You gave me the name of a hotel north of the Park and I must
look back and find it. Assuming that we should be over there for
about four months, do you think we must have hotel and travel
reservations all planned out? I'd hate it, but I'd better know. We don't
even know where we want to go. To Paris, I hope, and to other
places on the Continent, but which? A bit of England here and there
and even Scotland, but not by train. How does one do these things?
And what about food? After all you can't very well consume food
parcels in hotels. Laundry? Soap? Can one buy shirts and socks
and so on freely? This is a big thing to me; I don't want it to go sour.
I am not a very patient person, I've had a lot of illness, none serious,
and I haven't much stamina. Cissy, my wife, has more, but she is no
ironhorse either. Damn it, all this must sound very silly to you, but
we have lived a long time in a soft enervating climate. It's all so

difficult, perhaps I had better just go quietly back to bed. (I have a feeling amounting to a conviction that I am becoming a frightful bore.)

.   .   .

I don't think there is much chance of any motion picture outfit here buying the screen rights to *LS*.[1] They're tired of the private dick stories (having run them to death with a series of imitations) and the book is not too admiring of Hollywood. Fundamentally it is probably a question of money. Lots of stories are now sold for five or ten thousand dollars. I'm asking fifty. There was one producer at Warner's named Harry Kurnitz wanted to do it, but Jack Warner evidently said no. Nor do I think there is any feeling against me as an anti-Semitic. After all I dealt with dozens and dozens of Jews in Hollywood and was never accused by any of them of any such feeling. The people who do raise the point belong to that extreme fringe who resent anyone's using the word Jew at all. Some of my most stalwart supporters are Jewish. My favorite doctor is Jewish. He once said, "There's a bit of the anti-Semitic in all of us, Jews and Gentiles alike." What they seem to resent is the feeling that the Jew is a distinct racial type, that you can pick him out by his face, by the tone-quality of his voice, and far too often by his manners. In short, to some extent the Jews are still foreigners, especially the middle-Europeans. It was not so in England when I was a schoolboy. I must have known Jewish boys at school, but I can't remember which were which. One just didn't think about it. The only time I ever heard a man called a Jew in England was by one of his closest friends, and all he meant was that he was an orthodox Hebrew. Over here it is different. They are of all religions or no religion. When you call a man a Jew you are not thinking of his religion, but of certain personal characteristics of appearance or behaviour, and the Jews don't like that, because they know that is what you mean. They want to be like everyone else, indistinguishable from everyone else, except that they want to be Jews to themselves, and they want to be able to call non-Jews by the name of Gentiles. But even then they are not happy, because they know very well you can't insult a man by calling him a Gentile, whereas you *can* insult him by calling him a Jew. As long as

1. *The Little Sister.*

that is so I don't see how you can expect the Jews not to be
oversensitive, but at the same time I don't see why I should be so
unnaturally considerate of this oversensitiveness as never to use the
word Jew. It's not so one-sided. I've lived in a Jewish neighbourhood,
and I've watched one become Jewish, and it was pretty awful. I
don't know the answer, and I'm pretty sure it will take a long time to
find it. It really seems at times that the Jews ask too much of us.
They are like a man who insists upon being nameless and without an
address and yet insists on being invited to all the best parties.

Yours ever,

Ray

TO SOMERSET MAUGHAM

6005 Camino de la Costa
La Jolla, California
Jan. 13, 1950

Dear Mr. Maugham:

In passing, but apparently not lightly enough, I mentioned to
Jamie Hamilton that if I knew you, which was extremely unlikely, I
should ask you for an autographed copy of *Ashenden*, and that this
would be the only time I asked for or even desired such a thing from
any author. But a suggestion to Jamie is as electric as a kick in the
teeth to some people. The book now arrives with a very handsome
inscription for which I can only wish in vain that I might thank
you in words as graceful and unique as the person to whom they
would be addressed. But, disdaining not to strike an attitude, I can
only thank you quite simply and say that the nearness of your name
to mine on the title page of a book is as near as I am likely to get
to distinction, and a good deal nearer than I deserve.

Why *Ashenden* rather than something you probably value much
more highly? Because I am a bit of a connoisseur of melodramatic
effects and because *Ashenden* is unique. However great a novel you
may claim, or others may claim for you, there are other great novels.

[208]

There are not other great spy stories—none at all. I have been searching and I know. It's a strange thing. The form does not appear so very difficult. Evidently it is impossible. There are a few good tales of adventure with a spying element or something of the sort, but they always overplay their hand. Too much bravura, the tenor sings too loud. They are as much like *Ashenden* as the opera *Carmen* is like the deadly little tale that Merimée wrote.

I think it's rather a pity that somewhere along the line, seeing you have had time for so many things, you did not write a detective story. Not only would it have given us something to shoot at, but it would have quieted my long annoyance with those who gabble about the "classic" detective story. We should have had at least one specimen to which the term might be applied without idiocy.

To the esteem in which you are held I can add nothing. But I can be grateful for the kindness which permits me to write to you.

Yours most sincerely,

Raymond Chandler

TO DALE WARREN

6005 Camino de la Costa
La Jolla, California
Jan 15th. 1950

Dear Dale:
Bernice sent me the enclosed, which looks like an original, with no instructions about how to deal with it (mean keep it or return it). So I'm playing it safe.[1]

This is the sort of document that makes writers dog themselves out in a velveteen smoking jacket, a cap with a tassel, a pipe full of Craven Mixture, and lollygag around admiring themselves instead of putting out a little careful but uneven prose. The piece is a miracle

1. Presumably a biographical statement to be used on a dust jacket.

[209]

of overstatement. What about my classical profile, my head of wavy brown hair scarcely thinning at the temples, my erect bearing, and smiling Irish eyes and my unfailing courtesy to my social inferiors? What about those early days in the back of a Fifth Street bar, cleaning spittoons with the tail of my shirt, dining off the debris of the free lunch mixed with sawdust. A butt of bullies, a familiar of courtesans, a whipping boy for shamed alcoholics? What about the time I spent under the shadow of Saint Sulpice in that short but intoxicating affair with a demoiselle from Luxembourg—the one that afterwards became known the world over—but no, this is dangerous ground. Even in Luxembourg they have libel laws—in three languages as a matter of fact. And what about that lost six months I spent in the Höllenthal, trying to persuade a funicular railway to run on the level? You fellows leave so much out that happened and put so much in that didn't. What about those May mornings outside the Dôme—Garcon, deux Pernods, s'il vous plait, and ask that gentleman with the calvados to tuck his shirt in and stop flicking the muleta in my eyes. It wouldn't hurt him a lot to shave that grizzle off his muzzle either, and I see a spot for a hot bath if you can interest him at a very low price.

.   .   .

I should say that the fellow you write about appears to be knowable. When you are discussing writers that is a great deal. Most of them are what you said we had the biggest of in Washington.

Yours ever,

Ray

TO SOMERSET MAUGHAM

6005 Camino de la Costa
La Jolla, California
Feb 15, 1950

Dear Mr. Maugham:
    Herewith the tear sheets from a *Pocket Atlantic* with a

somewhat revised version of the article you desired.[1] I am delighted to send it and I have a number of other pieces which I should be glad to send you (if I may have them back) in case you had not seen them. I'd have to look them up to be sure what I have, but I know there are two pieces by Edmund Wilson from the *New Yorker*, a piece by Joseph Wood Krutch, one by Jacques Barzun from *SRL*[2] and a whole number of some avant-garde magazine called *Chimera* devoted to various praise and abuse. I have your own old piece from the *Post* and I've never forgotten the picture of Edith Wharton. Wouldn't she have been embarrassed if you had mentioned *The Turn of the Screw* to her? She would have *had* to like that, being a sort of road company Henry James herself. And if it isn't a thriller, I'd like to know what is.

I should have double-spaced this letter, but I'm a rotten typist and at the moment have no secretary.

Yours sincerely,

Raymond Chandler

TO CARL BRANDT

6005 Camino de la Costa
La Jolla, California
Feb 26, 1950

Dear Carl:

.　　　　.　　　　.

Here are a couple of samples of unconscious humor that fascinated me. 1. Our cook lives at home and she has been taking the magazines home as we finish with them, mostly for a girl to read who is staying with her. She took home some *SRL's* along with

1. Maugham was preparing his essay "The Decline and Fall of the Detective Story," and he had asked Chandler for other writings on the subject.
2. *Saturday Review of Literature.*

others and I discovered there was missing a number in which Dale Warren had said he had a piece.[1] I asked her to bring it back. She brought it and several others and reported that her friend, on looking into the *SRL*, had remarked with a mixture of bewilderment and indignation: "There's nothing to read in here. It's all authors." 2. Somewhere in this town of La Jolla there dwell a couple of gnome-like females who always dress with large pulled down felt hats on their heads, bunchy shapeless garments under old raincoats and carry walking sticks. They walk past our house every single day and they never walk abreast, always one several paces behind the other as if they were not on speaking terms, but were held together by some unbreakable tie. They look like something out of Grimm's Fairy Tales. One day as they passed a real estate man who was here to size up the house happened to glance out of the window and see them. He stared open-mouthed for a couple of seconds and then said suddenly: "What country are we in?"

Ray

TO DALE WARREN

6005 Camino de la Costa
La Jolla, California
April 4, 1950

Dear Dale:

.   .   .

It's a good thing I did catch your piece because I'm discontinuing my subscription to the *Saturday Review*.[1] It bores me further and further.

---

1. *Saturday Review of Literature.*

---

1. Warren had written an article on masters of ceremony.

The reviews are absolutely no good. Their editorials I skip. Some of the letters are amusing and some of Cerf's stuff too.[2] But that's hardly enough reason to bring another magazine into a house already overloaded with them. I guess they do a great job in selling what looks like the intellectual point of view to people who think they are intellectuals. But I must be one of the few living Americans who do not crave to have their minds improved. I know too much already. I would be happier knowing less. What decided me to drop this roadshow version of the cultured mind from my mailing list was a debate between Mr. Eric Johnston and Mr. Norman Cousins on the subject of the movies.[3] This item was strictly an affair of a couple of four-round prelim fighters accidentally boosted into the main event. Mr. Cousins has some fine qualities, including the courage to get up at that red symposium in New York and tell the Communists where to get off. Believe me, that takes courage. But he has such an extreme case of social consciousness that he is, and cannot help being, a good deal of a bore to my type of mind. As for Mr. Eric Johnston, Hollywood's ambassador-at-large, I think he does a terrific job of making the motion picture business look just exactly as silly as its worst enemies call it. I remember a few years back, at an Academy Award's affair, he glued himself to a microphone and announced in clear, ringing accents that the motion picture was the greatest art form since the Greek drama. You could have knocked me down with a baby Austin. I was inspired to write an unpaid contribution to the *Screen Writer*, now defunct alas, recommending that this statement not be allowed to die but that it be engraved on an old bottle cap and handed for safekeeping to one of the monkeys in Griffith Park zoo.

.   .   .

Yours ever,

Ray

2. Bennett Cerf, publisher, had a column in *The Saturday Review*.
3. Eric Johnston, director of the Motion Picture Association, whose Production Code governed the sexual and moral content of Hollywood films. Norman Cousins was editor of *The Saturday Review*.

TO MORRY RABIN[1]

6005 Camino de la Costa
La Jolla, California
April 11, 1950

Dear Mr. Rabin:

Thanks for your letter and I'm damned if I see any reason why I should be on your sucker list. No thanks to whoever put me there. I was never a working newspaper man. I was once a free lance journalist and a book reviewer for a literary weekly in London.

With the greatest possible reluctance I am enclosing a check for twenty-five dollars ($25.00). The amount is large enough to annoy me and too small to make you hysterical. The only reason I send it is that if I spent this much taking some one to dinner at Romanoff's (deductible, naturally) I shouldn't think very hard about it. Why should you be less expensive?

Do you want any copy? From time to time, especially around the time the bills come in, I have projected an essay on La Jolla entitled *A Sweet Little Town and You Can Have It*. But as long as I live here, wiser not. I have a silly piece called *Advice to a Young Critic* knocking around in my files somewhere. I thought of fixing it up for the *Atlantic* but I never got it to jell just right. But as the farm boy said when he brought the bucket of thin milk over to the neighbor, "Maw says it's only skim, but it's good enough to give away."

I should add that I want no publicity of any kind. "Before you clicked and became a name," quoted from your letter, meaning me. If I ever clicked, I never heard it. If I became a name, that is one mistake I should have liked to rectify. I always despised pseudonyms, and I found out too late that I was wrong.

Yours,

Raymond Chandler

---

1. President of the San Diego Newspaper Guild. This letter probably was never sent.

TO LEROY WRIGHT

6005 Camino de la Costa
La Jolla, California
April 12, 1950

Dear Mr. Wright:

In common with a lot of other people I find that I quite often don't know what I am talking about. After writing stories for years about the Los Angeles Police Department, Homicide Bureau, etc., I did some actual research and found out how it really operated. I was somewhat surprised at the modesty of the facilities. Same with private dicks. I want to check up. Some time when you are not to busy or when someone in your office is not too busy, would you be good enough to let me know the present status of the licensed private operative. Specifically (but not all inclusively):

What authority licenses him? How must he qualify? What are his rights, privileges and duties? What information does he give, and what shows on the license? Must it be in plain view on the wall of his office? How much is his bond? Are his fingerprints on record locally and in the FBI files? Has he automatically a right to carry weapons or must he qualify like anyone else? Is this within the discretion of the Sheriff or whom? Are his weapons registered and testfired? By whom?

How is a complaint made against him (a) by a private citizen, (b) by a police authority? What is the procedure in hearing such a complaint (assuming the matter to be short of a criminal charge)? On what grounds may his license be canceled? If it is for a specific period (what is the fee?) is it automatically renewed, or must he re-qualify?

To what extent is information given him by a client a privileged communication? (A lot of stories turn on this.) Has he any greater power of arrest than the ordinary citizen? Can he be held without bond as a material witness at the discretion of the D.A.? Has he any kind of badge (not being a uniformed special officer such as the men who patrol baseball parks, movie lots and so on)? What identification, etc. is he *required* to carry?

The private detective of fiction is, of course, pure imagination.

[215]

He does not and could not exist. He is the personification of an attitude, the exaggeration of a possibility. But that is no reason why he should not know the rules under which he operates. (The real life private dick is often quite vague on the subject, incidentally.)

Yours

Raymond Chandler

TO HAMISH HAMILTON

6005 Camino de la Costa
La Jolla, California
May 18, 1950

Dear Jamie:

I have to thank you for the Turgenev in your Novel Library and for Eric Partridge's *Here There and Everywhere*. By the way where does this spelling of Turgenev come from? Why is the "i" dropped after the "n"? In Russian there is a letter which is pronounced like "ny," like Spanish "n" with a tilde or Portuguese "nh." I wonder who started this crackpot modern custom of transliterating foreign names with no regard to the fact that the foreign letters, although the apparent equivalent of the English, do not correspond in sound.

Partridge is interesting but makes me uneasy. These scholars of the vernacular, cant, slang, etc. cover an awful lot of ground and one wonders how accurately they do it, if one happens to have any special knowledge of a small part of their field and find their report on that shading a little off the exact. Take p 104 1.16 "chiv": This does not mean a razor. Chiv, or more commonly shiv means a knife, a stabbing or cutting weapon, perhaps (but I don't think so) including a razor; but that is not the meaning. P. 105 1.15 "flop" means to go to bed and perhaps includes the idea of sleep, but doesn't mean sleep. Flophouse is a cheap transient hotel where a lot of men sleep in large rooms. I also question the translation of "gay-cat" as "look-out man or finder." A gaycat is a young punk who runs with an older tramp and there is always a connotation of homosexuality. Again he could be a "look-out" (outside man) or a "finder" (finger or finger man), but that is a derived or occasional meaning and not exact. On the same page "piped" does not mean "found" but saw or spotted (with the eyes). Flivvers are not "cheap cars;" they are Fords and only Fords, at least in my part of the country. I never heard the word applied to any other make. Of course when this piece was written, 1926, there were no other cars as cheap. The nearest was a Chevrolet, always "chevvy." (A couple of flivvers and a chevvy.) Page 107 1.18 "case dough." This means the same as nest egg really, not money for a trial which would be only one of many, many uses. It is the theoretically untouchable reserve for emergencies—that and nothing more. ("I'm down to case dough" means I've spent all my spare money and have nothing left but a getaway stake, etc.) In his analysis of "queer" Partridge is no doubt historically correct and all that, but it has only two meanings in modern American slang: counterfeit and sexually abnormal. Somewhere along in here he uses or quotes "beak" several times as meaning judge. In England, yes, but not in America. Anyone who has looked at an elderly judge with his wig on knows why he might be called a beak. There is no point in it here. Also, Walla Walla (page 106) is *not* a penitentiary for women. It is the Washington state penitentiary, just like Sing Sing or San Quentin. In his chapter on soldiers' slang he covers a lot of ground that I don't know. But some of his remarks don't click with me. P.B.I. (page 64) he says "a term rarely used by the 'poor bloody infantry' themselves." It was constantly used in my unit. And doesn't he overlook some of the most constantly used words? E.g. "bomb-proofer," "cushy job," "bivvy;" and above all, "napoo," "strafe's long's," for bombardment (The morning strafe), "street cars" or "tram cars" for heavy long range shells, "whizbangs" for rapid small shells, and the inimitable American "goldbrick" which is as superior to English "lead-swinger," as "milk run" (from the last war) is to "piece of cake."

What always gets me about these scholarly excursions into the language of the underworld, so to speak, is how they smell of the dictionary. The so-called experts in this line have their ear to the library, very seldom to the ground. They do not realize what a large proportion of these cant terms (using cant a bit too broadly) is of literary origin, how many of them crooks and cops use *after* writers have invented them. It is very difficult for the literary man to distinguish between a genuine crook term (like "back-door parole," prison slang for dying in prison) and an invented one (like "Chicago overcoat" for coffin). How do you tell a man to go away in hard language? Scram, beat it, take off, take the air, on your way, dangle, hit the road, and so forth. All good enough. But give me the classic expression actually used by Spike O'Donnell (of the O'Donnell brothers of Chicago, the only small outfit to tell the Capone mob to go to hell and live): What he said was "Be missing." The restraint of it is deadly.

Throughout his play *The Iceman Cometh* O'Neill used "the big sleep" as a synonym for death. He used it, so far as one can judge from the context, as a matter of course, apparently in the belief that it was an accepted underworld expression. If so, I'd like to see whence it comes, because I invented the expression. It is quite possible that I re-invented it, but I never saw it in print before I used it, and until I get the evidence, I shall continue to believe that O'Neill took it from me, directly or indirectly, and thought I was using a standard term. The whole tenor of his writing in this play shows that he knows very little about his subject.

.   .   .

My apologies to Mr. Partridge, but if he enters the field he must expect to get mixed up with people like me.

.   .   .

TO DALE WARREN

6005 Camino de la Costa
La Jolla, California
June 14, 1950

Dear Dale:

・　　　　・　　　　・

It must be about twenty years since I stopped wearing a hat. I remember that for years after I did people were always asking me if I hadn't forgotten my hat. And why does a man who hasn't worn a hat for years always look like a clown in one? Or did he always look that way?. . . . Strange things the eyes. Consider the question of the cat. The cat has nothing to express emotion with but a pair of eyes and some slight assistance from the ears. Yet consider the wide range of expression a cat is capable of with such small means. And then consider the enormous number of human faces you must have looked at that had no more expression than a peeled potato. What a waste of material is here.

I have a publisher in my new book, of which I have written the first chapter and I am inclined to think the first chapter will also be the last. It never occurred to me that you would want me to send you a copy of my novelette. Anyhow, I don't think I have a copy to send you. The *Cosmopolitan* has just rejected it, so I feel rather deflated. It appears they are having some kind of change in trend or tone, or whatever they call these things in a magazine. Why the hell can't they once in a while reject something just because it stinks?

"Dear Sir: Your story *Midnight at Dawn* has been carefully read by our editorial staff. We are returning it herewith and suggest you use it to line a bureau drawer."

・　　　　・　　　　・

Very disconnected letter. Sorry.

Yours, Ray

TO HAMISH HAMILTON

6005 Camino de la Costa
La Jolla, California
June 23, 1950

Dear Jamie:
Your Paris trip sounds like a typical publisher's jaunt, every

meal an interview, and authors crawling in and out of your pockets from morning till night. I don't know how publishers stand these trips. One writer would exhaust me for a week. And you get one with every meal. There are things about the publishing business that I should like, but dealing with writers would not be one of them. Their egos require too much petting. They live over-strained lives in which far too much humanity is sacrificed to far too little art. I think that's why I decided years ago that I should never be anything but an amateur. If I had the talent to be first-class, I would still lack the hard core of selfishness which is necessary to exploit that talent to the full. The creative artist seems to be almost the only kind of man that you could never meet on neutral ground. You can only meet him as an artist. He sees nothing objectively because his own ego is always in the foreground of every picture. Even when he is not talking about his art, which is seldom, he is still thinking about it. If he is a writer, he tends to associate only with other writers and with the various parasitic growths which batten on writing. To all these people literature is more or less the central fact of existence. Whereas, to vast numbers of reasonably intelligent people it is an unimportant sideline, a relaxation, an escape, a source of information, and sometimes an inspiration. But they could do without it far more easily than they could do without coffee or whiskey.

.   .   .

Yours ever,

Ray

TO JAMES KEDDIE

6005 Camino de la Costa
La Jolla, California
August 15, 1950

Dear Mr. Keddie:

[220]

Thank you also for the report of the proceedings of *The Speckled Band*. No, I don't think you could convert me. This is not due to any superciliousness on my part towards the faithful, nor towards the great Sherlock. It is just that I do not seem to find any hollow place in my life which the cult of the master alone could fill. If I were drawn into any esoteric activity of this sort, I think it would probably be a group devoted to the desperate analysis of certain actual crimes which have never been satisfactorily explained and of course never will be. For example, the Maybrick case, the Julia Wallace case, the disappearance of Judge Crater, and so forth and so on. Or to put it another way, an examination into how and by what grotesque process of legalistic reasoning the best legal minds in England (with one exception) were able to convince themselves that the late William Joyce, Lord Haw Haw, owed allegiance to his sovereign majesty the King, and so thinking were able to convict him of the crime of bearing aid and comfort to the King's enemies on the testimony (and this was the only evidence adduced in the trial) of one detective inspector, who had once heard William Joyce speak at a meeting in England and had once heard a broadcast of Lord Haw Haw's and said it was the same man.[1] The history of actual trials is so full of these beautiful and impossible tangles that a devotion to the minutiae of the life of Sherlock Holmes seems to me rather a waste of energy— nothing against it of course. I should say it was comparable with the composition of Sapphic odes or a study of Provençal French.

With kindest regards,

Raymond Chandler

---

1. Joyce was convicted for having broadcast propaganda for Germany during World War II.

TO BERNICE BAUMGARTEN

6005 Camino de la Costa
La Jolla, California
September 13, 1950

Dear Bernice:

   .   .   .

  I'm still slaving away for Warner Brothers on this Hitchcock thing, which you may or may not have heard about.[1] Some days I think it is fun and other days I think it is damn foolishness. The money looks good, but as a matter of fact it isn't. I'm too conscientious and, although I do not work nearly as fast as I would have worked twenty years ago, I still work a good deal faster than the job requires or has any right to expect. For the most part the work is boring, unreal, and I have no feeling that it is the kind of thing I can do better than anybody else. Suspense as an absolute quality has never seemed to me very important. At best it is a secondary growth, and at worst an attempt to make something out of nothing.

   .   .   .

With kindest regards,

Ray

TO HAMISH HAMILTON

6005 Camino de la Costa
La Jolla, California
September 28, 1950

Dear Jamie:

1. The screenplay for *Strangers on a Train*, to be directed by Alfred Hitchcock.

[222]

Well, here we are (as the debonair character in the operetta said) back on the scene of our former triumphs. I sent in the last of my movie script Tuesday night.[1] It arrived at Warner Bros Wednesday morning—apparently about 8.30 A.M. At nine I received a wire from my agent telling me I was off salary. Just imagine the frantic speed these boys moved at and so early in the morning too, to avoid having to pay me for an extra half day or so! The bastards, no wonder nobody ever, or hardly ever, tries to deal ethically with them. One week I got a touch of food poisoning and didn't do much work, so I refused to accept any pay. Nevertheless to meet a deadline I knew nothing about when I took the job I worked Saturdays and Sundays to clean it up. I could just as easily have held on to the final pages to the end of this week. But I said to myself, I'm not dealing with pikers. I was wrong. They're all pikers. They hire writers as a necessary evil because all the brilliant second guessers, who can tell you what is wrong with what you do, can't do anything themselves. They hire writers, I said, and sometimes at a high salary (mine is very high for present conditions in Hollywood) but they hate them every minute. They would rather save a thousand bucks by cutting off a writer before he has time to catch his breath than save fifty thousand by using their brains during production.

The picture will hardly be any better than *Stage Fright*, which was not rated very highly here. There seems to be a general feeling about Hitchcock that he has shot his wad, but that is always a dangerous assumption with a man of any talent. He is definitely a man of talent, but he belongs to the type which is rather dull outside its particular skill. Some movie makers, like some writers, seem to do their work without committing more than a small part of their real abilities. These belong to the class I call the amateurs; when they are big enough, they are geniuses. Others can do some particular thing extremely well, but you would never think they had it in them merely by meeting them. These are the technicians. I'd say Hitch belongs to this group, but of course I don't really know the man. I had a few discussions with him and then he went blank on me. It's very unusual for a writer to do an entire screenplay without one single conference with the producer. He may have decided this was the best way to handle me. In one sense he was clever about it. I

1. Screenplay for *Strangers on a Train*.

worked very fast for me. Even if my script was not as perfect as it might have been with more discussion of knotty points, he got it pretty cheap, considering how little there was to go on. The book had one idea, and that was all. But I didn't work fast just to please Hitchcock or Warners. I worked fast because of a feeling about 10 or 12 weeks was the most I could give to a film job. After all I'm drawing on capital now. The job's not worth any more time. Most of the boys have the attitude that as long as they are working they are being paid, so let's make it last, fellows. I have the attitude that film work is too valuable a connection to discard completely but not valuable enough to let it dominate your life. Hack work is all right in small doses, but they must be kept small. I know that mystery writers are regarded as hacks in certain quarters simply because they are mystery writers. This is a confusion of thought, to my mind. A writer who accepts a certain formula and works within it is no more a hack than Shakespeare was because to hold his audience he had to include a certain amount of violence and a certain amount of low comedy, no more a hack than the Renaissance painters were because they had to exploit the religious motives which were pleasing to the church. My definition of a hack is a man who lets someone else tell him how and what to write, who writes, if he is a writer, not to an accepted formula, but to some editor's definition of it. But the frontier is always vague.

·   ·   ·

Yours ever,

Ray

TO JAMES KEDDIE

6005 Camino de la Costa
La Jolla, California
September 29, 1950

Dear Mr. Keddie:

Yes, I know the books of Austin Freeman and Freeman Wills Crofts very well. I think my favorite Freemans are *Mr. Pottermack's Oversight* and *The Stoneware Monkey*. Freemans are very hard to get hold of. I haven't been able to get *The Stoneware Monkey* at all since I first read it. *Pontifex, Son and Thorndike* is also very good. The hansom cab era appeals to me very much. And I always enjoy the long walks across London which Thorndike and Jervis seem to take as a matter of course. Their legs never become tired apparently. As a matter of fact, Freeman is rather a poor writer compared with Conan Doyle. If you read him out loud he makes you laugh, he's so stilted. And Thorndike at times is a bit of a bore, especially when explaining to Jervis that he now has all the facts and that if he sits down and studies them, he should come up with a few ideas. Can it be possible that the acute Dr. Thorndike would ever think Jervis would ever come up with an idea? Dr. Watson, though no mental giant, was on occasion capable of a moderately sensible remark. But not Dr. Jervis. His mind is a complete blank. Some of the most delicious moments in Freeman to me are when Thorndike politely inquires of Jervis whether he will be free from engagements on the following date to accompany him on some expedition. Jervis is always free of course. He will always be free. One can hardly imagine anybody employing him to do anything more exacting than copying out a laundry list. Whether or not Freeman writes really good detective stories is quite another matter. In cases where, as in the example of *The Mystery of 31 New Inn*, there is no analysis of scientific evidence, in spots they are extremely transparent. And where the solution of a mystery turns on the correct analysis of scientific evidence, there arises a question of honesty. I realize that this is a big problem in detective stories—just what honesty is. But if you accept the basic premise, as I do, that in a novel of detection the reader should have been able to solve the problem, if he had paid proper attention to all the clues as they were presented and drawn the right deductions from them, then I say that he had no such opportunity if, to evaluate said clues, he is required to have an expert knowledge of archaeology, physics, chemistry, microscopy, pathology, metallurgy, and various other sciences. If, in order to know where a man was drowned, I have to identify the fish scales found in his lungs, then I, as a reader, cannot be expected to tell you where he was drowned. I should not be expected to. And if to solve the mystery I must be able to solve this point, then so far as I am concerned the clue is suppressed just as effectively as though it had never been given. In spite of all this, I have a very high regard for Freeman. His writing is stilted, but it is never dull in the sense that Crofts's writing is dull. That is to say, it is never flat. It is merely old-fashioned. His problems are always interesting in themselves, and the expositions at the end are master-pieces of lucid analysis. Thorndike is a far more accurate thinker than Sherlock Holmes. He is the only expert in fiction who would have been a match, and I think rather more than a match, for the real experts such as Sir Bernard Spillsbury.

With kindest regards,

Raymond Chandler

TO DALE WARREN

6005 Camino de la Costa
La Jolla, California
October 4, 1950

Dear Dale:

.   .   .

I get it from a pal back East that I got a stinking bad review in the *New York Times* from one John Dickson Carr, about as stinking as the one I got from Anthony Boucher. *Time* speaks of his taking "deadly aim" at me. I have not seen the review. Obviously people like Boucher and Carr are committed in advance to disliking me, because they are well aware that I regard their kind of detective story as apt to be a crashing bore, even when it is a good deal better written than they could ever write it. The only thing deadly is the assumption that the proper man to review a book is somebody who is drooling for a chance to get his knife into the writer, a snide theory

[226]

of criticism, which can taste nothing but its own bile. If they don't like my opinions, why don't they sit down and refute them on the same level instead of waiting until I write something else and then take their spleen out on that? I could write a better defense of the deductive mystery than they could.

· · ·

There ought to be a few ethics in this reviewing business. If I were offered a book by Mr. John Dickson Carr—supposing I reviewed books at all—would I jump at the chance because I knew I was going to dislike it and would have a field day being nasty about it? I'd say no thanks, I'm not the man for this job. I'm prejudiced. A reviewer need not perhaps be as just as Aristides, but he should at least be able to see the good in books he may not personally care for. If the editor if the book section of the *Times* knows the facts and offers the assignment deliberately to somebody who has just got a sharp knife waiting for the author, then the editor of the book section of the *Times* is not an honorable man. Of course that's a silly way to put it. He's most probably some frightened hack who won't have a job if he doesn't pull in enough full-page ads. And of course you publishers back him up. You think space is all that counts. You'd rather have a good review, but a bad one is better than none. A bad one that takes a column is better than a good one that takes a quarter of a column. And for all I know, you may be right. I don't know how much space the *Times* gave to this last job. I think they gave a column to *The Little Sister*. But what I'm wondering is, did they give the space to Mr. John Dickson Carr, or did they give it to me, or did they give it to your full-page ad. Interesting thought, isn't it? God, what a sleazy business newspaper and magazine criticism has become. How many critics could you name whose opinions have any validity above the level of a fireside chat, or a tout for the lending libraries? How many who really know anything about writing beyond the fact that they pooped out at it themselves? How many could you name who could read a page of a man's book and know for sure whether he's a real writer, regardless of his opinions on the current social and political scene? Not very many I'm sure. Look what they've done to the old war horse, Hemingway, and what they've been doing to him for a good many years for that matter. He'd have quit writing a long time ago if he had the faintest suspicion that any of them knew what they were talking about, that they had no spite in their systems, and that they were not sniping at him just because he had made good. Let's face it. One of the penalties of any kind of success is to have the jackals snapping at your heels. They don't hate you because you're bad. They say you're bad because they want to hate you.

Yours always,

Ray

TO CHARLES MORTON

6005 Camino de la Costa
La Jolla, California
October 9, 1950

Dear Charlie:

Quite a lapse in our once interesting correspondence, don't you think? Of course it's my fault because the last letter was from you. And you are most correct in saying in it that I owe you a letter. For quite a long time, I have owed practically everybody a letter. Why? Apparently it is what the years do to you. The horse which once had to be driven with a tight rein now has to be flicked with a whip in order to make him do much more than amble. Instead of being ready to slug it out with all comers, you find yourself having to give yourself pep talks before you can get a glove up. "Come on, you dumb loafer, start hittin' them typewriter keys." So much energy is wasted in winding the clock, so little is left to make the clock run. We still have dreams, but we know now that most of them will come to nothing. And we also most fortunately know that it really doesn't matter. Walter Bagehot once wrote, (I am quoting from an increasingly unreliable memory) "In my youth, I hoped to do great things. Now, I shall be satisfied to get through without scandal." In a sense, I am much better off than he was because I never expected to do great things; and in fact have done much better than I ever hoped to do. But as your energies shrink, you become rather niggardly in spending them. Normally a man should do his day's work, whatever it is, and then write a couple of letters to keep in touch with people that he likes and doesn't see in person. But I find that when I have done what passes for a day's work, I am sucked dry. I have nothing to say in the damn letters. I start them but don't finish them. I have a box file stuffed solid with carbon copies of letters that I wrote to just one man somewhere around fifteen years ago. Gosh, what a lot I had to say, and on the whole how well I said it. Now, it is becoming a bit of an effort to say anything. I am only too well aware that I have said it all before, and said it better.

My compliments to Mr. Weeks on belonging to that very small minority of critics who did not find in necessary to put Hemingway in his place over his last book.[1] Just what do the boys resent so much? Do they sense that the old wolf has been wounded and that this is a good time to pull him down? I have been reading the book. Candidly, it's not the best thing he's done, but it's still a hell of a sight better than anything his detractors could do. There's not much story in it, not much happens, hardly any scenes. And just for that reason, I suppose, the mannerisms sort of stick out. You can't expect charity from knife throwers naturally; knife throwing is their business. But you would think some of them might have asked themselves just what he was trying to do. Obviously he was not trying to write a masterpiece; but in a character not too unlike his own, trying to sum up the attitude of a man who is finished and knows it, and is bitter and angry about it. Apparently Hemingway had been very sick and he was not sure that he was going to get well, and he put down on paper in a rather cursory way how that made him feel to the things in life he had most valued. I suppose these primping second-guessers who call themselves critics think he shouldn't have written the book at all. Most men wouldn't have. Feeling the way that he felt, they wouldn't have had the guts to write anything. I'm damn sure I wouldn't. That's the difference between a champ and a knife thrower. The champ may have lost his stuff temporarily or permanently, he can't be sure. But when he can no

1. Edward Weeks, editor of *The Atlantic Monthly*, had reviewed Ernest Hemingway's *Across the River and into the Trees.*

longer throw the high hard one, he throws his heart instead. He throws something. He doesn't just walk off the mound and weep. Mr. Cyril Connolly, in a rather smoother piece of knife throwing than most of the second-guessers are capable of, suggests that Mr. Hemingway should take six months off and take stock of himself. The implication here apparently is that Hemingway has fully exploited the adolescent attitude which so many are pleased to attribute to him, and should now grow up intellectually and become an adult. But why? In the sense in which Connolly would define the word, Hemingway has never had any desire to be an adult. Some writers like some painters are born primitives. A nose full of Kafka is not at all their idea of happiness. I suppose the weakness, even the tragedy, of writers like Hemingway is that their sort of stuff demands an immense vitality; and a man outgrows his vitality without unfortunately outgrowing his furious concern with it. The kind of thing Hemingway writes cannot be written by an emotional corpse. The kind of thing Connolly writes can and is. It has its points. Some of it is very good, but you don't have to be alive to write it.

·　　　　·　　　　·

With kindest regards,

R.C.

TO HAMISH HAMILTON

6005 Camino de la Costa
La Jolla, California
October 13, 1950

Dear Jamie:

·　　　　·　　　　·

No, I don't despise Hollywood. Why should I? They're tough

[230]

and hard-boiled about money matters, but they take an awful gouging themselves from agents, from the unions, for the exhibitors. Their manners are bad. As a friend of mine put it, "They are arrogant when they should be humble and timid when they should be bold." They are extremely friendly when they want something and brutally indifferent when they don't. After all I wrote a treatment and a screenplay on a story, with nothing usable except an idea, in a matter of ten weeks. I was told at the beginning there was no hurry at all; and halfway through the job I found out that there had been a deadline for commencing shooting. I worked some nights, Saturdays and Sundays in order to get the thing out on time. I refused salary for a week when I was partly incapacitated by a little food poisoning and didn't do a full week's work, although I did some work. I wrote this screenplay to the best of my ability exactly as Hitchcock wanted it as to story line, etc., and I didn't get a single word of appreciation or acknowledgement of any kind from Hitchcock or from anybody else at Warner. Perhaps they didn't like the script. But if they didn't, they could see it as it came in bit by bit, and they didn't have to keep me on it since I was on a week to week basis. I just don't think this is the way to treat people, and from a purely practical point of view, I don't think it's the way to treat people. You don't get the best out of them that way. But all this doesn't mean that I am lacking in respect for a lot of the people who do very good work in Hollywood, and try to do good work even when they can't do the best. After all, the intrigue and backbiting are no worse than they would be in most big corporations or in the higher echelons of the civil service. A couple of non-Semitic writers and myself were once discussing what a bunch of bastards they are, and one of them remarked cogently, "Well, after all, the Jews know how to pay for what they get. If a bunch of Irish Catholics were running the motion picture business, we'd be working for fifty dollars a week."

.   .   .

Yours ever,

Ray.

[231]

TO BERNICE BAUMGARTEN

6005 Camino de la Costa
La Jolla, California
October 16, 1950

Dear Bernice:

.   .   .

I gather from your note that this is a poor book season. According to Mr. Maugham (Somerset Maugham) the American public has ceased to read and now spends its time looking at television. Well, I've spent a little time lately looking at television for the first time, and my opinion is that the people who look at television for any length of time and with any regularity have not ceased to read. They never began. It's a great deal like the chimpanzee who played the violin. He didn't play it in tune; he didn't play anything recognizable as a melody; he didn't hold the bow right; he didn't finger correctly. But, Jesus, wasn't it wonderful that he could play the violin at all?

.   .   .

Yours always,

Ray

TO FINLAY McDERMID

6005 Camino de la Costa
La Jolla, California
Nov. 2, 1950

Dear Mr. McDermid:

I am a cad not sooner to have made acknowledgment of your two letters dated July 7 and August 22. I remember very well the time when you (at the ungodly hour of 9:30 in the morning) conducted me to a projection room where I sat alone and watched

[232]

The Big Sleep. I was trying to do a script on *The Lady in the Lake* for M.G.M. then, and we were very anxious to be sure that we did not imitate any effect which Warners had got in the Howard Hawks' picture.

As to the week for which I did not receive payment working on *Strangers on a Train*, was I a damn fool about that! I had had a touch of food poisoning, incurred in the course of duty at a lunch with Hitchcock; and for three days I just sat around and gloomed, although I did work the rest of the week including Saturday and Sunday. In fact I worked Saturdays and Sundays all the time I was on this assignment. What strange delicacy of conscience induced me to give any weight to this, I wonder. It must have been that I thought I was dealing with people as precise as myself in these matters.

When I took this assignment, I was told by Mr. Hitchcock that there was no hurry—no hurry at all; no pressure—no pressure at all. About halfway through it I heard from his factotum that there was a shooting date of October 1, because Mr. Hitchcock had to go East before the leaves fall and he would have to have, or at least very greatly desired, the completed script some little time before that; and that there was even the possibility (although this may have been just talk) that if a page marked "The End" was not received by the studio before October 1, then Mr. Hitchcock might not be allowed to begin shooting. So I, as the phrase is, exerted myself to the full and perhaps a little more than to the full. I completed the script on the evening of Tuesday, September 26, mailed it to you special delivery, and it must have been in your hands early the next day, because early the next day I had a wire from Ray Stark that I was off salary as of Monday night. Incidentally, or perhaps not incidentally, I was not paid for Tuesday, September 26. I have raised this point in several places and at several times, and still I am not paid for Tuesday, September 26.

Of course my thought had been that I would be paid for the whole week. In the circumstances surely this would have been only a minimum of decency. I could very easily have kept the work going until the end of the week. Almost any writer you would deal with would have done so. And in view of the way Hollywood treats writers, I think he would have been justified in so doing. I am aggrieved about this, Mr. McDermid. I am not particularly greedy for money, but I am greedy for fair treatment.

Are you aware that this screenplay was written without one single consultation with Mr. Hitchcock after the writing of the screenplay began? Not even a telephone call. Not one word of criticism or appreciation. Silence. Blank silence then and since. You are much too clever a man to believe that any writer will do his best in conditions like this. There are always things that need to be discussed. There are always places where a writer goes wrong, not being himself a master of the camera. There are always difficult little points which require the meeting of minds, the accommodation of points of view. I had none of this. I find it rather strange. I find it rather ruthless. I find it almost incomparably rude. And I think in your heart of hearts you would be very apt to agree with me.

Yours very sincerely,

Raymond Chandler

TO FLEUR COWLES[1]

Nov. 7, 1950

Dear Mrs. Cowles:

Thank you for your very handsome letter of October 21 and for taking the time to write. I have to admit that I have never seen a copy of *Flair*, and I suppose politeness suggests that I should add "to my shame." I had an idea that it was almost fantastically smart, clever, and sophisticated, and I make claim to none of these qualities. Of course I am going to get a copy, as I see I have been missing things, especially such items as "The New Expense Account Society" by John O'Hara, and "The New Society in Crime" by Robin Harris. As for trying to do a piece for you, I suppose you wouldn't suggest it if you didn't think I could do it, but I am very easily intimidated by cleverness. In the days when I read *Esquire*, I was rather appalled by the bright and brittle quality, especially of the letters in the "Sound

1. Editor of *Flair* magazine. The text of this letter is taken from a transcript.

and Fury" department. My God, I thought, if they can be as clever as that for nothing, what would they be like if they got paid. I had to give it up. First thing you know I'd have been demanding champagne with my bread and cheese and Caesar salads for breakfast.

I am sending a copy of your letter on to Carl Brandt in New York. It always pays to let your agent know that you have high-class friends.

TO HAMISH HAMILTON

6005 Camino de la Costa
La Jolla, California
November 10, 1950

Dear Jamie:

.   .   .

Why do people want biographical material? Why does it matter? And why does a writer have to talk about himself as a person? It's all such a bore. I was born in Chicago, Illinois, so damned long ago that I wish I had never told anybody when. Both my parents were of Quaker descent. Neither was a practicing Quaker. My mother was born in Waterford, Ireland, where there was a very famous Quaker school, and perhaps still is. My father came of a Pennsylvania farming family, probably one of the batch that settled with William Penn. At the age of seven I had scarlet fever in a hotel, and I understand this is a very rare accomplishment. I remember principally the ice cream and the pleasure of pulling the loose skin off during convalescence. I spent five years in Dulwich and thereafter lived in France and Germany for a couple more years. At that time I was thought to be a British subject, since my mother had regained her British nationality while I was still a minor. So that when I returned to the United States, the record shows that I was admitted as a British subject. It took a long, long struggle, and finally a law suit against the Attorney General of the United States to get it changed. The point

[235]

of law was that a minor cannot be expatriated, and I don't know why they found it so hard to accept this. It cost me quite a lot of money to force it on them. I had done several years free lancing in London in a rather undistinguished way. I did book reviews, essays, etc., for the old *Academy*, sketches and verses for the *Westminster Gazette*, odd paragraphs here and there, etc. I served in the First Division of the Canadian Expeditionary Force in what used to be called the Great War, and was later attached to the R.A.F., but had not completed flight training when the Armistice came. So far I had shown very little talent for writing, and that little was riddled with intellectual snobbery. I arrived in California with a beautiful wardrobe, a public school accent, no practical gifts for earning a living, and a contempt for the natives which, I am sorry to say, has in some measure persisted to this day. I had a pretty hard time trying to make a living. Once I worked on an apricot ranch ten hours a day, twenty cents an hour. Another time I worked for a sporting goods house, stringing tennis rackets for $12.50 a week, 54 hours a week. I taught myself bookkeeping and from there on my rise was as rapid as the growth of a sequoia. I detested business life, but in spite of that I finally became an officer or director of half a dozen independent oil corporations. The depression finished that. I was much too expensive a luxury for those days. Wandering up and down the Pacific Coast in an automobile, I began to read pulp magazines, because they were cheap enough to throw away and because I never had any taste at any time for the kind of thing which is known as women's magazines. This was in the great days of the *Black Mask* (if I may call them great days) and it struck me that some of the writing was pretty forceful and honest, even though it had its crude aspect. I decided that this might be a good way to try to learn to write fiction and get paid a small amount of money at the same time. I spent five months over an 18,000 word novelette and sold it for $180. After that I never looked back, although I had a good many uneasy periods looking forward. I wrote *The Big Sleep* in three months, but a lot of the material in it was revamped from a couple of novelettes. This gave it body but didn't make it any easier to write. I was always a slow worker. In the best month I ever had, I wrote two 18,000 word novelettes and a short story which was sold to the *Post*. For Gardner this would be the work of a couple of days, but for me it was a terrific production and I have never approached it since. I went to Hollywood in 1943 to work with Billy Wilder on *Double Indemnity*. This was an agonizing experience and has probably shortened my life; but I learned from it as much about screen writing as I am capable of learning, which is not very much. I was under contract to Paramount after that and did several pictures for them, including one original screen play, *The Blue Dahlia*, which was written from scratch (that is without any basic story) and shot complete in twenty weeks. I was told at the time that this was some sort of a record for a high budget picture. All my books, except *The Little Sister*, have been made into pictures, two of them twice. Like every writer, or almost every writer, who goes to Hollywood, I was convinced in the beginning that there must be some discoverable method of working in pictures which would not be completely stultifying to whatever creative talent one might happen to possess. But like others before me I discovered that this was a dream. It's nobody's fault; it's part of the structure of the industry. Too many people have too much to say about a writer's work. It ceases to be his own. And after a while he ceases to care about it. He has brief enthusiasms, but they are destroyed before they can flower. People who can't write tell him how to write. He meets clever and interesting people and may even form lasting friendships, but all this is incidental to his proper business of writing. The wise screen writer is he who wears his second-best suit, artistically speaking, and doesn't take things too much to heart. He should have a touch of cynicism, but only a touch. The complete cynic is as useless to Hollywood as he is to himself. He should do the best he can without straining at it. He should be scrupulously honest about his work, but he should not expect scrupulous honesty in return. He won't get it. And when he has had enough, he should say good-bye with a smile, because for all he knows he may want to go back.

By the end of 1946 I had had enough. I moved to La Jolla. Since then I have written two screen plays, one of them with only occasional visits to a studio to talk over the story, and one without any visits to the studio at all. I shall probably do others, and if so I shall do them as well as I know how; but I shall keep my heart to myself.

I have been married since 1924 and have no children. I am

supposed to be a hard-boiled writer, but that means nothing. It is merely a method of projection. Personally I am sensitive and even diffident. At times I am extremely caustic and pugnacious; at other times very sentimental. I am not a good mixer because I am very easily bored, and to me the average never seems good enough, in people or in anything else. I am a spasmodic worker with no regular hours, which is to say I only write when I feel like it. I am always surprised at how very easy it seems at the time, and at how very tired one feels afterwards. As a mystery writer, I think I am a bit of an anomaly, since most mystery writers of the American school are only semi-literate; and I am not only literate but intellectual, much as I dislike the term. It would seem that a classical education might be rather a poor basis for writing novels in a hard-boiled vernacular. I happen to think otherwise. A classical education saves you from being fooled by pretentiousness, which is what most current fiction is too full of. In this country the mystery writer is looked down on as sub-literary merely because he is a mystery writer, rather than for instance a writer of social significance twaddle. To a classicist— even a very rusty one—such an attitude is merely a parvenu insecurity. When people ask me, as occasionally they do, why I don't try my hand at a serious novel, I don't argue with them; I don't even ask them what they mean by a serious novel. It would be useless. They wouldn't know. The question is parrot-talk. The problem of what is significant literature I leave to fat bores like Edmund Wilson—a man of many distinctions—among which personally I revere most highly (in the *Chronicles of Hecate County*) that of having made fornication as dull as a railroad time table.

Reading over some of the above, I seem to detect a rather supercilious tone here and there. I am afraid this is not altogether admirable, but unfortunately it is true. It belongs. I am, as a matter of fact, rather a supercilious person in many ways. I shouldn't be at all surprised if it shows in what I write. And it may well be this which arouses such flailing anger in pip-squeaks like John Dickson Carr and Anthony Boucher.

.   .   .

Yours ever,

Ray

[238]

TO DALE WARREN

6005 Camino de la Costa
La Jolla, California
November 13, 1950

Dear Dale:

.   .   .

You don't sound completely satisfied with the Fitzgerald book.[1] I'm sad about that, because Fitzgerald is a subject no one has a right to mess up. Nothing but the best will do for him. I think he just missed being a great writer, and the reason is pretty obvious. If the poor guy was already an alcoholic in his college days, it's a marvel that he did as well as he did. He had one of the rarest qualities in all literature, and it's a great shame that the word for it has been thoroughly debased by the cosmetic racketeers, so that one is almost ashamed to use it to describe a real distinction. Nevertheless, the word is charm—charm as Keats would have used it. Who has it today? It's not a matter of pretty writing or clear style. It's a kind of subdued magic, controlled and exquisite, the sort of thing you get from good string quartettes. Yes, where would you find it today?

.   .   .

Yours ever,

Ray

TO EDGAR CARTER

6005 Camino de la Costa
La Jolla, California
Nov 15, 1950

Dear Eddie:

.   .   .

I am having a feud with Warners. I am having a feud with the

1. Probably a reference to Budd Schulberg's novel *The Disenchanted*, which was based on an episode in Fitzgerald's life.

[239]

gardener. I am having a feud with a man who came to assemble a Garrard changer and ruined two LP records. I had several feuds with the TV people. Let's see who else—oh, skip it. You know Chandler. Always griping about something.

Yours ever,

Ray

TO CHARLES MORTON

6005 Camino de la Costa
La Jolla, California
November 22, 1950

Dear Charlie:

.   .   .

Perhaps in some way the worse television is, the better. A lot of people are looking at it, I hear, who had long since given up listening to radio. Perhaps enough of these people will realize after awhile that what they're really looking at is themselves. Television is really what we've been looking for all our lives. It took a certain amount of effort to go to the movies. Somebody had to stay with the kids. You had to get the car out of the garage. That was hard work. And you had to drive and park. Sometimes you had to walk as much as half a block to the theater. Then people with big fat heads would sit in front of you and make you nervous. Reading took less physical effort, but you had to concentrate a little, even when you were reading a mystery or a western or one of those historical novels, so-called. And every once in awhile you were apt to trip over a three-syllable word. That was pretty hard on the brain. Radio was a lot better, but there wasn't anything to look at. Your gaze wandered around the room and you might start thinking of other things—things you didn't want to think about. You had to use a little imagination to build yourself a picture of what was going on just by the sound. But television's perfect. You turn a few knobs, a few of those mechanical adjustments at which the higher apes are so proficient, and lean back and drain your mind of all thought. And there you are watching the bubbles in the primeval ooze. You don't have to concentrate. You don't have to react. You don't have to remember. You don't miss your brain because you don't need it. Your heart and liver and lungs continue to function normally. Apart from that, all is peace and quiet. You are in the poor man's nirvana. And if some nasty-minded person comes along and says you look more like a fly on a can of garbage, pay him no mind. He probably hasn't got the price of a television set.

Yours ever,

Ray

TO GENE LEVITT

6005 Camino de la Costa
La Jolla, California
November 22, 1950

Dear Gene:

·   ·   ·

I'd like to have a television show, but I don't suppose I'll get it. A television contract was actually sent to me at one time from Century Artists. It was a new low, or high, in unmitigated gall. I am only a very recent possessor of a television set. It is a very dangerous medium. Radio was bad enough, but at least you didn't have to look at it. You didn't have to watch the kind of direction and camera work that would have been considered ridiculously incompetent in the movies twenty-five years ago. And as for the commercials—well, I understand that the concoction of these is a business in itself, a business that makes prostitution or the drug traffic seem quite respectable. It was bad enough to have the sub-human hucksters controlling radio, but television does something to you which radio never did. It prevents you from forming any kind of a mental picture

and forces you to look at a caricature instead. There's no escape.
Take the show that Ralph Bellamy is doing. "Man Against Crime" I
think it's called. The writing, I suppose, is no worse than it was in
lots of radio shows, but by being more intrusive it *seems* worse. It's
no more good enough for television than it would be for any but
the cheapest movies, the kind of thing PRC[1] makes, or the type of
western movie turned out wholesale by Republic and never shown in
neighborhood theaters. If you have spent fifteen years building up
a character, a fairly complicated character, you can't deliver him to the
sort of people that do these shows. I don't think the plots are terribly
important. But I think the actor and the dialogue are very
important—so much so that if I were offered a television show (which
I have not been) I would have to demand approval of the actor
playing Philip Marlowe and also script approval. I simply can't afford
to have this character murdered by a bunch of yucks. A voice like
Gerald Mohr's gave you a personality which you could fill out
according to your fancy. But television shoves the whole thing right
down your throat. And if the actor says one flat, stupid, trashy
line, it sticks out like a lighthouse in a storm.

.   .   .

With kindest regards to you both,

Yours ever,

Ray

TO ALFRED HITCHCOCK

6005 Camino de la Costa
La Jolla, California
December 6, 1950

Dear Hitch:
    In spite of your wide and generous disregard of my

1. Producers Releasing Corporation, or PRC pictures, which released such films as *Swamp Woman, Wife of Monte Cristo,* and *Why Girls Leave Home.*

[242]

communications on the subject of the script of *Strangers On a Train*[1] and your failure to make any comment on it, and in spite of not having heard a word from you since I began the writing of the actual screenplay—for all of which I might say I bear no malice, since this sort of procedure seems to be part of the standard Hollywood depravity—in spite of this and in spite of this extremely cumbersome sentence, I feel that I should, just for the record, pass you a few comments on what is termed the final script. I could understand your finding fault with my script in this or that way, thinking that such and such a scene was too long or such and such a mechanism was too awkward. I could understand you changing your mind about the things that you specifically wanted, because some of such changes might have been imposed on you from without. What I cannot understand is your permitting a script which after all had some life and vitality to be reduced to such a flabby mass of clichés, a group of faceless characters, and the kind of dialogue every screen writer is taught not to write—the kind that says everything twice and leaves nothing to be implied by the actor or the camera. Of course you must have had your reasons but, to use a phrase once coined by Max Beerbohm, it would take a "far less brilliant mind than mine" to guess what they were.

Regardless of whether or no my name appears on the screen among the credits, I'm not afraid that anybody will think I wrote this stuff. They'll know damn well I didn't. I shouldn't have minded in the least if you had produced a better script—believe me, I shouldn't. But if you wanted something written in skim milk, why on earth did you bother to come to me in the first place? What a waste of money! What a waste of time! It's no answer to say that I was well paid. Nobody can be adequately paid for wasting his time.

There are minor changes in this construction, or plot order or whatever, which don't bother me at all, such as the drunken professor on the train, although the notion is not original and I simply do not believe for a moment that the professor sober would not even remember the existence of the song he sang when drunk. The idea of having more things happen on trains is all right too. But I certainly thought I had you talked out of this Hennessy nonsense, the idea that the Washington police, or any police, would put a twenty-four hour

1. Chandler was sent the final script of *Strangers on a Train*. This letter was never sent.

watch on a man against whom there was no evidence except motive, and do it for no apparent purpose except that if Guy had committed one murder and they watched him closely enough, they might catch him committing another. The ease with which he evades this watch reduces the whole procedure to absurdity. Also, I think there is a serious mistake in your reversal of the scenes between Guy and Bruno and between Guy and the Burton family immediately after Miriam's murder. The great difficulty of the story always was to make it credible to an audience that Guy should behave in the damn-fool way in which he did behave. Even to approach a solution it was necessary to have the scene with the Burton family first, and to realize what kind of people they are and what their relationship is to Guy and to one another; so that when Guy finds out that Bruno is the murderer, the audience will realize he is not stopped from going to the police solely by fear for himself. I might add that the expressed realization by Guy and Anne, that now that Miriam has been murdered there is nothing to prevent them from being married, will probably be hooted at. Also, take such items as scene 134 on page 47. This is after the scene between Guy and Bruno. Consider the effect of Guy saying on the telephone to Anne, "But you sound upset. Is anything wrong?" You better take that out fast, Hitch. You really better.

Another thing which seems to me dramatically wrong is the failure to have Bruno state specifically why he's going back to Metcalf. You deduce and expect the audience to deduce it from the fact that he says he has a date with the moon—an idea so crazy that only Bruno would think of it. However, these things often look less irrational on the screen than when you are reading the script. I think you may be the sort of director who thinks that camera angles, stage business, and interesting bits of byplay will make up for any amount of implausibility in a basic story. And I think you are quite wrong. I also think that the fact that you may get away with it doesn't prove you are right, because there is a feeling about a picture that is solidly based which cannot be produced in any other way than by having it solidly based. A sow's ear will look like a sow's ear even if one hangs it on a wall in a frame and calls it a French modern. As a friend and well-wisher, I urge you just once during your long and distinguished career—or perhaps I should say just once again—to get a sound and sinewy story into the script and to sacrifice no part of its soundness for an interesting camera shot. Sacrifice a camera

[244]

shot if necessary. There's always another camera shot just as good. There is never another motivation just as good.

The characters have had things happen to them. Anne was always a bit of a stick, but now she's a piece of spaghetti. Mrs. Antony is nothing. Mr. Antony hardly exists. And I do think it's a pity to have removed the tennis motivation from Senator Burton—the idea that he was a sort of frustrated champion who wanted someone else to win the title he could never win. I guess this is about all. The final shot was in my notes, but I didn't put it in my script. I talked it over with my secretary, and we sort of agreed that this was a pretty grim story and should be kept pretty grim and that you couldn't end it with a joke. In any case, I wish you all good luck. No one can predict the fate of a picture, since it often depends on some gimmick which seemed relatively insignificant while the picture was being made. Good pictures fail and bad ones succeed. The shrewdest minds are never quite sure why. Sometimes it seems that a good picture has to fail (example *Night Must Fall*) in order that a whole trend of pictures later on may succeed by the same formula of making a heel or a murderer out of what was formerly a glamour star. After all, a Hitchcock picture always has something.

Yours very truly,

Raymond Chandler

TO JAMES SANDOE

6005 Camino de la Costa
La Jolla, California
December 7, 1950

Dear Jim:

.   .   .

You should by all means catch *The Bicycle Thief*, and if possible an English picture called *I Know Where I'm Going*, shot largely on the west coast of Scotland—the coast that faces the Hebrides. I've never seen a picture which smelled of the wind and rain in quite this way, nor one which so beautifully exploited the kind of scenery people actually live with, rather than the kind which is commercialized as a show place. The shots of Corryvreckan alone are enough to make your hair stand on end. (Corryvreckan, in case you don't know, is a whirlpool which, in certain conditions of the tide, is formed between two of the islands of the Hebrides.) But you'd better forget about the Hitchcock film, because I have seen the final script made up from what I wrote, but a good deal changed and castrated. It is, in fact, so bad that I am debating whether to refuse screen credit. I don't know what's happened to Hitchcock. You call him flabby. I'd be inclined to call him idiotic, because if he wanted the kind of script this thing has turned into, why one earth did he go to the expense of hiring me to write a script for him? The sort of stuff he is presumably shooting he could have got for one-fifth or less of the money Warners paid me.

.   .   .

I have just been reading a book called *The Beast Must Die*, by Nicholas Blake, the pseudonym of Cecil Day Lewis. Once again I am struck, you might even say shattered, by the devastating effect on the story of the entrance of the detective, Nigel Strangeways, an amateur with wife tagging along—this wife is one of the world's three greatest female explorers, which puts her in the same distinguished, and to me utterly silly, class as the artist wife of Ngaio Marsh's Roderick Alleyn. Up to that point the story is damn good and extremely well written, but the amateur detective just won't do. He wouldn't do even when his brother was a duke and he had a title and was a classical scholar of considerable attainments, and he won't do as Nigel Strangeways any better, or as well.[1] The private eye admittedly is an exaggeration—a fantasy. But at least he's an exaggeration of the possible. The amateur gentleman who outthinks Scotland Yard is just plain silly. From a plot point of view I think Blake made a bad mistake in allowing his protagonist, the author of the diary, to find his hit-and-run murderer so soon. It should have been a long hard job with many frustrations and should have taken up

1.   Reference to Lord Peter Wimsey, the detective in the novels by Dorothy Sayers.

about two-thirds of the book, or anyway half. It's not only that it's absurd that an amateur should so easily find someone the police could not find, because I could swallow that if necessary; it's that the search itself always has a built-in suspense, and not to prolong it to the limit is simply throwing away good material. However, in the matter of plotting I have to confess that every man is entitled to proceed according to his own taste.

Yours ever,

Ray

TO CARL BRANDT

6005 Camino de la Costa
La Jolla, California
December 11, 1950

Dear Carl:

.   .   .

I'm not going to discuss the credits on the screenplay, because the only point here was whether I should refuse any credit on the ground that the final script was so poor a job that I didn't want my name on it.[1] I may still do it or, for all I know, one of the other writers may be dissatisfied with the allocation of credits and ask for an arbitration. The fallacy of this operation was my being involved in it at all, because it is obvious to me now, and must have been obvious to many people long since, that a Hitchcock picture has to be all Hitchcock. A script which shows any sign of a positive style must be obliterated or changed until it is quite innocuous, even if that means making it quite silly. What Hitchcock does with his camera, his actors, and his stage business is quite all right. I haven't a thing against it. And I'm not going to suggest that he would do better if he

1. Screenplay for *Strangers on a Train*. Chandler wrote the first screenplay and then was replaced on the job by Czenzi Ormonde, with whom he eventually shared credit for the film.

had a little more sense of dramatic plausibility, because maybe he wouldn't do better. Maybe he'd do worse. Stark seemed to enjoy suggesting that my script was bad.[2] But it wasn't bad. It was far better than what they finished with. It just had too much Chandler in it and not enough Hitchcock. That is my considered opinion, and not mine alone. I feel annoyed that the lady who did the rewriting behind my back, and who is probably little more than a note-taker for Hitchcock, should have been supplied by Stark's office. It's bad enough to be stabbed in the back without having your agent supply the knife. But of course I admit this could happen with any agency.

.   .   .

With kindest regards,

Ray

TO HAMISH HAMILTON

6005 Camino de la Costa
La Jolla, California
December 11, 1950

Dear Jamie:

.   .   .

J. A. Spender was editing the *Westminster Gazette* in the days when I worked for it. I got an introduction to him from a very charming old boy named Blennerhassett, a landed proprietor in Ireland, a barrister with, I think, a House of Lords' practice. It seems to me that I have written to you about him before. He was the sort of man who could make a frightened young nobody feel at ease in the company of the cream of patrician society. Spender put me up for the National Liberal Club in order that I might have the use of its reading room, and I used to browse through the French and

2. Ray Stark, Chandler's Hollywood agent, assigned him by Carl Brandt, his literary agent.

[248]

German papers looking for odd paragraphs and news items which could be translated and adapted for a column the *Westminster Gazette* ran. Spender thought I could make six guineas a week out of this, but I don't think I ever made more than about three. I wrote quite a lot of verses for him also, most of which now seem to me deplorable, but not all, and a good many sketches, mostly of a satirical nature— the sort of thing that Saki did so infinitely better. I still have a couple of them somewhere, and they now seem to me very precious in tone. But I suppose they weren't so bad, considering how little valid experience I had to back them up. Of course Naomi Royde-Smith may have been connected with the *Westminster* at that time, but I never personally came into contact with her. As a matter of fact, I had only the most limited personal contact with Spender. I would send the stuff in, and they would either send it back or send me proof. I never corrected the proof, didn't even know whether I was expected to. I simply took it as a convenient form of acceptance. I never waited for them to send me the money but appeared regularly on a certain day each week at their cashier's office and received payment in gold and silver, being required to affix a penny stamp in a large book and sign my name across it by way of receipt. What a strange world it seems now! I suppose I have told you of the time I wrote to Sir George Newnes and offered to buy a piece of his trashy but successful weekly magazine called *Tit-Bits*. I was received most courteously by a secretary, definitely public school, who regretted that the publication was not in need of capital, but said that my approach had at least the merit of originality. By the same device I did actually make a connection with *The Academy*, then edited and owned by a man named Cowper, who had bought it from Lord Alfred Douglas. He was not disposed to sell an interest in his magazine, but pointed to a large shelf of books in his office and said they were review copies and would I care to take a few home to review. I wonder why he did not rather have me thrown down his murky stairs; perhaps because there was no one in the office who could do it since his entire editorial staff seemed to consist of one placid middle-aged lady and a mousy little man, named Vizetelly, who was (I believe) the brother of another and more famous Vizetelly—the one who was arrested in New York in connection with an obscenity complaint over the American publication of the translation of *Madame Bovary*. I met there also a tall, bearded, and sad-eyed man called Richard Middleton, of whom I think you may have heard. Shortly afterwards he committed suicide in Antwerp, a suicide of despair, I should say. The incident made a great impression on me, because Middleton struck me as having far more talent than I was ever likely to possess; and if he couldn't make a go of it, it wasn't very likely that I could. Of course in those days as now there were popular and successful writers, and there were clever young men who made a decent living as free lances for the numerous literary weeklies and in the more literary departments of the daily papers. But most of the people who did this work either had private incomes or jobs, especially in the civil service. And I was distinctly not a clever young man. Nor was I at all a happy young man. I had very little money, although there was a great deal of it in my family. I had grown up in England and all my relatives were either English or Colonial. And yet I was not English. I had no feeling of identity with the United States, and yet I resented the kind of ignorant and snobbish criticism of Americans that was current at that time. During my year in Paris I had run across a good many Americans, and most of them seemed to have a lot of bounce and liveliness and to be thoroughly enjoying themselves in situations where the average Englishman of the same class would be stuffy or completely bored. But I wasn't one of them. I didn't even speak their language. I was, in effect, a man without a country. Having passed third (and first on the classical list) in an open civil service examination, I could have had a life-long and perfectly safe job with six weeks' vacation every year and ridiculously easy hours. And yet I thoroughly detested the civil service. I had too much Irish in my blood to stand being pushed around by suburban nobodies. The idea of being expected to tip my hat to the head of the department struck me as verging on the obscene. All in all, perhaps I ought to have stayed in Paris, although I never really liked the French. But you didn't exactly have to like the French to be at home in Paris. And you could always like some of them. On the other hand, I did like the Germans very much, that is the South Germans. But there wasn't much sense living in Germany, since it was an open secret, openly discussed, that we would be at war with them almost any time now. I suppose it was the most inevitable of all wars. There was never any question about whether it would happen. The only question was when.

· · ·

I have just received my copy of the Old Alleynian Yearbook, and although Dulwich is not, I suppose, quite out of the top drawer as public schools go, there is an astonishing number of quite distinguished old boys with enormous strings of letters after their names, titles, peerages, etc. I notice that two of us, though quite undistinguished, have addresses in La Jolla. Apparently there is only one more in all of California, a fellow named Gropius, who seems to have had the same address in San Francisco for the past thirty years, and probably went to school sometime during the reign of William IV.

Yours ever,

Ray

TO H. N. SWANSON and EDGAR CARTER

6005 Camino de la Costa
La Jolla, California
Dec. 15th. 1950

Dear Swanie and Eddie:

· · ·

Our little black cat had to be put to sleep yesterday morning. We feel pretty broken up about it. She was almost 20 years old. We saw it coming, of course, but we hoped she might pick up strength. But when she got too weak to stand up and practically stopped eating, there was nothing else to do. They have a wonderful way of doing it now. They inject nembutal into a vein of the foreleg and the animal just isn't there anymore. She falls asleep in two seconds. Then, after a few minutes, just to make certain, they inject it into the heart directly. Pity they can't do it to people. I watched my mother die under morphine and it took almost ten hours. She was

[251]

completely unconscious, of course, but how much better if it took two seconds—if it had to be anyhow.

All the best,

Ray

TO BERNICE BAUMGARTEN

6005 Camino de la Costa
La Jolla, California
December 19, 1950

Dear Bernice:

I have just received a copy of the Italian translation of *The Little Sister* published by Mondadori. I hope you have a copy in your office to glance at. It looks to me like a rotten job. According to the contract, Paragraph 2, the publishers agree to publish a "faithful and accurate Italian translation." My Italian is admittedly very sketchy, but I can spot eight or ten mistakes on the first page—the sort of mistakes which suggest that the translator may know schoolbook English but doesn't know the language I write at all. They appear to be mistakes of understanding. Also, the entire first paragraph of the book is omitted, and there are other omissions in the first chapter. In the cast of characters, for example, I think it's idiotic for them to put down that Mavis Weld is the sister of the Quests. This is something that should not be disclosed until it's disclosed in the story. They have Dr. Lagardie down as a functionary of the police along with the two detectives. This must be a complete misunderstanding. They have Ballou down as a producer instead of an agent. The description of the bluebottle fly is all fouled up; there isn't even an attempt to translate what I wrote. A "bar" is not a drugstore. To say the elevator "functions" is not to say it is free. After the line "Better try the University Club" on page 3 of my book here is what the translator puts instead of what I wrote: "I know that there are a pair of detectives there, but I do not think you would succeed in persuading them to work for you." This, if you please,

[252]

is supposed to be an Italian translation of "I heard they had a couple left over there," (gentlemen, that is) "but I'm not sure they'll let you handle them." At the end of this chapter they put "shut the door" instead of "lock the door." The whole thing is simply ridiculous. And all this in a column and a half on one page. God knows what it's like to go on with it.

I'm sure your agent on the spot, or Heath's agent on the spot, will confirm what I say here about the translation.[1] Most likely the translator did not understand what I wrote. If he did, he made no attempt to render it in Italian. I'm going to send my copy to Jamie Hamilton, whose wife is an Italian, and ask what they think of it. I certainly wouldn't want to have any more to do with this publishing house. There is too little money at stake to make it worthwhile to put up with this sort of thing. As for anything else being at stake, such as literary reputation, it is obvious that a translation of a book of mine into the same sort of Italian as the English used by Wilkie Collins is throwing away everything in it of any stylistic value. If the French can find translators who know the American language and can render it into idiomatic French—and they can and do—I should say that the Italians are capable of the same thing. If Mondadori can't or won't find the people to do it, then I should not have anything to do with Mondadori.

Yours ever,

Ray

TO CARL BRANDT

6005 Camino de la Costa
La Jolla, California
December 21, 1950

Dear Carl:

.   .   .

Your Night Letter just received shows that you are aware of

1. A. M. Heath and Company, Chandler's London agent.

the problem. I don't specifically dislike Ziff or Queen and I don't turn down five or six hundred dollars just to be cute, as you know.[1] What I see in this situation is purely and simply a question of the commercial value of prestige. In the literary market as in Hollywood it seems to me that a man's going price is largely determined by the kind of company he keeps. If you publish in cheap magazines, you are inevitably labelled for the qualities in your writing which coincide with cheap fiction. But it is precisely the qualities which do not belong to cheap fiction, which are overlooked or ignored by magazine and publisher alike, but not by the intelligent public, which finally make your reputation. Knopf did not realize this, neither does Houghton Mifflin, at least for promotion purposes. That is one reason why Jamie Hamilton consistently outsells them; to Jamie Hamilton I am not just a tough writer; I am the best there is in my line and the best there has ever been; I am tough only incidentally; substantially I am an original stylist with a very daring kind of imagination. To Jamie it is ludicrous that the *New York Times* should allow John Dickson Carr to sneer at me for not being able to handle the English language; he knows I can not only handle it in any style but that I am helping to make it. If I write an offbeat story like "Bingo," which admittedly may be good or bad, I do not think it is good business to accept a last chance publication when the better magazines turn it down. When this story comes out in a book, as it will with half a dozen others, I want no credits to pulp magazines on the back of the title page. I don't want the thought slid into the mind of the reviewer or reader that this is pulp material. I want him to take it on its merits as serious writing in a very difficult medium. And I want this, not because I am proud, but because in the long run I believe it pays. I am just as mercenary as you are—or as you pretend to be. It is rather that I have strong feelings about how best to be mercenary.

From now on I am going to write what I want to write as I want to write it. Some of it may flop. There are always going to be people who will say I have lost the pace I had once, that I take too long to say things now, and don't care enough about tight active plots. But I'm not writing for those people now. I'm writing for the people who understand about writing as an art and are able to separate what a man does with words and ideas from what he thinks about

1. Referring to offers to publish his work by Ziff-Davis and the *Ellery Queen* detective story magazine.

Truman or the United Nations. (I have a low opinion of both.) If I feel like writing a fast tough story, I'll write it, but not because there is a market for it and because I've done it before. If I feel like writing a poetic or ironic fantasy, I'll write that. You have to get some fun out of this job and you can't get it by filling orders. You can't get it by forcing yourself to do something you have lost interest in doing. At least I don't think you can. Obviously I don't think very much of even the big magazines, since I never read their fiction. But they pay the kind of money you can't refuse.

.   .   .

Yours ever,

Ray

TO SOMERSET MAUGHAM

6005 Camino de la Costa
La Jolla, California
January 5, 1951

Dear Mr. Maugham:
　　Herewith a few tear sheets of articles about the detective story which I promised to send you and which you are now ready to receive.[1] My file is not as complete as I thought it was, a couple of items apparently having gone astray. One of these was an article by Joseph Wood Krutch, but I find that it is included in a book called *The Art of the Mystery Story* edited by Howard Haycraft, published by Simon & Schuster in 1946. This book, in case you don't know it— and I don't think you do or you would have some of the material you wanted from me—contains a great many articles in various moods about mystery stories. If you have any difficulty in getting a copy, I should be only too glad to lend you mine. But your New York agent can probably dig one up and get it to you much more quickly than I could. If not, please drop me a line.

1. Maugham had asked Chandler for help on his article about detective fiction called "The Decline and Fall of the Detective Story."

I have seen a number of the television films of your stories and, admirable as the material is, I cannot help feeling a dissatisfaction with the way in which it is presented. There is something wrong with this medium as it is now used. For one thing the acting is not casual enough. The emphasis of stage acting (one might even call it over-emphasis) had to be enormously reduced for films, and it seems to me that it must be still further reduced for television. The slightest artifice glares. The feeling of a restricted space is so intense that one almost expects the dialogue to be carried on in whispers as by a couple of people hiding in the clothes closet. The camera work seems to me to be pretty bad, as bad as the camera work in those English films of the '30's of which we see so many on television now. The settings are so poor that one feels it might be better to do without them altogether and play against a back drop. But the worst thing to me is that the actors, instead of interpreting the story and making it come alive, seem to bulk right between the story and the audience. Their physical presence is overpowering. Their slightest motion distracts the eye. It strikes me that good acting is very much like style in a novel. You should not be too conscious of it. Its effect should be peripheral rather than central. But in television you can hardly be conscious of anything else.

With kindest regards,

Yours very truly,

Raymond Chandler

TO HAMISH HAMILTON

6005 Camino de la Costa
La Jolla, California
January 9, 1951

Dear Jamie:

.   .   .

All my life I have had cats and I have found that they differ almost as much as people, and that, like children, they are largely the way

[256]

you treat them except there are a few here and there who cannot be spoiled. But perhaps that is true of children also. Taki had absolute poise, which is a rare quality in animals as well as in human beings. And she had no cruelty, which is a still rarer quality in cats. She caught birds and mice without hurting them, and had no objection whatever to having them taken away from her and released. She even caught a butterfly once. In a group of people she would march straight up to the one cat lover in the room, and she would ignore absolutely the occasional individual who was pronouncedly anti-cat. I have never liked anyone who disliked cats, because I've always found an element of acute selfishness in their dispositions. Admittedly, a cat doesn't give you the kind of affection a dog gives you. A cat never behaves as if you were the only bright spot in an otherwise clouded existence. But this is only another way of saying that a cat is not a sentimentalist, which does not mean that it has no affection.

. . .

Yours ever,

Ray

TO EDGAR CARTER

February 5, 1951

Dear Eddie:

The Picture Post is for people who move their lips when they read. Surely they can get anything they want from my English publisher, Hamish Hamilton, Ltd., 90 Great Russell Street, London, W.C. 1. The questions you quote would seem to me to indicate the intellectual level of the editorial department of the *Picture Post*. Yes, I am exactly like the characters in my books. I am very tough and have been known to break a Vienna roll with my bare hands. I am very handsome, have a powerful physique, and change my shirt regularly every Monday morning. When resting between assignments I live in a French Provincial chateau of Mulholland Drive. It is a fairly small place of forty-eight rooms and fifty-nine baths. I dine off gold plate and prefer to be waited on by naked dancing girls. But

[257]

of course there are times when I have to grow a beard and hole up in a Main Street flophouse, and there are other times when I am, although not by request, entertained in the drunk tank in the city jail. I have friends from all walks of life. Some are highly educated and some talk like Darryl Zanuck.[1] I have fourteen telephones on my desk, including direct lines to New York, London, Paris, Rome, and Santa Rosa. My filing case opens out into a very convenient portable bar, and the bartender, who lives in the bottom drawer, is a midget named Harry Cohn.[2] I am a heavy smoker and according to my mood I smoke tobacco, marijuana, corn silk, and dried tea leaves. I do a great deal of research, especially in the apartments of tall blondes. I get my material in various ways, but my favorite procedure (sometimes known as the Jerry Wald system) consists of going through the desks of other writers after hours.[3] I am thirty-eight years old and have been for the last twenty years. I do not regard myself as a dead shot, but I am a pretty dangerous man with a wet towel. But all in all I think my favorite weapon is a twenty dollar bill. In my spare time I collect elephants.

Yours respectfully,

TO CARL BRANDT

6005 Camino de la Costa
La Jolla, California
February 13, 1951

Dear Carl:

.　　　　　.　　　　　.

I've known a number of these not-quite writers. No doubt you have also. But in your profession you would get away from them as fast as possible; whereas I've known several of them quite well. I have spent time and money on them and it's always wasted, because even if they make an occasional sale it turns out that they have been traveling on somebody else's gas. I guess these are the hardest cases,

1. Head of Twentieth Century-Fox Studio.
2. Head of Columbia Pictures.
3. Of Warner Brothers Studio.

because they want so hard to be professionals that it doesn't take very much encouragement to make them think they are. I knew one who sold a short story (most of which, incidentally, I had written for him) to that semi-slick MacFadden publication that Fulton Oursler used to edit—I forget the name of it.[1] Some cheap outfit bought the picture rights for five hundred bucks and made a very bad B picture with Sally Rand in it. This fellow thereupon got drunk and went around snooting all his writer friends because they were working for the pulps. A couple of years later he sold a short story to a pulp magazine, and I think that is the total of his contribution to literature in a commercial sense. To hear this fellow and his wife discussing and analyzing stories was a revelation in how much it is possible to know about technique without being able to use any. If you have enough talent, you can get by after a fashion without guts; and if you have enough guts, you can also get by, after a fashion, without talent. But you certainly can't get by without either. These not-quite writers are very tragic people and the more intelligent they are, the more tragic, because the step they can't take seems to them such a very small step, which in fact it is. And every successful or fairly successful writer knows, or should know, by what a narrow margin he himself was able to take that step. But if you can't take it, you can't. That's all there is to it.

.   .   .

Yours,

Ray

TO HAMISH HAMILTON

6005 Camino de la Costa
La Jolla, California
February 14, 1951

Dear Jamie:

.   .   .

Priestley descended on me out of the skies yesterday without

---

1. Fulton Oursler (1893–1952) was editor of *Liberty* and vice-president of MacFadden publications.

warning, except a telegram from Guadalajara just before he came, and at a damned inconvenient time, because my wife is not well and unable to entertain him.[1] However I have done the best I could. I drove down to Tijuana and picked him up, a damned long unpleasant drive, if there ever was one, and have installed him in our best hotel since we have no spare room. He is a likable, genial guy; fortunately a great talker, so about all I had to do was click my tongue against my teeth. He was not entirely satisfied with my company, for which I do not at all blame him, and suggested gently as I departed from him late last night at the door of his hotel that tonight possibly we might meet some of the fellows. So this morning I burst into tears and threw myself at the feet of Jonathan Latimer, who knows everybody and likes everybody (whereas I am just the opposite); so tonight I am going to take him over to Latimer's house, where will be gathered a reasonable selection of what passes for intelligent humanity in our city.[2]

.   .   .

Yours ever,

Ray

TO H. F. HOSE

[February 1951]

Dear Hose:

.   .   .

It is most unlikely that I should quarrel with your reading tastes or habits. If I didn't write detective stories, I should probably not read them. And I don't recall offhand that I ever read more than three or four before I began to write them. As you remark, most of them are very badly written and even those which have, at least in an academic sense, a certain purity of style are usually ridiculous in other ways. I agree with you that most contemporary writing is

1. J. B. Priestley, the English novelist.
2. Jonathan Latimer, a mystery writer, also lived in La Jolla.

rubbish. But hasn't that always been true? The situation is no different over here, except that hardly anyone pays much attention to Latin and Greek any more. I think the English writers generally speaking are apt to be much more leisurely and urbane than ours, but these qualities do not seem to carry them very far. I suppose a generation gets the literature it deserves, just as it is said to get the government it deserves.

Most of us become impatient with the messiness that is around us and are inclined to attribute to the past a purity of line which was not apparent to the contemporaries of that past. The past after all has been sifted and strained. The present has not. The literature of the past has survived and it has prestige on that account, apart from its other prestige. The reasons for its survival are complex. The past is our university; it gives us our taste and our habits of thought, and we are resentful when we cannot find a basis for them in the present. It is just possible that they are there just the same. You can't build a Gothic cathedral by assembly line methods; you can't get artistic stone masons from the union. For myself, I am convinced that if there is any virtue in our art, and there may be none at all, it does not lie in its resemblance to something that is now traditional, but which was not traditional when it was first produced. If we have stylists, they are not people like Osbert Sitwell—Edwardians who stayed up too late; nor are they pseudo-poetic dramatists like T. S. Eliot and Christopher Fry; nor bloodless intellectuals who sit just at the edge of the lamplight and dissect everything to nothing in dry little voices that convey little more than the accents of boredom and extreme disillusion. It seems to me that there have been damn few periods in the history of civilization that a man living in one of them could have recognized as definitely great. If you had been a contemporary of Sophocles, I think you might have thought of him almost as highly as you do now. But I think you might have thought Euripides a little vulgar. And if you had been an Elizabethan, I am quite sure you would have thought Shakespeare largely a purveyor of stale plots and over-elaborate rhetoric. I don't know why I'm saying this. I'm not trying to defend anything, and I certainly would not wish to diminish your pleasure in that which gives you pleasure, even if I could.

Yours ever

[261]

TO JAMES SANDOE

6005 Camino de la Costa
La Jolla, California
February 20, 1951

Dear Sandoe:

For once I don't know whether I owe you a letter or you owe me a letter, or whether it is a Mexican stand-off. I am not even sure that I have been polite enough to thank you for sending me that book. I am still a little dizzy from the descent on me of the English novelist, playwright, etc., J. B. Priestley. He cost me a good deal of time and a good deal of money, and I'm not quite sure what I got out of it if anything, except the satisfaction of having been as polite as possible to a friend of my English publisher. He likes my books, says he smiling politely in order to get the subject out of the way and forget it, then he wishes I would write something without murders in it. Now isn't that a typical attitude? You slam murder mysteries a la Edmund Wilson, because they are usually written, you say, by people who can't write well. And the moment you find someone who you are willing to admit can write well, you tell him he should not be writing murder mysteries. Meantime, have you been reading any good trash lately?

I have been having another look at the Adelaide Bartlett case, God knows why.[1] I think one of its most confusing elements is that Sir Edward Clarke's defense was so brilliant in contrast to the rather uninspired defense of Maybrick and Wallace that you are almost fooled into ignoring the facts. But the facts, if you look them straight in the eye, are pretty damning. For example:

Edwin Bartlett died of drinking liquid chloroform. Adelaide, his wife, had liquid chloroform procured for her surreptitiously by Dyson, the clergyman, who, if not actually her lover in a technical sense, was certainly doing some very high-powered necking. Her stated reason for wanting the chloroform is nonsense. Edwin was an

---

1. Adelaide Bartlett was brought to trial at the Central Criminal Court in London in 1886 for murdering her husband. The case was known popularly as the Pimlico Poisoning case.

unattractive and unnecessary husband and was a dope as well. If he died she got Dyson and Edwin's money. Edwin's health was excellent in spite of his constant complaining. It was more than usually good the night before he died. His insomnia seems to have been severe, but is not consistent with his hearty appetite. Morphia and chloral hydrate had both been tried on him without effect. He was obviously a hard person to drug. See about the gas at the dentist's. The wine glass which was found smelled of chloroform behind brandy. The chloroform bottle was not found. According to Adelaide it had been on the mantel earlier. The house was not searched, and Adelaide was not searched. Adelaide had opportunity to hide what remained of the chloroform. She admitted to disposing of it later. There are three principal arguments against her guilt: (1) her nursing care seemed genuine and fairly self-sacrificing; (2) she urged a quick post mortem and herself scouted the chance of his having taken the chloroform himself; (3) the difficulty of poisoning Edwin by this method was enormous according to medical testimony, and there was no previous record of murder by this means. But assuming her guilt, the first argument is meaningless. What else would you expect? How else has any poisoner ever acted? As to the second argument, there is no reason to assume, as the judge did, that she *knew* a delay in the post mortem would be in her favor. How about the theory of "methinks thou dost protest too much"? He didn't die of jugged hare. There was bound to be an investigation. If you know that and if you have murdered him, how best can you look innocent? The way she did. The judge disposed of the third argument. If she murdered him, it was by a method which had one chance in twenty of succeeding. But she didn't know that. To her it may have looked easy.

The insomnia makes me laugh. I have had insomnia—quite severe insomnia. I did not want a big meal of jugged hare. I did not want a supper of oysters and cake. I did not want a haddock for breakfast—a large haddock—so badly that I would have been willing to get up an hour earlier in order to start eating. I think this guy was a neurotic insomniac. That is to say, if he didn't feel as fresh as a daisy in the morning, he said he hadn't slept more than twenty minutes the night before. But if I don't believe his insomnia was severe, I can't believe he would be desperate enough to take the chloroform himself, even though the unpleasantness of it is not a conclusive argument because people used to take castor oil. If you hold your nose, you can swallow almost anything without tasting it. But you do have to believe that this guy was desperate from insomnia and yet had a very fine appetite for his food. It is quite true that the stuff burns. But if you have sniffed enough of it to make you woozy, it might be that your senses would be blunted. Apart from murder, this seems to be the only possiblity. And it is not a very convincing one.

Assuming Adelaide's guilt, her behavior with the bottle must have been entirely to protect Dyson, because if she admits possession of the chloroform, she has to tell how she got it. If she is willing to do that, her best bet is to leave the bottle where it was and stand on the insomnia and Edwin's desperate attempt to overcome it. Dr. Leach, the dope, will certainly back her up. Some of the medical history is in favor of it (but not the jugged hare). It makes a neat little problem all right. If she makes him sniff enough chloroform to put him almost under but not quite, and then gives him a nice fat drink of it in circumstances where he doesn't exactly know what he is drinking, just takes things on trust, then he swallows the chloroform and it kills him. The doctors say that if he had been quite unconscious, he wouldn't have swallowed it, that his swallowing would not be working. But they also seem to think that if he had swallowed it while he was conscious, he would have thrown it up. What they really mean is that they would, or you would, or I would. Edwin is a little bit different from us. You can feed anything to Edwin, and all he wants is to get up an hour early the next morning and start eating more. I think the man had a stomach like a goat. I think he could digest sawdust, old tin cans, iron filings, and shoe leather. I think he could drink chloroform just like you and I could drink orange juice. Anyhow, any argument against his being able to retain it in his stomach is nonsense, because he did retain it in his stomach; so the only real argument is against the difficulty of getting it down his throat. And in Edwin's case that doesn't seem to me a very strong argument. He probably thought he was drinking ginger wine.

Yours ever,

R.C.

[264]

TO HAMISH HAMILTON

6005 Camino de la Costa
La Jolla, California
February 27, 1951

Dear Jamie:

.   .   .

    I wouldn't say that I found Priestley tactless, and I certainly
haven't any quarrel with him. He plays the part of the blunt-spoken
Yorkshireman very well. He was very pleasant to me and went
out of his way to be complimentary. He is rugged, energetic,
versatile, and in a way very professional; that is, everything that
comes his way will be material and most of the material will be used
rather quickly and superficially. His social philosophy is a little too
rigid for my taste and a little too much conditioned by the fact that he
finds it impossible to see much good in anyone who has made a lot
of money (except by writing of course), anyone who has a public
school accent or a military bearing, anyone in short who has speech or
mannerisms above the level of the lower middle class. I think this
must be a great handicap to him, because in his world a gentleman of
property is automatically a villain. That's a rather limiting viewpoint,
and I would say that Priestley is a rather limited man, and that his
point of view as a writer does not arise from any artistic perception,
but that his artistic perception, such as it is, is strictly limited by a
point of view he already had. Of course I don't like socialism,
although a modified form of it is inevitable everywhere. I think a
bunch of bureaucrats can abuse the power of money just as ruthlessly
as a bunch of Wall Street bankers, and far less competently. Socialism
so far has existed largely on the fat of the class it is trying to
impoverish. What happens when the fat is all used up? What happens
when economic prosperity depends on the profits of industries run by
bureaucrats, and when those industries don't show a profit but more
likely a deficit? What happens when what Roosevelt called the
"wukkahs" find out that there's no one left to pay for their luxuries
but themselves and that they're paying the kind of income taxes the

[265]

rich used to pay? Well, I don't know and I don't think Priestley knows.

.   .   .

Yours ever,

Ray

TO JAMES SANDOE

6005 Camino de la Costa
La Jolla, California
March 6, 1951

Dear Sandoe:

.   .   .

I don't know whether you have a television set, or whether having one you could have seen films of the Kefauver committee hearings.[1] I saw part of those held in Los Angeles and found them fascinating. Obviously nothing that a mystery writer could dream up could be more fantastic than what actually goes on in the hoodlum empire which infests this country. Kefauver himself is worth the price of admission any day—a big powerful guy with absolute poise of manner and unfailing politeness to the witnesses, no trace of Southern accent whatever. He was hardly ever even sarcastic. Nevertheless, he made these racketeer witnesses very nervous, much more nervous I think than if he had been really tough with them. Even when he produced a piece of documentary evidence which made nonsense of what they had been saying, he didn't do it with any air of pouncing but in an offhand, casual manner as if it didn't really matter what they said, because it had all been decided somewhere else what was going to happen to them. I hope it has, although it is pretty obvious that under our present laws only income tax evasion could ever really be proved against these fellows. There was one fascinating little session in which an ex-sheriff of San Bernardino county described

1. Senator Estes Kefauver (Democrat of Tennessee) was chairman of a Senate committee investigating the influence of organized crime.

[266]

a visit to Big Bear Lake up in the mountains, where he heard two women mourning over some gambling losses their husbands had sustained locally and he found out where the gambling house was and went there. He said there were about a hundred and fifty people in the place, two roulette wheels were operating, at least one crap table, and numerous slot machines. He circulated around, determined who the managers and gamblers were, then talked to them and found out that the house was owned by a man named Gentry, who was the foreman of the grand jury. He then arrested all the gamblers, confiscated all the gambling equipment apparently with no opposition at all, although he was alone and not young, took the gamblers down to the justice of the peace, where they pleaded guilty and paid fines. Thereafter he was approached by emissaries of Mr. Gentry offering him money to get the gambling equipment back. Kefauver then put Mr. Gentry on the stand, the former foreman of the grand jury. Mr. Gentry said: (a) that he had never owned any gambling equipment and therefore had never sent anybody to try and buy it back from the sheriff; (b) that he had never owned this house in Big Bear Valley, although he had once had a twenty-six hundred dollar mortgage on it; (c) that he had never lived in it; (d) that the house consisted of a rather small living room, a bedroom, a small kitchen and a bathroom, and that if you could get fifteen people into it, the walls would bulge. Senator Kefauver smiled politely, thanked him, and left it at that.

Yours ever,

Raymond Chandler

TO HAMISH HAMILTON

6005 Camino de la Costa
La Jolla, California
March 19, 1951

Dear Jamie:

.   .   .

I had a friendly note from Priestley, flawlessly typed on Gracie Fields' stationery.[1] I hear she is giving up California and going to live in Capri. She seems to feel about Los Angeles very much as I do: that it has become a grotesque and impossible place for a human being to live in. Priestley left me with one uncomfortable and probably exaggerated idea, but it is one in which he seems to believe implicitly. He thinks the entertainment world in England and the literary world for that matter, at least from the critical side (stage, films, radios, television, reviewing, etc.) is completely dominated by homosexuals, and that a good fifty per cent of the people active in these things are homosexuals; including, he says, practically all the literary crtitics. . . . He also mentioned several rather distinguished writers as pansies, whom I had never thought of in that way. And when I said, "Well, if there are so many of them, why doesn't somebody write a really good novel about it?" he mentioned the name of a *very* distinguished novelist, a notorious case according to him, and said that he had retired from publication for several years and written a long novel about homosexualism from the inside by an expert, but that nobody would publish it. Well, well. These are dangerous thoughts to implant in a young and impressionable mind like mine. Now, every time I read one of these flossy and perceptive book reviewers, I say to myself, "Well, is he, or isn't he?" And by God, about three-quarters of the time I am beginning to think he is. *The Saturday Review of Literature* published an article a couple of weeks ago about twelve new and presumably promising novelists of 1950, together with their photographs. There were only three whom, on their physiognomy, I would definitely pass as male. From now on I'll be looking for them under the bed like an old maid looking for burglars. Maybe I ought to try an article for *The Atlantic* on the subject. I could call it, "You Too Could Be A Pansy"; or perhaps simply, "Homo Sapiens."

.   .   .

Yours ever,

Ray

1. English comedienne and motion picture actress.

TO BERNICE BAUMGARTEN

[April 1951]

Dear Bernice:
        Your reaction to Eric Ambler's book is extremely interesting
to me, because of your great professional gift for judging a piece
of writing within a narrow context, and yet not losing sight of the
fact that that narrow context is far from all there is.[1] It would seem to
me that Ambler has fallen between two stools and that he has
succumbed to a danger which afflicts all intellectuals who attempt to
deal with thriller material. I know I have to fight it all the time.
It is no easy trick to keep your characters and your story operating on
a level which is understandable to the semi-literate public and at the
same time give them some intellectual and artistic overtones which
that public does not seek or demand or in effect recognize, but which
somehow subconsciously it accepts and likes. My theory has always
been that the public will accept style provided you do not call it style
either in words or by, as it were, standing off and admiring it. There
seems to me to be a vast difference between writing down to the
public (something which always flops in the end) and doing what you
want to do in a form which the public has learned to accept. It's
not so much that Ambler let himself get too intellectual in this story
as that he let it become apparent that he was being intellectual. That
seems to be the fatal mistake, although I myself liked the book, just as
I did not particularly like Helen MacInness' book *Neither Five nor
Three*. She offends me by dealing with very complicated issues in a
sort of half-baked manner like a school girl analyzing Proust. You
can't laugh Communism off just as a dirty conspiracy. You have to
justify its intellectual appeal to some very brilliant minds and destroy
it nevertheless. I guess the lucky writers are those who can outwrite
their readers without out thinking them.

1. *Judgment on Deltchev.*

TO D. J. IBBERSON[1]

April 19, 1951

Dear Mr. Ibberson:

It is very kind of you to take such an interest in the facts of Philip Marlowe's life. The date of his birth is uncertain. I think he said somewhere that he was thirty-eight years old, but that was quite awhile ago and he is no older today. This is just something you will have to face. He was not born in a Midwestern town but in a small California town called Santa Rosa, which your map will show you to be about fifty miles north of San Francisco. Santa Rosa is famous as the home of Luther Burbank, a fruit and vegetable horticulturist, once of considerable renown. It is perhaps less widely known as the background of Hitchcock's picture *Shadow of a Doubt*, most of which was shot right in Santa Rosa. Marlowe has never spoken of his parents, and apparently he has no living relatives. This could be remedied if necessary. He had a couple of years of college, either at the University of Oregon at Eugene, or Oregon State University at Corvallis, Oregon. I don't know why he came to Southern California, except that eventually most people do, although not all of them remain. He seems to have had some experience as an investigator for an insurance company and later as investigator for the district attorney of Los Angeles county. This would not necessarily make him a police officer nor give him the right to make an arrest. The circumstances in which he lost that job are well known to me but I cannot be very specific about them. You'll have to be satisfied with the information that he got a little too efficient at a time and in a place where efficiency was the last thing desired by the persons in charge. He is slightly over six feet tall and weighs about thirteen stone eight. He has dark brown hair, brown eyes, and the expression "passably good looking" would not satisfy him in the least. I don't think he looks tough. He can be tough. If I had ever had an opportunity of selecting the movie actor who could best represent him to my mind, I think it would have been Cary Grant. I think he dresses as well as can be expected. Obviously he hasn't very much

1. An English correspondent.

money to spend on clothes, or on anything else for that matter. The horn-rimmed sunglasses do not make him distinctive. Practically everyone in Southern California wears sunglasses at some time or other. When you say he wears 'pyjamas' even in summer, I don't know what you mean. Who doesn't? Were you under the impression that he wore a nightshirt? Or did you mean that he might sleep raw in hot weather? The last is possible, although our weather here is very seldom hot at night. You are quite right about his smoking habits, although I don't think he insists on Camels. Almost any sort of cigarette will satisfy him. The use of cigarette cases is not as common here as in England. He definitely does not use bookmatches which are always safety matches. He uses either large wooden matches, which we call kitchen matches, or a smaller match of the same type which comes in small boxes and can be struck anywhere, including on the thumbnail if the weather is dry enough. In the desert or in the mountains it is quite easy to strike a match on your thumbnail, but the humidity around Los Angeles is pretty high. Marlowe's drinking habits are much as you state. I don't think he prefers rye to bourbon, however, He will drink practically anything that is not sweet. Certain drinks, such as Pink Ladies, Honolulu cocktails and crème de menthe highballs, he would regard as an insult. Yes, he makes good coffee. Anyone can make good coffee in this country, although it seems quite impossible in England. He takes cream, and sugar with his coffee, not milk. He will also drink it black without sugar. He cooks his own breakfast, which is a simple matter, but not any other meal. He is a late riser by inclination, but occasionally an early riser by necessity. Aren't we all? I would not say that his chess comes up to tournament standard. I don't know where he got the little paper-bound book of tournament games published in Leipzig, but he likes it because he prefers the continental method of designating the squares on the chess board. Nor do I know that he is something of a card player. This has slipped my mind. What do you mean he is "moderately fond of animals"? If you live in an apartment house, moderately is about as fond of them as you can get. It seems to me that you have an inclination to interpret any chance remark as an indication of a fixed taste. As to his interest in women as "frankly carnal", these are your words, not mine.

.   .   .

[271]

Marlowe cannot recognize a Bryn Mawr accent, because there is no such thing. All he implies by that expression is a toplofty way of speaking. I doubt very much that he can tell genuine old furniture from fakes. And I also beg leave to doubt that many experts can do it either, if the fakes are good enough. I pass the Edwardian furniture and pre-Raphaelite art. I just don't recall where you get your facts. I would not say that Marlowe's knowledge of perfume stops at Chanel Number 5. That again is merely a symbol of someting that is expensive and at the same time reasonably restrained. He likes all the slightly acrid perfumes, but not the cloying or overspiced type. He is, as you may have noticed, a slightly acrid person. Of course he knows what the Sorbonne is, and he also knows where it is. Of course he knows the difference between a tango and a rumba, and also between a conga and a samba, and he knows the difference between a samba and a mamba, although he does not believe that the mamba can overtake a galloping horse. I doubt if he knows the new dance called a mambo, because it seems to be only recently discovered or developed.

Now let's see, how far does that take us? Fairly regular film-goer, you say, dislikes musicals. Check. May be an admirer of Orson Welles. Possibly, especially when Orson is directed by someone other than himself. Marlowe's reading habits and musical tastes are just as much a mystery to me as they are to you, and if I tried to improvise, I'm afraid I would get him confused with my own tastes. If you ask me why he is a private detective, I can't answer you. Obviously there are times when he wishes he were not, just as there are times when I would rather be almost anything than a writer. The private detective of fiction is a fantastic creation who acts and speaks like a real man. He can be completely realistic in every sense but one, that one sense being that in life as we know it such a man would not be a private detective. The things which happen to him might still happen to him, but they would happen as the result of a peculiar set of chances. By making him a private detective, you skip the necessity for justifying his adventures.

Where he lives: in *The Big Sleep* and some earlier stories he apparently lived in a single apartment with a pull-down bed, a bed that folds up into the wall and it has a mirror on the under side of it. Then he moved into an apartment similar to that occupied by a character named Joe Brody in *The Big Sleep*. It may have been the same apartment, he may have got it cheap because a murder had taken place in it. I think, but I'm not sure, that this apartment is on the fourth floor. It contains a living room which you enter directly from the hallway, and opposite are French windows opening on an ornamental balcony, which is just something to look at, certainly not anything to sit out on. Against the right-hand wall as you stand in the doorway is a davenport. In the left-hand wall, nearest to the hallway of the apartment house, there is a door that leads to an interior hall. Beyond that, against the left-hand wall, there is this oak drop leaf desk, an easy chair, etc; beyond that, an archway entrance to the dinette and kitchen. The dinette, as known in American apartment houses or at any rate in California apartment houses, is simply a space divided off from the kitchen proper by an archway or a built-in china closet. It would be very small, and the kitchen would also be very small. As you enter the hallway from the living room (the interior hallway) you would come on your right to the bathroom door and continuing straight on you would come to the bedroom. The bedroom would contain a walk-in closet. The bathroom in a building of this type would contain a shower in the tub and a shower curtain. None of the rooms is very large. The rent of the apartment, furnished, would have been about sixty dollars a month when Marlowe moved into it. God knows what it would be now. I shudder to think. I should guess not less than ninety dollars a month, probably more.

As to Marlowe's office, I'll have to take another look at it sometime to refresh my memory. It seems to me it's on the sixth floor in a building which faces north, and that his office window faces east. But I'm not certain about this. As you say, there is a reception room which is a half-office, perhaps half the space of a corner office, converted into two reception rooms with separate entrances and communicating doors right and left respectively. Marlowe has a private office which communicates with his reception room, and there is a connection which causes a buzzer to ring in his private office when the door of the reception room is opened. But this buzzer can be switched off by a toggle switch. He has not, and never has had, a secretary. He could very easily subscribe to a telephone answering service, but I don't recall mentioning that anywhere. And I do not recall that his desk has a glass top, but I may have said so. The office bottle is kept in the filing drawer of the desk,—a drawer, standard in American office desks (perhaps also in England) which is the depth of two ordinary drawers, and is intended to contain file folders, but very seldom does, since most people keep their file folders in filing cases. It seems to me that some of these details flit about a good deal. His guns have also been rather various. He started out with a German Luger automatic pistol. He seems to have had Colt automatics of various calibers, but not larger than .38, and when last I heard he has a Smith & Wesson .38 special, probably with a four-inch barrel. This is a very powerful gun, although not the most powerful made, and has the advantage over an automatic of using a lead cartridge. It will not jam or discharge accidentally, even if dropped on a hard surface, and is probably just as effective a weapon at short range as a .45 caliber automatic. It would be better with a six-inch barrel, but that would make it much more awkward to carry. Even a four-inch barrel is not too convenient, and the detective branch of the police usually carries a gun with only a two and a half-inch barrel. This is about all I have for you now, but if there is anything else you want to know, please write to me again. The trouble is, you really seem to know a good deal more about Philip Marlowe than I do, and perhaps I shall have to ask you questions instead of your asking me.

With kindest regards,

Yours ever,

TO JUANITA MESSICK

[Easter week-end 1951]

Memo to J.M.

Office will be closed Thursday and Friday. On Friday you should go to church for three hours. On Thursday you will have to be guided by your conscience, if any. Leona[1] won't be here from Wednesday night until the following Monday but she doesn't get paid this time. Some damn nonsense about the child getting married. I suppose the nuns have told her she is to become the bride of Christ. Do Catholics get confirmed at the age of 8? I thought you had to

1. Leona was the maid.

have some idea what it was all about. I was confirmed by the Bishop of Worcester. He had a beard.

RC

TO JUANITA MESSICK

n.d. [1951]

This is a completely useless uncommercial story but I had fun writing it and you may as well copy it off and I'll annoy Carl Brandt with it.[1] It might make the *New Yorker* or one of the monthlies.

I estimate it runs about 6000 words. Make three carbons, please.

RC

TO SOL SIEGEL

April 27, 1951

Dear Sol:

.   .   .

I'd like to submit a couple of thoughts to you, although they are probably both present in your mind already. The first is that there are basically two kinds of screen writers that the industry can use (leaving out the hacks). There are the adept technicians, who know how to work with the medium and how to subordinate themselves to the use of the camera and the actors by the director. Their work is polished, effective, and entirely anonymous. Nothing they do bears any stamp of individuality. Then there is the writer whose personal touch must be allowed to come through, because his personal touch is what makes him a writer. Obviously a writer of this kind should never

1. "A Couple of Writers."

[275]

work for a director like Hitchock, because there must be nothing in a Hitchcock picture which Hitchcock himself might not have written. It is not merely a question of how Hitchcock uses his camera and his actors; the point is that there must be nothing in his pictures which is outside of his range. Eventually there will be a type of director who realizes that what is said and how it is said is more important than shooting it upside down through a glass of champagne.

The second thought I would like to express is that the public is getting increasingly tired of the kind of film which explores the technical resources of the medium with relentless cleverness, but contains nothing which could be acted out on a bare stage and still make its effect. There was a time when all the tricks were interesting in themselves, just as there was a time when the mere fact of movement was fascinating. The chase through the sewers or up the steel girders of a bridge or in the depths of Boulder Dam or what have you, all this is getting old hat. What remains is characters and their relationships to one another and what they have to say. And you will never get this from the technicians. There is a fade in *Sunset Boulevard* where the camera moves in close on a window, and then a hand reaches up and pulls the blind down over the window and the blind fills the screen and is dark, and that is the fade out. To the people in the business that's a clever fade. To the public it means absolutely nothing. What they want to know is what's going to happen next. And the only camera angle they care a nickel about is that which lets them see what's going on without fuss or calling attention to itself. Writers—whatever they cost, however much they are overpaid—are still the cheapest element in picture making. But of course it is not the business of story editors to admit that.

Best of luck and kindest regards.

TO SOMERSET MAUGHAM

6005 Camino de la Costa
La Jolla, California
May 4, 1951

Dear Somerset Maugham:

[276]

Thank you for returning the material about detective fiction. By all means use any quotes from my stuff you find useful. But I think most of it has already been quoted all over the place.

Priestley was in La Jolla a couple of months ago, and was kind enough to tell me that I wrote well and that I should write a straight novel. Of course I have heard this before in other connections. If you write well, you should not be writing a mystery. Mysteries should only be written by people who can't write. I regard this as vicious propaganda from the Edmund Wilson crowd. Obviously you can't expect detective fiction to be anything but sub-literary, to use Edmund Wilson's word, if you insist on weeding out from that field anyone who shows any pretensions to skill or imagination in the use of words.

With kindest regards,

Yours,

Raymond Chandler

TO HAMISH HAMILTON

6005 Camino de la Costa
La Jolla, California
May 9, 1951

Dear Jamie:

.　　　　.　　　　.　　　　'

I suppose you have been hearing a lot about the big fuss over MacArthur.[1] In some ways he reminds me of a story I used to hear in Hollywood about Cecil B. DeMille. It seems that DeMille died and went up to heaven and St. Peter met him at the gates with a beaming smile and outstretched hand. "I can't tell you how glad we are to see you up here, Mr. DeMille," said St. Peter. "Your organizing ability has been admired by us for a very long time, and I think you

1. General MacArthur had recently been relieved of his Korean War command by President Truman.

will find heaven just the field your talents can do the most with. We really do need a bit of reorganizing after all this time." "Well, I'll be delighted," DeMille says to St. Peter, "and I'll get to work right away. You can expect a detailed report from me within a few weeks. I'm a very fast worker when I'm interested, but I warn you I'm also very meticulous." "Just what we want," says St. Peter. So DeMille goes to work and about six weeks later he seeks out St. Peter. He is carrying under his arm, neatly bound in a blue cover, a thorough analysis of conditions in heaven and a blueprint of a proposed reorganization. St. Peter is delighted, takes the report and promises to read it that very night. The next morning he seeks DeMille out. "This is wonderful, Mr. DeMille. Wonderful," he says enthusiastically. "Such a gift for analysis. Such clear thinking. And such a wonderful talent for design." DeMille is very pleased. St. Peter adds in a slightly altered voice, "But there's just one small thing, Mr. DeMille, just one small thing. I don't really think God is going to like being vice-president."

.   .   .

Yours ever,

Ray

TO H. R. HARWOOD[1]

July 2, 1951

Dear Mr. Harwood:

I could not advise any man either to become a writer or not to become one. Contrary to popular belief, it is a very arduous profession and only a small fraction of those who attempt it ever succeed in making any kind of a decent income. The decline of the pulp magazines makes it more difficult for beginners even than it used to be, and it was never anything but difficult. I gather, however, that your special circumstances are such that this writing trade is

1. A correspondent from Missouri.

[278]

physically within your means, and I am hoping that you do not have to make a living out of writing at least for a long time to come, since the chances that you will are very, very slight. You say you are arranging "for immediate schooling in the fundamental principles of the narrative technique that any beginner should have." Let me warn you out of such experience as I have that any writer who cannot teach himself cannot be taught by others, and apart from the extension courses of reputable universities, I take a very dim view of writing instruction in general, above all the sort that is advertised in the so-called writers' magazines. They will teach you nothing that you cannot find out by studying and analyzing the published work of other writers. Analyze and imitate; no other school is necessary. I admit that criticism from others is helpful and sometimes even necessary, but when you have to pay for it, it is usually suspect. Since you are a grown man, you ought to be able to figure out why.

As to methods of plotting and plot outlines, I am afraid I cannot help you at all, since I have never plotted anything on paper. I do my plotting in my head as I go along, and usually I do it wrong and have to do it all over again. I know there are writers who plot their stories in great detail before they begin to write them, but I am not one of that group. With me plots are not made; they grow. And if they refuse to grow, you throw the stuff away and start over again. Perhaps you will get more helpful advice from someone who works for a blueprint. I hope so.

Yours sincerely,

TO CHARLES MORTON

6005 Camino de la Costa
La Jolla, California
July 5, 1951

Dear Charlie:

.   .   .

Now as to this business of pre-publication plugs on book

jackets, where do you get this bittersweet stuff? I wasn't writing to you but to a man named Dana at Lippincott's.[1] Evidently somebody with an important name dropped dead or got jailed for mopery at the last moment, so he had to root around in the weeds for a substitute; so I just had a little fun with him, meaning no harm to anyone. Secretly of course I was delighted that he hit me when I didn't have time to think, because I hate the whole lousy racket. The proper time to praise a writer is after his book has been published, and the proper place to praise him is in something else that is published. You must be well aware that there is practically a stable of puff merchants back in your territory who will go on record over practically anything including the World Almanac, provided they get their names featured. A few names occur with such monotonous regularity that only the fact of their known success as writers keeps one from thinking this is the way they earn their groceries. As a matter of fact I know that payment is sometimes made, because my Hollywood agent once called me up from New York and carefully propositioned me on the subject. My personal reaction to complimentary remarks on dust jackets, other than those quoted from reviews, is to refuse to have anything to do with the book enclosed in the jacket. But that's only personal, and of course I don't claim to be the most amiable character in the world. Over in England they carry this quote business, though not pre-publication so much, to the point where it is absolutely meaningless. The currency of praise has been so depreciated that there is nothing to say about a really good book. It has all been said already about the second, third, and fourth rate stuff which appears, circulates briefly, and then is forgotten. Anyhow if some thing comes along that you feel a sort of moral compulsion to praise to all the world if you have the opportunity, are you going to do it through the medium of a promotion department? I should hope to kiss a duck you're not.

.   .   .

Yours always,

Ray

1. Chandler had written Morton's publisher a somewhat begrudging blurb for his latest book.

TO LEROY WRIGHT

6005 Camino de la Costa
La Jolla, California
July 6, 1951

Dear Leroy:

Referring again to the 1945 income tax refund claim recently disallowed, I have dug up some 1939 diary entries which have a bearing on the case. I have no good explanation as to why I did not dig them up before, except that I seem somehow to have derived the impression that since the book *The Lady in the Lake* was published in 1943, we were only concerned with the two years prior to that, that is to say an attempt to establish that during the three years ending with 1943 I was working on the book.

.   .   .

Now the novel *The Lady in the Lake* was based on two novelettes called "Bay City Blues," published in June, 1938, and *The Lady in the Lake*, published January 1939. But in order to demonstrate method, I think it might be necessary to go beyond this. *The Big Sleep* was written in the spring of 1938 and was based on two novelettes called "Killer in the Rain," published January, 1935, and "The Curtain," published September, 1936. Included in this book also was a fairly long sequence taken from a novelette called "The Man who Liked Dogs," published March, 1936. *Farewell, My Lovely* was based on two novelettes called "Try the Girl," published January, 1937, and "Mandarin's Jade," published November, 1937. In the early part of 1939, that is to say up to April 12, I seem except for fumbling around with plots to have been writing novelettes and short stories. There is evidence of about four of them, not involved in this case, being written or partly written in that time. On April 12 I have an entry "Page 10—'The Girl from Brunette's'" with a question mark after it. This is evidently *Farewell, My Lovely*, because almost immediately the title was changed to "The Girl from Florian's" on April 18, when I'd reached page 52. Florian's is the Negro dive on Central Avenue involved in the beginning of the book. There is on March 31 an entry called "Page 14—'Law is Where You Buy It.'"

[281]

That apparently died right there and frankly I'm not sure what it refers to, since later in the year in the diary there is some evidence that I switched the titles around and applied this particular title to more than one book, although the idea of the title evidently derives from the story "Bay City Blues." That is a story which happens in a town so corrupt from the law enforcement point of view that the law is where you buy it and what you pay for it. To resume, on April 23 I am at page 100 with the notation "First lap—'The Girl From Florian's.'" On April 29 I am at page 127 and there is a reference to a girl named Anne Riordan who appears as a character in *Farewell, My Lovely*. This sort of thing goes on intermittently to May 22, when I'm at page 233, with a notation, "This story is a flop. It smells to high heaven. Think I'll have to scrap it and try something new." After that for several days I seem to have been toying with a story called "Tony Gets Out." I think this eventually developed into the short story called "I'll Be Waiting." On May 29 there is a notation "Tomorrow get out draft of 'The Girl From Florian's.'" On May 30 I evidently did this because I am checking the draft up to page 87, but that's as far as it goes. I didn't like it. Now come the entries, although this foregoing explanation is going to be necessary later on. On June 1, "Page 4—'Murder Is a Nuisance.'" This in itself means nothing except there is a mention of a character named Adrian Fromsett who is a character in *The Lady in the Lake* book and nowhere else. Next day, June 2, I'm at page 10 and I'm calling it *The Lady in the Lake*. This apparently died on me, because on June 5 I wrote 18 pages of a novelette called "Goldfish," but immediately dropped that for the time being. There are many notations that show that I didn't feel well. On June 12 I'm up to page 30; June 13, page 50; June 14, Page 60, and here is a notation "Leave photo of Fromsett," which seems to indicate what I am writing; June 15, page 71; June 16, page 127; June 17, page 148; June 18, page 169; June 19, page 191, and the damned thing is now called "The Golden Anklet." Now this ties it clearly to *The Lady in the Lake* because on the chapter headings of *The Lady in the Lake* novelette, inserted by the magazine editor, (I never used chapter headings myself) was "The Golden Anklet," and a golden anklet does figure in the story. June 20 I am at page 203, I'm now calling it "Deep and Dark Waters." That title is self explanatory. On June 28 I'm up to page

[282]

337. On June 29 there is this notation, "Tragic realization that there is another dead cat under the house. More than three-quarters done and no good." This certainly refers to the draft of *The Lady in the Lake* by whatever provisional title I might happen to have been calling it at the time. Now I write on half sheets of paper, turned endwise, and they figure out about six to a thousand words. Therefore 337 of these pages would make about 55,000 words of rough script, which is a very substantial hunk even though all done within a month.

. . .

The year 1940, partly from reasons of health and still more from the state of the world, seems to have contained an abnormal amount of vacillation. By the end of November I had made less real progress than I sometimes would make in a week. I also puttered with at least three other stories, only one of which was ever finished. The end of the year finds me having written 157 pages of the novelette "No Crime in the Mountains." I bring all these matters up just to show that I never worked on just one thing at a time for very long. *But* eventually somehow I would finish practically all these projects, no matter how long it took nor how many things I did in the meantime.

. . .

Mostly, but not without interruption, I worked on *The Lady in the Lake* for the rest of that year 1942, but not until April 4, 1943, is there any indication that I finished it. From the foregoing it is clear that from 1929, specifically the month of June, to April, 1943, I had this story in hand and worked on it intermittently, except possibly in 1940. It may be that I did no work on it in 1940. However, I certainly did do work on it in 1939, 1941, 1942, and 1943, and it seems almost certain that during the year 1940 I at least took it out and looked at it and thought about it. On the evidence of these entries and taking into account the method of work—a very bad method one must admit—although in my case it has proved successful—the job of writing the book *The Lady in the Lake* was definitely in hand from 1939 to 1943, that a very substantial amount of writing was done on it as early as 1939 (excluding the novelettes entirely), and that insofar

[283]

as the denial of the refund claim was based on lack of proof of facts, this deficiency can now be repaired.

. . .

Yours very truly,

Ray

TO FREDERIC DANNAY

July 10, 1951

Dear Frederic Dannay:

No, I would not care to nominate the ten best living detective-story writers. I don't mind sticking my neck out, but the point is, one has to agree on a few fundamentals before one starts picking lists of ten bests. For instance, does the category include writers of suspense stories in which there is little mystery, or none at all? If it does not, you eliminate some of the best performers, such as Elisabeth Sanxay Holding, certainly one of my favorites. And if it does, why call them detective stories? Charlotte Armstrong's *Mischief* contains no puzzle element whatever. On the other hand, some puzzle merchants, the people who have timetables and ground plans and pay the most meticulous attention to details, can't write a lick. There is a saying that a good plot will make a good detective story, but I personally question whether you can have a good plot if you can't create any believable characters or situations. My list, if I made it, would probably leave out some of those names which will inevitably appear on your ten best list. I just don't think they're any good, because by my standards they can't write. And it may also happen that single book, such as *The 31st of February* by Julian Symons, or *Walk the Dark Streets* by William Krasner, or the aforesaid *Mischief*, or *Mr. Bowling Buys a Newspaper* by Donald Henderson, will immediately put the writer above and beyond a whole host of writers who have written twenty or thirty books and are extremely well known and

[284]

successful, and from a literary point of view entirely negligible. I
don't particularly care for the hard-boiled babies, because most of
them are traveling on borrowed gas, and I don't think you have any
right to do that unless you can travel a little farther than the man
from whom you borrowed the gas. I don't care about the had-I-but-
known girls, because I don't care whether dear little Lucille gets
her neck stretched or not. But that's not quite honest. If I had a
choice, I'd prefer that she did get it stretched. I don't care for the
week-end chichi either here or in England. I don't seem to care who
conked Sir Mortimer with the poker, nor why, nor who set the
grandfather's clock twenty minutes slow. How did Frank Fustian
come to be eating fly agaric in the locked room? I couldn't care less. It
isn't that I don't like puzzles, because I like, for example, Austin
Freeman. I like him very much. There is probably not one of his
books that I haven't read at least twice, yet he bores a lot of people
stiff. I even like his Victorian love scenes. And I have liked some very
pedestrian stories, because they were unpretentious and because their
mysteries were rooted in hard facts and not in false motivations
cooked up for the purpose of mystifying a reader. I suppose the
attraction of the pedestrian books is their documentary quality and
this, if at all authentic, is pretty rare, and any attempt to dish it up
with chichi and glamour turns my stomach immediately. I think
you are up against a difficult problem, because I think we may take it
as granted that a mystery fan would rather read a bad mystery than
none at all. You are bound to give some weight to volume of
production, and strictly speaking volume of production means
absolutely nothing. A writer discloses himself on a single page,
sometimes in a single paragraph. An un-writer may fill a whole shelf,
he may achieve fame of a sort and fortune of a sort, he may
occasionally concoct a plot which will make him seem to be a little
better than he really is, but in the end he fades away and is nothing.
All good writers have a touch of magic. And unless we are to agree
with Edmund Wilson that detective fiction is on the sub-literary level,
and I personally do not agree with this, we demand that touch of
magic; at least I do, although I am well aware that the public does
not.

Yours very truly,

[285]

TO JOSEPH HINES[1]

August 13, 1951

Dear Mr. Hines:

Once in awhile I get a special delivery letter. Sometimes they are put into my box, since that is my official address, and sometimes they are delivered to the house. Whoever does this lately seems to have developed a habit of arriving at 7:30 in the morning and trying to batter the front door down, thus arousing my wife from sleep which she badly needs. I don't criticize the man at all, since he is probably impelled by a strong sense of duty. But may I, in all courtesy and friendliness, point out: first, that a special delivery letter is hardly that urgent, as anything really urgent would come by wire or telephone; and second, that there is a mail slot in the side door of our house at ground level, and that simply dropping the letter in that slot would be my idea of a beautiful job accomplished with tact and consideration. If this should prove impossible to accomplish or should be in violation of any postoffice rule, then may I request that special delivery mail be deposited in my box, No. 128, just like any other first-class mail. In my case at least it does not really require the red light and siren treatment. When this house was built the mail slot was put in the side door deliberately so that the mail man would not have to climb any steps. Usually whoever delivers special delivery mail does not know this, so he climbs to the front door, finds no mail slot and is thereby stung to fury.

Yours very sincerely,

TO S. J. PERELMAN

September 4, 1951

Dear Sid:

If you are still interested in Rancho Santa Fe and haven't forgotten all about it by this time, there is no objection there to your keeping tropical birds and a few tropical animals, provided you keep them off the main street and out of the dining room at the

1. Superintendent of the US. Post Office in La Jolla.

[286]

Rancho Santa Fe Inn. Rancho Santa Fe is part of the San Dieguito high school district, the school being located back of Encinitas, which you passed on the Coast Highway not very far north of Del Mar. And there is a school bus from Rancho Santa Fe. I don't know anything about the scholastic standing of this school, if any. I have heard the California high schools range from putrid to rotten, and I have one relative, fortunately distant, who graduated from the Fairfax high school in Los Angeles while still struggling with the alphabet. As to the La Jolla schools, which might be representative of this part of the state, the only authentic comment I have heard is from a party living across the street from my sister-in-law. This party has four children and is thinking of moving back to Kansas where there is a possibility of their being educated. It seems that they all get "A's" out here, although they know nothing and do no work. She regards this as very suspicious, inasmuch as before coming to California they did some work and got nowhere near any "A's" at all. I don't know much about this personally, and I resent the suggestion that we who live in California are cultural imbeciles.

.   .   .

I am still reading your brutal account of your family's efforts to keep you from being certified as a lunatic, and by God there are times when you don't speak of them at all nicely. Needless to say I enjoyed seeing you tremendously, although I realize that the gibbons will always come first.

Yours ever,

TO HAMISH HAMILTON

6005 Camino de la Costa
La Jolla, California
September 19, 1951

Dear Jamie:

.   .   .

I don't know if you have ever been to a dude ranch. I had

[287]

never been to one before. This one is called the Alisal, which in Spanish means a grove of sycamores, according to the publicity. It is a small part of a 10,500 acre cattle ranch, which is one of the few intact Spanish land grants of California and was originally made to the Carrillo family. It has a lovely climate, at least at this time of year. It is situated in an inland valley, the Santa Ynez valley just north of Santa Barbara, and is almost as dry as a desert, very hot in the daytime, very cool in the mornings, in the evenings and at night. I should think it must be pretty awful in the summer. We found the place both very amusing and intensely boring, expensive, badly run but nicely laid out with the usual swimming pool, tennis courts, etc. The kind of place where the people who work in the office wear riding boots, where the lady guests appear for breakfast in levis riveted with copper, for lunch in jodhpurs with gaudy shirts and scarfs and in the evening either in cocktail gowns or in more jodhpurs and more gaudy shirts and scarfs. The ideal scarf seems to be very narrow, not much wider than a boot lace, and run through a ring in front and then hangs down one side of the shirt. I didn't ask why; I didn't get to know anybody well enough. The men also wear gaudy shirts, which they change constantly for other patterns, all except the real horsemen, who wear rather heavy wool or nylon and wool shirts with long sleeves, yoked in the back, the kind of thing that can only be bought in a horsy town. I imagine the place is a lot of fun for the right sort of people, the kind who go riding in the morning, swimming or tennising in the afternoon, then have two or three drinks at the bar, and by the time they arrive for dinner are able to be quite enthusiastic over the rather inferior and much too greasy cooking. For us who were rather tired and out of sorts and consequently much too finicky, the place was a trial. But it was fun to see a whole army of quail strolling unconcernedly past the bungalows in the evening and to see birds that looked like jackdaws, which we never see anywhere else, not even in the mountains. While I was there I read three of the Hornblower novels by C. S. Forester, bound in one large pocketsize book. I had never read any of his stuff before and I don't think I could read it here at home. The detail of the handling of the ships, the maneuvers for battle and all that sort of thing seems to me quite fascinating and wonderfully exact. I don't suppose I had ever before realized the immense amount of skill that goes into the

[288]

handling of a sailing ship. Apart from that the stuff is appallingly dull to my mind. The emotions are about on the level with G. A. Henty.[1] He has no conception of character, and I say this with the full knowledge that Captain Horatio Hornblower is probably thought to be quite an achievement in character drawing. To me he is nothing of the sort. Except for his seamanship Forester never gets above the level of slick magazine writing, which I have always detested. But I know Forester must be a publisher's delight, and I may be a little unfair to him, even in a literary sense. If so, it was probably because I had just read Popski's *Private Army*.[2]

I suppose you have by now seen the *New Yorker's* profile of your boy, John Dickson Carr. They seem to have done him rather well, at least without condescension, very much in the way in which they handled Rex Stout some time ago. He sounds like a fellow for whom one could have a certain remote admiration without much affection. One sentence I found illuminating. After describing his fondness for the macabre and his ingenuity in plot making, the writer said in effect, I can't quote the exact words, "He hates the actual writing." This explains to me in a flash why I can't read the man, because a writer who hates the acutal writing is as impossible as a lawyer who hates the law, or a doctor who hates medicine. Plotting may be a bore even if you are good at it. At least it is something that has to be done so that you can get on with the real business. But a writer who hates the actual writing, who gets no joy out of the creation of magic by words, to me is simply not a writer at all. The actual writing is what you live for. The rest is something you have to get through in order to arrive at the point. How can you hate the actual writing? What is there to hate about it? You might as well say that a man likes to chop wood or clean house and hates the sunshine or the night breeze or the nodding of flowers or the dew on the grass or the songs of birds. How can you hate the magic which makes of a paragraph or a sentence or a line of dialogue or a description something in the nature of a new creation? Well, apparently you

---

1. British author (1832–1902) known for boys' adventure tales.
2. Popski is a pseudonym of Vladimir Peniakoff.

can and be successful in spite of it. But it certainly depresses me to feel that this is possible.

⋅ ⋅ ⋅

With all my best,

Yours ever,

Ray

TO JAMES SANDOE

6005 Camino de la Costa
La Jolla, California
September 25, 1951

Dear Sandoe:

⋅ ⋅ ⋅

I am glad to hear that you are going back to reviewing again, although I don't exactly envy you the job of reading the stuff. I guess my tastes must be changing because I find it very difficult to get any fun out of most of them. I have neither your tolerance nor your catholicity of taste. If the stuff doesn't vibrate, the hell with it. I don't care how ingenious the plot is, it seems to me to mean nothing unless the prose has that glimmer of magic. Well, you can't often expect that. Why should you? And frankly the general run of serious fiction leaves me just as flat, if not flatter. Since I have now arrived at an age where I should normally be a laudator temporis acti, and in fact in most things I am, I am pleased to declare that this does not apply to mystery stories. The good ones are far better than they ever were. They have more atmosphere, more character, more style, more wit, more color, more sense of detail, more background. But the good ones are extremely rare. Many is the time I've come home from the rental library with three or four books and returned them all unread. You are going to have to help me out if you find anything good. If you can't, no one can. Anyhow this is one metier in which the so-called giants of the past look pretty puny to me, and not only

[290]

the giants of the remoter past but the giants of the immediate past. Not long ago I made an effort to reread Dorothy Sayers's *Gaudy Night*. God, what sycophantic drivel. A whole clutch of lady dons at an Oxford college all in a flutter to know about Lord Peter Wimsey and to know about the plot of Harriett Vane's latest mystery story. How silly can you get? And yet this is far from being a silly woman.

    With kindest regards,

Yours ever,

Ray

TO HAMISH HAMILTON

6005 Camino de la Costa
La Jolla, California
October 5th. 1951

Dear Jamie:

       •   •   •

    I do hope to have a book in 1952, I hope very hard. But dammit I have a great deal of trouble getting on with it. The old zest is not there. I am worn down by worry over my wife, and that is why I am writing this myself and keeping no copy. We have a big house, rather, hard to take care of, and the help situation is damn near hopeless. For months after we lost our last cook, Cissy wore herself out trying to get someone, to endure what we got, to give up and start again. We cannot live here without help. Cissy can do very very little, she has lost a lot of ground in the last two years. She is a superb cook herself and we are both pretty much overfastidious, but we can't help it. I have thought that the sensible thing might be to get a small house and do for ourselves, but I'm afraid she is no longer capable even of that. When I get into work I am already tired and dispirited. I wake in the night with dreadful thoughts. Cissy has a constant cough which can only be kept down by drugs and the drugs destroy her vitality. It is not TB nor is it anything cancerous, but

I am afraid it is chronic and may get worse instead of better. She
has no strength and being of a buoyant disposition and a hard fighter,
she fights herself to the point of exhaustion. I dread, and I am sure
she does, although we try not to talk about it, a slow decline into
invalidism. And what happens then I frankly do not know. There are
people who enjoy being invalids, being unable to do anything, but
not she. She hates hospitals, she hates nurses, and she does not greatly
love doctors. In bad moods, which are not too infrequent, I feel the
icy touch of despair. It is no mood in which to produce writing with
any lift and vitality.

   You say nice things about what I write and I know you mean
them, but I have never felt important as a writer. In every generation
there are incomplete writers, people who never seem to get much
of themselves down on paper, men whose accomplishment seems
always rather incidental. Often, but not always, they have begun too
late and have an overdeveloped critical sense. Sometimes they just
lack the necessary ruthlessness and think other people's lives as
important as their own, other people's happiness more essential than
the expression of their own personalities, if any. I guess maybe I
belong in there. I have enough material success to see through it, and
not enough sense of destiny to feel that what I do matters a great deal.

   Don't think I worry about money, because I don't. There are
always ways to make money if you really need it. I rather envy
people who think art and literature worth any sacrifice, but I don't
seem to feel that way. My salute to posterity is a thumb to the end of
the nose and the fingers outspread. Publishers read too many critics,
in the course of business, naturally. And just who are the critics after
all? People of small accomplishment, mostly, whose dignity in life
depends on the perpetuating of a set of artificial values conceived by
other critics who were also people of small accomplishment. My
standards are too high for me to admire the successful hacks very
much, and too unorthodox for me to care what the pundits say. Also,
I have blind spots. I admit it. I think your Nancy Mitford is probably
a charming and clever woman but the stuff means nothing to me. The
wit is not real, the satire is not of the vintage year, the whole
performance tries to be something it is not capable of being. An
absolutely trivial writer, but you don't agree and you shouldn't. This
is strange (that I feel that way) because as a rule I admire the good
second-raters, like Marquand and Irwin Shaw and Herman Wouk, etc.

I like to read them and *while* I read them they seem very good. It is only afterwards that the quality fades. Same for Nicholas Montserrat. Or Priestley. Essentially one good chunk of Flaubert or Hemingway at their best is worth the whole pack of them. I had almost said Faulkner, but I think he is overrated. Well, all this matters nothing, except that a writer to be happy should be a good second-rater, not a starved genius like Laforgue. Not a sad lonely man like Heine, not a lunatic like Dostoevski. He should definitely not be a mystery writer with a touch of magic and a bad feeling about plots.

We still hope for "Europe in the spring," but is it more than hope now? Anyhow, Churchill will be in and I hope he doesn't make an ass of himself. These great men can be awfully silly in their dotage. It doesn't show in the rest of us. Nobody is looking.

I look upon you as a dear friend, Jamie. I am sorry to be such a depressing bore.

Ray

TO MR. INGLIS

[October 1951]

Dear Mr. Inglis:

I practically always answer letters eventually, but in your case I'm afraid the eventually is the key word. Anyhow thank you for yours of July 12th and for taking the trouble to cover so much paper at a time when you had a stiff wrist.

I'm afraid I can't give you much of an argument about your concept of what you call maturity, just as I cannot recall having used the expression or in fact the idea behind the expression in that essay of mine to which you refer. It may be that your "advanced psychology student" friend was pulling your leg a little, or it may be that the advanced psychology itself has got him into a state of confusion in which he will probably remain for the rest of his life. We seem to be somewhat over supplied with psychologists nowadays, but I suppose that is natural enough, since their jargon, tiresome as it is to me personally, seems to have the same attraction for muddled minds that theological hair-splitting had for people of a former age. I don't think my friend Philip Marlowe is very much concerned about whether or no he has a mature mind. I will admit to an equal lack of concern about myself. But it is very natural that you, being what you term a "shabby twenty-three," and having had apparently a fairly hard time of it should be more concerned than I am with what the boys in their sweet lingo call the social orientation of the individual. Don't take it too hard. Very few people are capable of straight thinking on any subject. If being in revolt against a corrupt society constitutes being immature, then Philip Marlowe is extremely immature. If seeing dirt where there is dirt constitutes an inadequate social adjustment, then Philip Marlowe has an inadequate social adjustment. Of course Marlowe is a failure and he knows it. He is a failure because he hasn't any money. A man who without physical handicaps cannot make a decent living is always a failure and usually a moral failure. But a lot of very good men have been failures because their particular talents did not suit their time and place. In the long run I guess we are all failures or we wouldn't have the kind of world we have. But you must remember that Marlowe is not a real person. He is a creature of fantasy. He is in a false position because I have put him there. In real life a man of his type would no more be a private detective than he would be a university don. Your private detective in real life is usually either an ex-policeman with a lot of hard practical experience and the brains of a turtle or else a shabby little hack who runs around trying to find out where people have moved to. It is obvious that the more highly organized police work becomes, the leaner are the pickings left for the private operator. I think I resent your suggestion that Philip Marlowe has contempt for other people's physical weakness. I don't know where you get the idea, and I don't think it's so. I am also a little tired of the numerous suggestions that have been made that he is always full of whiskey. The only point I can see in justification of that is that when he wants a drink he takes it openly and doesn't hesitate to remark on it. I don't know how it is in your part of the country, but compared with the country-club set in my part of the country he is as sober as a deacon. As for your questions, and I hope you kept a copy of them, the answer to Number One is: Yes. I wanted to be a barrister, but I didn't have enough money. The answer to Two is: So far as I know the cops read

[294]

my stories and don't resent them in the least. Question Three: My comments on the film production of my work are that it was probably as good as could be expected. My stories are about a man, and no one can satisfactorily recreate another man's character. I worked on *The Lady in the Lake* myself, although I refused screen credit because I didn't like the final script, but curiously enough I found that in writing the screen play I was almost entirely indifferent to the story I was supposed to be working from, and it was the producer of the picture who kept telling me, and not me him, "Look, stick to the book a little more." Question Four: Practically all the screen work I've done has been for other films. I always use my own name, but you don't always get your name on the picture and you don't always want your name on the picture. I have never been in police business properly speaking, although at one time I worked with a district attorney's investigator on an embezzlement case. It is true that Dashiell Hammett was once a Pinkerton agent, and I certainly owe a good deal to him, which I have admitted very publicly. Yes, I have met him, but I can't say that I'm a friend of his. I only met him once. He had at that time a shocking capacity for liquor, which I am frank to say I envied as I was never much of a drinker myself. Question Eight: You are not annoying me or I would not be writing to you.

Yours very sincerely,

TO CARL BRANDT

6005 Camino de la Costa
La Jolla, California
October 27 1951

Dear Carl:

. . .

I am having a hard time with the book.[1] Have enough paper

---

1. *The Long Goodbye.*

written to make it complete, but must do all over again. I just didn't know where I was going and when I got there I saw that I had come to the wrong place. That's the hell of being the kind of writer who cannot plan anything, but has to make it up as he goes along and then try to make sense out of it. If you gave me the best plot in the world all worked out I could not write it. It would be dead for me. Perhaps a year later I might tackle it, but no sooner.

.   .   .

All the best to you.

Ray

TO JAMES SANDOE

6005 Camino de la Costa
La Jolla, California
October 31, 1951

Dear Sandoe:

.   .   .

I gather that you didn't think much of the Bingo story, and you could be right.[1] But I'm not going to allow myself to worry about it. I think possibly it was a little too grim for a fantastic story and a little too fantastic for a grim story. But when you say why in hell would Joe bother, I don't get the point. Why wouldn't he? Anyhow I had fun writing the story, although it didn't turn out quite the way I expected. I started out to do a burlesque on the locked room mystery and somewhere along the line I lost interest in the burlesque angle and became preoccupied with the thought that a miracle is always a trap. As you know, good fantastic stories are extremely rare, and they are rare for a rather obvious reason, that in them it is almost impossible to turn the corner. Once you have exposed the situation, you have nowhere to go.

.   .   .

1. "Professor Bingo's Snuff."

I don't deny the mystery writer the privilege of making his detective any sort of a person he wants to make him—a poet, philosopher, student of ceramics or Egyptology, or a master of all the sciences like Dr. Thorndike. What I don't seem to cotton to is the affectation of gentility which does not belong to the job and which is in effect a subconscious expression of snobbery, the kind of thing that reached its high-water mark in Dorothy Sayers. Perhaps the trouble is that I'm an English Public School man myself and knew these birds inside out. And the only kind of Public School man who could make a real detective would be the Public School man in revolt, like George Orwell. But if English people and others like this sort of thing, there is no reason why they shouldn't have it.

Dale Warren, one of Houghton Mifflin's editors, writes me that you are doing a fine job for the *Herald Tribune*. And how are all your cats? We have a new black Persian who looks exactly like our last one, so exactly that we have to call him by the same name, Taki. He is going to be a very large fellow I think when he gets his full growth, as he weighs eight pounds at seven months. I had a Siamese kitten for awhile, but he chewed everything to pieces and was so much trouble to handle that I had to give him back to the breeder. I felt rather bad about it, because he was an affectionate little devil and full of life. But he chewed up blankets, chewed up my clothes, and he would have chewed up all the furniture. We just couldn't let him run loose, and a cat who can't run loose in our house has no business in it. We never let them run loose in the street, but in the house they own everything.

Yours ever,

R.C.

TO DALE WARREN

6005 Camino de la Costa
La Jolla, California
November 7, 1951

Dear Dale:

You asked me how anyone can survive Hollywood? Well, I

must say that I personally had a lot of fun there. But how long you can survive depends a great deal on what sort of people you get to work with. You meet a lot of bastards, but they usually have some saving grace. If you are a writer, most of your work is wasted it is true. And when it isn't, somebody else grabs most of the credit. A writer who can get teamed up with a director or producer who will give him a square deal, a really square deal, can get a lot of satisfaction out of his work. Unfortunately that doesn't happen too often. A really creative writer ought to become a director, which means that in addition to being creative he must also be very tough physically and morally. Otherwise by the time he has been kicked around enough to have learned to write a script that can be shot, that is camera-wise and not just writing, he has probably lost all his bounce. If you go to Hollywood just to make money, you have to be pretty cynical about it and not care too much what you do. And if you really believe in the art of the film, it's a long term job and you ought to forget all about any other kind of writing. A preoccupation with words for their own sake is fatal to good film making. It's not what films are for. It's not my cup of tea, but it could have been if I'd started it twenty years earlier. But twenty years earlier of course I never could have got there, and that is true of a great many people. They don't want you until you have made a name, and by the time you have made a name, you have developed some kind of talent which they can't use. All they will do is spoil it, if you let them. The best scenes I ever wrote were practically monosyllabic. And the best short scene I ever wrote, by my own judgment, was one in which a girl said "uh-huh" three times with three different intonations, and that's all there was to it. The hell of good film writing is that the most important part is what is left out. It's left out because the camera and the actors can do it better and quicker, above all quicker. But it had to be there in the beginning.

I should say these thoughts ought to be rambling enough to suit you.

Yours ever,

Ray

[298]

TO JUANITA MESSICK

November 15 [1951]

.　　　　.　　　　.

Messick—I forgot—the Community Chest. This bothers the hell out
of me. I don't feel the slightest desire to contribute to it. I don't
like their method of coming around and handing you a numbered
pledge with your name on it. The organization is not what it was
supposed to be in the beginning, and more and more drives outside
the Community Chest are accumulating. Also, they say openly that
90% of the money collected by the Community Chest goes in one
way or another for the care of children, which seems to me entirely
out of balance. What is the reaction among your friends and
acquaintances to the Community Chest? And what is the cause of this
latent hostility that one meets here and there. I often wonder and I
shall probably end by sending them a token contribution of not more
than $25, but I'd really like to tell them to take the whole thing and
shove it.

TO JUANITA MESSICK[1]

[1951]

We are going to cut out afternoon tea for a while and see how
we manage without it. It often interrupts Cissy in a nap. She doesn't
particularly care about it. Neither do I, and it is one more chore in a
day already overloaded with them so far as I'm concerned. I'm sure
you won't mind making youself a cup with tea bags if you want
it. . . . There seems to be no immediate prospect of our getting our
help. The one we had coming in the morning and in the evening
was a rotten cook, in fact to call her rotten is flattery. So we had to
cut out the evening and that discouraged her and now she won't come
in the morning. . . . There just doesn't seem to be the kind of help
we want, the only kind we can tolerate. And it looks to me as if until
my wife gets better, I'm going to have to do most of the cooking.

1. The ellipses in this communication appear in a transcript made by Dorothy Gardiner.
The original note has disappeared.

I'm a pretty good short order cook. I can cook steak, chops and vegetables far better than the restaurants can . . . and I rather like the idea of learning to be a little more of an accomplished cook, though I prefer to stop short of the elaborate stage. But it's a grind and there's no doubt about that. . . . I get up at 8 o'clock in the morning. . . . It takes me until 10 o'clock to get the two breakfasts and tidy. That gives me until one o'clock to try to do a little writing. That's not very much but it's probably as much as I'm good for the way things are. Then I have to go uptown and market, which doesn't matter because I was never any good at working in the afternoon, even as a schoolboy I was always dead in the afternoon. Then I come back and the minute I'm inside the house, there's this damn tea. . . .

By 5 o'clock, even on the short order basis, I have to get busy in the kitchen preparing the vegetables and so on. Then after dinner there are the dishes. If we had somebody really good to come in the morning, I think I might leave the dinner dishes—stick them down in the dishwasher, something of that sort. But it's almost as much trouble to do that and tidy up and wash off the stove and sink and drainboard as to do the whole job. . . . I've got to face the fact that Cissy hasn't got any stamina. . . . she's never going to get back to where she once was. And I dare say she knows it, although we don't talk about it. There's no sense in our relying on getting good help or on relying on keeping one if you did happen to get a good one. There's always something the matter with them. If they can cook, they're crotchety and spoiled, and very few of them can cook even moderately well. . . . So I guess it's up to this tired character as long as he holds out. Of course these things are not so hard when you get into a routine. You learn not to waste motion and not to do unnecessary things and not to walk your legs off.

TO JUANITA MESSICK

[1951]

JM

.   .   .

The use of present participles to avoid relative clauses should be very cautiously approached. "A man wearing a green hat came up the steps." This is fine because a lot simpler and less cumbrous and doesn't make too much of the green hat. "A man who was wearing a green hat came up the steps." Seems to hit it too hard. It seems that Tidwell's trouble is not poor syntax (what he writes is correct enough) but lack of feeling for the weight of words.[1] A statement as portentous should not be made with such a light and passing construction. It's getting towards a thing like: "De Musset was thirty three years old that day, being guillotined at two in the afternoon." Obviously what is wrong with that is the style, not the grammar. His age is made more important than the fact that he had his head chopped off. I should say—correct me if I am wrong—that this, next to the cliché, is the greatest fault of writing, important enough in its content, which is turned out by scientists, some scholars, and technical writers generally, and is the result of the separation of the Humanities from the special departments of knowledge. Not true of the best, of course. A really first class mind can always express itself. Why do we go on wasting our school years the only years we have in which to learn how to use our brains and minds and tongues? Why? Is it a question of money, of politics in the schools, or are we really intellectually a second-class people? And if so, do we want to be? Do we think it more manly to stumble over simple syntax provided we can reassemble a Ford or throw a football 45 yards?

RC

Why don't I shut up!

TO PAUL McCLUNG[1]

December 11, 1951

Dear Mr. McClung:
    It may be better for me to answer your letter by mail rather

1. This communication arose through Chandler's query to Juanita Messick raised in a newspaper column entitled "Take My Word" by Frank Colby. In this column James Tidwell, a contributor to a publication of the American Dialect Society, was criticized for infelicitous phrasing and misplaced emphasis.

---

1. Of the Dell Publishing Company.

[301]

than wire. The doctor on whose point of view I founded the opinion you quote has been dead for several years. In any case I doubt very much whether he would have appreciated my revealing his identity to a magazine or a newspaper in connection with an opinion which his profession as a group would probably consider defeatist and most improper. I remember his saying to me in effect: "The toughest thing about trying to cure an alcoholic or a user of dope is that you have absolutely nothing to offer him in the long run. He feels awful at the moment no doubt; he feels shamed and humiliated; he would like to be cured if it is not too painful, and sometimes even if it is, and it always is. In a purely physical sense you maybe say he is cured when his withdrawal symptoms have passed, and they can be pretty awful. But we forget pain, and to a certain extent we even forget humiliation. So your alcoholic cured or your former dope addict looks around him, and what has he achieved? A flat landscape through which there is no road more interesting than another. His reward is negative. He doesn't suffer physically, and he is not humiliated or shamed mentally. He is merely damned dull." Obviously such a point of view is inconsistent with the Pollyanna attitude we impose on the medical profession. They know better, but they have to live too, although there are times when in particular cases one doesn't quite see why.

I put my opinion, which you seem to have taken rather seriously, in the mouth of a crook. In times like these only a crook may safely express opinions of this sort. Any medical man of standing would have to add something like: "Of course with proper psychiatric treatment, blah, blah, blah—" He would have to leave you on the up-beat. And by mentioning psychiatry he would, for me at least, instantly destroy the entire effect of any frank statement into which he may have ventured, since I regard psychiatry as fifty per cent bunk, thirty per cent fraud, ten per cent parrot talk, and the remaining ten per cent just a fancy lingo for the common sense we have had for hundreds and perhaps thousands of years, if we ever had the guts to use it.

.   .   .

Yours very truly,

[302]

TO EDGAR CARTER

December 13, 1951

Dear Eddie:

.   .   .

I think a man ought to get drunk at least twice a year just on
principle, so he won't let himself get snotty about it. But I don't seem
to want to. When Priestley was here I threw a party for him at the
Marine Room, the guests being mostly Annie Oakleys invited by Jack
Latimer and his wife, people I had never seen before with one
exception, and have never seen since and don't care if I never see
again. I think I had about eight Scotches that night, which was well
below the average of the participants, but this was purely self-
protection on my part. If I hadn't had them, I would probably have
wanted to call the cops to throw the bastards out. It just goes to
show, but I'm not sure what, because I've forgotten what I was
talking about.

.   .   .

Yours ever,

TO HAMISH HAMILTON

6005 Camino de la Costa
La Jolla, California
December 21, 1951

Dear Jamie:

.   .   .

Well, Christmas with all its ancient horrors is on us again. The
stores are full of fantastic junk and everything you want is out of
stock. People with strained, agonized expressions are poring over

[303]

pieces of distorted glass and pottery, and being waited on, if that is the correct expression, by specially recruited morons on temporary parole from mental institutions, some of whom by determined effort can tell a teapot from a pickaxe.

My love and best wishes to you and yours.

Yours ever,

TO BERNICE BAUMGARTEN

6005 Camino de la Costa
La Jolla, California
December 21, 1951

Dear Bernice:

.   .   .

I finally the other day made it through Irwin Shaw's book, *The Young Lions*. The first time I tried it a couple of years back, I floundered and gave it up. It's a powerful and effective book, and I must say that I thought that most of it was damnably well done. But I do admit to a certain weariness with the sensitive young Jewish boy who gets kicked all over the lot by crude and brutal people. Couldn't we just once have one who does not get into a company of Georgia Crackers with an uncouth C.O., who does not have to get battered to pieces by a half dozen men twice his size in order to prove his manhood, who is not called a kike by anyone, and who does not have to carry the two thousand years of Jewish martyrdom on his shoulders every time he crosses the street?

.   .   .

Yours ever,

Ray

[304]

TO JAMES SANDOE

6005 Camino de la Costa
La Jolla, California
Dec 27 1951

Dear Sandoe:

Many thanks for letter and books. The one on Gertie seemed to me as subtle as all hell, a bit over my head, in fact.[1] Frankly I don't think the old girl was worth the effort but I can see that an English prof who has to dish out a book now and again is wise to champion a cause that is not too lost and not too won. My own views of Gertie come closer to those of Mrs. Porter. She talked a great game, but if she ever cracked ninety, she moved her ball. She has the sort of reputation that depends less on what she did than on what the intellectuals said about her. When I read Eliot's play *The Cocktail Party* I wondered what all the fuss was about. But of course I knew. There are always enough sterile critics looping around hunting for a piece of stale cake they can wrap up in a distinguished name and sell to the host of snob-fakers that infest all semi-literate societies.

.   .   .

Happy New Year

RC

TO CARL BRANDT

6005 Camino de la Costa
La Jolla, California
Dec 27, 1951

Dear Carl:

Secretary on vacation, the typing will be very bad. Excuse

1. By Donald Sutherland, *Gertrude Stein: A Biography of Her Work*, 1951.

[305]

please. So sorry. We had a lousy Christmas, thanks. The cook took sick, and the turkey didn't get cooked, and my wife is either in bed or lying down most of the time, trying to slough an obstinate bronchitis. Swanie sent me a tie for Christmas.[1] It is all covered with Sherlock Holmeses and bloody footprints. I wish Hollywood agents didn't feel they had to give Xmas presents to clients— especially as the presents are a far too accurate register of client's standing. A guy who worked up to a wrist watch and then slid back to a tie knows exactly what his rating is; he ought to be working for Republic. (By the way, do you know anybody dopey enough to wear a tie all covered with S.H.'s and bloody footprints. Be so happy to unload it. I wouldn't wear the thing to a post mortem on an Ozark sharecropper.)

.　　　　.　　　　.

Cheerio,

Ray

TO WILLIAM TOWNEND

January 3, 1952

Dear Bill:

.　　　　.　　　　.

Your publishers are probably quite right to ask you to cut your book. I think we all grow a little more prolix as we grow older. Our memories are so packed with experiences and emotions that all our perceptions are overlaid by a patina of memory. We lose interest in plot which is kindergarten stuff mostly, and we forget that the public has interest in very little else. I hope you will always go on believing that your next book is going to be a big success. Even a hundred thousand words seems to me too long; eighty thousand

1. H. N. Swanson, Chandler's Hollywood agent.

ought to be the limit. Only a very rich writer, rich that is in style and illusion, should go beyond eighty thousand words. As for Priestley's book, *Festival*, I confess that I did not read it nor did I want to read it. He wrote it very quickly and was very proud of having written so long a book in such a short time—I think about three months. I think there is a good deal to be said for his point of view that a man should write a great deal in volume and variety, and write fast. Certainly some of the best writers have done just that. But you have to be a genius to do it consistently well, and I do not think Priestley is a genius or anywhere near a genius. I quite agree with Wodehouse that most novels would benefit by being cut; and yet there is a sort of writing, which one might call peripheral writing, which cannot be cut without destroying the whole effect of a book. You couldn't cut Proust or Henry James for example, because the things you would be apt to cut would be the very things that make these men worth reading.

I also agree that it is perfectly absurd that Wodehouse cannot go back to England.[1] Surely a Conservative Government makes some difference. After all Churchill was one of the men who boosted the fund for the defense of von Manstein.[2] And plenty of people both in England and in America are beginning to think that the War Crimes Trials were a bad mistake regardless of whether the people who were tried deserved hanging, which of course most of them did. They were bad because they assumed the Germans were bound by laws which did not exist and do not exist now; they were bad because they removed the defense of obedience to superior orders, and in effect made a soldier decide whether an order was proper to be obeyed even though refusal to obey it might result in his being summarily shot. Even if the Hitler government was vicious, it was still a government legally constituted in its own country, and we recognized it as such. Yet in these trials we now say that generals who had sworn an oath of allegiance to their government had no right to be bound by an oath of allegiance. Also, the trials were in effect drumhead court-martials by the victors. An American general writing in the *Saturday Evening Post* about the Battle of the Bulge told how

1. P. G. Wodehouse, English humorist, also a schoolboy at Dulwich. During World War II, while a captive of the Germans, he made five radio broadcasts for them.
2. Field Marshal Erich von Manstein served on the Russian front until he was discharged by Hitler during the retreat.

after a bunch of American prisoners had been murdered in cold blood by German tank crews, various American units were taken to see their bodies laid out in the field. He went on to say that thereafter we, that is the Americans, took the two prisoners a day required by Intelligence and no more. That's just another way of saying that we shot every other German who tried to surrender. That in any fair view of the matter is just as much an atrocity as many of the things the Germans did. And if the Germans had won the war, they could just as easily have tried our generals for crimes against international law. Men attacking under fire often shoot prisoners, or rather men who try to make themselves prisoners, for the simple reason that they cannot let the surrendered men get behind them and that they have no way to handle them. Also, under the Charter of the United Nations most of these war trials would now be impossible, because the evidence under which a great many of the convictions were obtained would be inadmissible in any real international court of justice. So it is all the more absurd that a man like Wodehouse should be tried for a few unwise remarks, probably distorted at that. I can't even agree that a man like [William] Joyce, Lord Haw Haw, was legally convicted. I think he was judicially murdered, because he could only be convicted by a declaration of law to the effect that a man on a falsely obtained British passport owes allegiance to the British crown. Joyce was convicted of giving aid and comfort to the enemy at a time when he was an American citizen and when America was not in the war. This was held to be treason because he held a British passport, which he was not entitled to hold and which he had obtained by a false declaration. That of course was a crime, but it was not a capital crime. In this country it would mean five years penal servitude in a federal prison at most, and actually that would probably mean about two and a half years. But the British had to hang Joyce, and in order to hang him they had to accuse him of treason. And in order to accuse him and convict him of treason they had to put forward the fantastic legal fiction that the possession of a British passport wrongfully acquired put him in exactly the same position as though it had been legally acquired, and although he was not a British subject he was still capable of treason towards a country of which he was not a citizen. I don't think they would try Wodehouse. And if they did, I think they would just make themselves look silly and the whole thing would blow up in their faces. But that doesn't

[308]

solve his problem. And you could hardly expect the authorities to give him an assurance in advance that if he went back to England he would not be tried.

.   .   .

Yours ever,

TO S. J. PERELMAN

January 9, 1952

Dear Sid:

A fellow I know has a theory that if you delay long enough in answering somebody's letter, the guy will ultimately write to you again and apologize for not writing before. I've known it to work once or twice, but you can't rely on it. Anyhow, I do owe you a letter in answer to yours from Key West, Florida, dated October 24, 1951. And you shouldn't give the stuff away like that when you can sell it, unless of course your letters are just rough notes for articles. I guess you've lost interest in Rancho Santa Fe and so have I, but only because in their efforts to keep the place from getting cluttered up with the conveniences of life, the property owners have gone so far in the other direction that there is only one store for food, and that not much of a store, no drugstore, no movie theater (this probably would not be a blow to you, but your children might dislike it) and the essential technicians of life, such as plumbers, electricians and carpenters, are probably so scarce that one would find the aristocratic hauteur of their manners even more trying than the union scale for tramping dirt into the best carpets. I do think Rancho Santa Fe would be a pretty ideal place in which to bring up children, not that I regard that as one of the essential occupations. As for Florida, there must be some attractive spots in it but evidently not those you visited. Why is your wife so mad at Hollywood? After all there are lots of nice people in Hollywood, far more than there are in La Jolla. The picture business can be a little trying at times, but I don't suppose working for General Motors is all sheer delight, and working for Henry Ford, if one can believe any of Harry Bennett's

book, must have been just about as restful as being a bodyguard for
Dutch Schultz.[1]

.   .   .

I am frankly not interested in your Florida sex hunger. Nobody
made you go to Florida. And don't tell me you have to earn a living,
because your children are certainly old enough and smart enough to
support you by now, even if your wife won't work. And I rather
gathered from your writings that about all she does is put perfume in
her hair and loaf around in a mink coat and slacks. And in the
meantime may I remind you of your promise to lend me that book of
Nathanael West's, which seems to be unobtainable here.

With kindest regards,

Yours ever,

TO DALE WARREN

6005 Camino de la Costa
La Jolla, California
January 11, 1952

Dear Dale:

.   .   .

Your advance notice on the novel in which the frustrated lady school
teacher jumps down the well after certain adventures with a Negro
janitor prompts me to implore you not to send me the book when
you publish it. I don't say it would not be successful; the taste of
the public is as mysterious as the taste of critics. Look at the success a
fellow called Mickey Spillane is having, a success comparable to
that in England of James Hadley Chase, the distinguished author of
No Orchids for Miss Blandish. Mickey Spillane is just about on the
same low level of phoniness, and as far as I'm concerned just as
unreadable. I did honestly try to read one just to see what made them
click, but I couldn't make it. Pulp writing at its worst was never
as bad as this stuff. It isn't so very long since no decent publisher

1. Harry Bennett, *We Never Called Him Henry*, New York, 1951. Dutch Schultz was a
famous gangster during the Prohibition years of the 1920s and early 1930s.

would have touched it. I suppose it won't be long until the Book of the Month Club selects a handsomely produced volume of French postcards as its contribution to the national culture. This Spillane stuff, so far as I can see, is nothing but a mixture of violence and outright pornography. He and his publishers have had the courage, if that is the correct word, to carry these a little further than anyone else without interference from the police. I can't see anything else in it. This sort of thing makes the home boys with their libraries of elegant erotica seem rather nice people.

Last night inveigled by the critics and the ballyhoo, although I should now know better, we went to see *A Place in the Sun*.[1] This morning, looking through the *Variety* anniversary number, I see it is listed as the number 8 top grosser for 1951, three and a half million dollars domestic gross, which is very high for these times. So for once the New York critics and the public are agreed. My sister-in-law, who likes practically any kind of picture except slapstick, hated it. And I despised it. It's as slick a piece of bogus self-importance as you'll ever see. And to mention it in same breath with *A Streetcar Named Desire* seems to me an insult.[2] *Streetcar* is by no means a perfect picture, but it does have a lot of drive, a tremendous performance by Marlon Brando, and a skillful if occasionally rather wearisome one by Miss Vivien Leigh. It does get under your skin, whereas *A Place in the Sun* never touches your emotions once. Everything is held too long; every scene is milked ruthlessly. I got so sick of starry-eyed close-ups of Elizabeth Taylor that I could have gagged. The chi-chi was laid-on not with a trowel, not even with a shovel, but with a dragline. And the portrayal of how the lower classes think the upper classes live is about as ridiculous as could be imagined. They ought to have called it "Speedboats for Breakfast." And my God, that scene at the end where the girl visits him in the condemned cell a few hours before he gets the hot squat! My God, my God! The whole thing is beautifully done technically, and it reeks of calculation and contrivance emotionally. Mr. Montgomery Clift gives the performance of his career, which is not saying a great deal, since he had already demonstrated in *The Heiress* that he didn't

1. Film based on Theodore Dreiser's *An American Tragedy*. It was produced by George Stevens and starred Montgomery Clift and Elizabeth Taylor.
2. Film based on the Tennessee Williams play, directed by Elia Kazan and starring Vivien Leigh and Marlon Brando.

belong on the same screen with first-class actors.[3] The picture was made by a guy who has seen everything and has never had a creative idea of his own. Not once but twice in the picture he uses that great trick which Chaplin used in *Monsieur Verdoux*, where instead of a fadeout to close an act he shoots out of a window and watches the darkness turn to daylight. But this slab of unreal hokum makes three and a half million dollars and *Monsieur Verdoux* was a flop. My God, My God! And let me say it just once more. My God!

.　　　　.　　　　.

Yours ever,

Ray

TO THE EDITOR OF *SEQUENCE*[1]

February 15, 1952

Dear Sir:

I have *Sequence* 7, 13 and 14, and if you have any copies of 4, 8 and 11 remaining in stock, I should be glad to receive them. I think you owe me two issues on my subscription, but that is not important. I'll be glad to pay for any copies you send me if you need the money.

I hate to see the magazine fold. There is so little intelligent writing about films, so little that walks delicately but surely between the avant garde type, which is largely a reflection of neuroticism, and the deadly commercial stuff. I think you have been a little too hard at times on English films, which even when not top-notch do give you the feeling of moving around in a civilized world—something which the Hollywood product fails pretty short of as a rule. Even if you had been less intelligent, I should be sorry to see you go. *Sight and Sound* is all very well so far as it goes. I suppose it is subsidized, and everything that is subsidized compromises, and everything that compromises ends up by being pretty negative.

Yours with admiration and regret,

3. Based on Henry James's *Washington Square*, this film was directed by William Wyler and starred Olivia de Havilland and Ralph Richardson.

---

1. A film magazine.

TO H. N. SWANSON

March 10, 1952

Dear Swanie:

What do you mean do a trailer plugging a picture named *The Ragged Edge*? You want I should be a man of indistinction or something sitting behind a borrowed desk, looking straight into the camera and giving a spiel? Or is it that I should write the stuff for fifty dollars a week maybe, like a publicity man? I think that Sherlock Holmes tie you sent me has gone to your head. Seriously, the only thing about this proposition, if you could call it a proposition, that interests me is the fact that anybody would want me to do it. They're crazy anyhow. I have about as much publicity value as a fuzzy caterpillar. After five and a half years in La Jolla I don't think I even got my name in the local paper.

Yours disgustedly,

TO DALE WARREN

6005 Camino de la Costa
La Jolla, California
April 25, 1952

Dear Dale:

.   .   .

As for a cook book, for God's sake if you wanted a La Jolla cookbook, why didn't you apply to me? Except for my wife and one or two others, I am probably the best cook in La Jolla.

Kidding aside, somebody really ought to write a cookbook and put in all the things that the regular cookbooks leave out, the things which, if you're a beginner, the cookbooks don't tell you. They take too much for granted. Also, any decent cookbook should have a few special recipes, a touch of the unique. And this I could easily supply. My Swordfish Mascagni is famous for all of three blocks, and that just in a light breeze. With a good stiff one off the ocean practically the whole of La Jolla is reeling. And my apples baked in cider are vociferously admired by practically everyone who owes me money. How do you make soup without a can opener? Well, that's a mystery of the trade to which very few people know the answer. But it can be done. Just as it is possible to bake a cake out of plain ordinary flour if you have a little cornstarch around the house. You don't really have to buy the cake half baked in a cellophane bag at the A & P. Most people think you do, but it's an error. Why, in my cookbook I could even tell people how to poach an egg in open water. And if you think that's easy, we've had fifty or sixty cooks who couldn't do it. Most of them couldn't even poach an egg in an egg poacher, which doesn't really poach an egg at all.

·　　　·　　　·

TO BERNICE BAUMGARTEN

6005 Camino de la Costa
La Jolla, California
May 14 1952

Dear Bernice:

I'm sending you today, probably by air express, a draft of a story which I have called *The Long Goodbye*. It runs 92,000 words. I'd be happy to have your comments and objections and so on. I haven't even read the thing, except to make a few corrections and check a number of details that my secretary queried. So I am not sending you any opinion on the opus. You may find it slow going.

It has been clear to me for some time that what is largely boring about mystery stories, at least on a literate plane, is that the characters get lost about a third of the way through. Often the opening, the mis en scene, the establishment of the background, is very good. Then the plot thickens and the people become mere names. A very good example of this is a current work called *Reclining Figure* by my friend Harry Kurnitz, (Marco Page.) It begins so well, but in the end it is the same old hash. Well, what can you do to avoid this? You can write constant action and that is fine if you really enjoy it. But alas, one grows up, one becomes complicated and unsure, one becomes interested in moral dilemmas, rather than who cracked who on the head. And at that point perhaps one should retire and leave the field to younger and more simple men. I don't necessarily mean writers of comic books like Mickey Spillane.

Anyhow I wrote this as I wanted to because I can do that now. I didn't care whether the mystery was fairly obvious, but I cared about the people, about this strange corrupt world we live in, and how any man who tried to be honest looks in the end either sentimental or plain foolish. Enough of that. There are more practical reasons. You write in a style that has been imitated, even plagiarized, to the point where you begin to look as if you were imitating your imitators. So you have to go where they can't follow you. The danger is that the reader won't either.

.   .   .

Yours ever,

Ray

TO BERNICE BAUMGARTEN

6005 Camino de la Costa
La Jolla, California
Sunday May 25, 1952

Dear Bernice:

You will have received my wire by now and I hope it has been in time to stop the script from being copied and to withhold same from Jamie.[1] I thank you for your letter and needless to say I regret having sent the script out when I did. I was just too impatient to get rid of it. I knew the character of Marlowe had changed, and I thought it had to because the hardboiled stuff was too much of a pose after all this time. But I did not realize that it had become Christlike, and sentimental, and that he ought to be deriding his own emotions. It may be that I am no good any more. God knows, I've had enough worry to drive me off the beam. Being old-fashioned

1. Bernice Baumgarten and Carl Brandt had written Chandler making numerous suggestions for changes in *The Long Goodbye*.

[315]

enough to be deeply in love with my wife after twenty-eight years of marriage I feel the possibility that I have let emotion enter my life in a manner not suitable to the marts of commerce, as the cliché has it. Of course there is also the possibility—faint as it is, I admit—that you could be a little wrong.

I'll take a quick trip through the script when I get it back and then lay it aside for long enough to get perspective. I've always wanted to do that. I was never able to. I was always afraid that if I did I would junk the whole thing when I came back to it. I'm not afraid of that now. I know that whatever errors of emphasis or plot and so on the story contains it is fundamentally all right for me. I've never ridden with a loose rein before. That may be more of a trick than I know.

I am dropping a note to Jamie because he cabled me. If by any chance you have sent him a script, I shall ask him to return it to me direct.

Curiously enough I seem to have far fewer doubts about this story than I had about *The Little Sister*. Why that is I haven't the remotest idea. It has been said, I think, that writers always like the wrong things in their own work.

My thanks again and my apologies for putting you through it.

Yours ever,

Ray

TO HAMISH HAMILTON

6005 Camino de la Costa
La Jolla, California
May 25, 1952

Dear Jamie:
I am withdrawing the script of my book for revision. I have wired Bernice to return all copies to me and not to show it to anyone. I'm sorry and it's a damn nuisance. But Houghton Mifflin could not (apparently) have published this year anyhow. If a script should have been sent to you, please disregard it, and send back to me just any old way. No hurry.

[316]

This happens as the result of criticisms made by Bernice and concurred in by Carl Brandt. Some of these comments, if correct, are devastating, and if incorrect, are intolerable. Surely they are more likely to be the former than the latter. The character of Marlowe has become "Christlike" and sentimental, and he should be deriding his own emotions all through the book, or words to that effect. There are also detailed criticisms of no particular importance.

It's all my fault, of course. I should have put the damn thing to one side and let it simmer on the stove for awhile. Instead of that I hurry it out in an unregenerate condition and get slapped in the face for being so careless. It happened to me once before with Sydney Sanders, and much more brutally. It was over the book called *The High Window*, original and proper title *The Brashear Doubloon*, and changed as an effort of superb idiocy on the part of Knopf who thought my title sounded like a boy's story. That book is usually considered my weakest effort to date (I will no doubt surpass it and may have already—in weakness), although there are people who think it the best. It is still selling here and there, but you know how ignorant the public is. Compared with an agent the public knows nothing.

Another talent in which agents are greatly gifted is imploring you to let them see work in progress or unfinished or unedited, and when you succumb to their pleadings, hitting you in the face with it. And all for so modest a fee.

Yours ever

Ray

TO ERIC PARTRIDGE

May 29, 1952

Dear Eric:

.   .   .

Incidentally, it doesn't follow that a man who has been in stir writes

[317]

the best prison lingo any more than it follows that a man who has
been a police officer writes the best detective stories. My experience is
to the contrary. As you say, the lingo varies from place to place,
and it also varies from year to year. And there is no doubt that a large
part of it is of literary origin, literary here being used in a very
generous sense. Cops and crooks are readers of crime literature, and I
have no doubt that many a Western sheriff has ornamented his
language and perhaps even his costume from a study of six-gun
literature.

.　　　　.　　　　.

Yours ever,

TO CARL BRANDT

6005 Camino de la Costa
La Jolla, California
June 11, 1952

Dear Carl:

.　　　　.　　　　.

I am doing a good deal of revising on my book, especially
toward the end, which I think I shall change. But I probably do not
have the same confidence that I had before I received Bernice's
remarks. Some of the things she said are matters which I would
automatically have taken care of on revision. Some seem to me quite
without point. As to the character of Marlowe, I may be all wrong
but I was trying to write the book the way I wanted to write it and
not the way somebody else thinks I ought to write it. The irony
of a writer's career—I suppose most writers are confronted with it in
some form—is that he may write a couple of books which pass
with little notice at the time of their publication, and then as time
goes by they slowly build up a reputation and in the end are used as
yardsticks by which to measure his later work, sometimes by the
very people who were quite unable to discuss any merit in the early
performance at the time. A writer of my type should never show

[318]

unfinished work to anyone. He should wait until he is sure that he has what he wanted, or as near to it as he is capable of producing.

 With kindest regards,

Yours ever,

Ray

TO BERNICE BAUMGARTEN

6005 Camino de la Costa
La Jolla, California
July 20th. 1952

Dear Bernice:

 Thanks for note, but I see no reason why you should, even as a matter of form, apologize for speaking what was in your mind. You were probably, almost certainly, quite right. One never knows what sort of impact a letter will make, since one never knows the mood or very much of the circumstances in which it will be read. Complete tact requires more knowledge than is given to us. It was all my fault anyhow, as I've said. My present trouble is that I don't know where I am at, don't know whether there is anything in all this mess worth salvaging, or whether it would be cleverer to throw it away and start fresh. I am not much good at tinkering or revising. I lose interest, lose perspective, and whatever critical sense I have is dissipated in trivialities such as whether it is better to put in "he said" or let the speech stand alone.

 My kind of writing demands a certain amount of dash and high spirits—the word is gusto, a quality lacking in modern writing— and you could not know the bitter struggle I have had the past year even to achieve enough cheerfulness to live on, much less to put into a book. So let's face it: I didn't get it into the book. I didn't have it to give.

.   .   .

All the best,

Ray

[319]

TO PAUL BROOKS

The Connaught Hotel
Carlos Place, London W.1.[1]
September 28, 1952

Dear Paul Brooks:

Thanks for your letter which was forwarded to me here.
Today is an English Sunday and by God it's gloomy enough for a
crossing of the Styx. I thought England was broke but the whole
damn city is crawling with Rolls Royces, Bentleys, Daimlers and
expensive blondes.

Never thought I'd get sick of the sight of a grouse on toast or a
partidge, but by God I am.

On my return Oct. 7 via *Mauretania* shall be at the Hampshire
House for a few days and will call up to say hello, if you are
available. The book (seen from here in perspective) is all right. It had
a few changes here though. Bernice is an idiot (I hope).

In England I am an author. In the USA just a mystery writer.
Can't tell you why. God knows I don't care one way or the other. I
have met:
(1) An Oxford don who writes bad Westerns under a pen name.
(2) A secretary who lunches on bread and butter and straight gin.
(3) A valet who enters without knocking while my wife is having a
     bath.
(4) A publisher who makes the world's worst martinis.
     And so on.

Yours ever

Raymond Chandler

---

1. Chandler and his wife Cissy visited England for a month in the autumn of 1952. They
sailed from Los Angeles on a Swedish motor ship via the Panama Canal and returned on
the *Mauretania* of the Cunard line. It was Chandler's first visit to England since 1918.

TO LEONARD RUSSELL

6005 Camino de la Costa
La Jolla, California
October 29, 1952

Dear Leonard:

I hope I am not too forward in so addressing you.

Herewith the story about which we spoke briefly the night before my wife and I left the Connaught Hotel for Southampton. You expressed a desire to see it. I warned you that it had not been received with the slightest trace of enthusiasm on this side of the Atlantic. So if you don't like it, I shall not be in the least chagrined; I shall simply feel that there is something in the story which I did not succeed in getting on paper. To me it seems in some vague way one of the best things I ever wrote, but an author is a very poor judge of his own stuff.

I can't tell you how much I enjoyed meeting you and Dilys Powell.[1] The reason I can't tell you is that I feel it requires a much more ample expression than I am capable of at the moment. Today the style is not worthy of the subject; perhaps later on it will be, and you will hear from me again. My wife and I both feel that the evening we spent at your house, alcoholic as it was, was one of the high spots of our visit to London. And nothing would give us greater pleasure or joy than to repeat it at least twice a week for the rest of our lives.

Yours ever,

Ray

---

1. Russell's wife and film critic for the *Sunday Times*.

TO J. FRANCIS

6005 Camino de la Costa
La Jolla, California
October 30, 1952

Dear Frank:

.   .   .

As to Maugham's remarks about the decline and fall of the detective story, in spite of his flattering references to me, I do not agree with his thesis.[1] People have been burying the detective story for at least two generations, and it is still very much alive, although I do admit that the term "detective story" hardly covers the field any more, since a great deal of the best stuff written nowadays is only slightly if at all concerned with the elucidation of the mystery. What we have is more in the nature of the novel of suspense. I'm going to write him a long letter one of these days and take up the argument with him. I may even write an article in reply if anybody wants to print it. I should have valued his references to Philip Marlowe even more if he had remembered to spell Marlowe's name correctly. Some of this stuff of Maugham's was published a long time ago. The fascinating and acid little vignette of Edith Wharton for example was published in the *Saturday Evening Post*, and I still have the tear sheets (I think) from the issue. And I seem to recall that Edmund Wilson took rather nasty issue with Maugham about Maugham's claim that the writers of straight novels had largely forgotten how to tell a story. I hate to agree with such an ill-natured and bad mannered person as Edmund Wilson, but I think he was right on this point. I don't think the quality in the detective or mystery story which appeals to people has very much to do with the story a particular book has to tell. I think what draws people is a certain emotional tension which takes you out of yourself without draining you too much. They allow you to live dangerously without any real risk. They are something like those elaborate machines which they used to use and probably still do use to accustom student pilots to the sensation of aerial

---

1. Published in *The Vagrant Mood*, 1953.

[322]

acrobatics. You can do anything from a wing over to an Immelmann in them without any danger of going into a flat spin out of control. Well, enough of that for now.

.   .   .

Kindest regards to everyone,

Yours ever,

Ray Chandler

TO HAMISH HAMILTON

6005 Camino de la Costa
La Jolla, California
November 5, 1952

Dear Jamie:
You people over there write one another so many little polite notes on all sorts of occasions that I suppose I was very stupid not to realize that I should not have waited until I had time to do a more substantial kind of letter. I am extremely sorry to have hurt your feelings inadvertently. There have been certain excuses but not any complete excuse. I could have written to you on the *Mauretania*, illegible as my writing is. I could have written to you from New York. I could have written to you on the train coming across the country. As soon as I got back here I wrote a couple of duty notes: one to Francis, who made me a present of a book just before I left and I had not time to thank him for it in person, the other to Leonard Russell. But these were short and not at all the kind of letter I should have liked to write to you. I think letter writing is more of a chore to me than it is to you, because I cannot write longhand so that anyone can read it. I don't like typing letters myself, because I don't type well enough, although I type rapidly, and I have fallen into the habit of dictating. But none of this is any adequate excuse for me to have been so neglectful that your feelings were hurt. And I do apologize

[323]

most sincerely. As for my being offended about anything, you cannot use that word to me with impunity. *I just simply am not the type that gets offended,* even when there might be thought to be some justification and certainly there could never be from you. You were kindness itself, and I'm sure you spent far more hours worrying about me than you should have. I have had my feelings hurt, sometimes intentionally. Like most writers I have occasionally been sneered at and maligned. I don't say I have never been hurt and never discouraged, but I have never felt it a personal matter. I never sulk. I am never huffy. Sometimes, I admit, I can be pretty irritable, but this is perhaps more the fault of a nervous temperament than of any innate vice.

It seemed natural for Cissy to write to Roger, because he sent flowers to the boat and she certainly had to thank him, though if they had been sent to me, I might well have waited until I got home to do it. I can see now that that would have been wrong. So please, dear Jamie, try to understand that I think you and yours were all utterly kind and charming to us, and that even though certain things about our stay in London were a little annoying at the time, they are all very pleasant in retrospect. The annoying things were mostly things that could not be avoided. There was the desperate struggle on Cissy's part (when she was in no fit condition to do it) to find something to wear, and not merely something to wear to a dinner party but things which she badly needed and things which she simply could not find in the West End of London. She couldn't even find a decent pair of shoes to put on. At fantastic prices they were selling what we should over here regard as quite second-rate English goods. Of course I do understand why, but it was annoying just the same. I couldn't find a decent pair of woolen socks. The only things I found were fit for lumberjacks. I thought the hotel charges were pretty outrageous for a not too comfortable room. But all that is to be expected and I am sure as things go it is a pretty damn good hotel. Next time, however, I should like to try another, possibly Claridge's. And compared with New York, which is an abominable place in far too many ways, I think London is a paradise of charm and good manners. Soon after we reached London, although we said very little about it at the time, Cissy hurt herself getting into a taxi, just because the damn doorman wouldn't take the trouble to get the taxi up to the curb, and the strap on one of her shoes slipped. She developed a very serious bruise which should have been bandaged at once if we had realized how serious it was. But as a matter of fact it was not bandaged until she got on the *Mauretania*. She has been wearing bandages ever since. Evidently a large vein was broken and there was a great deal of subcutaneous hemorrhage which refused to absorb. On the way back on the train she developed some kind of infection, probably due to the use of harsh towels washed in detergent and insufficiently rinsed. I should say it was allergic in origin, but just the same it was bad and still is bad, very hard to shake off. I have been under the weather myself, but I'm all right now. And we were in such appalling difficulties from a domestic point of view that we had to ask Cissy's unfortunate sister to come right back and help us out, when she had been away from her own home for two months and was pretty fed up with being here. Also, I have been deeply depressed about my book. I felt, and I still feel, that Bernice was wrong in all but a few rather insignificant details. But there was always the chance that I was wrong and she was right. And when you're not feeling well, these things are apt to loom very large. After all I'm not getting any younger and I haven't turned out a book for quite a while and this sort of thing can't go on indefinitely. But I think I see now the answer to what problems there are, and that if we can have some peace in our home, things will start to move.

I didn't like the *Mauretania*. It wasn't a ship at all. It was just a damned floating hotel. I didn't like the hotel we stayed at in New York, and Cissy disliked it even more than I did. I suppose there is an amiable and pleasant side to New York we just didn't happen to see, except that I have one very good friend who took the trouble to come down from Old Chatham and meet us and stay several days with us. But frankly it seems to me a dirty, lawless, rude, hard-boiled place. It makes even Los Angeles seem fairly civilized. The New York taxi drivers were a bunch of hard-boiled, dirty-looking Jews except for an occasional grizzled and civilized Irishman. And most of them are crooks into the bargain. I have never been in any place that gave me such an acute feeling that no one had the time or inclination for even a modicum of good manners unless there was a quick buck in it for him. Oh yes, I will make one exception in favor of the customs inspectors. They are supposed to be tough. I found them charming and extremely clever. The one we got (after waiting an hour and a half because the Cunard people lost one of our suitcases and didn't even take the trouble to apologize when they finally found it) made a great to-do about the Berenson book, which I think was the only thing in our ten pieces of luggage he even looked at. But I had a very strong impression that his looking at it and talking about it and asking questions about it was simply a device for sizing up his customer, and that after a few moments of this he made up his mind what sort of people he was dealing with, and from then on he didn't want to see or know anything at all. He didn't even ask us to open our bags. I had declared this book on the customs declaration as a gift and put an estimated value on it, because it was the sort of expensive thing that I didn't want them to find without being told. But at the same time I wouldn't try to fool with these people. They caught a slick-looking Jew with a fine batch of very expensive looking French costume jewelry wrapped up in an old shirt. And they took no time at all in marching him off to a senior officer, the Jew remarking plaintively as he departed that he wasn't trying to get away with anything. Famous last words.

Well, Jamie, let's face it. We loved London and we had a lovely time there. What little inconveniences we happened to have suffered were all due to our own inexperience and probably would not happen again. All your people were wonderful to me. It was really extremely touching. I am just not used to being treated with that much consideration. There are things I regret, such as losing several days over my vaccination, such as not going to any of the picture galleries, such as only seeing one rather poor play, such as not having dinner at your home. I spent too much time talking about myself, which I don't enjoy, and too little time listening to other people talk about themselves, which I do enjoy. I missed seeing something of the English countryside. And childish as it may sound, I missed very much not having hired a Rolls Royce and a driver for a day and driven to Oxford or Cambridge or some place like that. But all in all there was a hell of a lot I did not miss, and all of it good. And for that you above all others are to be thanked. I'll be writing you again soon. In the meantime my best love to you and Yvonne, and that goes for Cissy too. I think the trip did her a lot of good. She had bad luck, but psychologically she was buoyed up no end.

Yours ever,

Ray

[326]

P.S. The Maugham book just came, and thanks ever so much for sending it. Francis had sent me a bound copy of the proof. I wish Maugham had taken the trouble to spell Marlowe's name right, and I don't agree with his thesis that the detective story is dying. That's just an elderly gentleman's point of view. Such predictions have been made periodically ever since one can remember. I'm sure I did thank you for the Berenson book, which I shall have a hard time getting away from Cissy, and for the *Journal* of Delacroix. But what's this about a Partridge book? You didn't send me a Partridge book, or if you did, I haven't received it.

R.

TO W. TOWNEND

November 11, 1952

Dear Bill:

.   .   .

The London of 1952 probably struck me as a much more amiable and attractive place than you found it, because I probably never saw it at its best, at least not since I was a very young man. The present generation of English people impressed me very well. There is a touch of aggressiveness about the working classes and the non-Public School types which I think is something new and which I personally do not find at all unpleasant, since it is even more emphatic in this country. And the real Public School types, or many of them, with their bird-like chirpings are becoming a little ridiculous, I thought. I grant you that English food is pretty dreary. There was no shortage of anything at the hotel, but we did find the menu pretty monotonous and the cooking not too good. We thought at the time this was probably due to the shortage of some of the necessary cooking materials and ingredients, the little things that give flavor. But on the *Mauretania* where there is no shortage of anything, in fact where there is far too much food and far too great a variety, we found the same sort of dullness in the cooking, so I am driven to the conclusion that it is just English. Compared with the Swedes, even on a modest ship like a passenger-freighter, the English are no cooks at all. For instance, at the Café Royale we had pork chops, pork apparently being the only unrationed fresh meat. Now pork chops are not particularly difficult to cook. I can cook them myself. You cook them in their own fat, they bring with them everything that is necessary except salt and pepper. Yet these pork chops were badly cooked and were messed up with some kind of sauce, which added nothing to their flavor and probably took away what little they had left. It's this sort of bastard imitation of French cooking, a fussiness without the skill or the grace, which I found so trying at the hotel and in London generally. I don't suggest that there are no good English cooks. Far from it. But in a general way it seems to me they cannot take a piece of perfectly good meat or fish or fowl and cook it simply and properly so as to bring out its natural flavor and let it go at that. All in all I think the best thing that they cook is oysters on the half-shell. Whitstable oysters are very good indeed, every bit as good as Blue Points or Cape Cod oysters back East in the U.S.A.

Yes, I met a few of the literary and theatrical people who are big names in London. We had lunch with Priestley, and a very good lunch it was. We had dinner with Leonard Russell, and his wife, Dilys Powell. It wasn't much of a dinner, but it was elegantly served by a butler, and the company was very nice indeed. Dilys Powell I found charming; Leonard Russell, Cissy found charming. Not that I didn't like him, but I didn't go overboard for him the way she did. Also present were Val Gielgud, who is head of dramatic productions for BBC; Nicolas Bentley, the son of the fellow who wrote *Trent's Last Case*,[1] his wife, who is the daughter of Sir Patrick Hastings; one of the daughters-in-law of H. J. Massingham, who used to edit the great liberal weekly, *The Saturday Review*; Campbell Dixon, who is some kind of a film reviewer and has been a foreign correspondent and a special feature writer in many places, and his wife, who also works for the BBC and has some connections with Korda.[2] I had lunch with Eric Partridge, and we did happen to miss a dinner at

1. E. C. Bentley.
2. Sir Alexander Korda.

which Cyril Connolly and Peter Ustinov[3] were to have been present.
I can't say I met all the bigwigs, even very many of them. But
those I did meet were all very nice people and made an unnecessary
amount of fuss over me. No, I haven't read Cary's book, *Prisoner of
Grace*, and don't think I shall; so if that makes me a nitwit, I'll be one
right along with you.

·   ·   ·

Of all the people we met in London, that is those we had not known
before, I think we liked best Roger Machell, a director of Hamish
Hamilton, a cheerful, rather pudgy, light-hearted character, with a
droll sense of humor and the sort of off-hand good manners which
you rarely find except in a genuine aristocrat. This fellow is an old
Etonian, which of course is not conclusive. He is a great grand-
nephew of Queen Victoria, he is the grandson of Prince Hohenlohe,
and his mother, Lady Something or Other Machell, lives in St.
James Palace. Just why, I don't know, because none of this
information came from Machell himself. He was badly wounded in
the war and made a joke of it. He seemed to think it was
characteristic that he should have been wounded while telephoning
London from a French pub. A bomb dropped on it and blew a piece
of a wall through his chest. It just missed killing him, but he seems to
show no ill effects now. He said he got a commission as a major in
some guard's regiment, but he didn't know how, probably pure luck
or else someone made a bad mistake. When he reported one morning
to a barracks in London in uniform he found them in the act of the
changing of the guard. He said he didn't know whether he was
supposed to salute the guard or if the guard was supposed to salute
him, so he just sat in his car outside until it was all over. He has
the sort of humorous, self-deprecating manner which by sheer magic
of personality is never overdone or posey or artificial. He lives
handsomely in chambers in the Old Albany, drives a ramshackle old
car, mixes perfectly awful Martinis in a two-quart water pitcher
(two of them would knock you out for a week) and took us on a
wonderful tour of London, including the East End bombed-out
district, making all the time such comments as, "Well, let's run down
and take a look at the Tower, supposing I can find it," and "over

3. Cyril Connolly, critic and author; Peter Ustinov, writer and actor.

[329]

there is St. Paul's or something of that sort." He had us in giggles the whole time, yet he is in no sense of the word an intentional comedian. I claim that a man who can get away with this sort of thing and be perfectly natural about it is a bit of a genius.

With much love from both of us to both of you,

Ever yours,

TO DALE WARREN

November 13, 1952

Dear Dale:

.   .   .

I owe an apology to Paul Brooks for failing to call in at your New York office as he asked me to and meet a couple of people there. This is going to sound rather corny, but the simple fact is I forgot all about it. I don't know why, and I have no excuse. It simply happened. I think possibly I developed a certain amount of subconscious reluctance to have anything to do with New York taxi drivers. Those that don't whine or bluster want to make a travelogue out of a ten-block ride. I suppose New Yorkers get used to them, just as hotel doormen get used to standing out in the middle of the street, blowing whistles all day long; just as you get used to seeing cars double and triple parked all over the place and the police taking no notice; and just as you get used, or do you, to going out into the middle of the street to get into a taxi and never by any chance getting one at the curb. I see in the current *New Yorker* that Sacheverell Sitwell, that visiting virtuoso of the quill pen, remarks that New York traffic is better managed than that in London, about as idiotic a remark as I have ever heard or read. New York traffic isn't managed at all. It is absolute chaos. London traffic, generally speaking and considering the fantastic pattern of the streets, is superbly managed. Of course the system wouldn't work in New York because it depends on a certain element of decency and obedience to the law. The only real fault I found with the London traffic system was their allowing left turns from places like Oxford Circus during rush hours. With which gripe I conclude.

Yours ever,

TO MR. SHEPPARD[1]

November 14, 1952

Dear Mr. Sheppard:
Whatever happened to my photographs, those that were taken on October 6th last by the Russian-Armenian lady in the smock and the Apache style coiffure? You remember the proofs were to have been sent to you by the following Friday, which would have been October 10th; and unless they were on the face of it quite impossible, were to have been sent to me. It was agreed, you remember, when I submitted myself to this degrading ordeal that I should have the privilege of passing on the proofs and that nothing should be used which I did not like. Experience has taught me to be very sensitive about photographs. I am no fuzzy chicken and I can be made to look pretty ghastly, as was well demonstrated by the *Sunday Times*. All questions of personal vanity apart (and I do not consider them very much, although I do not say I don't consider them at all) I am convinced as a member of the reading public myself that bad photographs are bad business. I have been put off reading books, which otherwise looked rather attractive, by the puss of the author printed on the back of the dust cover. It is not a question of making you handsome when you are not, or of making you young when you are not. It is a question of not presenting the reader with an image which will turn his stomach at the worst, and at the best haunt him with just enough distaste for the personality of the author to give him a bias against the author's writing. I don't think publishers pay enough attention to this sort of thing. I do think, and positively, that a poor photograph is worse than none at all. In his writing, if he is going to get anywhere, an author has to present the public with an attractive personality. It may be and often is an artificial

1. Publicity director of Hamish Hamilton, Chandler's London publishers.

[331]

personality, something the author as a human specimen cannot live up to. But time and time again publishers will destroy the effect the author has managed to achieve in his writing by presenting a photographic study of him as a conceited ape or a flat-faced homunculus whom you would not on his looks think capable of a BBC talk about the sex life of a caterpillar.

It is obvious from this letter that a mere discussion of the disastrous effects of photographing authors can bring out the worst in at least one of them. Anyhow, it was delightful to meet you. It was very kind of you to trundle me down the street to the sordid neighborhood of the Garrick Club and to suffer with me in that bleak little studio. But I would like to know what happened—that is if anything happened.

With kindest regards,

Yours ever,

TO HOWARD HUNT[1]

November 16, 1952

Dear Mr. Hunt:

Your letter to the editors of Pocket Books, accusing me of self-plagiarism, was sent on to me by them without comment. Since the letter was not addressed to me, there is no real reason why I should answer it, but I will take up a couple of points. First, as to *The Hard-Boiled Omnibus*, you were perfectly right. As a matter of fact I suggested the idea of this anthology to Joe Shaw, a former editor of the *Black Mask* and a long-time friend of mine, and I signed a permission to him for this story when I was very busy at Paramount and not paying any particular attention to it. That is to say, I relied on his good faith. Later I read the story and immediately raised a howl and secured his undertaking in writing not to use it but to substitute something else which had not been, as I term it, "cannibalized."

1. At the time, attached to the American Embassy in Mexico City. Later, as an aide to President Nixon, he was embroiled in the Watergate scandal.

When the book came out he explained somewhat lamely that the editors of Simon & Schuster had overruled him. Legally of course I had no remedy, although I spent several hundred dollars in lawyers fees trying to find one. I had signed the permission. The most I achieved was to prevent the inclusion of this story in the English edition of that anthology.

You should not blame the editors of Pocket Books, because the volume of their business is so great that they naturally take these things on trust from the publishers from whom as a rule they secure the reprint rights. I consider that my confidence was abused, but that is just my personal opinion.

As to your broader charge of self-plagiarism, based on the use by me of scenes, characters, incidents, background, color, etc., from old *Black Mask* novelettes: first of all, let me say that I have a perfect right to use them; I am the copyright owner, I can use my material in any way I see fit. There have been many instances of short stories being expanded into books which were published, and then being dramatized into plays which were published, and so on. Where the novel takes over the essential plot and story line of the briefer story, I would say that the reader should be put upon notice of this, particularly if the title is changed. Where the material used is merely character and incident, there is no fraud on the public because the thing is re-created in another form. Even if occasional lines of dialogue are used, there is no fraud. There is no moral or ethical issue involved. You may dislike the procedure, but that's as far as you can go.

There is another consideration which may have escaped your attention. That is that these old stories of mine were written for the most ephemeral possible kind of publication, one which had a life of thirty days and then was as dead as Caesar. At the time it would never have occurred to me that any of these stories would ever be resurrected, remembered, republished again in any form. I am not sure that they ever should have been republished in their original form, but I took a wide selection of opinions on the subject before I consented. It was brought home to me that a whole generation had grown up that had never known the *Black Mask*, and that that generation might just possibly want to read these stories, and certainly would not be able to read them unless they were republished. There might happen to be a few odd copies of the magazine obtainable in some secondhand magazine store, but who would be likely to look for them except a fanatic. I was even assured by a somewhat austere critic of this type of fiction, James Sandoe by name, that even people who knew the stories and had perhaps kept them in some other form would still be very likely to want them in hard covers.

I have a further remark. As you may know, writers like Dashiell Hammett and myself have been widely and ruthlessly imitated, so closely as to amount to a moral plagiarism, even though the law does not recognize anything but the substantial taking of a plot. I have had stories taken scene by scene and just lightly changed here and there. I have had lines of dialogue taken intact, bits of description also word for word. I have no recourse. The law doesn't call it plagiarism. Against this background you must pardon me if I find it just a little ludicrous that you should object to my using what is mine in the way that seems to me most suitable and most convenient. If my early stories had been published in a magazine of prestige and significance, the situation would have been rather different, and I would have been much more reluctant to do what you complain of. But as it is, I wish I had carried the process much further and used more of my old novelettes as material instead of republishing them with all their crudities, some of which crudities I now find almost unbearable.

I think my principal reason for writing this letter is that in all these years you are the only person who has ever raised this objection, that is to say, the only person other than myself. I have a file of pretty bitter correspondence on the subject of the first paragraph of your letter.

Yours very truly,

TO LEONARD RUSSELL

6005 Camino de la Costa
La Jolla, California
December 11, 1952

Dear Leonard Russell:

Remember me? Chandler? We met once briefly in London. We had dinner at your house, and very charming it was. And you had a couple of pink gins at my hotel, and very charming that was, except that it led me to send you a story called "A Couple of Writers," which was dispatched by airmail on October 29, 1952. And the rest is silence. Don't think I'm anxious. Don't think I'm disheartened. I told you the worst about the story. And after all, you asked me to send it to you. I think some brief acknowledgement might be in order, if the story ever reached you. I'm beginning to wonder if it did.

My wife has been very ill. She is back home from the hospital, but still very frail and still in bed. Mostly on that account we have decided to forget all about Christmas this year, cards included. So may I now wish you and Dilys Powell whatever in this sad world remains of peace and happiness, such as red sunsets, the smell of roses after a summer rain, soft carpets in quiet rooms, firelight, and old friends.

Yours ever,

Ray

TO ERIC PARTRIDGE

January 19, 1953

Dear Eric:

.   .   .

The best shaggy dog story I know, it tops them all I think, was published a long time ago in *Collier's*, but it was published in a way that suggested that it was not original but that somebody had heard it from somebody else who had heard it, etc. It seems that on a very hot summer afternoon a couple of hippopotamuses, or hippopotami if you want to be a purist, were basking in the muddy water of the Nile with their noses just showing above. They appeared very contented and even a little drowsy. Finally one of the hippopotamuses raised his snout out of the water enough so that he

[335]

could open his mouth. He said dreamily, "Somehow you know, I can't help thinking this is Thursday." End of story.

I know a wonderful story which probably doesn't quite qualify as a shaggy dog story. As a matter of fact, the definition of a shaggy dog story is pretty vague to me, except that it's supposed to be pure nonsense and yet somehow funny. It seems that a Polish farmer had murdered his wife and her lover. He had been tried, convicted, and the judge before sentencing him asked him if he had anything to say. The Polish farmer had quite a lot to say, but I will not attempt to reproduce his dialect, nor do I know what dialect a Polish farmer uses. He said in effect, "Your Honor, I'm a hard working man. I work hard in the fields all day. I come home six o'clock. I wash my hands and face at the pump. I go in house. Dinner on table. I sit down with wife. Eat dinner. Look at the paper a little while. I go to bed. I sleep. Get up at five o'clock. Work hard in the fields all day. Well, one night I come home. Wash face and hands at the pump. Go in house. Dinner on table. It six o'clock. No wife. Go upstairs. Wife in bed with lover. Go downstairs. Eat dinner. Look at paper. Lover go way. I go to bed. Get up at five o'clock in the morning. Work hard in the fields all day. I get home six o'clock. Wash hands and face at the pump. Go in house. No dinner on table. Go upstairs. Wife in bed with lover. I kill wife and lover." Then he raised his voice to a shout, pounded his fist in his palm and said, "Dinner must be on the table at six o'clock!"

·   ·   ·

With all best wishes for the New Year to you and yours,

Sincerely,

TO AN UNKNOWN CORRESPONDENT[1]

March 13, 1953

Thank you so much for sending me *The Mind of the Maker* by

1. Unidentified carbon in Chandler's files.

Dorothy Sayers. I must say that I find it pretty damned dull. Either my mind is completely vitiated, or this is a pretty fair example of the oversubtilized kind of thinking that really is a neurosis of the intellectual. Take an example at random: "The criterion is, not whether the associations are called up, but whether the spirits invoked by this kind of verbal incantation are charged with personal power by the magician who speeds them about their new business." Or to put it more simply: does it contain irium. She is talking about people like T. S. Eliot who use a great deal of classic and other quotation and allusion in their poems. I once had a radio program, a summer replacement for thirteen weeks, which was sponsored by the Pepsodent people. I tried very hard to find out what irium was. I don't think they know because I don't think it exists. It's just another name for the ineffable. So the criterion, as Miss Sayers puts it, seems to be not whether the ingredients in the poems of T. S. Eliot (or in Pepsodent toothpaste perhaps) are good in themselves but whether when they are put together there is something there that wasn't there before. It hardly seems to me worth arguing about. The answer always has to be yes. I long ago made up my mind that subtlety was not a dimension of thinking but merely a technique, and not a particularly difficult technique at that.

Thank you so very much anyhow.

TO H. N. SWANSON

6005 Camino de la Costa
La Jolla, California
Mar 14 1953

Dear Swanie:

.   .   .

Playback is getting a bit tired.[1] I have 36,000 words of doodling and not yet a stiff. That is terrible. I am suffering from a very

1. Chandler's last novel, not published until 1958.

[337]

uncommon disease called (by me) atrophy of the inventive powers. I can write like a streak but I bore myself. That being so, I could hardly fail to bore others worse. I can't help thinking of that beautiful piece of Sid Perelman's entitled "I'm Sorry I Made Me Cry."

Did you ever read what they call Science Fiction. It's a scream. It is written like this: "I checked out with K 19 on Aldabaran III, and stepped out through the crummalite hatch on my 22 Model Sirus Hardtop. I cocked the timejector in secondary and waded through the bright blue manda grass. My breath froze into pink pretzels. I flicked on the heat bars and the Brylls ran swiftly on five legs using their other two to send out crylon vibrations. The pressure was almost unbearable, but I caught the range on my wrist computer through the transparent cysicites. I pressed the trigger. The thin violet glow was icecold against the rust-colored mountains. The Brylls shrank to half an inch long and I worked fast stepping on them with the poltex. But it wasn't enough. The sudden brightness swung me around and the Fourth Moon had already risen. I had exactly four seconds to hot up the disintegrator and Google had told me it wasn't enough. He was right."

They pay brisk money for this crap?

Ray

TO ROGER MACHELL

6005 Camino de la Costa
La Jolla, California
Sunday March 15th [1953]

Dear Roger:

This is going to be awful because I'm balling the jack myself and on a Corona yet. On Sunday nobody works but Chandler and he breaks his heart seven days a week and without no music.

.   .   .

Please thank Jamie for sending me *The Big Change* and tell him I shall be writing to him anon. And thank you for the stuff from

[338]

John O'London's and the piece from the Westminster Bank.[1] In most ways I liked that better. As to Peter Forster, every interview makes a different man, and that is one reason why I don't like them. The photo is rather ugly. The hands are obviously those of a strangler. But Ida has rather cleverly minimised the hump on my back. The physical description of Chandler is unrecognizable by anyone who knows him. He calls me small. What is his standard? I have hardly ever weighed less than twelve stone—is that small in England? I have often weighed almost 13 stone. Attired for the street I am an inch short of six feet. My nose is not sharp but blunt, the result of trying to tackle a man as he was kicking a ball. For an English nose it would hardly be called prominent. Wispy hair like steel wool? Nuts. It is limp. Walks with a forward-leaning lope, huh? Chandler cantered gaily into the cocktail lounge, rapidly consumed three double gimlets and fell flat on his kisser, his steel wool hair curling gracefully against the pattern of the carpet. No wonder this man Forster thinks me observant. By his standards anyone who noticed how many walls the room had would be observant.

. . .

Yours ever,

Ray

TO JUANITA MESSICK[1]

[1953]

That is a lot of bunk—removing the grid while preheating. Because why? The grid gets hot very quickly during cooking. The meat splatters grease all over it. The meat has to be turned and

1. Interviews. The one by Peter Forster is called "Gentle Tough Guy," *John O'London's Weekly*, March 6, 1953.

---

1. In answer to a note from Juanita Messick on cleaning the stove.

therefore does not always lie in the same place. What drivel sales people do talk! Take cigarette advertising. Every favorite brand is milder and less irritating than every other. The ideal cigarette has no taste at all. Therefore why smoke? What we need for broiling is a non-spattering steak, a steak containing no grease, fat, or other injurious ingredients, and incidentally, no flavor. What we need is a steakless steak to be broiled on a heatless broiler in a non-existent oven and eaten by a toothless ghost.

TO JUANITA MESSICK

[1953]

Did you find "neg-otiator"[1] somewhere? It looks all wrong to me. Some words are very hard to split and probably should not be split at all unless there is an obvious place. You can split a word after a prefix or before a suffix, you can split it after a root, but how else? There must be some rule about it.

The "neg" in negotiate has nothing to do with the neg in negative. The big Webster gives the syllable split on all words, some in four or five places, but they don't all look right when you put them down on paper. It seems to me that the first part of the split word, that at the end of the line, should at least suggest a meaning of some sort, or a word association which could become a meaning. The mind rejects a meaningless syllable, like the first two letters ("ne-") although this might be technically right. There should be enough of the word to show its probable shape. Somehow it seems better for the split-off part to suggest the wrong meaning than no meaning at all.

RC

1. Webster's Second and Third New International Dictionaries both divide the word as ne-go-ti-a-tor.

TO ALAN K. CAMPBELL

April 22, 1953

Dear Mr. Campbell:

I am replying to your kind letter of April 1st, inviting me to have something to say at a conference of the Harvard Summer School. Naturally I am grateful and flattered that you should think of me, and I am regretful that largely for personal reasons I cannot be in Boston in August. I say largely for personal reasons, and these reasons are compelling. But I do not say entirely, since it is not within my scheme of living, and I don't see how it ever could be, to get up on a platform and tell anyone about anything. Perhaps I am trying to make a virtue out of diffidence. I hope that is not entirely true, but it may be. I am not a lecturer nor have I any qualifications to be one. Too bad. It would be a nice one to drop into the still pool of respectful attention, "You know I lectured at Harvard last summer. It was rather fun." Thank you again, and believe me

Yours most respectfully,

TO HAMISH HAMILTON

Box One Twenty Eight
La Jolla, California
May 11, 1953

Dear Jamie:

Two things I am annoyed about in *The Journal of Eugene Delacroix*: one is the India paper, which of course I like very much in some ways but when the tops of the pages are painted they are so hard to turn; the other is reading a book as fine as this is in English when I might just as well be reading it in French. I suppose that this is an excellent translation, but the style seems to me a bit stuffy compared with the French. Take any sentence at random. Take the second one in the book: "My keenest wish is to remember that I am writing only for myself." What a heavy lump of suet that is compared

[341]

with the lightness and ease of the French, the casual arrangement of the words and so on. Damn translations anyway. We have to have them because there are so many languages we don't know, but they're never the real thing, not even the best of them. Thank you so much for Eric Partridge's book on punctuation just received. What a frightfully industrious old bird he is! Makes me nervous just to think of him spending day after day, month after month in the British Museum with mountains of books stacked all around him.

.   .   .

As to my own efforts, I should say I am about four-fifths of the way through *Summer in Idle Valley*, which I no longer like as a title, almost completely rewritten because of my unfortunate inability to edit anything except changing a word here or there.[1] If it isn't right, I always have to start all over again and rewrite it. It seems easier to me; it isn't easier I know, it just seems easier. Every now and again I get stuck on a chapter, and then I wonder why. But there's always a reason, and I have to wait for the reason to come to me. I got about halfway through the other book before I decided that that needed a very drastic revision also. This one is no longer any fun; I've been too close to it too long, and it may turn out not to be any good.

.   .   .

Yours ever,

TO ALFRED KNOPF

Box One Twenty Eight
La Jolla, California
July 16, 1953

Dear Alfred:

.   .   .

No, I am not on strike against publishing methods. I'd be

1. The title was later abandoned, and the book was published as *The Long Goodbye*.

foolish to criticize them too much, since I don't know the problems behind them well enough. I don't agree and I never have agreed that a publisher is entitled to collect more money in reprint rights than he pays out in royalties on his trade editions. He probably wouldn't be doing it, or not in all cases, if the silly old Authors League hadn't put everybody's back up by delivering ultimata with nothing to back them up but screams of anguish. Nor do I agree that a book is in print within the meaning of the terms of a publisher's contract when it is only in print in some paper-back edition which the publisher did not publish. But these may well be matters of opinion. I have just finished a book, as a matter of fact. I was never very productive, and I am not as productive as I used to be. I am much harder to satisfy than I used to be, also more easily tired. I am no longer with Brandt & Brandt, and in a way I regret that I was ever persuaded to leave you, although I realize I was no great financial asset to your publishing house. But I did, and a man can't keep jumping about from publisher to publisher. Anyhow, you have your hard-boiled writer now, and for a house of your standing one is enough.[1] I'm a little tired of the kick-'em-in-the-teeth stuff myself. I hope I have developed, but perhaps I have only grown tired and soft, but certainly not mellow. After all, I have fifty per cent Irish blood.

Yours with best wishes and kindest regards,

Ray

TO ROGER MACHELL

Box One Twenty Eight
La Jolla, California
July 17, 1953

Dear Roger:

.   .   .

I should especially like you to check me on two points that are outside

1. Probable reference to Ross Macdonald.

[343]

my territory: one, that it is neither quick nor easy for an enlisted man on active service to get permission to get married; and two, what is the procedure for getting married at the Caxton Hall Registry Office?[1] I am assuming that it is still in business. If it isn't, please suggest another that would be suitable. I have assumed that although a person making a false declaration is liable for perjury, it would not be very difficult to get married under a false name if you weren't afraid of being hooked for perjury. If there's anything else I should know that would involve any alterations in the script, would you please tell me. And remember that this is in war time. To cut it short, all I want to know is that what I said happened could have happened, because if it couldn't have happened, then I have to think of something else. It's always like this. You state one fact, but you have to have twenty other facts that you don't state to back it up.

Yours ever,

Ray

TO PHILIP GASKELL

Box One Twenty Eight
La Jolla, California
July 17, 1953

Dear Mr. Gaskell:

.   .   .

I will send you the information about the films as soon as I can. I don't suppose you are in any hurry for it. It's amusing that you should have mentioned Montgomery's version of *The Lady in the Lake* having nothing much to do with the book of that name.[1] I wrote the first script for this, but as I was under contract to Paramount

---

1. The questions relate to the typescript of *The Long Goodbye*.

---

1. Robert Montgomery, director and star of the film version of *The Lady in the Lake*.

and was only permitted thirteen weeks' work for another studio, this was not long enough for me to do the second and final shooting script. I didn't like the way that was done and refused to have my name on it. The amusing part is this—when I was working on the script I kept forgetting all about the book, because it was so much easier to do it ab initio. And it was the producer who kept saying to me, "Let's stick to the book a little here and there." This is the only published fiction of mine which I have tried to adapt for films. And it would take a lot of money to make me try it again, and I don't think that kind of money would be paid me now from Hollywood. When a man has written a book and rewritten it and rewritten it, he has had enough of it.

Yours very truly,

Raymond Chandler

TO JUANITA MESSICK

August 8 1953

Nita: I have a rather sad message for you. I'm afraid that the end of this month you and I are going to have to part company on the present basis, but I sincerely hope are not going to have to part company completely. The simple fact of the matter is that I cannot, as things now are, afford the luxury of a secretary who costs me nearly 2000 dollars a year. I just can't do it and that's all there is to it. You know my circumstances perfectly well and you know that except for windfalls on which no one can count, I can hardly look forward to an income of more than 10 or 12 thousand dollars a year, gross. You know that I'm getting older and more tired, and that I have many worries. It is just not in the picture that I should be able to spend a fifth or a sixth of my gross income for a secretary. I should go it alone—entirely alone—for a month and see what kind of help, the extent of the help I most urgently need and should have. And I should then like, if possible and convenient to make some kind of an arrangement with you. Of course if I had a script to be copied, I'd need somebody to copy it. I mean even want, say a day a week from you for letters. But I think I write many unnecessary letters and many unnecessarily long letters. And I think these letters consume a great deal of your time. The keeping of the books and the writing of the checks is nothing to me. The files are something else. They will probably be neglected unless you help with them. The same with the royalty statements. But after all, I'm pretty well on the downgrade and does it really matter so seriously? I am a worn, tired, man. I have lost my appetite and I have lost so much weight that I've had to punch two fresh holes in my belts. My clothes don't fit me any more. I'm depressed often and sleep badly. I have a sick wife who is not getting any better. I hope she will, and above all I hope that by the spring of this next year she will be well enough to go away somewhere for a long time. I'd like to go to Europe for a year. The cost of living in this country is so outrageous that when you begin to get old and have a little money saved up, it seems ridiculous not to go somewhere where life is a little cheaper. We have no very binding ties. I have found out that in my need nobody helps me. I'm not complaining. Nobody has that obligation.

.   .   .

I don't want to have to work in Hollywood or in television, nor in fact in any way at all except the writing of fiction. And I don't want to be driven in that. Well, if that is the situation, there is only one answer. You have to cut down on your expenses if you're going to cut down your output. Cissy has been going through a very bad time. And nobody helps her either, least of all the doctors. Perhaps they can't. They're not miracle workers. The fact is they don't. And I don't think any L.J. doctor will.[1] And I'm not sure that any doctor anywhere will.

I was 65 years old on my last birthday. As things go nowadays that's not old age exactly, but it does mean that you slow down, that you tire more quickly, that you have less ambition, that you are more easily irritated by business matters. And above all, you would occasionally like to sit in the sun and do nothing. Getting the breakfast, then driving myself to the typewriter for 3 or 4 hours, then almost at once going out to do the marketing, coming back and

1. La Jolla.

[346]

immediately starting to prepare the dinner, cooking it, washing the dishes, cleaning up afterward—this is not easy for me. It's not easy at all. I do it willingly, for I'd rather do it than have the kind of tramps in the house that we've had for the most part. But it's not easy. It takes its toll.

TO JUANITA MESSICK

August 12, 1953

Dear Nita:

Thank you for your note and all the rest of it, and I'm sure that we shall be able to work something out which won't interfere too much with what you are doing, and will not be unnecessarily elaborate from my point of view.

Please don't drive yourself too hard. If you are not comfortable, don't come. Don't be too conscientious about anything. It's always easy to overdo it. A certain amount of selfishness is necessary to the business of living. This is difficult for unselfish people to achieve, but it is very necessary, believe me.

By clearing out the files I meant mostly getting rid of the purely formal letters, etc., which contain no substantial material of any kind. I would not of course expect you to destroy any masterpieces of letter writing. Once in a while I run across one myself in the files, and I'm a little staggered if I happen to be the author of it to think I could have been so brilliant for no money. What a pity it is that there is nothing in essay writing. I could have been a very fine essayist, and should thoroughly have enjoyed that. Much more so than murder stories, which part of my mind always looks on with a certain condescension.

.   .   :

As to when you take a week off to take a trip, I should say you should take it when you can get something out of it. I may need a little help around Christmas time—that is the week before Christmas, but it isn't anything that couldn't be done the week before that if that should happen to be the week you want to take—I mean that if the week before Christmas should happen to be the week you want to take. I don't see that it really matters very much. We don't have to file another income tax estimate until the 15th of January and that one should be practically final. That is to say, the books should be posted and balanced up to the end of the year, the allocations of expense distributed, etc.; the depreciation schedules worked out.

As to your being a bore—or rather as to its being a bore to have somebody here all the time, that depends on the person. I did find it so with Mildred Onstine, because although she was an extremely likeable and efficient person, she had a sort of officy personality. I kept wondering if I was doing her justice and realizing that I was not. Your being here doesn't bore me; it doesn't bore my wife; and it doesn't bore Leona; and I'm quite sure it doesn't bore Taki.[1] But if in a tactfully indirect way you happen to be nudging at the suggestion that there are some things that you want to do or some activities that you want to follow which you find yourself cramped in attending, then I say you know how to arrange your work. Go ahead and do what you want to do and take the time you need to do it. This is not a factory. As you have probably realized by now, my greatest problem in life is to do any work. More and more, as the years go by, I am distracted and irritated by gardeners, plumbers, electricians, painters, carpenters, insurance men, and all the types that you have to have to do things for you, and that a man who is really a business man (which I am not) should be able to take in stride and then put them out of his mind. To me, each of these things is an operation. I get tired much more easily than I used to. Unfortunately I have a rather pugnacious temperament and I lack the stamina that ought to go with it to make it effective. I was once a main eventer, but I'm strictly a four-round prelim boy now. So the more of this stuff you can accustom yourself to handle, the more happy I shall be and the more productive my life would be. It costs a lot of money to live in La Jolla; it costs a lot of money to live the way we live, although I don't think we live extravagantly. And I can't make that money wrangling with technicians. I don't know why the hell I write so many letters, and I don't know why the hell when I do write letters, I have to write such long letters. I guess my mind

1. Leona the cook; Taki the cat.

is just too active for my own good. I have too much in me that never gets a chance to get said. It's probably not worth saying, but then that doesn't help me to realize that.

There is another thing you are probably well aware of, although I'm a little reluctant to mention it. And that is that my wife is not able to do what she did only a few years ago. When we came down here in 1946, sometimes she did all the housework, or almost all of it, with some daily help. She cooked the meals; she did the marketing; she dealt with painters and people of that sort; and she liked doing it. And I know that secretly she feels a little bit depressed that she can't do it now, and I wouldn't even talk to her about it. Won't mention it to her. But the fact is, she can't. For instance, she would say to me "Well you forget about the gardener. I'll get a gardener and handle him and attend to him. Just put it out of your mind." Then she'd get busy on the telephone and wear herself out talking to various people and finally get a gardener and he'd come and she'd follow around with him and spend a lot of time with him. And I could see it was tiring her too much. And then I'd gradually edge in and take over, and I wouldn't like it. I mean I wouldn't like to have to do it. I'm a man who takes very little lightly.

Now a secretary in the home is in an awkward position, that is an awkward position for most people. I don't think it is so for you, because it's not only the place where the man works. It's also his wife's home, and she doesn't like to take on herself things which she may not think are her business. So I should suggest to you that if the thought occurs to you "Well I could do that if he'd let me or he wants me to," or "I could do that for Mrs. Chandler, if she wants me to." Then I suggest that you say so right off, and that you ask my wife if she wouldn't like you to do so and so. But never hint to her that you don't think she's able to do it. And if you see me starting to do something which you know is going to end in my getting mad at somebody, why come right out and say, "You'd better leave me to do that. I think I can handle it. And if I can't I'll tell you." Or something to that effect. You can be even blunter. You don't have to be so damn polite. And as for being bored, again, with having somebody around all the time, I'm not bored, and I shan't be bored. But I'm perfectly well aware that there are times when it would be very natural for you to be bored. And when those times come, I suggest you simply get up and say "Well, I'm going out for awhile."

[349]

Or, "I'm going to San Diego this afternoon, and if you don't like it, to hell with you." Of course I shan't mind in the least, because you'll know better than I do whether it is going to be difficult or inconvenient.

Ten years ago I could have looked after this garden all by myself and enjoyed it. I'd have put in three or four hours a day on it probably. And though there would have been times when it would have bored me a little, on the whole I should have got a lot of fun and satisfaction out of it. I don't think I could do it now. One of the penalties of having enough money—and you never realize it until you have enough money—is that you don't get any satisfaction out of doing the things that save money. I admire the man who can paint his own house and roof and get a lot of healthy exercise and save himself a good big painter's bill. But saving that painter's bill probably means a lot to him—a lot more than it could possibly mean to me. That's something people don't think about. In my business it's a great deal easier to make money than it is to save it. But for some reason, or set of reasons I don't quite understand, I haven't lately been very successful in getting myself in the right mood to make money. It's my own fault. I shall never be able to change my temperament now. The most I can hope for is to outfox it occasionally.

Message ends.

TO H. F. HOSE

Box One Twenty Eight
La Jolla, California
Sept. 16 1953

Dear Hose:

I should write to you oftener. I have lost weight lately and I tire easily. I do a little work, then business letters, and after that no energy. No doubt you know the feeling. After sixty a man should not worry about trifles, but I do. (I don't mean that writing you is a trifle, but rather that worrying about trifles saps one's energies.) The best doctor I know has told me that I shall probably die of

[350]

exhaustion, as there is nothing else to kill me, no deterioration. I don't remember as well as I did. I have to make notes and lists. Sometimes quite familiar names slip off the edge of memory and hang out of sight, then pop back grinning.

When I was in London Slacker[1] told me that they retired masters at 60 (I believe that is the ridiculous age) because it was so much cheaper to employ a young man. That struck me as a ridiculous way of looking at things. He also said men of that age were out of touch with the boys. I should reply that in most cases any adult is out of touch with the average or even rather better than average boy. One of the weird problems of our time is the juvenile delinquent. Gangs of young crooks pop up in the most exclusive neighborhoods. Atlanta, Georgia, had a wave of burglaries and vandalism and it was traced to the young of some of the wealthiest families in the city. Our local high school (realschule or grammar school) had a Thieves Club among the children of the best families. Those who have much to do with the young tell me the delinquents come from the very poor and the rich, seldom from the ordinary middle class people. I happen to know it is not true. They come from any level of income. The wars have had a lot to do with it, no doubt, but much of it would have happened anyhow. There is no discipline in the schools because there is no means of enforcing it. And in the home parents argue with their children, they don't tell them. If I had children, and thank God I never had any, I should send them abroad to school. American schools are rotten, especially in California. If your boy won't behave himself, you can try a military school where he will be taught to behave himself (or expelled), but he won't learn anything else. You can send him to one of the New England snob schools like Groton, if you can afford it but unless you are well off it is not a kind thing to do. He will meet boys who drive Jaguars and Rileys and have too much spending money and he will feel inferior. Or you can send him to a Jesuit school, regardless of religion. The public schools are trash. About all they learn there is the increasingly simple art of seduction. The state universities have laughable standards of scholarship as a rule. One of my wife's nephews graduated (they say 'was graduated' over here, but I dislike the locution intensely) from high-school with the mental equipment of the Lower Fourth, say the

---

1. A mutual friend from Chandler's Dulwich days.

middle third of that form. But he has turned out very well. He couldn't have got into a state university, much less a place like Stanford or Pomona, but he faced the problem of earning a living without any trouble at all. I find that curious, and very American. He did fourteen months in Korea without any trace of old soldier nonsense about him, he is married, and he is very scrupulous about money. But you couldn't talk to him for five minutes about anything which assumed a knowledge of history or literature or even an awareness that such things exist.

.   .   .

No. I have never published anything under a pseudonym. I'm sure I don't know how the rumor you heard came about. I'd like to know. I have been ruthlessly imitated and even plagiarized of course, but there is nothing one can do about it. A few years ago a man wrote a story which was a scene by scene steal from one of mine. He changed names and incidents just enough to stay inside the law, which is not difficult as the courts have a very primitive attitude on plagiarism. The publisher to whom the book was sent demanded indignantly of the agent submitting it how he dared send them a book by Chandler under a pseudonym without saying so. When he learned that I had not had anything to do with the book he demanded certain changes to tone down the blatancy of the imitation and then published it. It did very well too. Someday an enlightened jurist of the type of Curtis Bok or Learned Hand may announce that the plagiarism of style is the most nefarious of all forms of plagiarism and the shabbiest. But it would be very difficult to draw the line between the natural imitativeness of a writer influenced by another and the deliberate attempt to steal his characteristic mise en scene. After all if another writer can really steal your style, it can't be very important. The answer is that he can't, he can only produce some of the superficial characteristics.

.   .   .

And so to bed, but without any particular content of mind.

Yours ever,

Ray

[352]

TO J. B. PRIESTLEY

Box One Twenty Eight
La Jolla, California
December 10, 1953

Dear Priestley:

Many thanks for yours of November 25th and the comments therein. In thinking I should write a Marlowe story without a murder or any violence in it you are one with my wife who thinks exactly the same thing. Would it be all right if he got conked on the head with a Scotch bottle just once? On the other hand, the whole business of writing demands a lot of verve, and I just don't have it any more. It doesn't seem to matter.

I never did thank you for arranging that showing of *Last Holiday*, to which we were conducted by a furious character named Peters, coldly furious I should add, who would make a perfect superintendent of police at Scotland Yard. His manner was impeccable, but the whole deal was obviously a crashing bore to him and he could hardly wait for it to be over. We enjoyed the picture immensely, but I had some qualms about the ending. I don't mean that it was wrong, and I'm quite sure you gave it plenty of thought. But the irony did seem a little factitious. The picture hasn't shown up out here, although it is playing in New York, but when and if it does, I'd like very much to see it again. It has some lovely scenes.

My wife remembers the luncheon with you with a great deal of pleasure. I regret to say that she is not at all well, as she was not when you were here. I am hoping but rather against hope that we shall be able to make to Europe again next spring. She felt very badly all the time we were in London but tried hard not to show it.

With kindest regards,

Yours ever,

Ray

[353]

TO HAMISH HAMILTON

Box One Twenty Eight
La Jolla, California
Jan 16, 1954

Dear Jamie:

Thank you so much for the bound copy (I should have said specially bound) of *LG*.[1] I don't really think my books are worth so handsome a binding and I have moments when I feel like hiding them—except that it would look rather ungrateful to you. I have visions as it were of some snooty character looking over my bookshelves and saying to himself: "Does this type really think his books belong in calf with gold edges and gold tooling?" However, what is a man to do?

.   .   .

Los Angeles has nothing for me anymore. It's only a question of time until a Gentile has to wear an armband there. The story I am fitfully working on at the moment is laid in La Jolla and will be much shorter and more light-hearted than *LG*. But I'm fed up with the California locale.

I don't know whether this true story will have any meaning for you, but it amused me no end. A woman and her small boy were in the local bookshop and the woman was browsing and the kid was trying to tell her about a dog that was hurt by a car. She was giving him the usual absent, "Yes, darling," while really thinking of something else. "The poor little dog was hurt awful bad, Mummy," the kid said. "He was hurt awful bad." "Was he, dear?" "Yes, Mummy, he was hurt awful bad but he dragged hisself all the way home, Mummy. He was hurt so bad but he dragged hisself all the way home, Mummy." "Did he, dear? Well, that's nice." The kid looked up at her sadly, then said, "He got home all right Mummy. But he passed on."

.   .   .

When duller letters are written, Chandler will write them.

Ray

1. *The Long Goodbye.*

P.S. Your letter with clippings arrived just as I was about to post this, so I have opened it to add a little. I don't begin to understand this reference to Henry James (of whom once I was a desperately ardent admirer). Over here I have never been treated otherwise than as a rather good second-rate thriller writer and I thought the same was the attitude in England and I assumed that these desires for interviews were more the result of your kindly machinations than any spontaneous wishes on the part of newspapers, etc. It has always been clear to me that if the good Lord had intended me to be an important writer, he would not have allowed me to waste twenty years of my life in offices, almost ten of them as the factotum of a corrupt multi-millionaire. (Anyone who thinks I don't understand rich people of a certain type is wrong.) There are things about writing that I love, but it is a lonely and ungrateful profession and personally I'd much rather have been a barrister, or even an actor. It is always a misfortune to be taken seriously in a field of writing where quality is not expected nor desired. The highbrows find it hard enough to forgive popularity, even moderate popularity such as mine, but popularity plus pretentions to any kind of literary distinction—that is too, too much. How they must have suffered over Maugham!

TO MR. LOVELL[1]

Box One Twenty Eight
La Jolla, California
Feb 9, 1954

Dear Mr. Lovell:

.   .   .

I suppose in the history of writing there must have been quite a few one book writers. *Delay in the Sun* by Anthony Thorne (he has written other books but ng.) The most impressive examples I recall are *The Unbearable Bassington* by Saki (of course he wrote a lot of

1. A book collector

[355]

short pieces but I think no other novel) and a book you probably never heard of called *The Great Humpty-Dumpty* by Daniel Chaucer.[2] When one is young one has love affairs with books as with girls. I recall this book with delight but should be afraid to read it now, just as I should be afraid to reread another early darling of mine called *The Loves of Edwy* by Rose Ceil O'Neill. (She was really a gifted illustrator, but this book got to me when I was at the impressionable age.) Chaucer's book was to have been called *The Dark Forest* but he found out Hugh Walpole had published a book with that title. Hence the regrettable substitution.

A la recherche du temps perdu—that way lies disillusion. Like the fellow who wanted to take his bride to see the little lake near Saint Cloud with the swans on it that he remembered so vividly from a childhood in France. It was to be one of the high lights of their honeymoon. When they arrived there and established the location—no lake, no swans. There never had been a lake there and there never had been any swans.

The swans of our childhood were probably just pigeons.

Yours,

Raymond Chandler

TO JAMES M. FOX[1]

Box One Twenty Eight
La Jolla, California
February 16, 1954

Dear Fox:

.   .   .

I don't know why I should write an autobiography. My English publisher said once I should, but I fail to agree with him. If I

2. Pseudonym used by Ford Madox Ford for this book *The New Humpty-Dumpty*.

1. Author of *Dark Crusade* and other books.

did it, it would be full of lies. I don't think anyone else could do it, though, and I shouldn't care for the idea. What your arguments are I have no idea, but they will almost certainly not convince me. There is no reason why a man should not write his autobiography if he can make it interesting enough. He doesn't have to be a person of any vast distinction. The only point is, is it a book? Like Neville Cardus (not sure of the way he spells his first name).[2] You don't read it because you are curious about him, but because he makes his life interesting. It is quite another matter for a man to assume that he is so much of a personality that a biography is a matter of public interest, regardless of who writes it.

     .   .   .

As to the ending or denouement not being a surprise, what ending is to someone in the trade? You are opening up a large box of crackers here. I could exhaust myself discussing it because it is one of my favorite beefs. I claim that no "honest" mystery plot will fool the aficionado. The operative word here is "honest" and I mean it in a very rigorous sense. You don't write for just one kind of people. A mystery subtle enough to come near fooling the analytical mind will make no sense to the ordinary rental library ghoul. So you have a choice. Either assume that your denouement is going to be transparent to some people or else cheat. Very often you do both without realizing it. The cheat may be merely a matter of over or under-emphasis, the burying of the essential clue in a mass of trivia, the revelation early in a book of a certain abnormal facet of character which is then immediately dropped until the end. The first person story is assumed to tell all but it doesn't. There is always a point at which the hero stops taking the reader into his confidence. There is the solution which turns on a recondite piece of knowledge, as in Austin Freeman. There is the solution which depends on something not disclosed to the reader until almost the end, such as in Sayers's *Have His Carcase*. That is a cheat for two reasons; one, because it was withheld too long, the other because the police surgeon, unless he was an idiot, would have known the dead man was a hemophiliac. I don't want to labor the point. I never bother about who bumped off Sir Montague Core-Cavendish in the gun room with the doors

2. Music critic, journalist, and author of books on cricket.

and windows all locked. Very often just for the fun of it I look at the end and then amuse myself with watching the author trying to smudge his fingerprints. And a surprise ending is no good if you don't believe it. If the reader doesn't think he *should* have known, he has been had. And what doesn't fool you will fool all sorts of other people, including reviewers. The typical mystery novel is like that thing on Studio One last night. An obvious suspect is presented and played up and you immediately eliminate her just because she has been played up. An old man in a wheel chair can get out of it to snitch a drink at the sideboard. Another red herring. The old housekeeper is obviously just what she pretends to be. The youngest sister is in love with the doctor who is going to solve the mystery. So who is left? The sister who got the poison pen letters. So she wrote them to herself. Why? No reason that makes sense. So she did it without knowing what she was doing. At that point I didn't give a damn and was far more interested in speculating why the doctor went out of the room leaving his medical bag open in the presence of a loony and what drug he would have with him that worked almost as fast as cyanide and yet gave the dear girl time to use her exit line. I had to give up on that one.

So long,

R.C.

TO HARDWICK MOSELEY

Box One Twenty Eight
La Jolla, California
March 23rd, 1954

Dear Hardwick:

    I'm sick as a dog, thank you, with one of these lousy virus infections the doctors have invented to cover up their ignorance. But I know you want an answer. I missed seeing Paul Brooks two weeks ago and I'm still rocking. I also missed a *Time* photog but they intrinsically lied. He was from the San Diego *Union-Tribune* and there is no worse murderer than a newspaper flash gun artist. They did one of me in London that made me look like Grandma Moses and I swore I'd never have another. (By the way where did you get that beastly thing you put in your spring list?) Of course *Time* doesn't matter because the fact that they interview you or photograph you is no guarantee. Imagine those lice in *Newsweek* not even paying for the photographs they ordered![1]

You better do a damn sight better with *The Long Goodbye* than you did with *Little Sister*. I realize the appalling situation but I also realize that the publishers are not indefinitely going to be able to make their profits if any by their share of the reprints. Writers of forgettable fiction will simply be forced into the paperback market. How the hell can you expect anyone to pay dollars three for a mystery novel? I might be the best writer in this country, and with two exceptions I very likely am, but I'm still a mystery writer. For the first time in my life I was reviewed as a Novelist in the London *Sunday Times* (but Leonard Russell is a friend of mine and may have leaned a little out of kindness). I was discussed on the BBC by as addled a group of so-called intellectuals (among whom Dilys Powell hardly got a word in) as ever had soup on their vests. But over here? *The New York Times* which surely should know what it is doing if any newspaper does has twice given books of mine for review to mystery writers who had been waiting for years for the chance to knife me because I have ridiculed the sort of thing they write themselves (not mentioning them by name in any sense nor even by suggestion). Neither had either the guts or the ability to make a reply on the same level as the original article. It could be that the *Times* has it in for me because I have persistently refused to review books for them; on the other hand they change personnel so often that they probably don't even know I refused. But what I'm getting at is that if a paper of that quality can't judge a book by its quality as a piece of writing rather than by its news value or subject matter, how in hell can one expect a semi-literate public to do anything more intelligent?

.　　　　.　　　　.

We are still trying to sell this house, much as we like it. My wife is far from well, domestic help is unobtainable unless you have,

1. Chandler had been promised a *Newsweek* cover story, but it was never published.

as we have, a treasure. But we have her only five days a week, she is not too well herself, and she has troubles which may end her for us at almost any time. If I get sick over a week end, it is a catastrophe. My wife almost fainted two or three times last weekend trying to take care of me. We can't live here indefinitely. We are thinking of the south of France. The climate would be good for Cissy. But it's a pretty risky adventure all the same. I have an operative working on it. What acquaintances tell you is no good unless you know their own standards. I'm not terribly fond of French people but I know the language and they at least do their own thinking and can express it in language. A stevedore on the docks is more articulate in France than most senators and Congressmen are here. And McCarthy would last over there about the length of time necessary to uncover the cesspool.[2]

I salute you finally with two animal stories, one true, one not. A family on the street behind us has a black French poodle, small, toy size, I guess. The animal is taking piano lessons, $35 a month. As of now he can play Peter, Peter, Pumpkin Eater, not technically very exacting, but one has to begin, n'est-ce pas? Little steps for little feet. Later one hopes he will make his debut in Carnegie Hall. The people can afford it and that's all it takes. One looks forward, perhaps a little hesitantly, to his scintillating performance of Chopin's Barcarolle, a difficult piece seldom played and never played really well since de Pachmann.[3] Rubinstein is supposed to be a Chopin virtuoso, but to me he is very in and out. The poodle has a pretty clear field there. It's nice to have ambitious neighbors, and to live in a milieu where money is spent on Art, not just on Cadillacs, Jaguars, and colored butlers. This is true. $35 a month for lessons. Black toy French poodle.

The other one is about a guy who went to the *Cinema* (English accent please) and was annoyed by a large, tall and far too wide fur coat in front of him. Leaning over he perceived that the fur coat was a bear. He tapped the man beside the bear on the shoulder.

"I say, old man, is that your bear?"

"He's with me."

"Well get him out of here right away, old man. This is no place to bring a bear."

2. Senator Joseph McCarthy.
3. Vladimir de Pachmann (1848–1933), eccentric Russian pianist and champion of Chopin.

"I shall do nothing of the sort. He's paid for his ticket and he's enjoying himself."

Man subsides, very annoyed. Picture ends finally, lights go up, man with bear seems about to leave. Objecting man has a change of heart.

"I say, old man, sorry I spoke like that about your bear. Seems dashed well behaved. But why bring him to the pictures, old man?"

"Oh, he's very fond of the *cinema*, very fond indeed. And he particularly wanted to see this film. He liked the book so much."

Ray

TO ROGER MACHELL

Box One Twenty Eight
La Jolla, California
March 24th. 1954

Dear Roger:

There's quite a bit to answer in your good letter but before I get on to it, two or three items I'm afraid of forgetting. 1. For God's sake save your people the anguish and expense of sending me 8 copies of Finnish translations. Four would be more than enough. My wife keeps one (she has a new issue of everything of mine ever published, even pulp magazines), I keep a so-called file copy and it's always possible in this polyglot country that I may run across someone who would like a book in Finnish. They do a nice job on them, but Jesus what a language! Everything is backwards. I once hoped to be a comparative philologist (just a boyhood fancy no doubt) and dabbled in such strange lingos as Modern Greek (there's a debased language for you—it just *looks* like Greek, all the richness and variety is gone, all the subtlety, all the charm), Armenian, Hungarian, besides the simpler and more obvious Romance tongues and the Germanic group. I slept with a chart of the 214 key ideographs of the Chinese Mandarin language pinned to the wall at the head of my bed in the Pension Narjollet, 27 Boulevard St. Michel, au cinquième. But Finnish, hell it's worse than Turkish.

[361]

As for Commercial TV, here is a small true story of the kind of atmosphere the domination of the big advertising agencies can create. A few years back the Pepsodent Company took over sponsorship of a radio series on Philip Marlowe as a summer replacement. Their agency was a big firm which also at the time handled Chesterfield cigarettes. The producer of the show is the brother of a very well-known actor. He told me the story. A company big shot (partner) visited the L.A. office on business, a severe and elegant gentleman immaculate and grey, one of these extraordinary people of our time who seem to be able to reconcile wealth, position, blameless private lives and perfect manners with an idiotic devotion to the latest brand of skin-poisoning detergent or face cream (if the manufacturer is their account, natch). This geek happened to see a junior executive entering the premises that morning smoking a Philip Morris cigarette. He stopped him and said: "I observe, Mr. Jones, that you do not care for the product of our sponsor." Mr. Jones flushed and looked at the cigarette he was holding. Oh, I'm extremely sorry, Mr. Blank. I was rather in a hurry this morning and instead of my own Chesterfields I must have grabbed up one of my wife's cigarettes." Mr. Blank stared at him in silence for a long moment, then, as he turned away, he remarked icily: "I presume that your wife has an income of her own."

You know, that sort of thing makes a cold shiver run down my spine.

Ray

TO DOROTHY GARDINER[1]

April, 1954

As a writer of 20 years' professional experience I have met all kinds of people. Those who know most about writing are those who can't write. The less attention you pay to them the better. They

---

1. Former secretary of the Mystery Writers of America. This statement was written for *The Third Degree*, the bulletin of that organization.

are on the outside looking in and what they see is no good to the man inside; it is in a different category of mind. So I have made three rules of writing for myself that are absolutes: Never take advice. Never show or discuss work in progress. Never answer a critic.

TO HARDWICK MOSELEY

Box One Hundred Twenty Eight
La Jolla, California
May 6, 1954

Dear Hardwick:

.   .   .

No one has ever attacked me so far and yet in every book I have written there is what is described by more perceptive friends as a "thinly disguised portrait" of some notorious local character. In every case, the thinly disguised etc. has been a portrait of someone I didn't even know existed. In *The High Window* I had an Italian mortician on Bunker Hill who was a political boss on the side. Well, whaddaya know, there actually was an Italian mortician on Bunker Hill who was a political boss, and a pretty crooked one, on the side. But I never heard of him. I invented him. I suppose it's an old story. And yet when you do use some really notorious person as a model nobody spots it.

.   .   .

Some crazy idiot at Little Brown sent me a book called *Freak Show*.[1] I haven't the slightest intention of reading it nor have I the faintest idea why they published it. So it may easily be a bestseller. I would say the guy might be a road show James Cain except that James Cain is a road show James Cain himself.

With malice towards all,

Yours always,

Ray

1. *Freakshow*, by Jacquin Sanders.

TO ROGER MACHELL

Box One Twenty Eight
La Jolla, California
May 25, 1954

Dear Roger:

Thanks for your letter and statements and for the remittance which the Canadian Bank of Commerce has duly confirmed. I'm enclosing a letter from a Portuguese agent in Lisbon which will possibly be of no interest to you. The only point that stuck me, if it is valid, was his statement that Portuguese readers do not like Brazilian translations. I'm sure this is very likely since the South American languages must have departed considerably from the standard of the mother country.

I see that Cassells had an ad in the *Sunday Times* which quoted part of Mr. Iles' gratuitously offensive remarks ("snide" is our word for that sort of thing) but did leave out the slur about nymphomaniacs.[1] Somebody ought to tell these dessicated creeps what a nymphomaniac is. They apparently seem to think the word is synonymous with promiscuity, or even with a mild fling at adultery. Of course I ought not to pay any attention to them and usually I just take the bad with the good and realize that I have probably had more than my share of the good. But if I were somewhat younger and heartier, I might take a fling at it anyhow, realising the weakness of the legal position (it would be far weaker here) but also realising that it is one thing to slam a book when it has been handed to you for review and quite another to keep sniping at a writer under cover of reviewing somebody else. There is a certain class of 'tec writer or ex-'tec writer who will never forgive me for having blown up their pretense of writing deduction. In this class are Anthony Boucher over here, John Dickson Carr, Lenore Glen Offord, Anthony Berkeley and so on. There are no doubt many others, but I mention those who review books. "Oh that mine enemy would write a book!" I've often been asked to review books that seemed more or less up my alley but I have always declined—The *N.Y. Times* was especially

1. Francis Iles and Anthony Berkeley are pseudonyms for Anthony Berkeley Cox, a reviewer and critic.

[364]

persistent—because I am aware of having prejudices and I don't think I have any right to exploit them at the expense of some struggling writer.

The practical effect of all this sneering at me is to make me self-conscious to the point where it is difficult for me to write anything in my somewhat bravura manner without wondering whether I am not just making an ass of myself. That is the writer's cross and few bear it without getting weary. Theoretically he should be as hard as nails, as insensitive as the pavement. If he were, he would have no magic, and without some magic there is nothing. He does not expect everyone to like him and, in fact, he is often enough surprised that anyone likes him. No matter how successful he has been, he always starts from scratch on the next job. The public or whatever small fraction of it reads him expects from him always much the same thing. He is supposed to deliver a staple article. But the critics expect him to break new ground with every new effort. Of course if he did, they would be most happy to announce that he would have been wiser to stay within the established formula.

Yours ever,

Ray

TO ROGER MACHELL

Box One Twenty Eight
La Jolla, California
Sunday July 11, 1954
Tuesday July 13, 1954

Dear Rog:
This is what they would call you if you lived over here. We are so goddam busy watching TV that we don't have the time to speak anyone's full name.

.   .   .

THE UCLA Library (University of California at Los Angeles)

[365]

has asked for the typescript of any of my books, but I never have kept it. However they got *The Long Goodbye* from Houghton Mifflin. What on earth they want it for I can't imagine. They also wanted to purchase a first edition of *Farewell My Lovely*. I didn't have one but offered them the first English edition of which I had a copy, and they accepted it with an ornate scroll. By the way this title, which I thought entirely original, turned up as the title of a piece by E. B. White (under a pseudonym—Lee Strout White) about the Model T Ford. This was, I think, originally published in the *New Yorker*, but long before I ever looked at the magazine. It wasn't until I went to work in Hollywood that I knew the magazine existed and I have never really liked it. There is an undertone of spitefulness about too much of its writing—not all, of course—that is quite missing from *Punch*. *Punch* you have to read; the *New Yorker* you just glance through. I don't know how these things happen. One would think I had seen the magazine in a doctor's office but no. My memory for that sort of material is much too good. It happens just as people happen to steal your story ideas before you even use them. Certain things are in the air.

    Leave us all go home.

Yours ever,

Ray

TO HAMISH HAMILTON

July 15th, 1954

Dear Jamie:

    Thank you so much for sending me the books; *Pompadour*, *The Long Beat Home*, *The Woman with No Past*, and the pseudo-Victorian novel which Cissy has and I forget the title.[1] *The Long Beat Home* looks like a nice try, but it doesn't seem to me to have that crisp something that gets you by the throat and holds on. I don't know whether we Americans (I always feel like a phoney when I say 'we

---

1. *Madame de Pompadour*, by Nancy Mitford; *The Long Bear Home* by Peter Gladwin; *The Woman with No Past*, by Serge Groussard.

Americans' because basically I never have and never will feel quite a native) are more mentally lazy than you English; I rather think we are, but I'm not sure; but I do think we are more resentful of having to do the donkey work of getting interested in something—unless we know in advance that is worth the effort. For instance *The Go-Between* was a very highly praised book, but I started it and dropped it and went back half a dozen times before I got far enough into it to give a damn about anyone.[2] And even then I did a lot of skipping. And I never quite believed the book. I tried to see the world through the eyes of this boy, but I was a twelve year old myself and in much the same period and it just didn't look that way to me. Somehow for me the novel lacks a dimension. Or I lack one. I've read Maugham's articles in the *Sunday Times* as far as they have come this way.[3] Maugham would have done that story to perfection, but he wouldn't have written it through the eyes of a 12 year old boy. He would have known damn well that it is not possible and he is much too acute to attempt the impossible. Sometimes one thinks that is rather a pity. So long and distinguished a career deserves at least one magnificent failure.

Pompadour is a lot of fun. What a woman, what a world, what a waste! But the world I grew up in is almost as remote. A wonderful world if you were born into exactly the right family, a blasted cold hypocritical cruel world if you were not. Still, at least part of the population had a good time. No one has nowadays except the crooks and the oil millionaires (there may be a slight distinction here but I was in the oil business for about ten years and the distinction is very fine), and perhaps some of the higher civil servants, but they are usually too stupid to know it. What a strange sense of values we had. What godawful snobs! My grandmother referred to one of the nicest families we knew as "very respectable people" because there were two sons, five golden haired but unmarriagable daughters and no servant. They were driven to the utter humiliation of opening their own front door. The father painted, sang tenor, built beautiful model yachts and sailed a small yawl all over the place. My grandmother was the widow of an Irish solicitor. Her son, very wealthy later on, was also a solicitor and had a housekeeper named Miss Groome who sneered at him behind his back because he wasn't a barrister. The

2. By L. P. Hartley
3. A series on the authors and their novels.

Church, the Navy, the Army, the Bar. There was nothing else. Outside Waterford in a big house with gardens and gardens lived a Miss Paul who occasionally, *very* occasionally invited Miss Groome to tea on account of her father had been a canon. Miss Groome regarded this as the supreme accolade because Miss Paul was County. It didn't seem to bother Miss Paul but it sure as hell made a wreck of Miss Groome. It would be some comfort to add that she was a capable housekeeper, but she was not. My uncle had a succession of awful Irish Protestant maids and cooks and so on—always Protestants, as they and the Catholics had little or nothing to do with one another on any level. I remember playing a cricket match with one of my cousins and one of the boys was a Catholic from some probably rather important family. Anyhow he came in a carriage with a coachman and footman and after the game immediately departed without even having tea with the teams. My uncle was a man of rather evil temper on occasion. Sometimes when the dinner did not suit him he would order it removed and we would sit in stony silence for three quarters of an hour while the frantic Miss Groome browbeat the domestics below stairs and finally another meal was delivered to the master, probably much worse than the one he had refused; but I can still feel that silence.

A strange and puzzling thing, the English snobbishness. I was a poor relation and one of my cousins had a short job as some kind of companion to a very well-to-do family living in a suburb not very far away. Later on when I was about seventeen, I think, I was invited over to their house to play tennis. They were rather gaudy people, except the father. A number of the guests were very young girls and young men, all expensively dressed, and several rather drunk. I was in no way expensively dressed, but far from feeling inferior I realized at once that these people were not at all up to the standard even of Dulwich, and heaven knows what Eton or Rugby would have thought about them. The boys and girls had gone to private schools, but not the right kind. There was a little something about their accents, and more than a little about their manners. (One sicked up in the drawing room.) During the course of an afternoon of rather studied courtesy on my part the family dog chewed up my straw hat with the school ribbon on it. When I left, the head of the family, a very nice little man in some kind of "trade" in the City, insisted on paying for the hat. I coldly refused to accept his money, although in those times it was quite usual for the host to tip a schoolboy at the end of a visit. But this seemed to me different. This was taking money from a social inferior: not to be thought of. Yet they were kind people and full of fun and very tolerant and, as I look back on it now, probably much more worth knowing than my stupid and arrogant grandmother. Of course the genuine top drawer people were quite different, insofar as I ever got close to them for a few brief moments.

Yours ever,

Ray

What a lot of drivel!

TO EDGAR CARTER

September 21, 1954

Dear Eddie:
    Herewith the CBS contract, signed, and signed also the declaration that I am not, have not ever been, and do not intend ever to be a hole in a piece of Swiss cheese.[1] My God, what is this country coming to? What are we afraid of? As a charter member of the C.B.S.A. (Colored Baby Sitters of America, Inc.) I resent the suggestion that I am not a four hundred per cent loyal American and that I must sign a document of this type in order that something which I once wrote may be transmuted into something that somebody else has since rewritten, and no doubt abominably, for the purposes of television, which has, by a far less brilliant mind than mine, been described as "infinite boredom in a little room." Nevertheless, the soft buck is paramount; nothing must be allowed to interfere with its oleaginous progress into the bank account. However, for the moment I think we are fairly safe. Of the seventeen decorations I received from Stalin, fifteen are buried in an old salmon can under the third

1. Anti-Communist loyalty oath.

juniper tree to the left, and the other two are buried in the back of my
neck. And after all, the stuff I stole wasn't very important really. I
think the best find the FBI made was that scribbled greeting, "Good
morning, chief," which I had rather inefficiently concealed behind
the lining of my second-best silk hat. But I don't think they ever
would have found that if they hadn't happened on an agent with two
heads who insisted upon wearing two silk hats all the time.
Something besides his ears must have rustled in one of them.

Yours ever,

TO H. N. SWANSON

Box One Twenty Eight
La Jolla, California
September 22, 1954

Dear Swanie:

.   .   .

I know that you can make a lot of money out of the big magazines if
you have the right approach and the temperament to accept their
suggestions and fit yourself into their ideas of what makes good
fiction. Half a dozen third-rate mystery writers are getting their
stories serialized in the slicks regularly, and more power to them. You
spent about three months trying to get some bid for the serial rights
of *The Long Goodbye*, whereas you ought to have known in the
beginning it never would be serialized. Or perhaps you did know and
didn't want to trust your own judgment. I don't know what the
difference is; I don't know just what it is that I haven't got, but it is
something. I guess maybe there are two kinds of writers; writers
who write stories and writers who write writing. There are a hundred
clever plot architects for every writer who can do you a paragraph
of prose with a touch of magic to it on whatever level, in whatever
vein you happen to be interested in. Perhaps some of the better
magazine editors know the difference, but I'm damned sure the critics

don't. . . . You're a sweet guy, Swanie, one of the nicest I ever met. In fact, until I met you I didn't think it was possible for an agent to be a nice guy, and in that I should like to include Eddie.[1] But don't believe very much the magazine editors tell you. Some day you might do me a favor, if you felt inclined. Get some of these fiction writers to write me a letter direct and tell me, if they have happened to have read anything I have written, just what I would have to do to please them. I don't know, and I don't think you do either.

Yours ever,

Ray

TO HAMISH HAMILTON

Box One Twenty Eight
La Jolla, California
September 27, 1954

Dear Jamie:

Yours of September 13th contains a word which I had to look up in the dictionary, "inspissate."[1] This annoyed me very much, as although there are many words in fairly common use which I probably do not know accurately, having but a cloudy idea of their exact meaning, it isn't often that I come across a word that I don't know at all. It was some relief to find that Webster's Unabridged marks the adjectival form, which you used, as obsolete. Please don't think that I grudge you the word; you probably picked it up from some antique and over erudite pansy decomposing in an Italian villa amid a welter of fake masterpieces.

.   .   .

When I write to Roger [Machell] I shall have the pleasure of giving him a detailed account of how I broke my toe, because he, as a victim of gout, would probably have some small sympathy for me.

---

1. Edgar Carter, Swanson's associate.

---

1. It means to thicken, usually by evaporation.

I've got nowhere with the recital over here. Some little time ago I was in the garage where we send our cars to be serviced and having about fifteen minutes of spare time on my hands to converse with the assistant manager, I thought this might be a good opportunity to tell him all about my toe. But I didn't even get a complete sentence out. As soon as he realized what I was leading up to he started on a long and detailed account of how he dislocated his thumb. I think the foundations for the accident went back to his childhood and to a time when he was about five years old, and from then on the detail was copious. I left him with many expressions of sympathy and by this time I don't think he even knew I had broken my toe. It's been the same everywhere. Nobody wants to hear about my toe.

.　　　　.　　　　.

As to writing my memoirs, Jamie, and you are not the only one who has suggested it to me nor is this the first time you have suggested it, I can only say that I don't think I could face it. It seems to me there are people who can write their memoirs with a reasonable amount of honesty, and there are people who simply cannot take themselves seriously enough. I think I might be the first to admit that the sort of reticence which prevents a man from exploiting his own personality is really an inverted sort of egotism.

.　　　　.　　　　.

If you really want to know what I should really like to write, it would be fantastic stories, and I don't mean science fiction. A dozen or so of them have been rattling around in my head for a great many years, pleading to be put down on paper. But they wouldn't make a thin worn dime. That would just be a wonderful way to become a Neglected Author. God, what a fascinating document could be put together about these same Neglected Authors and also the one book writers: fellows like Edward Anderson who long ago wrote a book called *Thieves Like Us*, one of the best crook stories ever written. John Houseman made a picture from it for Howard Hughes and Anderson wrote to Houseman and said that he was trying to build himself a house somewhere down in Texas and could they possibly give him another hundred dollars! Then there is James Ross who wrote a novel published by Houghton Mifflin, called *They Don't Dance Much,* a sleazy, corrupt but completely believable story of a

[372]

North Carolina town about the size of Raleigh. I've read the book several times and I've never heard that he ever wrote anything else. When I was a boy a man named Daniel Chaucer wrote a book called *The Dark Forest*, and then found out that there was a novel of the same name by Hugh Walpole and had to change the title to *The New Humpty-Dumpty*.[2] It was a better book than Walpole could ever hope to write, and I don't think Chaucer ever wrote anything else. And there's Aaron Klopstein. Who ever heard of him? I don't suppose you have. He committed suicide at the age of 33 in Greenwich Village by shooting himself with an Amazonian blow gun, having published two novels entitled *Once More The Cicatrice* and *The Sea Gull Has No Friends*, two volumes of poetry, *The Hydraulic Face Lift* and *Cat Hairs in the Custard*, one book of short stories called *Twenty Inches of Monkey*, and a book of critical essays entitled *Shakespeare in Baby Talk*.

Well, I guess that's enough for now, Jamie. All the best to you.

Yours ever,

Ray

TO LEONARD RUSSELL

December 29, 1954

Dear Leonard:

Your letter of December 15th has just reached me, the mails being what they are around Christmas time. I have received much sympathy and kindness and many letters, but yours is somehow unique in that it speaks of the beauty that is lost rather than condoling with the comparatively useless life that continues on.[1] She was everything you say, and more. She was the beat of my heart for thirty years. She was the music heard faintly at the edge of sound. It was my great and now useless regret that I never wrote anything really

2. Chaucer was Ford Madox Ford.

1. Chandler's wife Cissy died on December 12, 1954.

worth her attention, no book that I could dedicate to her. I planned it. I thought of it, but I never wrote it. Perhaps I couldn't have written it.

She died hard. Her body fought a hundred lost battles, any one of which would have been enough to finish most of us. Twice I brought her home from the hospital because she hated hospitals, and had her in her own bed in her own room with nurses around the clock. But she had to go back. And I suppose she never quite forgave me for that. But when at the end I closed her eyes she looked very young. Perhaps by now she realizes that I tried, and that I regarded the sacrifice of several years of a rather insignificant literary career as a small price to pay, if I could make her smile a few times more.

No doubt you realize that this was no sudden thing, that it had been going on for a long time, and that I have said goodbye to my Cissy in the middle of the night in the dark cold hours many, many times. She admired and liked you very much. I'm not sure that she liked Dilys as much as I did, because possibly she suspected that I liked her too much. And it is just possible that I thought she liked *you* a little too much.

I hope that you are both well and prosperous and that I may have the privilege of seeing you again in the not too distant future, with or without the butler from the Ritz. And I hope I am not being too sentimental if I sign myself,

Yours affectionately,

TO HAMISH HAMILTON

Box One Twenty Eight
La Jolla, California
January 5, 1955

Dear Jamie:
It was nice to talk to you on the telephone. It was the first and probably the only time I shall ever permit myself the luxury of a trans-Atlantic telephone call. The occasion seemed somehow to justify

it, and it did not cost as much as I expected. Thank you for your several kind letters and also for the books you sent. Please don't send me any more books, as they will only have to go into storage. I don't recall whether I told you that I have sold the house, but I have, and I will be out of here about March 15th or before. I don't think I can make it to New York early in February. In fact, I don't think that the trip would be worthwhile, because I am planning to take a Swedish boat through the Canal about the first or second week in April. The dates of sailings are not fixed yet so I can't be absolute. I'll let you know as soon as I know myself about when I shall be in London. I gather from your letter that you would like me to stay with you at your house for a little while. But if I may say so without sounding ungrateful, I should rather be on my own. I'd like to be at a hotel—any good hotel, even the Connaught—until you can help me find a service flat. And I don't want to spend a fortune. I should like to stay in Europe about six months, and spend as much time in England as I can without incurring the risk of being called a resident. I should also like to go to Paris, and perhaps though not certainly, to the South of France for part of the time. I don't want to be a burden or a nuisance to anyone. I am pretty badly broken up, and for me it may last a long time, as my emotions are not superficial. I have friends with me, and they are going to Europe with me, although I do not think that in the beginning they will go to England. We hope to come on one of the new Swedish cargo boats, which are about fifty per cent more expensive than the other ships of the type, and for that reason it is easier to get reservations on them. They probably go to Antwerp, Rotterdam and London, but God knows where in London, very likely the East India docks.

I hope the answer to your cable about *The Big Sleep* was satisfactory. I don't really care what they do with it. I assume the *Daily Sketch* is the type of paper you and I don't read.[1]

Leonard Russell sent me a very touching letter which I have already answered. If it is convenient, you might telephone Eric Partridge and tell him that I know I owe him a letter, and tell him why I have not so far been able to write to him. You probably realized when we were in London that Cissy was in rather frail health. When we got back she looked and felt better than she had in a couple

1. Proposal to serialize the book.

of years, but it didn't last. She got weaker and weaker and more and
more tired. She tried to drive herself, and there were a few occasions
when she actually drove her car out, and on several others I drove her
somewhere she wanted to go, or just out of doors for the air, or to
do some shopping for clothes she badly needed. But even that ceased.
Usually, until about a month before she died, she was able to get
up part of the day and to dinner. She had an obscure and rather rare
ailment, I am told, called fibrosis of the lungs. I don't think they
know very much about it or what causes it. It's a slow hardening of
the lung tissue, starting at the bottom of the lungs and progressing
upwards. The part that is fibrosed returns no oxygen to the blood,
which of course puts more strain on the heart and the breathing.
As far back as 1948 her X-rays showed the condition as existing, but
it was quite a long time before I realized that it could only have
one ending. I don't think that she herself ever quite gave up hope, or
if so during the last weeks, she didn't let anyone else know that she
had given up hope. We tried a number of doctors. Mostly they just
gave up without saying why. Late in October we tried a Dr. Neber,
whom we had known when we first came to La Jolla but had given
up because his medicine had never seemed to agree with Cissy,
and he started her on cortisone. We tried him principally because he
had three or four cases of fibrosis of the lungs, which is unusual
for one doctor to have in a small place like La Jolla. With his other
patients he had had great success with cortisone. A couple of them
that had been bedridden had been able to get up and go about their
business almost normally. But it is a very strong medicine, and Cissy
was always peculiar about drugs. It affected her brain, and especially it
affected her memory and made her very uncomfortable. She couldn't
remember anything for five or ten minutes. I had to measure out all
her medicines, or else she would take them twice or three times over
without realizing she had already taken them. The cortisone didn't
work, so at the end of the first week in November he took her off
that and started her on ACTH, and this, after the first shots, I was
able to give her myself hypodermically, as I had been used for several
years to give her hypodermic shots of various vitamins. This didn't
do very much good either. She got lower and lower and more and
more depressed, and she was not an easily depressed person. On
November 30 she developed pneumonia and had to be taken to the
hospital in an ambulance. Early the next morning she was clamoring

[376]

to be taken home in an absolute fury of indignation. From seven o'clock on she called repeatedly or had her nurse call. I managed to persuade her to stay there that day and until the following morning, and then her temperature being normal and the penicillin having apparently aborted the pneumonia, the doctor reluctantly allowed me to bring her home, which made her very happy. But the next day she had already forgotten about the horrors of the hospital—and no one ever hated hospitals more—and was wanting to go back again. The doctor furthermore wanted to try a medicine called ruwaulfia, or African snake root, which apparently has the property of inducing a condition of euphoria without any damage and can be taken indefinitely. He told me at the time that she would have to spend the rest of her life in a sanitarium and that he was hoping the ruwaulfia would put her in such a complaisant mood that she would accept that. The next morning again she called up early and demanded to be taken home. So I got in touch with the doctor and I said I couldn't stand her mental suffering, and he again reluctantly allowed me to bring her home. By this time she was very ill and very weak, had to be helped to the bathroom, had to have someone stay there with her. Her sister Vinnie and I were just about done in, especially Vinnie, because we got very little sleep. I then managed to get nurses around the clock to take care of her, but she was very miserable, gasped all the time, coughed violently, and said she was in great pain. By December 7th I realized she was dying. In the middle of the night she suddenly appeared in my room in her pajamas looking like a ghost, having evaded the nurse somehow. We got her back to bed and she tried it once more, but this time the nurse was watching. At three A.M. on the morning of December 8th her temperature was so low that the nurse got frightened and called the doctor, and once more the ambulance came and took her off to the hospital. She couldn't sleep and I knew it took a lot of stuff to put her under, so I would take her sleeping pills and she would tie them in the corner of her handkerchief so that she could swallow them surreptitiously when the nurse was out of the room. She was in an oxygen tent all the time, but she kept pulling it away so that she could hold my hand. She was quite vague in her mind about some things, but almost too desperately clear about other. Once she asked me where we lived, what town we lived in, and then asked me to describe the house. She didn't seem to know what it looked like. Then she would turn her head away and when I

[377]

was no longer in her line of vision, she seemed to forget all about me. Whenever I went to see her she would reach her handkerchief out under the edge of the oxygen tent for me to give her the sleeping pills. I began to be worried about this and confessed to the doctor, and he said she was getting much stronger medicine than any sleeping pills. On the 11th when I went to see her I had none and she reached out under the edge of the oxygen tent with the handkerchief, and when I had nothing to give her she turned her head away and said, "Is this the way you wanted it?" About noon that day the doctor called me up and said I had better come over and talk to her as it might be the last chance I would have. When I got over there he was trying to find veins in her feet to inject *demerol*. What an irony that I should have written about *demerol* in my last book! He managed to get her asleep, but she was wide awake again that night. That is she seemed to be wide awake, but I'm not even sure that she knew me. She went to sleep again while I was there. A little after noon on December 12th, which was a Sunday, the nurse called up and said she was very low, which is about as drastic a statement as a nurse ever makes. Vinnie's son was here then with Vinnie, and he drove me over to the hospital at fifty miles an hour, breaking all the traffic regulations, which I told him to ignore as the La Jolla cops were friends of mine. When I got there they had taken the oxygen tent away and she was lying with her eyes half open. I think she was already dead. Another doctor had his stethoscope over her heart and was listening. After a while he stepped back and nodded. I closed her eyes and kissed her and went away.

Of course in a sense I had said goodbye to her long ago. In fact, many times during the past two years in the middle of the night I had realized that it was only a question of time until I lost her. But that is not the same thing as having it happen. Saying goodbye to your loved one in your mind is not the same thing as closing her eyes and knowing they will never open again. But I was glad that she died. To think of this proud, fearless bird caged in a room in some rotten sanitarium for the rest of her days was such an unbearable thought that I could hardly face it at all. I didn't really break until after the funeral, partly because I was in shock and partly because I had to hold her sister together. I am sleeping in her room. I thought I couldn't face that, and then I thought that if the room were empty it would just be haunted, and every time I went past the door I would have the horrors, and that the only thing was for me to come in here and fill it up with my junk and make it look the kind of mess I'm used to living in. It was the right decision. Her clothes are all around me, but they are in closets or hidden away in drawers. I have a couple of very old friends staying with me, and they are patient and kind beyond any expectation. But the horrors are all mine just the same. For thirty years, ten months and four days, she was the light of my life, my whole ambition. Anything else I did was just the fire for her to warm her hands at. That is all there is to say.

I'm afraid my Christmas orders were put in a little late, but I hope they arrived in time to cheer you all up a little. I don't know how things are over there now, but I gather from Roger that they are a lot better than they used to be.

Love to all,

Yours ever,

Ray

TO HAMISH HAMILTON

6005 Camino de la Costa
La Jolla, California
Jan 22 1955

Dear Jamie:

.   .   .

I try not to think too much about Cissy. Late at night when people have gone to bed and the house is still and it is difficult to read I hear light steps rustling on the carpet and I see a gentle smile hovering at the edge of the lamplight and I hear a voice calling me by a pet name. Then I go out to the pantry and mix a stiff brandy and soda and try to think of something else. Unfortunately I cannot read poetry except by daylight. Poetry is too sad. You are always running across lines like:

Or shredded perfume, like a cloud
From closet long to quiet vowed,

[379]

With mothed and dropping arras hung,
Mouldering her lute and books among.
As when a queen, long dead, was young.

I dug out some of my own old poetry and was rather startled to find
some of it not too bad. It lacks the acerbity and I-dare-you-to-
understand-what-I'm-talking-about of the modern stuff. It is, I
suppose, Grade B Georgian. I'll send you a couple one of these days. I
never regarded myself as a publishable poet, of course, although a
certain amount of it was published a long time ago in the *Westminster
Gazette*, etc.

As to the service flat I'd rather go to a hotel for a time and get
a chance to look around. The location of the flat is important to
me and I am not sure just what is meant by service flat. How far does
the service go? Do they come in and make your bed and wash dishes
in the morning? Is there a restaurant in the building? That sort of
thing.

.   .   .

That should be enough for now.

> With love to all
>
> Ray

TO ROGER MACHELL

> 6005 Camino de la Costa
> La Jolla, California
> Jan 28, 1955

Dear Roger:
Just a quick chit to let you know that I'm changing my ideas
about going through the Canal in spite of my fondness for Swedish
cooking. I have something the matter with one of my sinuses and half
the time I have no voice. I think the natural venom of my disposition
is slipping down on to my vocal chords at night and making me

cough and get hoarse. I could be dying, but I think not. Anyhow I may need attention from a nose wrecker for some time and better not get holed up on a 12 passenger ship. They might even refuse to take me. The captain probably has a supply of narcotics on board but might be stingy with them. He also, no doubt, has a set of carpenter's tools for setting broken bones, and a bottle of aspirin. Apart from all that the idea of going through the Canal without Cissy has a certain sadness. So I'm going east in late March and I have a single cabin on the Hotel Cecil (*Mauretania* to you) sailing April 12th. She should get to Southampton some time on April 18th unless we meet a large iceberg. You will know all about that as I shall myself a little later. Anyhow I shall confirm it to you when the ticket is in my possession.

. . .

I had a charming letter from Jamie. He should be in New York by next Wednesday, but if my voice is not better than it is now, I shan't be able to talk to him by telephone with much success. I hope he can bring back some good books with him. Things are really weird over here in the publishing racket. A friend of mine had two books turned down because they were submitted to the paperback people before the publisher would take them on, and the paperback people are being very cagey just now. Bankruptcies and mergers are imminent. Prostitution, flagellation and the dope racket seem quite sound still, but trade editions of books—ye gods, look at the current bestseller list. It is headed by an item called *Love Is Eternal* by one Irving Stone. No doubt as a business venture you would be glad to publish it, I know the man and I read one of his early books, the one about Van Gogh. Since then I have given him none of my business. Not that he needs it. However, bestsellers at their worst are not as asinine as English critical writing. That seems to be done entirely by exhumed corpses suspected of containing arsenic.

You can see that I am coming along pretty well. I still sleep badly but the old spirit is returning slowly. Seldom a day without its reasonably well-phrased insult.

Yours ever

Ray

[381]

TO ROGER MACHELL

Feb 7 1955

Dear Roger:

.   .   .

The *Mauretania* takes six days, so I should arrive in England on
the 18th. of April, but at what hour of the day I have no idea. Could
you contrive a hotel room and bath for me for about a week from
then on? I think I'd like the old Connaught well enough. The only
thing I really had against them was that I paid a service charge on
the bill including the bar bill (which was quite large) whereas the bar
people get nothing from it, since they are a concession. This hardly
seems quite fair. Also in spite of the fact that this service charge was
supposed to take the place of tipping, I couldn't make myself let
it go at that and actually I tipped everyone I had any dealings with,
and even gave five quid to the dining room staff without so much as
an acknowledgement from the maitre d'hotel. I rather resent that.
Maybe the black tie character I gave it to pinched the lot. I need some
advice on this point. Tipping is really the horror of travel. I never
know how much to give and I always for that reason give too much.
Of course I do that here also. I always overtip. I like to think of it
as generosity, but it is probably exhibitionism.

Then comes the problem of a service flat. Just what the hell *is* a
serivce flat? How much service do you get, what do they do for
you, how much does it cost and so on. Jamie says you are an expert
in these matters. Frank Francis wrote to me that the Whitehall Court
expects about 30 guineas a week. That is a bit steep even if they
supply naked dancing girls. And do these places have dining rooms?
And can you make as much noise as you like? For instance I sit up
half the night playing records when I have the blues and can't get
drunk enough to feel sleepy. My nights are pretty awful. And they
don't get any better. I've been alone since Saturday morning when
Vinnie went home. Alone except for Mable the Marble, my
Pennsylvania Dutch cook and housekeeper. She has a lot of fine
qualities, but she is not much company. She is not even beautiful.
She's as fat as a porpoise and when she bends over you see a pair of
gams that an all-in wrestler would envy. For size, if not for shape.

[382]

I'd like to go to Paris for two or three weeks at a good time of year and possibly also to Nürnberg. But by that time Europe will be so loused up with Americans that it will be impossible to get a flea in with a shoehorn. I don't want any Georges Cinq stuff, but a decent hotel where I can have a room and bath, assuming such luxury is possible for a struggling writer who owns no oil wells in Texas. What I particularly do not crave is a load of American tourists all over the place. Je m'en foute pas mal des touristes Américains. I understand the current phrase is: Sortez les, sortez les, sortez les!

Perhaps when I get away from this house and all its memories I can settle down to do some writing. And then again I may just be homesick and to be homesick for a home you haven't got is rather poignant.

Tomorrow is or would have been our thirty-first wedding anniversary. I'm going to fill the house with red roses and have a friend in to drink champagne, which we always did. A useless and probably a foolish gesture because my lost love is so utterly lost and I have no belief in any after life. But just the same I shall do it. All us tough guys are hopeless sentimentalists at heart.

> All the best,
>
> Ray

TO ROGER MACHELL

> Box One Twenty Eight
> La Jolla, California
> March 5th 1955

Dear Roger:

· · ·

I got off a short airmail letter to Jamie which should have reached him before he left for home. If it did not, it wasn't too important, just a few lines to tell him everything was all right with me, or as near as one could hope for.[1] I couldn't for the life of me tell you whether I really intended to go through with it or whether my subconscious was putting on a cheap dramatic performance. The first shot went off without my intending it to. I had never fired the gun and the trigger pull was so light that I barely touched it to get my hand in position when off she went and the bullet ricocheted around the tile walls of the shower and went up through the ceiling. It could just as easily have ricocheted into my stomach. The charge seemed to me to be very weak. This was borne out when the second shot (the business) didn't fire at all. The cartridges were about five years old and in this climate I guess the charge had decomposed. At that point I blacked out. The police officer who came in then told me later that I was sitting on the floor of the shower trying to get the gun into my mouth, and then when he asked me to give him the gun I just laughed and handed it to him. I haven't the slightest recollection of this. And I don't know whether or no it is an emotional defect that I have absolutely no sense of guilt nor any embarrassment at meeting people in La Jolla who all knew what happened. It was on the radio here, on the wire services, in papers all over the country, and I had piles of letters from all over the place, some kind and sympathetic, some scolding, some silly beyond belief. I had letters from police officers, active and retired, from two Intelligence officers, one in Tokyo and one in March Field, Riverside, and a letter from an active professional private eye in San Francisco. These letters all said two things: 1, they should have written to me long before because perhaps I hadn't known what my books meant to people, and 2, How in the name of wonder did a writer who had never been a cop come to know them so precisely and portray them so accurately. One man who said he had served 23 years on the Los Angeles Police said he could put an actual name to practically any cop I put in any of my stories. He seemed to think I must actually have known all these men. This sort of thing staggered me a little because I had always supposed that if a real live police officer or detective read a mystery, it would be just to sneer at it. Who was it— Stevenson possibly—who said, Experience is largely a matter of intuition?

1. Chandler had attempted to commit suicide on February 22, 1955, by shooting himself in the bathroom of his house in La Jolla. He was in despair over his wife's death.

In England, I believe, and in some other places, including New York State, attempted suicide, or what looks like it, is a crime. In California it is not, but you have to go through the observation ward at the County Hospital. With a more than able assist from a friend of mine who does a column in the San Diego paper, I talked myself out of it the next noon but on condition I went to a private sanitarium.[2] This I did. I had more trouble talking myself out of that. I stuck it for six days and then got a feeling I was being strung along with half promises. At that point I announced that I was going to discharge myself. Upheaval. This simply wasn't done. All right, I said, Tell me the law that keeps me here. There wasn't any and he knew it. So finally he conceded that I could leave any time I wished, but would I come to his office and talk to him. I said I would, not because I expected any good from it, but because it would make his case record look better, and in addition, if he was perfectly frank with me, I might be able to help him.

So I came home and since then nothing has mattered to me about the whole business except that they shot me so full of dope to keep me tractable that I still have a little hangover from it. Isn't it amazing that people should sit around depressed and bored and miserable in those places, worried about their jobs and their families, longing to go home, subjected every other day to Electrical Shock Treatments (they didn't dare try that on me) and in between insulin shock, worrying about the cost of it all and the feeling of being a prisoner, and yet not have the guts to get up and walk out? I suppose it is part of what's the matter with them. If they had more guts, they wouldn't be there in the first place. But that's hardly an answer. If I had had more guts I shouldn't have let despair and grief get me so far down that I did what I did. But when I found myself dealing with people and with a lot of psychiatric claptrap and with a non-existent authority that tried to make me think it had power, I didn't find that it took any special amount of daring to tell them all what I was going to do and to do it. And in the end strangely enough they almost seemed to like it. The head nurse kissed me and said I was the politest, the most considerate and cooperative and the most resilient patient they had ever had there, and God help any

2. Neil Morgan was the person who arranged for Chandler's release.

doctor who tried to make me do anything I wasn't convinced I ought to do. And so much for that.

> Love
>
> Ray

TO WILLIAM GAULT

Hotel Del Charro
2380 Torrey Pines Road
La Jolla, California
[n.d. April 1955]

Dear Bill Gault:

I'm answering your letter on the hop, not because it is kind, which of course it is, and I have had a hundred kind letters from all parts of the world (nothing in this is deprecating), but because of your idea that I look down on the mystery story. I don't know how this notion came to you. I can't recall ever having written or said anything of the sort. It's possible that had I been a little younger when I started to write fiction, had I been a better observer and a better rememberer, I might have made a reputation as a straight novelist. It never occurred to me to try. I thought I was extremely lucky to get as far as I did in our field, and believe me when I say lucky I am not talking to the birds. Talent is never enough. The history of literature is strewn with the corpses of writers who through no fault of their own missed out on the timing or were just a little too far ahead of their generation. An old and wise friend of mine once said the world never hears of its greatest men; the men it calls great are just enough ahead of the average to stand out, but not far enough ahead to be remote.

I believe there is a peculiar kind of satisfaction in taking a type of literature which the pundits regard as below the salt and making of it something which the fair-minded among them are forced to treat with a little respect. You must never admit to yourself that the kind of writing you and I do is by definition inferior. It is as good as the man who writes it and the record proves it will outlast 99.44 per cent of the touted best sellers.

Yesterday I finished the rather agonizing business of getting the furniture out of my house and closing it up for the new buyer. When I walked through the empty rooms checking the windows and so on I felt a little like the last man on a dead world. But it will pass. On Wednesday I leave for Old Chatham, New York to stay with my best friend and on April 12th I sail on the *Mauretania*. I expect to be back about the end of October and to find a house in La Jolla—much smaller of course—because it is an easy place to live in and everybody knows me here.

Thank you for writing to me and for what you say and I hope you are not exaggerating too much, unconsciously. It would not matter so much to me, since I am a naturally modest fellow, but it would not be good for you. Because you have it in you to be as good as the best. Don't ever write anything you don't like yourself and if you do like it, don't take anyone else's advice about changing it. They just don't know. All the best

Ray

TO HARDWICK MOSELEY

The Connaught Hotel,
Carlos Place, London, W.1.
April 24, 1955

Dear Hardwick:

Thank you for your kind wire. I am here at least until May the 8th. after which I may have to sleep in Green Park. I am not happy and I am terribly hoarse from laryngitis. The racket here is just too intense also; you go to a luncheon with eight people and next day five of them invite you to a dinner party. So dine, drink and drab is about all you do. I love this hotel, though, but I do not love being stared at and being pointed out to people, and I do not love newspaper interviews.

[387]

It seems quite likely now that I shall never accomplish anything here and that I shall come back, if I can arrange it, early in June. I am already quite homesick.

Yoursever,

Ray

PS This is a new Olivetti and I haven't quite mastered it. It's a beautiful piece of work.

TO HAMISH HAMILTON

The Connaught Hotel
Carlos Place
London, W.1.
27.4.1955

Dear Jamie:

Would you please have someone tell the *Daily Sketch* that not only would I not do a piece of writing for them but that I wouldn't use their rotten rag even to stuff up a rat hole. Our press is no bargain, but your gutter press is fantastically bad. You might also call that nice Mr. Harris of the *Standard* and tell him I'm sorry but cannot now put my mind to what he wants, don't feel well enough and simply cannot get my private letters written. I'll write him a note and send him back his tear sheets because I liked him personally more than anyone in his peculiar profession that I happened to meet.

The whole thing last night was rather weird. Natasha Spender is a charming and devoted hostess and served up a magnificent meal and everybody got tight. They poured it on me a little too thick, I imagine. A Sonia[1] somebody . . . said that I was the darling of the British intellectuals and all the poets raved about me and that Edith Sitwell sat up in bed (probably looking like Henry the IVth, Part 3) and read my stuff with passion. They said [Cyril] Connolly had

1. Sonia Orwell.

written a piece about me which was considered a classic. The funny part of it was that they seemed quite sincere. I tried to explain to them that I was just a beat-up pulp writer and that in the USA I ranked slightly above a mulatto.

Well anyhow it was a lot of fun.

This morning the BBC, always a little slow, called up. I'm not talking to anyone I don't know anymore until they write and explain what they want and I get a chance to check with you.

Yours,

Ray

This typewriter is much better but still a bit strange to me.

TO NEIL MORGAN

116, Eaton Square
London S.W.1.
June 3rd. 1955.

Dear Neil,

I tried for almost three days to get you on the telephone, and then became so disgusted that I cancelled the call. I know I have owed you a letter for a long time, as I owe you for other things, which I shall never forget.

I don't think you would recognise me if you saw me now. I have become so damned refined that at times I loathe myself. I still don't sleep well and often get up at 4 or 5 in the morning, and lately have been indulging in a form of polite pornography, which would probably interest you mildly and I am, therefore enclosing a couple of samples.[1] You should understand that the basic motif behind this is an attempt to spoof the upper-middle class sort of talk. There can be no greater mistake than to think that we and the English people speak the same language.

1. These sketches were called "Routines to Shock the Neighbors," and were written to help prepare Chandler to write for the English stage. Two are printed in *The Notebooks of Raymond Chandler*, 1976.

Mostly I run around with the St. John's Wood–Chelsea literary, artistic crowd, and perhaps they are a little special. Of course I know some cockneys too, but the people that I do run around with have expressions of their own which need translating. For instance: "I simple adore her" means "I'd stick a knife in her back if she had a back." "They are absolutely and utterly precious" means "What rubbish, but that woman never did have any taste." "I rather care for that" means "Give it to me quick." And "I'm simply impossibly in love with him" means "He has enough money to pay for the drinks."

It has been a wonderful spring, the squares flaming with the most gorgeous tulips three and even four feet high. Kew Gardens is a paradise of green and color, rhododendrons, azaleas, amaryllis, flowering trees of every kind. It catches you by the throat after the hard dusty green of California. The shops are beautifully dressed and full of all kinds of wonderful things. Harrods is easily the finest department store in the world. Nothing in New York or Los Angeles can equal it. The traffic control system here is superb. The one thing lacking is tender meat. They simply haven't got the storage to age it. You get it at very good hotels like the Connaught, the Savoy or Claridge's, but almost nowhere else. What they call a filet in most places eats like round steak.

But the women! If they ever had buck teeth I don't see them now. I've seen glamour girls at parties that would stun Hollywood. And they are so damn honest they won't even let you pay their taxi fares. If you know them well enough you can give them the money privately, but you can't give it to the driver. If you want them to go to bed with you, you have to say "please" five times. A CIC officer I know was a bit worried about this.[2] He was asking me how to get a really topdrawer, refined English girl—no G.I. bait—into bed. So I told him what I just wrote. "But what if she refuses?" he asked. "Brother, if you can't tell in advance by her eyes, the way she moves and looks at you or doesn't look at you, by the tone of her voice, you're lost." He was rather depressed. Americans are not as a rule successful with the best type of English girls and women. They move too fast and too roughly. There is far too much of this "Come on, baby, let's hit the hay" motif. They don't like it. They expect

2. Probably Counterintelligence Corps.

to be treated as ladies. They are perfectly willing to sleep with you if they like you and if you treat them with deference, because in a country where women outnumber the men so excessively that is almost inevitable, but they don't want to be treated as easy lays. They want you to work up to it slowly and fastidiously, and I certainly think they are right.

. . .

Ray

TO THE EDITOR OF *THE EVENING STANDARD*

June 30, 1955

Dear Sir:

As a part-time resident and full-time friend and admirer of England, I have always, until now, respected its legal system—as has most of the world. But there is at times a vein of savagery that repels me.

I have been tormented for a week at the idea that a highly civilized people should put a rope around the neck of Ruth Ellis[1] and drop her through a trap and break her neck. I could understand perhaps the hanging of a woman for bestial crime like a multiple poisoning, and axe murder (à la Lizzie Borden) or a baby-farm operator killing her charges, but this was a crime of passion under considerable provocation. No other country in the world would hang this woman.

In France she would get off with light sentence or none. In America it would be first or second degree manslaughter and she would be out of prison in anywhere from three to seven years.

This thing haunts me and, so far as I may say it, disgusts me as something obscene. I am not referring to the trial, of course, but to the medieval savagery of the law.

Raymond Chandler

1. Ruth Ellis, a convicted murderer, was condemned to be hanged. Chandler's letter contributed to a public outcry over her punishment and questions were raised in Parliament. Nevertheless, the sentence was carried out in July.

[391]

TO JESSICA TYNDALE

116 Eaton Square
London, S.W.1.
SLO 3691
Sept. 17th., 1955

Jessica, darling, you worry about me far too much. Your letter of
Sept. 13th. just came and the conclusions you draw are really quite
exaggerated. I'll come to Helga later, but first let me say that I have
written things to you I would not have written to any other human
being, because I could feel in you absolute sincerity and trust.[1] You
know, you never really saw me sober and I have been sober now for
some weeks—absolutely bone-dry sober. Dull as it may be I intend to
remain that way. Something in my chemistry will no longer accept
alcohol. There is some sort of chain reaction. I start off with a drink
of white wine and end up drinking two bottles of Scotch a day.
Then I stop eating. After four or five days of that I am ill. I have to
quit and the withdrawal symptoms are simply awful. I shake so that I
can't hold a glass of water. I can't stand up or walk without help.
One day I vomited eighteen times. I wasn't sick at all, but something
kept dropping down at the back of my throat from inflamed sinuses
and every time that happened I gagged my life out. For three days I
could drink nothing but sips of ice water. Well, that's thirty for
me. My father was an alcoholic and I have lived all my life in the fear
of becoming one but until my wife died I could always quit drinking
on my own power when I felt there was a real need for it. For three
years before she died I was as dry as a bone. The funny thing is I
don't mind in the least. It's other people who mind, some even resent
it a little. But they will just have to take it. I suspect that all people
who drink more than the odd cocktail are secretly a little aware of
weakness and resent anyone who doesn't share that weakness.
Certainly it has nothing to do with morality. I know men who can
drink enormous quantities of liquor without any apparent damage.

1. Helga Greene, a friend of Jessica Tyndale's, who later became Chandler's literary agent.

They will probably all die of cirrhosis of the liver, but one has to die of something.

.   .   .

With much love and please stop worrying,

Ray

TO JESSICA TYNDALE

c/o Barrow
Old Chatham, N.Y.
10/21/55

Dearest Jessica:

.   .   .

Any one who can drink a great deal steadily over a long period of time is apt to think of himself as an alcoholic, because liquor is part of his life and he is terribly let down without it. Yet he is not an alcoholic, because he is the same guy even with a load on. . . . The problem comes when our physical systems can't oxydize the stuff fast enough and we have to cut down or stop. If we stop, we feel awful, because our emotional systems are tuned to the stimulation and the sedative effect of alcohol. Yet, if we can, we stop altogether for a while (hating it every minute) until we are completely free of it and then we try to learn to drink. How much can we absorb without either feeling high at the time or let down the next day? That is what we have to find out and we have to be rather cautious about it. If we don't get enough to feel cheered up, it's a waste. It seems to me that there is a certain level to find, and if you find it, you are all right, even if you sometimes slop over a little. If I had found out all about this when I was twenty years old (I did almost no drinking then) I think I should have cut it out absolutely and I shouldn't have felt any the worse, because of the resilience one has at that time. But at my age, that no longer makes sense. At my age, there is

[393]

nothing to replace it. . . . Drinking, after all, except when it is a social ritual, is rather a negative business.

.   .   .

Much, much love,

Ray

TO HELGA GREENE

Box 958
La Jolla, California
November 13th. 1955

Dear Helga:

It seems funny to be writing a businessy letter to you. I am sitting on two bed pillows at the writing desk in my room at the Del Charro Hotel (but address me only at the above), I am smoking a Craven A cigarette which is no match for the Benson and Hedges Superfine but imported cigarettes here are just a little too steep. Am I comfortable? No. Am I happy? No. Am I weak, depressed, no good, and of no social value to the community? Yes. Outside my window is an illuminated swimming pool. Phooey on it! The service here is excellent, the food fair, the price of my room slightly above what I paid at the Connaught, but an infinitely better room. Light wood furniture, two wide couch beds set in a right angle triangle with the heads against a roomy built-in stand with two of those focussed reading lights. There is a chest of six drawers (not enough), three closets, a dressing room with side lights at the table, and a beautiful bathroom, bathtub with sliding glass doors for the shower. There is a built-in electric heater in the bathroom and a built in gas heater in the bedroom, which is really a bed-sit. It is cheap compared with New York.

.   .   .

Much love,

Ray

TO NEIL MORGAN

Nov 18 1955

Dear Neil:

On the eve of my departure into regions where Eskimos starve and the polar bears wear mittens and goloshes and are still dissatisfied (Anybody ever see a polar bear that liked anybody?),[1] and on the eve of your dive into marriage with a lovely girl—I'm not sure that dive was the word I wanted—may I wish for you the kind of magic that Maeterlinck's donkey could hear: the roses opening, the grass growing and the day after tomorrow coming. May I wish for you the kind of magic vision that birds have, such as on a morning after rain seeing a worm make love to its other end. (This joke was stolen from me and somehow finally got to Groucho.)[2] May I wish for you the knowledge (I'm getting a little heavy-handed here) that Marriages do not Take Place, they are made by hand; that there is always an element of discipline involved; that however perfect the honeymoon, the time will come, however brief it is, when you will wish she would fall downstairs and break a leg. That goes for her too. But the mood will pass, if you give it time. Here are a few words of sound advice. I know.

1. Ride her on a short rein and never let her think she is riding you.
2. If the coffee is lousy, don't say so. Just throw it on the floor.
3. Don't let her change the arrangement of the furniture more than once a year.
4. Don't have any joint back accounts unless she puts in the money.
5. In case of a quarrel, remember it is always your fault.
6. Keep her away from antique shops.
7. Never praise her girl friends very much.
8. Above all never forget that a marriage is in one way very much

---

1. Chandler was taking a polar flight to England. Although he had just returned from London, he felt he had to return almost immediately, because of his concern for Natasha Spender's health.
2. Groucho Marx

like a newspaper. It has to be made fresh every damn day of every damn year.

I'll be at the Connaught Hotel, Carlos Place, London W.1. in case I didn't tell you. For a while that is.

Love,

Ray

TO IAN FLEMING

49 Carlton Hill
London N.W.8.
11th April 1956

Dear Ian,

Thank you so much for your letter of Wednesday and if the payment for my outstanding review had been received a little earlier I should have been able to eat three meals a day.[1]

I thought my review was no more than you deserved and I tried to write it in such a way that the good part could be quoted and the bad parts left out. After all, old boy, there had to be some bad parts. I think you will have to make up your mind what kind of a writer you are going to be. You could be almost anything except that I think you are a bit of a sadist!

I am not in any Hampstead hospital.[2] I am at home and if they ever put me in a hospital again I shall walk out leaving corpses strewn behind me, except pretty nurses.

As for having lunch with you, with or without butler, I can't do it yet—because even if I were much better than I am I should be having lunch with ladies.

Yours affectionately,

Ray

1. Chandler had reviewed Fleming's *Moonraker* for the *Sunday Times*.
2. Chandler had been hospitalized for excessive drinking.

[396]

TO PAUL BROOKS

49 Carlton Hill
London N.W.8.
April 30, 1956

Dear Paul;

I'm sorry but our lunch date will have to be changed because my dentist, whom I need very badly, wants to push the appointment up an hour, which cuts it much too fine.

I also had the idea that Etoile is pretty stale to me and might be to you. Unless you have seen enough of the Garrick Club, we might have lunch there. The food is the best English food in London. They don't eat until 1.30. Up to that time they drink.

Then there is a rather little used place in Greek Street called Le Jardin des Gourmets. it has a very nice corner on the 1st floor (Anglicé).

I have no dates on the 5th. or the 7th. nor the following week. Since I am half-dead most of the time, I probably should not have any at all, but you can't get out of them in London.

Do you remember Mae Murray? I had a note from her asking me to lunch. I can't imagine why. I never met her.

With apologies profuse,

Ray

TO IAN FLEMING

The Grosvenor
35 Fifth Avenue
New York
June 9th. 1956

Dear Ian:

I didn't like leaving England without saying good-bye to the few friends I knew well enough to care about, but then I don't like saying good-bye at all, especially when it may be quite a long time before I come back. As you probably know, I long overstayed the six months allowed, but I had a compelling reason, even if I get hooked for British income tax. I am also likely to lose half my European royalties, which isn't funny. It's all a little obscure to me, but there it is. And it doesn't matter whether your stay in England is broken half a dozen times. If the time adds up to over six months within the fiscal year, you are it.[1]

I am looking forward to your next book. I am also looking forward to my next book.

I rather liked New York this time, having heretofore loathed its harshness and rudeness. For one thing the weather has been wonderful, only one hot day so far and that not unbearable. I have friends here, but not many. Come to think of it I haven't many anywhere. Monday night I am flying back to California and this time I hope to stick it out and make some kind of modest but convenient home there.

I am wondering what happened to all the chic pretty women who are supposed to be typical of New York. Damned if I've seen any of them. Perhaps I've looked in the wrong places, but I do have a feeling that New York is being slowly downgraded.

Please remember me to Mrs. Fleming if you see her and if she remembers me (doubtful). And how is His Grace and Duke of Westminster these days?[2] Painting lots of houses, I hope.

With love

Yours ever,

Ray

TO HELGA GREENE

Hotel Grosvenor
Fifth Avenue at Tenth Street
New York 3, N.Y.
June 10th. 1956

Dearest Helga:

1. Chandler had overstayed his permit because of his concern for Natasha Spender's health.
2. Fleming lived in Victoria Square in property owned by the Duke of Westminster.

I bet you haven't many boy friends who write you two letters in two days. And perhaps it bores you, but since Friday noon I haven't a damn thing to do but write letters, read, take a taxi or bus uptown and potter about a bit, or just go for a walk through the Village, which always fascinates me with its quaint houses, little culs-de-sac, iron railings painted in odd colors, innumerable hidden restaurants, and the people themselves, the way they dress and the look they have of belonging to another world from uptown New York.

. . . .

Ray

TO HAMISH HAMILTON

Hotel Grosvenor
Fifth Avenue at Tenth Street
New York 3, N.Y.
June 10th. 1956

Dear Jamie:

My deepest thanks to all for the very kind farewell telegram. I didn't see as much of the boys and girls this time as I should like to have (done, as the English say, a disgusting locution to me).

I've been in New York all this time. . . . When I first landed after a rotten twenty four hour flight via Iceland and Gander, on account of storms in mid-Atlantic—I always thought the BOAC prided itself on flying right through them—and an hour wait in the customs and the usual barbaric treatment, a sort of studied insolence (but not on the part of my particular inspector when I finally got him) I was willing to expatriate myself permanently. Surely no other country in the world makes you feel like a dirty immigrant from Central Europe. Not even the Spaniards and they are high-handed enough. I bought a copy of *Newsweek* and started to read the letters in the front. One of them went over to another page and believe me there were four solid pages of advertising before I got to the

[399]

conclusion of the letter. I knew where I was all right, but this country reeks of wealth. It is so different from England where almost everything is touched by a faint air of squalor. Not your house, of course, nor Roger's nor Helga Greene's, but I have been into many lavatories where a single dirty towel was thrown on the floor; grimy little kitchens such as I had in Carlton Hill, bath tubs that needed scrubbing and had needed it for quite a while, people dripping with amusing or intellectual small talk who don't wash their hands when they go to the bathroom. All this is bearable, and you would get it anywhere but in this country, if only the talk were not so malicious, if only there were not so goddam many queers all around you.

.   .   .

Yours ever,

Ray

TO HELGA GREENE

Hotel Del Charro
2380 Torrey Pines Road
La Jolla, California
June 14, 1956

Dear Helga:

.   .   .

    I went to dinner with some friends last night and it was a little trying to see them have three or four drinks and I nothing but tonic water with a little fresh lime in it. It wasn't that I wanted the alcohol—I didn't at all—but it kept them gingered up while I had nothing to support me but my beautiful if slightly tarnished character. That has always been the trouble with me during the many periods of my life when I was not drinking. The people who do outlast me and I get very tired and rather irritable. But there is no help for it.

[400]

I'm convinced that it has to be a permanent thing, and that for some strange reason alcohol is poison to me.

> . . .

> Love,

> Ray

TO HELGA GREENE

June 19, 1956

My Sweet Helga:

> . . .

I love fantastic stories and have sketches of perhaps a dozen that I should love to see in print. They are not science fiction. My idea of the fantastic story—possibly a little out of date—is that everything is completely realistic except for the basic impossible premise. Both those I have mentioned are concerned with vanishing or invisibility. I have one about a man who got into fairyland but they wouldn't let him stay. Another about a princess who traded her tongue for a ruby and then was sorry and it had to be retrieved. One about a young society novelist whose father was a magician and kept making a duke disappear so his son could make love to the duchess. I may add that the duke took it with good grace (a joke) although he was rather annoyed. That sort of thing. Quite rare nowadays.

> . . .

 I met Marcel Duhamel (of Gallimard's Série Noire) in New York and took them and Jessica to lunch at the Pierre. Lunch just average. Duhamel has a perfect command of English and is so energetic he tires me out. His wife is charming. I'd like to sleep with her. Right now I'd like to sleep with almost any pretty soft gentle woman, but of course I shan't do it (even if I had the chance) because there has to be love. Without that it is nothing.

[401]

．　　　　　．　　　　　．

Can a man not be genuinely in love with two women—especially a man who expects nothing but the privelege of loving them? And caring for them when he can, and always being devoted and kind? I am not an average man. There is nothing predatory in me. I am much more of a giver than a receiver. I don't think the sexual act is in itself so terribly important, but I do think compassion and tenderness are vastly important. My sister-in-law says I was the most wonderful husband a woman ever had. But isn't it easy to be a wonderful husband if you have a wonderful wife? And isn't it just because I loved her so much that now that she is gone I love all gracious and tender women. . . .

．　　　　　．　　　　　．

Goodnight, darling. Perhaps I have talked too much. I signed the lease today. Now, out of furniture for a house with a huge living room, a fancy powder room, a solarium (with rattan furniture) four bedrooms and four and a half baths, I have to select what I can use in two bedrooms, a reasonable but not large living room with a dining alcove, and one bathroom. Not so easy. And the books! Dear God, what on earth shall I do with books that overflowed a large house? I guess you have to be ruthless about possessions.

I love you dearly,

Ray

TO HARDWICK MOSELEY

Hotel Del Charro
2380 Torrey Pines Road
La Jolla, California
June 20, 1956

Dear Hardwick:

．　　　　　．　　　　　．

This place really has a climate. You have to go through an

[402]

English winter to appreciate it. Very seldom hot and very seldom cold, built on a point of land with the Pacific on three sides, with hills behind it, no railroad and only two roads of ingress. I have tried to use it as the setting for a story I am trying to write;[1] I have changed the topography a little and changed the name, and in doing this I have to accept the handicap of all English mystery writers: I can't make heavies of the cops, because they are nice cops and most of them are friends of mine. I call them "the boys with the beautiful shirts" because their tan shirts and slacks are always immaculately creased military style. The captain in charge is a grizzled veteran of long service and he told me he had never fired his Smith and Wesson .38 except to qualify on the police target range, as per the standing orders. Sometime last year a man shot his wife in a store here and the cop who came rushing in—too late—was so nervous that he shot a bystander by mistake. (He didn't kill him.)

Yours ever,

Ray

TO JESSICA TYNDALE

July 3rd. [1956]

Darling Jessica:

No one but you could have sent me the books and I thank you, thank you. *The Talking Bug* is neat, concise and to the point, an expert job without a trace of anything memorable. That's the nice thing about a good thriller. You can read it once a year. Mr. Bagby I have reservations about. I really don't care much for these chaps who try to use a European background without having absorbed it. I don't want to be too bitter, because some of the many mistakes in his very first chapter may be the fault of the publisher or printer. (One moment, please. There is a girl outside my window in a two-

1. *Playback.*

[403]

piece swimsuit. The bra is about two inches wide and if her pants shrink any more, I'll probably go right through the glass with a brush and comb).

No, she saved me by putting a loose white shirt on. The difference in types is very striking. When I first came here they were all sunburned coarse Californians. Now we are getting the hot weather refugees from Texas and the East and they not only have more delicate skins, but are more gracfully built. (Do you think I pay too much attention to such things? Possibly.)

Have you read *Bhowani Junction*?[1] I think you should. It's a damn good job and there are several effing scenes in it that I should have been proud to write, but God knows much prouder to have lived them. But I'm afraid I'm not that good any more.

.   .   .

Yours lovingly,

Ray

TO JESSICA TYNDALE

July 12th. 1956

Dearest Jessica:

If I sound a little as if I had been smoking reefers, I had a tooth out this afternoon and am still a little on the goof side. No pain at all, but beginning to feel feverish. I was pretty indignant about the whole thing because I have never lost a tooth but once, as a schoolboy with a tooth growing in behind two others. Also I felt that if the dentist had taken X-rays oftener, he could have stopped the decay before it reached a nerve. Wonderful how they do it though. I never knew it was out until he showed it to me. I supposed they had to strap you down and pull like hell. It was a molar too.

1. By John Masters.

[404]

This place is an unfurnished apartment on the ocean front. That is, it was unfurnished. It now has so damn much furniture in it that only a steeple-chaser would feel at home in it. But in spite of having all this lovely (and to me now detestable) furniture, a fine electric stove, a Frigidaire and some curtains, in spite of being full of nice yellow cartons which keep me from putting my shirts and underclothes away, in spite of having a small private patio and a large private storeroom, all I have to eat off of is one cup, one saucer, one plate, all borrowed. But a full set of sterling silver, oh my yes.

·　　　·　　　·

I know now what is the matter with my writing or not writing. I've lost any affinity for my background. Los Angeles is no longer my city, and La Jolla is nothing but a climate and a lot of meaningless chi-chi. I went to a cocktail party a week or two ago and my God there was a man there in a checked dinner jacket and another in a rose moiré dinner jacket. And today in Dutch Smiths shop I saw one in puce. This country is riding the crest of a boom, everybody is making fine wages and everybody is in debt to the ears from instalment buying. God help them if rearmament slows down. As far as I'm concerned the country is overpriced. I just can't afford to live here. There's nothing for me to write about. To write about a place you have to love it or hate it or do both by turns, which is usually the way you love a woman. But a sense of vacuity and boredom—that is fatal.

·　　　·　　　·

I send you large amounts of love and I know damn well I sound like a bitter and disappointed man. I guess I am at that. I was the first writer to write about Southern California at all realistically, as the UCLA Librarian admitted when asking for my original manuscripts for the Special Collections of their library. Now half the writers in the country piddle around in the smog.

·　　　·　　　·

With lots and lots of love,

Ray

[405]

TO HELGA GREENE

Helga Darling:

.   .   .

One thing I regret is never having based a story on the Palm Springs, Cathedral City desert locale. It is unique. Perhaps I may still do it from memory. At any rate my book about La Jolla is going to be much more brutal if I am safely in Europe.[1] There is really nothing here but a climate (wonderful, I admit, but I'd take the worst of London gladly in exchange) and a lot of very stupid chi-chi. How did the French expression chi-chi which means fuss come to have its American meaning of silly elegance? After all, puce dinner jackets! Or am I just getting too old? I am already sick to death of skins like burnt orange and smiles like gashes. I am sick of people who never put a glass down and cocktail parties where no one (but me) can sit down. Alas, not all my country is hopelessly vulgar, but this part of it certainly is.

Materially we have everything, and an English person would for a time be fascinated by our gleaming kitchens and bathrooms, by our beautifully designed houses, by the wonderful work of our decorators (if you can afford them). After a few weeks' visit they would return to their gloomy houses with glowing accounts. But this is all on the surface. Underneath is vacuity and boredom. TV, cocktails, bad cooking, and what do we do next except buy another and more garish car, go to some idiotic and exorbitant hotel in a resort, read the *Post*, *Time*, and *Ladies Home Journal*, and if one is exceptionally intellectual, one might even rise to the *New Yorker*. We are a very clean people. We take showers every day, which only rare people like yourself do in England. Our best restaurants are appallingly dull and expensive, not in the least equal either in menu or service to La Speranza, which I suppose is only second class in London. . . .

1. *Playback.*

I am really terrified of trying to live in France. I shall be most awfully lost. When I was a young man and very innocent I lived in a pension on the Boule Miche and was very happy wandering around, with very little money, but a sort of starry-eyed love of everything I saw. The only thing that upset me was the whores at the door of the apartment building if I happened to be out a little late. And I so innocent that I didn't realize that there were two girls at the pension that couldn't keep their feet off mine and were offering themselves to my innocence and I never even knew it. I knew so little about women then, I know almost too much now. And yet I have never become cynical about them, never ceased to respect them, never for a moment failed to realise that they face hazards in life which a man does not face, and therefore should be given a special tenderness and consideration. I have never seduced a virgin nor intruded upon a valid marriage. I think this feeling which I have about women, and which women obviously do not feel about themselves. . . . was the basis for my fury about the Ruth Ellis case. There is nothing to argue about here, so far as I am concerned. If a woman gives herself to me, for one night or for much longer, I regard the gift as a delicate and almost a sacred thing, and although I am, I suppose, subconsciously aware that she gets something out of it too, I always think of myself as the recipient of a royal favour. Women are so damned vulnerable to all sorts of hurts.

·   ·   ·

Terribly much love,

Ray

TO JESSICA TYNDALE

6925 Neptune Place
La Jolla
August 20th. 1956

My Darling Jessica:
    I have been neglecting you shockingly but not only you. I

don't think I've written a letter in three weeks until yesterday, when I wrote several business letters. I have just come back from the Las Encinas Sanitarium in Pasadena, a very wonderful place but frightfully expensive. Cost me over $1400. But hold your hat, I was *not* drunk and have two witnesses to prove it. It was much more serious really (if anything can be more serious). Twice in the past two years my world has crumbled to pieces around me. It was more than I could take. . . . After a little while I stopped caring about my meals, and then I stopped eating altogether, but I ask you to believe me—it was not drink. I was drinking very little and some days not at all. And if finally occurred to me: Boy, you may not know it in your conscious mind, but you've got a death wish. You're too proud to do it openly and directly again, but you are starving yourself to death because you want to die. Well, it was like a voice speaking softly in the night but it threw me. I had to find out if I was off my rocker and didn't know it. And Las Encinas is the place to find out. They have a psychiatrist there that an intelligent man can really respect. They treat all kinds of people, senile old people (with money, natch), incurable alcoholics, guys on benders . . . a few psychotics who have to be kept in a special locked bungalow, depressed people, etc. It's a beautiful place, carefully landscaped, all bungalows, and the atmosphere is absolutely uncritical. The doctors are very attentive, the food magnificent. They kept me in a state of semi-somnolence for several days until I started to eat, and God, how I did eat then. I had some of the best food I've ever had in my life. Then they went through the usual boring program of tests, and after that they went to work on me. I told them the whole truth very frankly. I said that I had been married so long and so happily that after the slow torture of my wife's death it seemed at first treason to look at another woman, and then suddenly I seemed to be in love with all women. I had no idea what I had to give them that they gave so much to me, that the most strict and puritantical woman I had ever met had been in bed with me a week after I met her. That the strange thing was that such affairs as I had had never ended. There was never any bitterness or boredom. I loved them all still and they seemed to love me. But I could not live alone. It destroyed me. Therefore I could not be completely faithful to any woman who could not share my life, but that I didn't regard this as infidelity, because after all sex is only a rather minor part of love, delicious as it is when it is right. I said I really didn't want to get married again because my heart was in too many places and a wife would never have more than a part of me.

. . .

They gave me tests, apperception tests, Rorschack tests, wood block tests. I haven't had the lowdown on them yet, but I think I was pretty brilliant except on the drawing. I never could draw, couldn't even learn under a drawing teacher at school.

Finally the head guy said: "You think you are depressed, but you are quite wrong. You are a fully integrated personality and I wouldn't dream of trying to intefere with it by psycho-analysis or anything of that sort. All that's the matter with you is loneliness. You simply cannot and must not live alone. If you do, you will inevitably drink and that will make you sick. I detect no signs in you of a suicidal impulse. You seem to me to be vibrant and full of ambition, but something has got in your way, and that something to my mind is that you can't live alone. After all it takes a long time for a man who has lived your life, always with a woman close to him, to get used to being a loner. And if you could make it, you would probably dry up in the process." I said: "Doctor, am I an alcoholic? They told me I was in New York." He said: "In the first place I have been studying alcoholics for twenty years, I have read all there is written on the subject, and discussed it with everyone who is preoccupied with the problem. There is no definition of an alcoholic. Nobody, but nobody, knows what an alcoholic is, except by a pragmatic definition. An alcoholic is a man who can't take the second drink because he can't take the first. One incontrovertible fact is that no alcoholic can ever become a controlled drinker. If you can become a controlled drinker, and personally I think you can with the right sort of life, you are not an alcoholic." "The right sort of life," I said. "But I don't want to get married." "Marriage is a religious and civil institution of great importance," he said. "People in love with each other should be married and should stay married. But morals are not my business. I am concerned with your mental health and stability, as I said. From that point of view, and especially at your age, I don't care whether you live with one woman or twenty, as long as you live with someone. That in my opinion is an absolute."

I thought he was damned clever to take me to pieces so

[409]

smoothly. I hadn't expected anything so penetrating. Well, you know
Chandler.

.　　　　.　　　　.

Ray

TO MICHAEL GILBERT

6925 Neptune Place
La Jolla, California
Sept. 6th. 1956

Dear Michael:

.　　　　.　　　　.

La Jolla is no place in which to live. The climate is all right
(although lately we have had a lot of thin fog) and the shops are
wonderful. The place has style—no billboards or advertising signs are
permitted. But it's too dear and too dull. There is no one to talk
to. All the well-to-do and almost well-to-do crowd accomplish in
their lives is an overdecorated home—the house beautiful for gracious
living—a wife who, if she is young, plays tennis at the Beach Club,
lies on the beach until her visible skin looks like brown sandpaper and
feels the same, I have no doubt, swills several cocktails before dinner
(almost always in company with friends), several highballs after
dinner and ends up either being pawed by some other girl's husband
or shrieking with laughter at some joke which hardly merits more
than a mild "huh." If she is verging on middle age, she is very chic in
a tasteless way, talks a great deal about how she is going to have
the guest room done over by some jerk with long sideburns, has her
husband so tamed that he is afraid to sit down in some of the chairs,
and however tired he may be, he must shower and shave and put on
his white dinner jacket (in summer) because Mr. and Mrs. Whoosis
are coming over to play bridge, which he hates almost as much as he
hates Mr. and Mrs. Whoosis. While waiting for dinner, cooked
with much supervision by the lady of the house, but all the coolie

[410]

labor done by some sulky coloured girl, he is compelled to read the funny paper to his brats, although they have read it four times already and made a crumpled mess of the part *he* wants to read. Then there are the quite elderly, quite rich retired people. They dress immaculately, are helped into Cadillacs by coloured butler-drivers and are driven to the Beach Club, where they sit in perfect silence, or converse in low monosyllabic voices with others of their kind.

There are also the working people, but most of them are, in any real sense, illiterates also.

The hell with me!

all the best to you,
Ray

TO WILLIAM GAULT

6925 Neptune Place
La Jolla, California
Sep 7 1956

Dear Bill:

. . .

I am feeling rather disgusted with life at the moment. One of my girl friends just got herself married to a lunkhead whom I found quite repulsive, and I'm afraid the poor girl has made a mistake. . . . I guess she is just damn well fed up with living alone.

So am I. If there is anything in life I hate it is going out to dinner alone. I could cook it, but that would be worse. Four days a week I have someone to go with, but the other three are hell. I feel like chucking the whole thing and going back to England to come a resident and pay their bloody taxes. The cost of living is so much lower there (except in the four or five best hotels) that the difference in that might easily equal the difference in tax, or even go beyond it. Also my secretary has abandoned me for schoolteaching, a pretty sensible idea or her part, but it involves her dumping files, contracts, books of account, cash journals, bills to pay, letters to write—all

[411]

bang in my lap and in an apartment where I have hardly enough room
to be halfway comfortable without all that. In London I had a hell
of a good secretary who cost me .70 an hour (five shillings) on a half
day job. She had more brains in one finger than most girls in that
line have in both legs.

Yours despondently,

Ray

TO ROGER MACHELL

6925 Neptune Place
La Jolla, California
Sep 12 1956

Dear Roger:

.　　　.　　　.

Jamie wrote me a long and pleasant letter about covers and
misprints and some great artist (for covers) whom many had tried to
bribe away from him. This incorruptible genius designed the cover
for *The Long Goodbye*. Jamie said that the booksellers liked pictures
on the covers of my sort of book. I still don't like it. I don't like
the blood, the arm and hand seem to me out of proportion (she has a
hand like a first baseman), the spray of roses that tall would not
stand up in a shallow dish, but these are not the point. My point was
and remains that the effect on me and on others I know was cheap.
Houghton Mifflin's covers tend to an extravagance of design which is
supposed to suggest something rather than hit you on the nose with
it.

.　　　.　　　.

A working man [in La Jolla] lives far better than most white collar
people in England—that is if you don't examine what is in his brain.
He has all the gadgets, a new car every year or so, and he is buying
his house on a government loan that he will pay off in twenty years,
maybe. He has TV, an automatic stove that does everything but
sing Tristan and Isolde, a garbage disposal thing in the sink, a

[412]

dishwasher which only nicks or cracks about fifteen dishes a month, a clothes washer, a dryer, an ironer, a deep freeze unit in his garage where he keeps enough food for six months, (he buys that on time too) and most of the other food he eats comes ready prepared and half-chewed. Unless his wife really wants to cook well, and I'm told by an authority that a great many of them really do want to cook well, all his wife has to do to make dinner and dessert could be done in ten or fifteen minutes. All our clocks are electric, all our heating is automatic, and in fact I sometimes wonder what the hell we are here for. Certainly not to use our minds.

Yours lovingly,

Ray

TO HAMISH HAMILTON

6925 Neptune Place
La Jolla, California
Oct. 26, 1956

Dear Jamie:

.   .   .

 Roger and I had some amiable growling about your covers, but it was all amiable—how could anything be otherwise with Roger—and I haven't changed my opinion in the least. Have you ever looked at the dust jacket of *The Little Sister*, for example? It portrays a desiccated schoolteacher or librarian of some 38 to 40 years of age, about as sexy as a rat-trap. Yet this little girl was young, and without her glasses or with smarter ones, looked good enough to fumble with. Some day, just for the hell of it, a dust jacket artist ought to submit to the excruciating agony of reading the damn book.

.   .   .

Much love to all,

Ray

[413]

TO HELGA GREENE

6925 Neptune Place
La Jolla, California
Nov. 20, 1956

Helga Darling:

.   .   .

They won't give you two bedrooms and a communicating bath in this damn hypocritical country. They don't refuse outright everywhere, they just don't have the vacancy. They will give you a suite with a sitting room, but when you arrive you are apt to find that what you have is two separate rooms with a sitting room in one, but no connection. Of course at a place like the ———— in Los Angeles it doesn't matter. They have a bordello wing, well away from the main building, in which no questions are asked. I was there once in an emergency and next door to me were two couples, obviously unmarried, all four union organisers, all four drunk and dirty and profane. First of all there was a loud and clear discussion as to which girl should sleep with which man. Then it appeared that both wanted the same man. Then there was a fight, at first with words, but in the end with more than words. The fight ended in tears and a reconciliation, after which the two couples obviously paired off and fornicated in the twin beds side by side. I heard all this, not because I tried to, but because I couldn't help it. Don't ever talk to me about union organizers.

.   .   .

I think of you constantly, and always with love
Ray

TO HARDWICK MOSELEY

6925 Neptune Place
La Jolla, California
Jan 5, 1957

Dear Hardwick:

[414]

How *are* you? I am very fit and have gained about ten pounds and have survived any and every kind of test. My doctor here regards me as some kind of freak and says he can't see any possible thing I could die of, except exhaustion. He says it is very unusual to give an exhaustive examination to a man of my age and not detect some clue as to what may eventually take him off. But enough of bragging.

Spent the time since December sixth until the last week taking an English friend all over Arizona and part of Nevada and then Palm Springs. Arizona never had such a going over; perhaps, since this friend is an incorrigible and insatiable sightseer, which I am not. Friend was entranced with the wild mountain scenery, which is unlike anything in Europe or California. The Dolomites are rugged enough, but the cypresses grow halfway up their sides, whereas everything in Arizona is barren, as though God had quit with the job unfinished.

Am going to Palm Springs again on Monday for three weeks. Address there General Delivery. Your two year-end remittances of royalties touched me deeply: one direct and one through Brandt and Brandt. They totaled forty some dollars. Almost at the same time I had a check from England for over $5000 net after commissions. No wonder the boys are selling direct to paperbacks. What in the world can be the matter? You put out a beautiful book on good paper and meticulously proofread. But who will pay the price? People can rent the damn book to read it and if they want it again later, they can get it in Pocket Books. An English publisher puts out a rather cheap book, not on very good paper, not well proofread, and sells 40,000 copies. Later he puts out a cheaper edition from the same plates and later still a paperback (my publisher does, anyhow) and also an English language Continental edition, like the old Tauchnitz books. I believe I could write a bestseller, American style, if I wanted to badly enough. I seems to me that all it takes is a gimmick. But I shouldn't have the reputation I have, especially in England, Germany and Scandinavia—it can't be any news to you that the Swedes buy more books, proportionately, than any other people. Somehow, if you write something deliberately aimed at the wide public, it always shows. I don't suppose that any mystery writer since Conan Doyle and perhaps Willard Huntington Wright (and what drivel *he* wrote) was ever a bestseller in a large way.[1] But I don't complain. Quite the

1. Wright wrote the Philo Vance detective stories under the pseudonym of S. S. Van Dine.

contrary, I think I have been very lucky, but not in trade editions, except that without them I could never have been paid $2500 a week in Hollywood or $100,000 for a screenplay. I've turned down quite a few movie offers lately because I didn't feel that I could take the beating.

.　　　　.　　　　.

Yours,

Ray

TO JESSICA TYNDALE

General Delivery
Palm Springs
Jan 18 57

Darling Jessica:

.　　　　.　　　　.

I have a couple of good friends in La Jolla (by good friends I mean people who take the trouble to keep in touch with you), and of course dozens and dozens of acquaintances. But the place is a desert intellectually. I met [Christopher] Isherwood in Santa Monica and liked him. I think he is the only queer I have felt entirely at ease with. I also met Gerald Heard (he wrote a very clever thriller called *A Taste For Honey*) and found him amusing and very learned, but much too pontifical. Americans generally seem to be quite content to be lectured at for a whole evening. I resent it, no matter how clever the talk is. N. [Natasha Spender] said I was very hostile to him, but her social standards and mine are quite different. *She* thinks I am rude when I am just blunt or sarcastic. *I* think people are extremely rude when they carry on a very private and intimate conversation (I call it "The Derek-Peter-Nigel Routine") which excludes another guest who may also, and it has happened to me, be the guest of honor. You can't interrupt these people, because they constantly interrupt one another and someone is always talking. You *could* interrupt them but it would take violence. Really one should, since once they realize

[416]

they are cornering the conversation they become apologetic. I am quite happy in a company of two or three or even four (including myself) but beyond that I tend to clam up.

.   .   .

Much love,

Ray

TO MICHAEL GILBERT

Palm Springs, California
Jan 26, 1957

Dear Michael,

.   .   .

Last night, since it was the last night, we went to the Starlite Room of the Chi-Chi Restaurant here. The technique is absolute, although rather demeaning. You make a booking in advance and say what sort of table you want. Since this place is on two levels, the back part just a matter of four or five feet above the front part, the ideal position is in the middle of the first row of the back section, from which you have an uninterrupted view of the stage and floorshow. The decor is rather magnificent in its way, with a semicircular curtain around the stage. Having booked the table you arrive and your car is taken by an attendant in uniform. You enter and are greeted by the maitre d'hotel (they have half a dozen captains) and you say, "Good Evening, I believe I had a reservation, but possibly you could not manage to give me the table I rather wanted." At the same time you slip a folded five-dollar bill into his hand. Now, in this part of the country very few people do that. They demand, they do not politely ask, and above all they do not themselves provide the maitre d'hotel in advance with a situation for which he may only have to offer the mildest apology. As a result of this approach (and the five bucks) you get the best table in the house, and the captains won't even let the waiters wait on you, or pour the wine. You can't light your own cigarette. The lighter is

[417]

already there as you put it in your mouth. It simply amazes me how few Americans understand the art combining generosity in tipping with demanding very little. But that is the whole point. These headwaiters are tough, callous and cynical, but they must behave with deference to the most impossible people. Then someone comes along who treats them with deference, and they simply can't do enough for you. I suppose my own approach is a bit calculated, but my manners are not, and when you are with a lady for whom you have a very high regard, you are not thinking in the least of yourself; you are trying to create around her an atmosphere of ease and graciousness. So that even in America you can achieve something that here is very rare: an attentiveness that will not allow a lady to unfold her own napkin, a realisation that her chair must be held by her escort and not by a waiter, so that a captain will deliberately stand back and wait for you to seat your guest, instead of, as is usual here even in the best places, holding her chair himself. He will not attempt to help her off with her coat or wrap, but when you have done it, he will be at your elbow to take it and put it in the cloakroom, and when the wine is brought, a Pontet Canet 1928 (I was a bit afraid of it, because we get all the bad years here, since we don't know the difference) no one is allowed to touch the bottle except the captain who originally conducted you to your table. Rather a farce in a way, but an English lady probably doesn't realise what a rare thing it is in America—or perhaps I should say, most of America—for this sort of thing to happen.

Unfortunately, the Pontet Canet 1928 costs just about as much as Krug Champagne costs at Boulestin's.

.   .   .

Yours always,

TO HELGA GREENE

6925 Neptune Place
La Jolla, California
Feb 11 1957

Helga Darling:

[418]

It's difficult enough to accept that your wife, or mine, had two other husbands, one of whom at least must have been a better lover than I. But to accept infidelity when one is totally committed is very very difficult. That is, if one regards marriage as a serious business. I personally, and am probably quite wrong, don't think infidelity is a matter of much importance if one has a casual view of marriage. But if you find an ideal and an inspiration, you don't cheapen it. It's not so much that an individual is hurt, but that one's whole level of being is hurt.

•   •   •

Much love, darling

Ray

TO JEAN DE LEON

6925 Neptune Place
La Jolla, California
Feb 11 1957

Jean Darling:

•   •   •

It was very sweet of you to send me some of your poems. Little as I am qualified, I should like to discuss them with you, but not without your permission. I shall say only that the one you wrote for me seems better than any of them. I think it is a very dangerous thing to criticize poetry, because a poet is so easily discouraged. As an offering to make myself vulnerable I am sending you three things I wrote myself. I never claimed to be a poet, although as a young man I wrote quite a lot of verse which was published in various English papers and magazines. I haven't any of it now, which might indicate a certain modesty. I don't even remember much of it. I suppose it was fair or it would not have been published, but that is as far as I could go.

I am very glad that you can accept your father's death without too much grief. But of course I know from my own experience

[419]

that it takes time, quite a lot of time, to reconcile oneself, and that so far you are being brave. I am one of those who do not believe in personal immortality, since I see no reason for it. God probably finds something to preserve, but what, I don't know. He might find even in me, a sensual, sardonic, cynical man, some essence worth preserving, but I don't really think it is anything I could recognize. So much of us is external, environmental, caused by our experiences here on earth, so little of us is pure and undiluted. God knows, but I don't. I share your antipathy to dogmas, but more than that I will just not surrender my right to examine, to dissect, to question. Creo quia impossibile seems to me just one of those devices the Catholic hierarchy is too clever at, and yet, taking it broadly and admitting the many corruptions, the Catholic religion is the only one in our world (I'm not considering the religions of the East) which really lives. The Church of England and our Episcopalian church here live in individual priests, but not as a faith. Its services have beautiful words (which it didn't write) and many of its priests are fine people; but the faith itself is barren and tired. (I ought to apologize for my typing, but I have three fingers bandaged, and that makes me clumsy.)

.   .   .

Your theory of poetry may be right; I don't know. I have no theories about writing; I just write. If it doesn't seem to me to be good, I throw it away. There is a certain quality indispensable to writing, from my point of view, which I call magic, but which could be called by other names. It is a sort of vital force. So I hate studied writing, the kind of thing that stands off and admires itself. I suppose I am a born improviser, I calculate nothing in advance, and I believe that whatever one may have done in the past, one always starts from scratch. Damn, I said this before.

I don't deny you your right to be tolerant of homosexuality; one more or less has to in England. But I do think that homosexuals (not bi-sexuals, that is a matter of time and custom), however artistic and full of taste they may seem to be, always lack any deep emotional feeling. They are wonderful with surfaces. I simply could not read Angus Wilson's novel, his last, because it seemed to me that he described his characters and did not create them. I just found the book dull.[1] ——— is always trying to write fiction, but he can't do it,

1. *Anglo-Saxon Attitudes*, 1956.

[420]

because people of his kind have no real emotional life. They see life through mirrors. As for their having a better understanding of women, be off with you. I know more about women than any of them will ever know, and yet I don't know very much. They like women who are sympathetic to them, because they are always afraid, even if they act arrogantly. Their physical bravery was proved in the war, but they are still essentially the dilettante type. Some of them, like Isherwood, are very likable, some of them are repulsive. My wife hated them and she could spot one just by walking into a roomful of people.

·   ·   ·

But I am not ashamed to be a lover of women. The difficult thing to make another person understand is that I have a code, that I adhere to it, that I have always adhered to it. There was a time in my life as a young man when I could have picked up any pretty girl on the street and slept with her that night. (Bragging again, but it is true.) I didn't do it because there has to be something else and a man like me has to be sure he is not hurting anyone, and he can't know that until he knows more about her. There are lots of cheap women, of course, but they never interested me. There are women who are inaccessible, and I can tell that in five minutes. I always could. There are women who could be had tomorrow night but not tonight. That I know also. There are women who for one reason or another would give themselves wrongly, and who would feel awful about it the next morning. That also I had to know. Because one doesn't love in order to hurt or destroy. There were girls who could have been scarred for life by giving way to a normal human impulse, but not by me. If by someone else, I expect I couldn't help it. There were girls who didn't care, but for them I didn't care either. I don't know whether it is a talent or a curse, but I always know. I don't know how I know, but I could give you specific instances in which, against all the outward appearances, I knew. Sometimes this haunts me. I feel as though I must be an evil man, that this intuition is given to me only to destroy me. But I guess I don't mind being destroyed very much any more. After all, I was a loving and faithful husband for almost thirty-one years, and I watched by wife die by half-inches and I wrote my best book in the agony of that knowledge, and yet I wrote it. I don't know how. I used to shut myself in my

[421]

study and think myself into another world. It usually took an hour, at least. And then I went to work. But I always listened. And late at night I would lie on the eight-foot couch reading because I knew that round midnight she would come quietly in and that she would want a cup of tea, but would never ask for it. I always had to talk her into it. But I had to be there, since if I had been asleep, she wouldn't have wakened me, and wouldn't have had her tea.

Do you think I regret any of this? I'm proud of it. It was the supreme time of my life.

Ray

TO EDWARD WEEKS

6925 Neptune Place
La Jolla, California
27-2-1957

Dear Mr. Weeks:

.   .   .

I expect to go back to London in a few months. I have had a few ideas for articles which you might have liked, but I don't know— I could be all wrong. You know I don't write articles for money but to express something which to me needs saying. When I wrote a couple of rather caustic things about Hollywood writers warned me that I had destroyed myself; but I never had a word of criticism from any important executive. In fact, it was after you published these things that I had the most lucrative assignments. I think Hollywood people are much underrated; they think, many of them, what I think, but they just don't dare say it, and they are really rather grateful to anyone who does. I always knew there was only one way to deal with them. In any negotiation you must be prepared to lay your head on the block. A writer never has anything to fight with but whatever guts the Lord gave him. He is always up against business organizations that have enough power to destroy him in an hour. So all he can do is try to make them understand that destroying him would be a mistake, because he may have something to give them.

I found it quite wonderful to deal with the Moguls. They seemed so ruthless, they conceded nothing, they knew they could throw me out, that in a sense I was nobody, that I said things to them that a writer in Hollywood simply does not say to the big bosses. But somehow or other they were too clever to resent it. And in the end I almost think they liked me for it. At any rate, they never tried to hurt me. And some of them are very clever people. I wish I could write the Hollywood novel that has never been written, but it takes a more photographic memory than I have. The whole scene is too complex and all of it would have to be in, or the thing would be just another distortion.

Well, I suppose all this is a bit boring and too long-winded. I'm not young any more and I am afraid of no one. I have been through hell and I still exist. I had a long and happy married life and I watched my wife die by half-inches and while she was dying, and I knew she was dying, I wrote my best book. I wrote it in agony but I wrote it. I suppose that is some sort of accomplishment. No doubt, other men have gone through the same ordeal. I'm not bragging at all (I hope). I am simply trying to say that all in all I have been a very lucky man, but that I have paid for that luck in the only way I knew how.

I'm afraid this letter may seem to you too personal. If so, may you forgive me? Sometimes I feel terribly alone.

Yours with kindest regards,

Ray Chandler

TO DEIRDRE GARTRELL

6925 Neptune Place
La Jolla, California
2nd March 1957

Dearest Deirdre:

.   .   .

Courage is a strange thing: one can never be sure of it. As a platoon commander very many years ago I never seemed to be afraid, and yet I have been afraid of the most insignificant risks. If you had to go over the top somehow all you seemed to think of was trying to keep the men spaced, in order to reduce casualties. It was always very difficult, especially if you had replacements or men who had been wounded. It's only human to want to bunch for companionship in face of heavy fire. Nowadays war is very different. In some ways it's much worse, but the casualties don't compare with those in trench warfare. My battalion (Canadian) had a normal strength of 1200 men and it had over 14,000 casualties.

· · ·

Ray

TO PAUL BROOKS

6925 Neptune Place
La Jolla, California
March 10, 1957

Dear Paul:

· · ·

As to the doctor book idea, it may be a little while before I can send you samples of the material, or at least samples of the sort of thing it would be.[1] The book would not be liked by the bigwigs in the medical profession, by the surgeons who perform all sorts of unnecessary operations to get the money, by the hospitals who charge patients for all sorts of unnecessary tests, by the "operators" who, although often very competent, put every patient they get into a long and expensive routine, no matter how simple his ailment may be to diagnose. Nor by the "come back boys" (I'd like to see you again on Friday) when there is nothing to come back about. Nor by the sort of doctor who wants to get you into a hospital so that he can pop

1. For a brief time, Chandler considered writing a nonfiction book on the medical profession.

[424]

in two or three times a day and say a few pleasant words and stick you ten bucks for every time he drops in. Nor by certain types who want to give every medicine by hypodermic and charge you for giving it to you and charge you for the material at (they say what it costs them) but at four or five times what it costs them. I know them all; I've had dealings with them all. There are many things people don't know about such practises, nor how to beat overcharges. They don't even know the various county medical associations have scales of fees. They don't know that no doctor has a right to make an unrequested call, unless he does not charge for it. They don't know how to beat an overcharge. Suppose you receive what you think is an exorbitant bill—it happened to me when my wife was ill, and she was ill many times—and I wrote that I considered it exorbitant and explained why. The next thing I knew I was served by a collection agency. Well, it so happened that one of the lawyers we used at that time (I was in the oil business then) volunteered to represent me and my wife, and refused any fee. So we went to court and the doctor sent one of his juniors to testify. On the stand he had to admit that he had not rendered any of the services involved and did not of his own personal knowledge know anything about them. The attorney immediately moved for a dismissal and he got it. He might not have got it from every judge—some of them almost automatically give judgment for a collection agency—but he got it this time. So I called the doctor and told him what I thought I should pay and he accepted gladly, although he had already lost half of it to the collection agency. I might add that he was personally a very charming man.

But my technique was all wrong. I should have called him up at once when I got the bill and told him I thought it was exorbitant, that he had made many unnecessary calls and done nothing when he made them, and that I proposed to file a complaint with the Los Angeles County Medical Association. He would almost certainly have said: "Oh, I'm very sorry, there must have been some mistake in the office. I'll be glad to send you a corrected bill for whatever amount you think fair."

There is the sort of doctor—I know one in New York—to whom you go for perhaps a sinus condition that you know is chronic, but is a little worse than usual, and he puts you in a hospital for a general check-up (although he knows very well from what you tell him that what you have is a chronic allergic rhinitis), gets another

[425]

doctor, an internist to supervise an exhaustive and very expensive series of tests, all most competently done, but all leading to nothing but a big bill. And every day you are there this ear, nose and throat man pops in pleasantly, although he has absolutely no responsibility for the check-up, and later sends you a bill for fifteen or perhaps even twenty dollars for every time he popped in.

The country is full of all these types, mostly in rather well-to-do (exclusive is the word they use) communities or in large cities. And then of course there is the driven, overworked honest doctor who makes at the most a very modest living, who never gets enough sleep, and never collects all or nearly all of his bills. And of course there are the "doctor's patients," mostly neurotic or elderly people, especially women, who just love to have doctor come and see them three times a week, even though there isn't a damn thing the matter with them that a kick in the pants might not help. These people pose a dilemma to the most honest doctor, is he really doing any good? If so, perhaps he is justified in making the calls, but if he does, in the end, he will find himself giving the patient the medicine she wants, and not anything he knows to be necessary.

My own doctor is too damned honest. After he had seen my wife a few times, and seen her X-Rays and knew she had advanced fibrosis of the lungs and that there was very little hope, he said: "I'm very sorry, Mrs. Chandler, I wish I knew how to help you, but I don't. If I were in New York, I could send you to a specialist who knows everything there is to know about cases like yours. But here I simply don't know of anyone to send you to, and it wouldn't be right for me to let you keep coming to see me when I know I can't help you." Well, she was mad at him. Of course he knew she was going to die, but he couldn't know how long it would take—perhaps years. If an honest doctor is certain that you are going to die in three or six months, say of an advanced inoperable cancer, he will think it his duty to tell you. But with a very slowly progressive but incurable disease such as my wife had, he doesn't know how long it will take, and it would be cruel for him to tell the patient or the patient's husband that there was no cure.

And there is the doctor I went to in La Jolla when I had about my fourth attack of angioneurotic edema, which is an inflamation of the skin of the neck (probably allergic in origin) with redness, swelling and the most unbearable itching. Sometimes it spreads up onto your face and sometimes the itching is so unbearable that you have to have morphine. Well, I knew how it had to be treated from previous experience, but this doctor didn't and said so. I told him I had to have injections of certain drugs. So he thought a moment and asked me if I was sure. "You can call a doctor in Los Angeles who has treated me and he will confirm it." "Well they are not drugs that could hurt anyone," he said. So he called the drugstore and made them send the stuff over and gave me the shots. Then he gave me back the two or three bottles, and what he charged me was, I think, about three dollars for an office visit and for the drugs, not what they would have cost me, but what they cost him.

Sorry to write at such length. I wanted to give you an idea of what it was all about. Later I'll send some actual and rather dramatic cases.

.   .   .

With kindest regards, and apologies too,

Yours always,

Ray

P.S. I'll finish the damn Marlowe novel one of these days.[2] I just got fed up with it.

TO JESSICA TYNDALE

6925 Neptune Place
La Jolla, California
March 14, 1957

Jessica Darling:

.   .   .

I promised to tell you about my struggles with the Alien Registration people in England. When I went to Italy I was due to

2. *Playback.*

[427]

report, and I tried the night I was leaving, but I couldn't get the damn passport pictures in time. When I came back I asked my solicitor what I should do. He told me to hurry over to the principal police station of the Westminster district—it was such an obscure place that the taxi driver had a hell of a time finding it. I went and the sergeant said, "Oh no, you don't report here. You have to go to the Alien Registration office in Piccadilly Place." I'd never heard of that either, but I finally found out that the building was the old Vine Street police station. An amiable young man looked at my passport and said, "Oh, you don't have to report. You've broken your residence." A couple of days later I received a stern letter from the Commissioner of the Metropolitan Police ordering me to report at once at the Alien Registration office with two passport photos, all my travel documents, and five shillings. So over I buzzed and the same amiable man introduced me in the office of, I suppose, the head guy, who shook hands with smiles all over him and said he was very pleased to make my acquaintance. Then the other chap came in with a day book that looked about three hundred years old and wrote something in and stamped my passport. They wouldn't look at the passport photos or the five bob.

The next time I had to report, early in 1956, I got the refugee treatment. Lots of questions, quite polite but quite firm, the passport photos and the five bob taken from me. The next day I had to go back again and was given a permit which I was required to show to any police officer who asked to see it. Naturally they never did. The whole thing is such a farce, because there is no liaison. The Home Secretary says one thing, the solicitor says another, the Alien Registration Office pays no attention whatsoever to any of them.

.   .   .

Ray

TO HELGA GREENE

6925 Neptune Place
La Jolla, California
March 19th. 1957

Helga Darling:

[428]

．　　　　　．　　　　　．

I agree with you about the word "affair," but what else can you say? The obvious word is not to be used except on very intimate occasions. I remember a hardboiled RAF chap in the war who said, "I don't fool around. If I see a nice dame (he was an American) I walk up to her and say, 'Madam, do you f-ck?'" Someone asked him if he didn't get an awful lot of ballings out. He said, "Sure, but I get a lot of the other thing too."

Personally, I am completely amoral, if it is possible to be that and at the same time to have a very exacting code about women. Women understand it, but most men wouldn't. Jessica [Tyndale] called me a "passionate moralist." But bourgeois morality is too hypocritical for my taste. I wasn't faithful to my wife out of principle, but because she was completely adorable and the urge to stray which afflicts many men at a certain age, because they think they have been missing a lot of beautiful girls, never touched me. I already had perfection. When she was younger she used to have sudden and very short-lived tempers, in which she would throw pillows at me. I just laughed. I liked her spirit. She was a terrific fighter. If an awkward or unpleasant scene faced her, and at times we all face that, she would march right in, and never hesitate a moment to think it over. And she always won, not because she deliberately put on the charm at the tactical moment, but because she was irresistible without even knowing or caring about it. So she had to die by half-inches. I suppose everything has to be paid for in some manner.

．　　　　　．　　　　　．

Much, much love,

Ray

TO DEIRDRE GARTRELL

6925 Neptune Place
La Jolla, California
March 20, 1957

Darling Deirdre:

．　　　　　．　　　　　．

Love is a strange thing. I smoked a pipe from morning to night when

[429]

my wife was alive and I loved it. I can't smoke cigarettes at the typewriter. I'm not much of a smoker anyhow. I used to drink a great deal of tea, and my wife loved that, just as she loved to see me smoking a pipe. I have a large collection of them, all English. Since she died I don't smoke a pipe or drink tea; I suppose it may be wrong, but everything intimately connected with her likes has died in me when she died. I don't mean I am unhappy—not at all. I was for a long time, but not now. The irrevocable can finally be endured. It would in a way be far worse if she had divorced me (this is just an example, we adored each other) and had married some other man and I had to think of her living with and loving that man, and saying to him the same tender things she said to me.

. . .

You pay me a great compliment in feeling sure and happy when you put your thoughts and feelings in my hands, but you are quite right. I do have a strange sort of instinct for understanding people, especially women. And I can always be trusted, although by bourgeois standards I am no moralist. I am more than twice your age and it may be out of place for me to be saying these things to you, but it is nevertheless a simple fact that I could never hurt, cheapen or demean a woman, and often, when I was young and unmarried, I had to think for the girl too, to prevent her sometimes from doing something which I knew would shame her later. I always seemed to know. I don't have any idea why. I don't go too far with this, because after all I am writing to a well-bred young lady, and I don't want to offend her. I could go much farther, but would it be right?

Surely you realize, that when you write so frankly to me, it is because I am far away and because we may never meet. I rather hope we shall, unless it destroys an illusion. You need the illusion. And it might be that if we did meet, and even if I didn't too much disappoint you, you would never again be able to open your heart to me. As for your being born too late or I too early, I shouldn't have had the marriage I had, if it had been otherwise. Do you understand what it is to love a woman so deeply and be so deeply loved that no day in thirty years was not in its way a courtship? I always held her chair for her at the dinner table—until she couldn't come to it any more. I always opened the car door for her and helped her in. I never

[430]

let her bring me anything. I always brought things to her. I never went out of a door or into a door before her. I never went into her bedroom without knocking. I suppose these are small things—like constantly sending her flowers, and always having seven presents for her birthday, and always having champagne on our anniversaries. They are small in a way, but women have to be treated with great tenderness and consideration—because they are women.

. . .

Ray

TO MICHAEL GILBERT

March 25, 1957

Dear Michael:

. . .

I always feel like a beginner when I start a new job. Of course I have been successful and of course I have made a lot of money, but these things may be largely luck. I don't feel any more important than when I was writing for the pulps. Why should I? Also, there is the background that I was a successful business executive, managed eight corporations, had perhaps the best office staff in Los Angeles, because I knew how to treat them and how to pay them. I don't think these are important talents, but they do make me realize that for a writer or author to be self-centred or arrogant, is just a sign of stupidity. What have we to be arrogant about? One does the best he can at the time, sometimes in very torturing circumstances. Perhaps it is good, perhaps it is bad. But he does his best, and if he has a big success, that doesn't make him anything he wasn't before. He still has his neck on the block. He can still flop or lose his touch. I am the same man I was when I was a struggling nobody. I feel the same. I know more, it is true, I break all the rules and get away with it, but that doesn't make me important. I may have written the most beautiful American vernacular that has ever been written (some people think I have),

[431]

but if it is so, I am still a writer trying to find his way through a maze. Should I be anything else? I can't see it.

TO JAMES HOWARD

6925 Neptune Place
La Jolla, California
March 26, 1957

Dear Mr. Howard:

.   .   .

Of course I was fortunate. I was in the oil business as an executive for years, and when I decided to give it up, I wasn't broke. I had written very highbrow stuff in London as a young man—my mother was British, but I was an American by birth—and I went to school in England, France and Germany. In 1931 my wife and I used to cruise up and down the Pacific Coast, in a very leisurely way, and at night, just to have something to read, I would pick a pulp magazine off a rack. It suddenly struck me that I might be able to write this stuff and get paid while I was learning. I spent five months on my first novelette, but I did something I have never been able to persuade any other writer to do. Writers who asked me for help or advice later on. I made a detailed synopsis of some story—say by Gardner, he was one of them, and he is a good friend of mine—and then tried to write the story. Then I compared it with professional work and saw where I had failed to make an effect, or had the pace wrong, or some other mistake. Then I did it over and over again. But the boys who want you to show them how to write won't do that. Everything they do has to be, they hope, for publication. They won't sacrifice anything to learn their trade. They never get it into their heads that what a man wants to do and what he can do are entirely separate things, that no writer worth the powder to blow him through a barbed wire fence into hell is ever in his own mind anything but starting from scratch. No matter what he may have done in the past, what he is trying to do now makes him a boy again, that however much skill in routine technical things he may have acquired, nothing will help him now but passion and humility. They read some story in a magazine and get a lift out of it and start banging the typewriter on borrowed energy. They get a certain distance and then they fade. They don't know why, so they come to someone like me, or perhaps someone like you, and ask what is wrong. You try to tell them, but you never get it home. They think all they need is some little twist; they never get it into their heads that writing is like an iceberg, for every foot that shows above water there are eight below.

.   .   .

Yours very truly,

Raymond Chandler

TO WILLIAM GAULT

6925 Neptune Place
La Jolla, California
March 31st. 1957

Dear Bill:

I am ashamed to confess that I haven't yet read the book you so kindly sent me. I hope you will forgive me. I want to read it, but I can't seem to catch up. I have had an awful mass of letters to write, I am in a tax hassle with the British government which has involved a lot of correspondence with the British Consulate and with my lawyer in London. Also, I have three very badly inflamed fingers—must be some kind of allergy—all the outer skin is gone and I have to bandage them rather heavily. Otherwise I couldn't type at all, and I can't type without making a lot of mistakes.

.   .   .

By evening I get so tired that I don't even want to read. I just lie on my back and look at TV until one or two A.M. Sometimes I go to sleep on the couch and sleep through a whole film. But I study the thing, because I believe it is worth it. A lot of programs are junk, but there is some very good writing. If I were a young man

I think I'd go into it seriously, but the pressure would be too much for me now. I loathe some of the commercials, but don't have to listen to them, because I have a blab-off, had one in 1950 before they were even on the market.

Your attitude to writing is probably right for you, but it wouldn't have been right for me. Once, because my agent worried me about it so long, I wrote a slick story.[1] It has been anthologized to death, and I lately re-read it in this paperback anthology, and I didn't like it very much. It was too studied, too careful. I just don't take to that sort of writing. The story was all right, but I could have written it much better in my own way, without trying to be smooth and polished, because that is not my talent. I'm an improviser, and perhaps at times an innovator. Some slick writing is very good, on the surface, but it seems to lack something for me. Also, it's dangerous. You can adapt yourself to a certain magazine and then the editor changes, the policy changes, and they don't want your stuff any more. And much to your surprise you find that you have lost your individuality, given away too much. Or, as has happened recently, the damn rag folds up. The angle boys may have a temporary success, but they spend so much time and effort pleasing editors that they never have a chance to find out what they can do best. But perhaps I have a different idea about writing and shouldn't be saying this.

I want to go to England to see if I can learn to write plays. London is the best place in the world to do it, they have so many active theatres, and they are not overawed by the critics. I need a change; I've probably written the best story of the kind that I could ever write. The thing becomes a routine in the end. The Gardners and the Christies can go on forever, but Chandler has to believe in something. To me writing is not a business or a racket, it is an art. Perhaps I talk too big. If so, I'm sorry. I know writers have to live and that it is not easy for them to make enough to live on, and I don't blame them for making concessions, but it's not for me. Screen writing is different, you're not even the author of what you write, and things are changed on you without your knowledge. It's not exactly hack work, because there are a lot of clever people in Hollywood, as well as some awful idiots, and sometimes you can do

1. "I'll Be Waiting," *Saturday Evening Post*, October 14, 1939.

something good, and if you have the right producer, it may even be kept that way. But however much money you get, and I got a hell of a lot, nothing you do ever really belongs to you. I once wrote an original screenplay in about three weeks, because the studio had three actors they had to pay and no film for them.[2] It was written, shot, cut and in the can in, I think some 41 days, and it was not a cheap picture at all. One of the actors was supposed to be called up and it had to be done quick. It was no wonderful job, but it had its points, and it made a lot of money. But I don't call that sort of thing writing. You do it for the money, and you do it in a constant struggle to keep some top heavy director from messing it up. If I could, I'd far rather write for the stage. A writer has some authority there; he may have to change lines because some temperamental actor or actress doesn't like them (and often they are right), but you have something to say about the casting and the direction. You are not a hired hand.

.   .   .

I've often tried to figure out what makes these teenagers what they often are. Do they think they live in a lost world? Even here in La Jolla, after a very nice party down somewhere at La Jolla Shores, the boys and girls amused themselves by slashing tires on the way home. Why? Why do highschool kids of decent families get fun out of destroying things belonging, for all they know, to people who may having a hard time getting by? Is it a sort of revolt against a world they don't believe in? Is it the result of the war? I don't know, but it is not just us. In London they have the Teddyboys, so called because they affect clothes of the Edwardian era. They are plenty tough and their girl friends too, but so far they stay out of the good residential districts, but for how long? I have a girl friend in London who likes to go walking late at night. She used to come to see me when I lived in Eaton Square, not far away from where she lived, and I was always afraid something might happen to her. It never did, but I thought it a bit dangerous all the same. She is my English agent, the daughter of an immensely rich man, but she works hard at being an agent and lives quite simply.[3] I used to have to go down and open

2. *The Blue Dahlia*, 1945. Produced by Joseph Sistrom and John Houseman, the film starred Veronica Lake and Alan Ladd, who was about to be drafted into the army.
3. Helga Greene.

the front door for her—it was always locked at ten P.M.—and I would see this lonely distant figure coming towards me along the deserted street, and I'd know damn well that couple of tough kids with knieves would be more than I could handle. But she was never afraid. We would sit and have a drink or two and talk about all sorts of things, and then she would go home the same way. I couldn't do a thing about it. A foreigner (and very few Englishmen) can't get a permit to carry or even own a gun in England, except a sporting gun, and even if you shoot a burglar in your own home, you have a tough time proving it was in self defense. So if I had walked her home, I should have been just an added attraction. They would have knocked me out or knifed me, taken my money, and she would have been worse off, because she was a witness. Finally I moved to where she would have to come to see me in her car. But you can't do much with English people of the sort I know. You can't scare them. Even during the worst part of the Blitz in the last war none of them ever went to air raid shelters. More likely, at a dinner party, if the bombs got too close and too loud, they would say in that offhand way they have: "A bit noisy tonight, isn't it?" And that's not affectation, that's the way they are. Sometimes I think they carry this stiff-upper-lip attitude a little too far, but they don't do it to show off; it's natural to them.

All this doesn't settle the problem of the juvenile hoodlums. I don't know the answer. Do You?

One of these days or weeks I have to go to the British Consulate in Los Angeles. When I do, I hope we shall get together.

Yours always,

Ray

TO LEROY WRIGHT

6925 Neptune Place
La Jolla, California
March 31, 1957

Dear Leroy:

I have gone as far as I can with the mystery story. I may have written the best one of its type ever written. Many people think so. The thing becomes routine; a man gets tired of producing the same sort of scenes and the same sort of effects. He begins to wonder if he is only imitating himself. But to attack a new and difficult kind of writing would do wonders for me, even if I failed. After all, I am a good dialogue writer.[1] Beyond that I should like to write an English novel, not as an American attempting a tour de force, but as a writer perfectly at home with the nuances of British English and yet ambitious to make it become a little more alive. For months I have been writing sketches in various kinds of stylized English (they are mildly pornographic, but that was only to make them fun to write). Some were exaggerated spoofs, some were self-conscious and off the beam, but the last I did has passed the criticism of one of the best writers I know in England. Not a word or an expression wrong, she says. If you think we and the upper-middle and upper-class English speak the same language, you couldn't be more wrong. The affectations, especially of some women, are very funny. Samples:

I rather care for that.	Meaning:	I'm crazy about it.
I'm madly in love with him.	"	He has enough money to take me to nice places
I simply adore your house.	"	The woman hasn't a shred of taste. A perfectly awful place.
Darling, it was absolutely sublime. Call me again soon, won't you?	"	Well, that's the end of that, Thank God.
Would you adore to have dinner with me on Friday? And so on.	"	She has lost a lover and is scouting for a new one.

·   ·   ·

With kindest regards,

Ray

---

1. Chandler had hopes of writing for the London stage.

6925 Neptune Place
La Jolla, California
April 16th, 1957

Helga Darling:

.   .   .

I remember my first love, but that was a different world. When we met my throat choked up and I could hardly get a word out. To have held her hand would have been ecstasy, to have kissed her would have been unthinkable. But I don't think at that point one is really in love with a particular girl; one is in love with love. Of course one never finds out, because when one meets her later on, if one does, she has long since been married, and usually to some dullard one considers quite unsuitable. Did you ever read a novel by Leonard Merrick called *Conrad in Quest of His Youth*? Probably not too good by our standards, but I liked it. The moral is, Never go Back.

.   .   .

love, love, love

Ray

TO JEAN DE LEON

6925 Neptune Place
La Jolla, California
April 18th. 1957

Dearest Jean:

.   .   .

No, I haven't read *The Light of Asia*.[1] I really feel that formal

1. A life of Gautama Buddha by Sir Edwin Arnold, 1879.

religions, however liberal in thought, are a little too late for me now. And perhaps—I hope so—I am not the type who runs crying to an Unknown God when he feels, alone, desperate, or facing death. I think I shall take it as calmly as I took the dangers in my war so long ago. But one never knows. Anyone can be broken by suffering. Perhaps, in a way, I am lucky to have reached the decision to take my own life and to have failed, since in a sense I have already known what it is to look death in the eye. Neither prayers nor religion could have helped me then. It was between me and myself, so to speak. Of course, torture is something else. I doubt very much that I could have put on as good a show as so many did.

Why would I not like your love poem? You and I might disagree about certain aspects of love, surely that could not affect what I thought about your poem. Poems are not sermons or thesis plays, at least, I hope not.

I don't know what I think of Billy Graham. I saw him once on TV and he seemed a well-dressed, pleasant sort of chap, young, good-looking, and so on. But in America we are inclined to regard all such people as "on the make," I suppose. There have been too many of them over here and they have made too much money. The flagrant cases seem to me Aimee Semple MacPherson and Father Divine.

.   .   .

Not long ago I wrote a column for a friend, Neil Morgan, who does a regular daily column for the *San Diego Tribune*, not much of a paper, but San Diego is still a hick town, even though the population is almost half a million. In the column I expressed my views about La Jolla (calling it a reluctant suburb of San Diego) and about the emptiness of life among the retired rich, but I also said nice things. The column made quite a stir and someone put up a painted sign at the southern limit of La Jolla—there is a permanent sign there too—and the sign read: YOU ARE NOW ENTERING RAYMOND CHANDLER'S RELUCTANT SUBURB OF SAN DIEGO. It was probably taken down by the first police car that passed, but not until someone photographed it and sent the photograph to Neil Morgan, who promptly printed an item in his column. I didn't think my column very good; it was hastily and easily written, and for nothing, of course. Morgan had the flu at the time (this was stated at the head of my column) and he says that since then people have been asking him, "Why don't you get sick more often?"

.   .   .

Ray

TO DEIRDRE GARTRELL

6925 Neptune Place
La Jolla, California
April 23, 1957

Deirdre Darling:

.   .   .

Most people make do with what is available and seemingly appropriate to their condition. Ferocious romantics of my sort never make do with anything. They demand the impossible and on very rare occasions they achieve it, much to their surprise. I was one of those, one of the perhaps two per cent, who are blessed with a marriage which is forever a courtship. I can't, as I think back, find any reason why I should have been so favoured. Above all, since as a young man I was anything but virginal.

.   .   .

You will never lose dignity with me, since it is obviously a part of you. To answer one question, I never proposed marriage formally to anyone. My wife and I just seemed to melt into each other's hearts without the need of words.

With much love,

Ray

[440]

TO HELGA GREENE

6925 Neptune Place
La Jolla, California
Easter Sunday, April 28th.
[1957]

Darling Helga:

.　　　　　.　　　　　.

When I was about sixteen I had an infatuation for a girl, but was too
shy even to speak to her about it. I used to write letters to her. It
would have been an ecstasy to hold her hand. A kiss would have been
almost unthinkable. Not that I was so damned pure. Very young I
belonged to a neighbourhood gang (not criminal in any way) and
found myself paired up with a nice little girl, whom I used to undress
up to a point, purely out of curiosity, and she rather expected it. I
also used to take down the drawers of a cousin of mine in Nebraska,
about my age, and since her four year old brother was with us, we
used to take down his pants just to get him into the act and make him
feel he was not excluded. The curious thing, as it seems to me now,
was that I wasn't in the least interested (so far as I knew) in her
genital organs, but only in her nice firm round backside. I suppose it
was a dawning sex feeling in a way, but it never appeared to me
as anything but naughty and rather nice. I think I was a strange boy
in some ways, because I had an enormous personal pride. I never
masturbated, thinking it dirty. (I had plenty of wet dreams however.)
The headmaster, who ran the pre-confirmation interviews, clearly,
to me, never believed that I had never masturbated, because
practically all boys did. I got hold somehow of a curious idea, must
have read or heard it somewhere. "When you do that, you think you
are holding in your arms a beautiful and unattainable woman. When
you get one really, you will find it very disappointing." Well I didn't,
perhaps partly because I had not filled myself with sexual fantasies
and partly because I was a rather intelligent boy. I have never known
a woman or girl who in any way disgusted me or made me feel
cheap, just as I never to my knowledge made a girl feel cheap.
Sometimes, afterwards, they would burst into sobs and tears, and that

[441]

would frighten me terribly, until they told me it was purely an emotional reaction, and not in the least because they were ashamed. God, how little any man can know about women.

.   .   .

Ray

TO HELGA GREENE

6925 Neptune Place
La Jolla, California
April 30, 1957

Helga Darling,

.   .   .

I hate to go against your advice, but I have fought many hard battles in my life, and I never found that there was any way to fight them except directly, accepting the risks, knowing that all I had to fight with was my brain and my courage, and that I could easily lose against much more powerful people than myself. But I did not become one of the three or four highest paid writers in Hollywood by letting anyone walk over me. I wasn't really ever a very good film writer, but I must have had something or other. I think today there are much better film writers than I could ever be, because I never quite saw things in the terms of the camera, but always as dramatic scenes between people. I suppose you know the famous story of the writer who racked his brains how to show, very shortly, that a middle-aged man and his wife were no longer in love with each other. Finally he licked it. The man and his wife got into a lift and he kept his hat on. At the next stop a lady got into the lift and he immediately removed his hat. That is proper film writing. Me, I'd have done a four page scene about it. What this chap did took a few seconds. It isn't a question of whether I might have written a good scene— taken as a scene—but whether I was really thinking for the camera. Somehow I don't think I ever was. Good film writers should become directors, as they do more and more. But in a sense they cease to be writers, because a writer creates his own world on his own terms, in his own way.

.   .   .

A schoolmaster of mine long ago said, "You can only learn from the second-raters. The first-raters are out of range; you can't see how they get their effects." There is a lot of truth in this. While I dislike calling myself anything more than I am, even to make a point, a fellow mystery writer quite a while ago told me that he had read my stories over and over again, line by line, and almost word by word, and he still didn't grasp how I achieved certain effects. I didn't either, to be honest. Nor did I know that I had achieved them. All I really know, and I'm sure I've said it before, is that for all of fifteen years a lot of quite good writers have been almost desperately trying to imitate me, and that not one of them has even come close. It's a sort of mystery. There are much better plotters than I am, and much better idea men, but it doesn't seem to matter. When they write the scene, there is no magic. Why?

.   .   .

All my love,

.Ray

TO HELGA GREENE

6925 Neptune Place
La Jolla, California
May 5th, 1957

Darling Helga:

.   .   .

I was an executive in the oil business once, a director of eight companies and a president of three, although actually I was simply a high-priced employé. They were small companies, but very rich.

[443]

I had the best office staff in Los Angeles and I paid them higher salaries than they could have got anywhere else, and they knew it. My office door was never closed, everyone called me by my Christian name, and there was never any dissension, because I made it my business to see that there was no cause for it. Once in a while, not often, I had to fire someone—not someone I had picked myself, but someone who had been imposed upon me by the big man—and that I hated terribly, because one never knows what hardship it may mean to the individual. I had a talent for picking out the capabilities of people. There was one man, I remember, who had a genius for filing. Others were good at routine jobs but had no initiative. There were secretaries who could remember everything and secretaries who were wonderful at dictation and typing, but whose minds were really elsewhere. I had to understand them all and use them according to what they were. There was one girl, not pretty and not too bright, who could have been given a million dollars in cash, and a month later, without being asked, she would have known the number of every bill and listed it, and would have, at her own expense, taken a safe deposit box to keep the money in. There was a lawyer on salary in our office (I didn't approve of the idea, but was overruled by the Board) who was very acute but also very unreliable, because he drank too much. I found out just how to use his brain, and he said often and publicly that I was the best office manager in Los Angeles, and probably one of the best in the world. (Eventually, he crashed a police car and I had to get him out of jail.) When I hadn't been long with the firms we had an embezzler. His method would only be possible in a badly organized office. But I found him out and at his trial I had to sit beside the Assistant D.A. and tell him what questions to ask. The damn fool didn't know his own case.

.   .   .

My only excuse for what I wrote of my business career was a hope of convincing you that I am not exactly a baby in these matters. I always somehow seemed to have a fight on my hands. At one time I employed six lawyers; some were good at one thing, some at another. Their bills always exasperated the Chairman; he said they were too high. I always paid them as rendered because they were not too high, in the circumstances. Business is very tough and I hate it. But whatever you set out to do, you have to do as well as you know how.

[444]

I remember one time when we had a truck carrying pipe in Signal Hill (just north of Long Beach) and the pipe stuck out quite a long way, but there was a red lantern on it, according to law. A car with two drunken sailors and two girls crashed into it and filed actions for $1000 apiece. They waited almost a year, which is the deadline here for filing a personal injury action. The insurance company said, "Oh well, it costs a lot of money to defend these suits, and we'd rather settle." I said, "That's all very well. It doesn't cost you anything to settle. You simply put the rates up. If you don't want to fight this case, and fight it competently, my company will fight it." "At your own expense?" "Of course not. We'll sue you for what it costs us, unless you pay without that necessity." He walked out of the office. We defended the action, with the best lawyer we knew, and he proved that the pipe truck had been properly lighted and then we brought in various bar men from Long Beach (it took money to find them, but it was worth it) and that they had been thrown out of three bars. We won hands down, and the insurance company paid up immediately about a third of what they would have settled for, and as soon as they did this I cancelled the policy, and had it rewritten with another company.

Perhaps all this sounds a little hard-boiled. But I wasn't like that really at all. I was just doing what I thought was my job. It's always been a fight, hasn't it? Everywhere you go, everything you do—it all takes it out of you. It takes more out of me than it did once, but still I have the same feeling.

.   .   .

Love, love, love,

Ray

6925 Neptune Place
La Jolla, California
May 7th., 1957

Darling Helga:
        I am sending you my story "English Summer" herewith. It is

[445]

about 8500 words long, not the best length commercially. It may not be commercial at all, but I enjoyed writing it and rewriting it very much. It might be a little over-written, but I think I'd rather have it that way.

.   .   .

If you go somewhere to study new surroundings, absorb new atmospheres, meet different types of people, you always have at the back of your mind at least a hope of getting some use from it all. I have lost Los Angeles as a locale. It is no longer the part of me it once was, although I was the first to write about it in a realistic way. Now half the writers in America live in or near it, the war has made it an industrial city, and the climate has been ruined partly by this and partly by too much vegetation, too many lawns to be watered, and in a place nature intended to be a semi-desert. It was hot and dry when I first went there, with tropical rains in winter, and sunshine at least nine-tenths of the year. Now it is humid, hot, sticky, and when the smog comes down into the bowl between mountains which is Los Angeles, it is damn near intolerable.

So naturally I look around for something else to write about. I can't write about England until I feel England in my bones. Love is not enough.

.   .   .

Ray

TO DEIRDRE GARTRELL

May 8th 1957

Deirdre Darling:

.   .   .

May I comment on the fact that in none of your letters to me have you ever told me about anything external to your own thoughts? You have never described your room, your university, the buildings,

[446]

the place, the atmosphere, the climate, what sort of place Armidale is. You may think this unimportant, but to me it indicates a state of mind; a state of mind which must be unhappy. I am interested in Australia, in everything about it, what it looks like, what its houses are like, how many rooms they have and what sort, what flowers grow there, what animals and birds are there, what the seasons are, what the ordinary life of people of your sort consists of. You tell me a great deal about your thoughts, but nothing about the life around you. Do you suppose I became one of the most successful mystery story writers of any age by thinking about me—about my personal torments and triumphs, about an unending analysis of my personal emotions? I did not. And you should know that very well. But from you all I hear is about you. This is not said to blame you or accuse you of being egocentric at all.

. . .

With much love and some hope,

Ray

TO HAMISH HAMILTON

6925 Neptune Place
La Jolla, California
May 16th., 1957

Dear Jamie:

First, greetings, salutations and love to all who might be interested in any of these, especially to yourself and Roger.

Next, I have a faint—really quite faint—recollection that at one time you thought my letters might be worth publishing. I raise the subject now only because I have such an accumulation of them that I must destroy them unless my recollection was right. A friend of yours called me a "flaming egotist." For a long time I thought myself to be a rather modest man, but I am beginning to believe this friend was right, that all writers are bound to be egotists since they drain their hearts and souls to write at all, and therefore become introspective. I think I have lately become worse, because I have been praised too much, because I live a lonely life and have no hope of anything else from now on.

As to the letters, some are analytical, some are a bit poetical, some sad, and a good many caustic or even funny. They reveal, I suppose, a writer's reaction to his early struggles and later his attempts to ward off the numerous people who seek to exploit him in some way. There are also love letters and letters to an unknown girl in Australia which were merely a rather kind attempt to resolve her problems after she had given me more of her heart than (as she said) she had ever given to any of her family. Naturally, many of them could not be to a name, and many of them would require a note of explanation about the circumstances which caused them to be written. A good many were to you.

It would be quite a job to sort them out and select those which might be worth while any one's attention. One editor of Houghton Mifflin wrote that I had revived the lost art of letter-writing. I make no comment on this, but it is true that in letters I sometimes seem to have been more penetrating than in any other kind of writing—at times—and that as I reread some of them, I am really astonished— astonished at the facility of expression and the range of thought I seemed to show even when I was only a struggling beginner. Please believe that I am not asking you to publish them at all, merely wondering whether they could possibly be of enough interest to be worth publishing. A real writer, and at times I think I am one, exists on many levels of thought. Perhaps as a result of my business training I always knew that a writer had to follow a line with which the public would become familiar. He had to "type" himself to the extent that the public would associate his name (if they remembered it) with a certain kind of writing. But that would not be enough for him in his own mind. So I suppose in my letters I more or less revealed those facets of my mind which had to be obscured or distorted in what I wrote for publication.

This may sound to you a little silly, but I hardly think so. For instance lately I sold a serious poem to the *Atlantic* and I have just written a longish short story with an English setting (but told by an

American). And I am now back on the Marlowe thing which I hope
to finish soon.[1]

I ask you about the letters because it will be quite a lot of work
to go through hundreds of them and pick out those which seem to
have something and then have them copied and make the necessary
notes. I don't want to do it, if it is of no interest. You must over
the years have received enough letters from me to get some idea
whether the project is worth the time and expense, although I should
never expect a publisher to commit himself in advance except in
general terms.

.   .   .

I'll send the carbon of this to Helga and then, dammit, I'll
probably forget what I wrote.

Love,

Ray

TO THE EDITOR OF THE *DAILY EXPRESS*

May 21, 1957

Dear Sir:

I have read in the Los Angeles *Times* Mr. Rene MacColl's
remarks on certain things which he does not seem to like about my
country, and with many of them I am forced to agree. There is
another side to America which Mr. MacColl seems to have
overlooked. We became too rich and too powerful through a sort of
genius of production technique, and as a result I think we placed
ourselves in a position to dominate the world before we had any real
knowledge of how to do it or any real desire to do it. We were just
stuck in the Number One spot. For 100 years, as you may remember,

1. The poem is called "Requiem" and the story is "An English Summer." The Marlowe
novel is *Playback*.

England dominated the world and was rather cordially detested by everyone else. That seems to be the price of power, however unwanted or undesired. The position we find ourselves in is almost impossible to maintain either gracefully or cleverly.

I admit that most of our values are quite wrong, but they result from something which we did not intend to be wrong. I admit that our motor cars tend to be absurd in their design, but we live in an economy of overproduction and fantastic advertising campaigns are waged to make us think that anything six months old belongs with the Pharaohs. I admit that the cost of living here has reached absurd levels, but at least we have clean kitchens and clean bathrooms—and we bathe. I admit our manners are not always what they should be, but with us a cab-driver has as much right to punch you in the nose as a marquess would in England. I admit that our grocery-store bread is tasteless, but what could be more awful than your coffee or your bacon? I admit that tea bags are offensive, but there is tea to be obtained in this country without bags and of a far better quality than anything you have.

Ours is a young, large, and variegated country. We don't know everything. Do you? We try, and have tried very hard, to do what we think we should do in the world, and our workmen occasionally do a day's work, which is more than yours do so far as I have observed. Once on Wimpole Street while waiting for a friend in a doctor's office, I watched two men moving those light-weight fireproof bricks which are extensively used in construction in England. It took two of them to move two of them across the pavement and drop them into a chute—and that seemed to make them very tired. We should have devised a machine to do it in twenty minutes. They were probably at it for two days.

Not everything about us is right, of course; but is everything about England right? It is so easy to write a newspaper article sneering at some other country; but it is not easy to create a civilization in that country, however many men of good will and great ability may try.

If Mr. Rene MacColl would like me to write a few comments on England as disparaging as his about America, I should not do it, although I could. It would be too cheap a victory over a friend.

Yours respectfully,

[450]

TO HELGA GREENE

6925 Neptune Place
La Jolla, California
May 25th. 1957

Darling Helga:

"Non-U Author desires the services of a private secretary (very private) who can cook, wash dishes, make beds, tidy flat, and do some secretarial work. Hours long (sometimes all night), seven days a week, salary liberal, employer American, fairly good manners, but not too reliable. Works like hell when he feels like it, but occasionally has other interests. Applicant, if interested, should be unmarried, reasonably pretty, approachable. Please send photograph, preferably in the nude. Lunches and dinners at good restaurants would be provided, and occasional trips abroad. Applicant should be university-educated and very refined, but not too damned refined. Should be adept at shorthand, a fast and accurate typist, have knowledge of filing (not on the floor). Good quality lingerie essential, and not too much of it. Working conditions will be pleasant, but not conservative. If interested, please apply in writing stating salary expected, height, weight, age and colour of mink stole. This is an exceptional opportunity. Don't miss it. Box Z-2098, *The Times*."

Helga, darling: I'd better start all over again. Your cut from the *Times* threw me. Your letter arrived at 7.30 A.M. I had been up until 3. But reading your letters was worth it. I think I have to agree that "English Summer" won't make a play, because by the time I had licked the difficulties, I'd have another story entirely. I really sent you the story to make you understand how difficult it is going to be for me, since plays, I think, need tight construction and a clear, not too complicated line. But I am by nature, so far, a rather discursive writer who falls in love with a scene or a character or a background or an atmosphere. Once, in a book that was not too good as a whole, although it had some cunning scenes, I wrote a description as an attempt to find out whether purely through the tone of the description I could render a state of mind.

.   .   .

Ray

TO EDGAR CARTER

June 3, 1957

Dear Eddie:

.   .   .

    I think you have the job of convincing these lunatics that if a show is to last, it must cost not too much and must have some sort of special quality, and that quality must be on terms the public can understand and appreciate.[1] I may be wrong, but to me Marlowe is a character of some nobility, of scorching wit, sad but not defeated, lonely but never really sure of himself. He will at any time, because he is that sort of a man, meet any danger, since he thinks that is what he was created for, and because he knows the corruption of his country can only be cured by men who are determined if necessary to sacrifice themselves to cure it. He doesn't talk or behave like an idealist, but I think he is one at heart; and I think that he rather hates to admit it, even to himself. I have written practically nothing about his sex life because I thought it was his own business, but I did in my last book break down a little. It is impossible to think that such a man would not have a sex life, but so many writers of this sort of story have made it too blatant and too vulgar. Since I am just about finished with the mystery story, I think I may confess that Philip Marlowe, unlike myself (he is not me, of course), would get almost any woman into bed with him by a certain obscure technique which depends almost entirely on making a woman feel that you respect her, that you never make any cheap gestures or suggestions, that you never—or almost never—touch her until you know. Ask your wife if I am right. Women always know so much more about these things than men.

    I suppose that a man who was married for almost 31 years to a woman he adored becomes in a sense a lover of all women, and is forever seeking, even though he does not know it, for something he has lost. You can never cheapen a woman. No man of my sort thinks of her exactly as she thinks of herself. After all, her body is to

1. Reference is to television adaptation of Marlowe material.

[452]

her a familiar thing; but to some men it is always a sort of shrine. Women are very subtle in these things. For hundreds and hundreds of years, they had to please men with their looks, their charm, etc. Inevitably it must have left somewhere in their minds a deep intelligence about sex, because once that was all they had.

Some of this had to go into Philip Marlowe if he is to be any good. Otherwise, he would be just another sharp-talking nobody. If it is not possible to achieve this, I think we should forget the whole thing. After all, a great many writers have been trying to steal him from me for 15 years or more, and they have never made it yet. I suppose all writers are crazy, but if they are any good, I believe they have a terrible honesty.

Yours,

TO MRS. DOROTHY BEACH[1]

6925 Neptune Place
La Jolla, California
June 3, 1957

Dear Mrs. Beach:
Thank you for your letter. I have no quarrel with Mr. Rene MacColl personally, but if he is pro-American, I am a two-headed chimpanzee. I was interviewed by him in the spring of 1955, and I think I am entitled to my personal impression of him. I am not a "great gentleman," kind as you are to say so. I am merely an ordinary American. If you count me on a par with Erle Stanley Gardner and Rex Stout, I am very sorry. I count myself far above them. This will prove to you that I am not a gentleman at all.

I entirely agree with you that understanding between Britain and America is vastly important to the future of the world, but of

---

1. A correspondent replying to Chandler's public letter on Rene MacColl.

course as one man I cannot achieve it. I can only resent things that seem to me to damage it.

Yours very truly,

Raymond Chandler

TO HELGA GREENE

6925 Neptune Place
July 11th. 1957

Darling Helga:

.   .   .

I think it would be impossible for me to live here. I am not surrounded by old friends, because in order to have friends you have to cultivate them and for years I almost never went out at night and never had anyone to the house. Also the sort of people one would expect to know are a stupid lot whose lives centre around the Beach and Tennis Club. You probably have exactly the same sort of people in England, but in London you can find others. Here there are no others. The furniture is a nightmare. The only thing to do with it is for me to get out and let someone sell it piece by piece on commission. I have over fifty cartons and a dozen barrels. I have so many clothes that the closets in both bedrooms won't hold them, nor all the drawers in all the chests. I have suits that I had forgotten, shirts beyond any possible need, underwear for all seasons, and about 18 pairs of shoes. Good God!

.   .   .

Love, love, love

Ray

[454]

TO DEIRDRE GARTRELL

6925 Neptune Place
La Jolla, California
July 25, 1957

Darling Deirdre:

.　　　　.　　　　.

It seems that I have a serious anaemic condition. Not fatal, but quite
serious. These diagnoses never make much impression on me, since I
have lived my whole life on the edge of nothing. Once you have
had to lead a platoon into direct machine-gun fire, nothing is ever the
same again.

.　　　　.　　　　.

I don't quite know why you are so close to my heart, but you
are. In some mysterious way you have put me inside of you, so
that I have to lie awake at night and worry about you—you a girl I
have not even seen. It must sound ridiculous to you. All I can say is
that in some strange way you have become a part of me, so that I
wake in the night and wonder what is Deirdre thinking or doing, is
she making a fool of herself with some nice but stupid man, and
if she is what can I do about it? All very silly, but there is a certain
devotion in it also, entirely because of your letters. I have had
thousands of letters, and I suppose I have written thousands. A
collection of my letters is to be published when I can weed them out.
But that is not the point. Why should I take Deirdre into my heart
when hundreds of charming people made no impression on me at all
deeply?
    The older you get, the less you know.

.　　　　.　　　　.

With all my love,

Ray

[455]

TO HELGA GREENE

6925 Neptune Place
La Jolla, California
Sept. 20, 1957

Helga Darling:

.   .   .

I haven't seen the *New Yorker* for months, just got tired of it. So I did not see the Angus Wilson story. I tried to read his fairly recent novel, but it didn't hold me. Like all people of his sort, however clever, he doesn't create his characters, he describes them. But I think I may have become a bit crotchety from loneliness, worry, illness and physical suffering. My ideas of what constitutes good writing are increasingly rebellious. I may even end up echoing Henry Ford's verdict on history, and saying to unlistening ears: "Literature is bunk." In the meantime, I don't think I should passionately care for either *The Last Angry Man*[1] or the one on the other side of the sheet you so kindly sent me. You are an agent, you have to keep abreast. I may satisfy myself with *Richard II* or a crime novel and tell all the fancy boys to go to hell, all the subtle-subtle ones that they did us a service by exposing the truth that subtlety is only a technique, and a weak technique at that; all the stream-of-consciousness ladies and gents, mostly the former, that you can split a hair fourteen ways from the deuce, but what you've got left isn't even a hair; all the editorial novelists that they should go back to school and stay there until they can make a story come alive with nothing but dialogue and concrete description: oh, we'll allow them one chapter of set-piece writing per book, even two, but no more; and finally all the clever-clever darlings with the fluty voices that cleverness, like perhaps strawberries, is a perishable commodity. The things that last—or should—I admit they sometimes miss—come from deeper levels of a writer's being, and the particular form used to frame them has very little to do with their value. The test of a writer

1. By Gerald Green, 1957

is whether you want to read him again years after he should by the rules be dated.

.   .   .

Much, much love,

Ray

6926 Neptune Place
La Jolla, California
Oct. 20th. 1957

Helga Darling:

.   .   .

    I don't know how many times I have taken the Marlowe story out and looked at it and put it away again with a sigh, knowing all too well that my heart was too sad to let me capture the mood and gusto and impudence which is essential to that sort of writing.[1] Perhaps you can help me out of it. It seems that I cannot learn to stand loneliness, and that is another reason why I dread Paris.[2] But perhaps we can talk of these things when you are here.

With all my love,

Ray

TO WESLEY HARTLEY[1]

Dec 3rd., 1957

Dear Mr. Hartley,
    My most humble apologies for not answering your letter much

---

1. *Playback.*
2. Chandler was thinking of living in France for tax reasons.

---

1. California schoolmaster who had sent questions to Chandler.

[457]

sooner. I had a rather bad virus sore throat, and on November 20th. I came down to Palm Springs with an English lady who is my agent for everything but Motion Picture stuff, if any (I don't much want to work in Hollywood), and TV.[2] This needs an American specialist. I've had three American agents, not counting Hollywood and the good ones do a good job in America, and their English opposite numbers are all right, except that they are careless about translation rights, don't really know who the best foreign language publishers are, and practically always use a local agent. Also they are careless about watching performance dates and payment dates. My agent, who speaks three languages fluently, can make deals directly on a ten percent to me instead of the usual 20 per cent. She is also brilliant and beautiful.

I was educated at Dulwich College, an English Public School, not quite on a level with Eton and Harrow from a social point of view, but very good educationally. In my time they had two "sides," a Modern Side intended mostly for boys who expected to go into some sort of business, and a Classical Side for those who took Latin and Greek and expected to go to Oxford or Cambridge. I went up the Modern Side to the top and then switched down to the lowest form (class) in the senior school on the Classical side. I went up that to the form next to the Sixth, the top form. You usually stay in the Remove, as they call it, for a year before being sent on to the Sixth. I left school at seventeen—the usual leaving age then was before one's twentieth birthday, which was compulsory, I mean one had to leave before the 20th. birthday.

After this I had six months each in Paris and Germany. In Paris at school and in Germany with a private tutor. I could speak German well enough then to be taken for a German, but not now, alas, and the language has changed a lot (but I don't think the Germans will ever change). French one never speaks well enough to satisfy a Frenchman. Il sait se faire comprendre is about as far as they will go. Or Il parle très bien le français, mais (a shrug) l'accent—horrible!

Now to answer your questions. College or university education is definitely not necessary, provided one learns anything in high school and only real students do. I have a nephew, really my dead wife's nephew, who was graduated from Fairfax High in L.A., and he

2. Helga Greene.

didn't know a bloody thing. In his last year he took an elective course in music appreciation and he knows as much about music and has as little interest in it as a horned toad. He said the seniors he knew talked of nothing much but sports and dates and girls, that some of them were secretly married, and many were having affairs all over the place. The same went for the girls, except that they substituted primping for sports.

You could tell your lively students, and I realize they must be of a very different type, that although I did a lot of writing as a young man in London (some publicity or jacket blurb writers have called me English, but I was born in Chicago of a British mother and an American father from a Pennsylvania Quaker family), but I couldn't write fiction to save my life. I couldn't get a character in or out of a room, I couldn't even get his hat off. I learned to write fiction by a method which I have recommended to other young struggling writers I tried to help, but no soap. Everything they did had to be for sale. What I did was take a novelette, I think it was by Gardner, and make a detailed synopsis of it. From this synopsis I wrote the story, then compared it with the original to see where he, Gardner, had got an effect and I had got nothing. I did this over and over again with the same story. I think I did learn a great deal that way. My first novelette for the *Black Mask* took me five months to write, and I got $180 for it. Another device I used, especially for the pulp field, was to write a straight story and then rewrite so that it *seemed*, just seemed, like something else. I concentrated on the detective story because it was a popular form and I thought the right and lucky man might finally make it into literature. My books are so considered in England and most of Europe. The Germans and Italians are a little inclined to look down their noses at this sort of fiction. The Germans are a rather stupid type of intellectual snobs, in spite of their language having a magnificent slang. Only the French and ourselves equal or surpass it. The Italians seem to want either tragic stories in which everyone is dirty, never has any decent clothes or money, and every one is rude to every one else; or else novels in which the hero spends practically all of his time in bed with some woman. Some years ago some girl wrote for *Esquire* an article called "Latins Are Lousy Lovers." It gave great offense and the issue was even banned in Cuba. But I happen to know that she was absolutely right. Latins talk a great game and make a rather dignified parade of love-making, but in the actual result the Northern nations and ourselves have them beat to a frazzle.

At the moment I can't think of much else to tell you. I am finishing up my seventh Marlowe story. It is not a very big production for a mystery writer, of course, but I take a great deal of trouble and am not naturally prolific. I do very little pencil or pen revising. If a scene seems wrong to me, I throw it away. I know that what was good in it, if anything, will stay with me when I rewrite it. I probably write ten thousand words for every thousand that get published. Early in 1958 I am going to England to try to write plays. There are forty active theatres in London and if the producers like a play, they will keep it on until the public has a chance to react. The critics in England are far less influential than the New York critics. The English are an old and wise and well-balanced people, and they don't seem to care a hoot in hell that some high-powered reviewer, so he thinks, doesn't get hysterical with delight over something the public comes to regard favorably. Often it takes a little time, and the English producers will as a rule give it time. Also, scalping is illegal in England. All an agency may charge is a quite reasonable service charge. In addition to all this, the Continent of Europe with its hundreds and hundreds of state-supported theatres, is always screaming for new plays.

That doesn't mean I'm giving up Marlowe. I'm far too fond of him. Apart from Marlowe, I have turned to poetry again. The *Atlantic* took a thing called "Requiem" from me—it hasn't yet appeared— and I have just finished a sequence of three sonnets in the classical manner which my agent thinks are very good. I wrote two devastating articles about Hollywood in the *Atlantic* and the writers, not the best of them told me I was through, and one of the trade papers which is dishonest (its reviews can be bought) printed that "Chandler was on a slow march to the guillotine." As a matter of fact, I made far more money after these articles than before. I also took the agents to pieces in an essay called "Ten Per Cent of Your Life." And I took the formal English detective story to pieces in another essay called "The Simple Art of Murder." My first agent was very annoyed with me because I didn't become "his top slick writer" to use his own phrase. I told him that a slick writer might die overnight because a magazine changed its policy, or changed editors and the new one didn't like some types of stories, or BECAUSE

[460]

A MAGAZINE, AS HAS ACTUALLY HAPPENED, PRINTS
FEWER STORIES AND MORE NON-FIction. (Sorry, the capitals
were not intended. I had the wrong key). I said it was my belief
that a writer should create his own public, if he could, even though
for a time he made far less money than he would get from the big
slicks. However, to be nice, I did write one story for the *Saturday
Evening Post* to please my agent.[3] They were very doubtful about
it at first—it got one NO, which rejects a story or did then, but the
Editor took it anyhow. They demanded extensive changes of all
sorts. I was still being nice so I made the changes. Then they printed
the story exactly as I had first written it, and for years they asked
me for more stories about the same character and simply could not
get it through their heads that he was a one-shot character, as he
was. Some of the best fun I had was writing a novelette which
lampooned my own kind of fiction.[4]

The great and difficult problem of the writer in our day—if he
wants to make a living—is to write something acceptable to the
public and yet at the same time write what he thinks is good writing.
A lot of big best sellers are very badly written. I am still getting
royalties on things written 25 years ago, so I do think I chose the
right way. Very few slick writers ever become good novelists.
Marquand did, although he has become a bit of a bore lately. I
finished *Yours Sincerely, Willis Wayde* by main force.[5] I think it is one
of the dullest books ever written.

If you have any questions, I'll try to answer them. I hope I
have not been boring or too egotistical. All successful writers, even
though they try to fight against it, inevitably become a little
egotistical. It is a lonely and uncertain life and however such success
you have had, you always start from scratch. So, I guess when you
achieve a certain amount of world-wide recognition, you inevitably
feel, "Well, I must be pretty good after all. It was a tough road,
and I haven't come to the end of it. But I've come a good long way
and perhaps I am entitled to give myself a pat on the back once
in a while."

Yours very truly,

3. "I'll Be Waiting."
4. "Pearls Are a Nuisance."
5. Title is actually *Sincerely, Willis Wayde.*

TO HELGA GREENE

6925 Neptune Place
La Jolla, California
Dec 4th. 1957

My Beloved Helga:

.   .   .

I thought Dwight Macdonald's piece on James Agee was piffling
compared with his slow and patient liquidation of *The Outsider*.[1] I
could only get half way through it. Perhaps I missed the best part.
(Why don't we do a book called A Child's Garden of Curses?) He
says: "Why are our (American) writers so much more at home with
children than with adults?" They're not. Very very few writers can
write effectively about children. Salinger, for example, can. Irwin
Shaw is not bad, but he doesn't quite get it. "The stained glass of the
L. and N. depot smoldered like an exhausted butterfly"[2] This is
Agee. He tried too hard and stuck his foot in his mouth. Anybody
seen an exhausted butterfly smoldering lately? The bit about the street
car, too long to quote, much admired by Macdonald, was a perfect
piece of pretentious and overstrained writing. "big drops, silent as a
held breath, and the only noise the flattering noise on leaves and
the slapped grass at the fall of each drop." More Agee. Macdonald
thinks this is magic. Make up your mind, Agee; was it silent as a
held breath or wasn't it? "All right, Mary I hate to go, but it can't be
avoided." Agee. "The last sentence, in rhythm and word choice,
seems to me perfect." Macdonald. What's the matter with the man?
About as perfect as, for example: "Why isn't dinner ready, Susan? I'm
so hungry I could eat the hind leg of a goat." It says what it says,
of course, but why rave about it? Would you rave about a sentence
like: "If we hurry, we may catch the next bus."?
　　　　Well, he read the book which is probably more than I could

1. Reviews in *The New Yorker* for November 16, 1957, and October 13, 1956. *The Outsider*
is by Colin Wilson.
2. Quotation from James Agee, *A Death in the Family*.

have done, because I loathe pretentious writing, and, after all, he got paid for it. Peace be unto him—and may he recover his mind.

.   .   .

I love you very dearly.

Ray

TO E. JACK NEUMAN

Harlow Haven
Palm Springs
Dec 9, 1957

Dear Jack:

.   .   .

To fill up the space a few of what I call my morning limericks, usually indecent.

A charming young lady of France
Had scorned my most careful advance
Till a sunny day
Made her feel very gay,
And I found she was wearing no pance.

A certain young charmer of Ghent
Was rather too clearly enceinte
When her father yelled: "Who??"
She replied with a coo:
"I don't know. He just came—and he went."

There once was a lady of Spain
Who regarded my love with disdain,
Till one night on champagne
She was feeling no pain,
And we did it again and again.

[463]

A lovely young charmer named Jean
Was dainty and tender and clean.
Her legs I adored,
But I always deplored
That I never could get in between.

Rather a single track mind, wouldn't you say. I make these up in a few seconds. I also write serious poetry at times.

R.

TO JESSICA TYNDALE

December 23rd., 1957

Darling Jessica:

.   .   .

Helga and I get along so perfectly that I am amazed. She seemed so aloof when I first knew her. We never quarrel, she takes everything in stride, and all is peace and happiness between us, as it never was with you know who. For reasons of her own life and temperament she doesn't want to get married again, and this is all right with me, as long as I can live close to her and go away with her.

.   .   .

I am flying to Palm Springs today to attend a very fancy party at the home of a rich woman to whom my doctor gave me an introduction. She begged me so hard to come that I finally gave in. She is a redhead (with assistance), about fifty, very easy to get along with and a fine dancer. I want to use her house in my next Marlowe story, which I plan to lay in Palm Springs, with Marlowe married to the 8 million dollar girl from *The Long Goodbye*. I think the struggle between them as to whether he is going to live her kind of life or his own might make a good sub-plot. Either she will give in, or the marriage will bust up. I don't know. But I do know that nobody, but nobody, is going to keep Marlowe from his shabby office and his unremunerative practice, his endurance, determination and his

[464]

sarcastic pity. She'll probably want to redo his office, but she won't get to first base with that either.

TO PAUL BROOKS

Harlow Haven
Palm Springs, California
Dec 28th 1957

Dear Paul:

.   .   .

By getting up at 6 A.M. and working 10 hours straight with no food but coffee and Scotch I finished the Marlowe book.[1] Haven't been over it yet but I think it will stand up. I plan to dictate the whole thing—as an experiment—from my rough draft. Helga should have it within a month unless I have made a mess of it somewhere. I don't really think so. I'll probably bring you a copy or two, but Helga is the boss.[2]

Love,

Ray

TO HELGA GREENE

6925 Neptune Place
La Jolla, California
January 7th. 1958

My Beloved One:

.   .   .

It was just like me to lose that piece that Robert Campigny (?)

1. *Playback.*
2. Helga Greene.

[465]

wrote in the Paris *Revue-Critique*, and also to lose the reply I had made to him, in the rough. I think I left them at the Ranch Club on Saturday night. On Friday night Jessie took me there and we had a very pleasant time. On Saturday I had a date with a tall and rather exquisite girl who is a waitress at the Doll House, but I don't think you ever saw her. I had noticed her several times, not so much for her looks, but for the way she carried herself and her swift exact movements. I knew at once that she must be a wonderful dancer, and I found out (through careful investigations) that she was. So one morning, when she happened to wait on me—her hours were very irregular—I asked her whether she would consider dining and dancing with me, and made it clear that I had no other intentions. She finally said she would think it over. This was very funny to me, as she obviously did not believe what I said. One night I was having dinner there alone and she ignored me completely until a certain man left, and then she came over to my table and was very nice, and slipped me her telephone number on a folded piece of paper. She said she was going to Las Vegas over the week-end, but would I call her when she returned. She didn't seem like a pickup at all, but I hardly expected her to be a virgin. She was very frank and told me that men made her all kinds of propositions and it was not easy for her to tell which were on the level and which were not. I said I had the same trouble with girls. They didn't seem to be able to believe that all I wanted was a dancing partner, and only a good one. I could tell she was very good indeed, just by watching her move.

So on Saturday last she was "available" and asked me to call for her at 8.30 P.M. This I did and found her dressed in a stunning white dress with plenty of cleavage. She put on a white fur wrap, which she certainly had not acquired as a waitress. Unfortunately, when we arrived at the Ranch Club, the joint was packed. I hadn't made a reservation because it had been so easy the night before. They offered me a table halfway into the kitchen which I promptly refused. We sat in the bar for a while, and then the hostess came and said they now had a good table for me. It proved to be quite a distance from the dance floor. I said I was used to a table at the edge of the dance floor, but I couldn't make it this time. I then said I should very much like to have the members of the band drop over to my table when they had time, as I had had a very pleasant experience with them the night before. They never came. The girl had a large

and healthy appetite and she told me a good deal about herself, .
more, really, than I wanted to know. She also called me "dear,"
which I didn't like too well, because it rather placed her. But she
behaved very nicely, held her liquor well, and looked really gorgeous.
We tried one dance, but it was impossible. No room to move. All
one could do was shuffle. At midnight we had enough and when they
came with the bill there was a further bill for drinks for the band. I
said: "What's this? I asked the boys over here for a drink of
champagne. As you can see, there is almost a full bottle left." "The
band had the drinks in the other room." I took the bill and tore it up.
"I'm sorry," I said, "But when I want to entertain my guests by
long distance, I'll let you know." They went away and after a
moment or two the head man of the band appeared and was very
apologetic and said there had been a mistake, and he was sorry, and
there would be no charge. The girl was quite amused. She said
they tried that sort of thing all the time, but very few people ever
called their hand. So we went back to her apartment. By this time I
think, but of course can't be sure, that she expected me to spend
the night with her. But I had no such intention and I rather think she
would have been a rather too practiced sleeping companion. At any
rate, she didn't let on, and we parted in front of her apartment with
excellent manners on both sides. It's rather sad about these girls,
although few of them have the looks and the style this one had. They
are so insecure and so vulnerable. She was 27 years old, had been
married and divorced, and with her looks, why was she still a
waitress? I suppose the only answer is that a girl in that position
thinks she is one day going to meet the right sort of man, but she
never does, because the right sort of man would never think of her as
anything but a waitress, unless, like me, he wanted to dance with
her and no more. And there are so few serious dancers.

But I have to admit that she never made the slightest attempt
to involve me in any way in anything I didn't want. The next
morning I called her up and asked her what colour roses she
preferred. She said: "Why should you send me roses?" I said: "When
a lady does me the honour to dine with me, I usually send her
roses." "Well, if you must—I like red ones," she said, and then she
burst into tears. "What's the matter? Have I offended you?" There
was a silence for a little while and then she said, "I guess, I'm just not
used to being treated this way. Usually—oh, the hell with it. What

[467]

can I say except thanks very much. Will I see you again?" "I'm afraid
not. I'm going back to La Jolla today, and in a little while to London.
I'm sorry about last night. I managed badly. I wanted very much to
dance with you, but I took you to the wrong place. So I guess this
is goodbye." Then she said a very strange thing. "I'm sorry we didn't
dance. But what can you do more for a girl than what you did?"

．　　　　．　　　　．

I'd better stop now, or I'll be writing another lousy sonnet, and
with 16 lines yet.

Ray

TO BERGEN EVANS

January 18th 1958

Dear Sir:
    I happened (and by this I don't imply that I feel superior to
TV, but only that the time is unusual for me, as I am usually working
then) to see part of your programme today.[1] I was particularly
interested because I am an admirer of Mr. Peter Ustinov, and we have
mutual friends in London. I barely missed a dinner party at the house
of my publisher, Hamish Hamilton, at which Mr. Ustinov was to be
present.
    If my memory is not at fault, and if there are no technical
reasons which I do not understand, then I confess to being puzzled by
your panel's attitude to the phrase, which I hope I quote correctly,
"All and everyone of the Persians drank their sherbet."
    As I remember it, the discussion, rather brief, turned on
sherbet. Sherbet can be a fairly solid thing which one eats with a
spoon, or in other parts of the world a liquid. No one, so far as I
remember, made what seemed to me the two essential points. The use
of "everyone" is quite incorrect, and "each and everyone," even *if*

1. The linguist conducted a television show called *The Last Word*.

[468]

correct, does not make a plural phrase. I know that it is far too easy to become puristic, or even pedantic, in these manners, and I, as an experimenter in the American vernacular, am perhaps not supposed to know anything about literary language. It so happens that I know a very great deal.

If the sentence had read: "Each and all of the Persians, etc." the sentence should have continued, "drank his or her sherbet." This assumes that the context does not make it clear that all were men. The sentence could also have read: "Each and every Persian," and would still have taken a singular verb. Mr. Ustinov made an amiable attempt to indicate that this was a compound phrase, but others of your panel were so busy showing off their learning, that he received little attention.

As for "He didn't go to the ball game on account of he was in bed with a virus sore throat,"—I'm making this up, but the point is not altered, this is an outright vulgarism.

I can't say that our language will not tolerate such locutions in the end. Once you let the bars down, you may as well forget that rules exist. But rules are not made by grammarians; they are recognized by grammarians. During the depression of the thirties, when Will Rogers was writing a daily column, it seems that some Bostonian type objected to his use of "ain't." His answer was, "A lot of people that ain't sayin' ain't, ain't eatin'."

If that's how you make a language which can be accurate, vital, elegant, colorful and imaginative, I quit. If a lot of moronic halfwits are to decide what is right or wrong (I'm not thinking of Rogers, who was a charming man), I quit twice. We have an educational system which is the laughing stock of the world. It will remain so as long as it is under the control of political appointees. We are nice people, but in some ways insufferably stupid. Of course the boy or girl who really wants an education will get it under any system. And there will always be those who cannot be educated, because (or on account of) there is no foundation on which to build. These exist everywhere, but however meaningless the pass degree at Oxford or Cambridge, at least a certain standard of polite behavior seems to go with it.

I don't really know why I am writing this. I have a hundred things to do which are more important to me personally. Perhaps I have more love for our superb language than I could ever possibly

[469]

express. Perhaps I don't like fools. Perhaps I don't like the theory that anything may become correct if enough halfwits insist on making it current. Much of our slang comes from such people; they do have their moments. But I hardly think that gives them the right to be arbiters.

There is an old story about us Americans which, to the right mind, tells a great deal. At a fork in the road there are two signs. One said, TO A CONCERT OF THE MUSIC OF BACH. The other said, TO A LECTURE ON THE MUSIC OF BACH. Guess which way the Americans went.

Sincerely,

TO JESSICA TYNDALE

6925 Neptune Place
La Jolla, California
February 3rd. 1958

My Sweet and Adorable Jessica:

Please pardon the effusiveness, but since I finished the goddam book I have been a little nutty. Tomorrow my copyist will go to work on the final copy. You know, if it hadn't been for Helga, I'd never have finished the damn book. She arouses my mind and my ambition by some strange quality in her own mind. She makes me want to conquer the earth, which of course I shan't do, but wanting do it is a lot different from my lackadaisical attitude of the past few years. There are many sweet and adorable women in the world, and you are one of the sweetest and most adorable, but there is some sort of chemistry between Helga and me that gives me a driving impulse. With Helga around I feel as though I could write anything— sonnets, love poems, idiocies, plays, novels, even cookbooks. What on earth happened between this rather cool, aloof woman and me? Something very strange. She has built for herself an oasis into which no one may intrude. I don't know why—whether it is an escape from a too domineering father, or a refuge from the pain of a lost

[470]

marriage. But I'd never intrude upon it; it's something she has to have, and I think she knows I would never try to intrude upon it, and that this knowledge brings us closer together, rather than creating a barrier. I don't believe in this day and age that any man should have the right to invade the privacy of a woman, however fond of her he may be. With me Helga will always be safe; she will never for an instant have to fear that I should try to take from her anything that belongs to her. But that is not exactly why I am writing in this fashion. It is what she does to me as a writer that I find so amazing. And I don't know how she does it, nor even that she makes the slightest attempt to do it. In fact, I am sure she does not. But somehow, just by the way she talks and acts, by her simplicity, her lack of pettiness, the keenness of her mind, she inspires me. And she does it without trying to. She is much more valuable to me as an agent and a friend than I could possibly be to her as a client.

·　　　　·　　　　·

With much love to both

Ray

TO ROBERT CAMPIGNY

February 7th. 1958

Cher Robert Campigny:

La Pièce que vous avez dernièrement écrit dans La *Revue-Critique*, sous la titre 'Raymond Chandler et le Roman Policier' m'a parvenu de la part de mon éditeur a Londres, and mon ami depuis longtemps, M. Hamish Hamilton, and aussi de la part de Mme. Helga Greene, qui est ce qu'en anglais on appelle 'my literary agent'. Je ne suis pas trop sûr du mot précis en francais.

Il va sans dire que j'ai eu grand plaisir en lisant ce que vous avez écrit, et je vous remercie plus que beaucoup pour l'honneur que vous m'avez fait en écrivant avec tant de soin sur une espèce de literature qui is souvent regardé comme peu de chose. Naturellement,

[471]

je ne sais pas écrire en francais avec la netteté de style que vous possédez. Mais ce que dis, c'est moi tout seul qui le dit.

Il n'est guère probable ni même à désirer que l'écrivain de romans soit toujours d'accord avec les opinions exprimées par l'écrivain-critique. Ce dernier doit créer quelque chose qui lui appartient, qui a une valeur unique, qui possède une vrai raison d'être. Au même temps je me trouve forcé de vous agréer sans reculement que le roman policier américain du genre 'hardboiled' peut bien devenir un cliché de style aussi ennuyant que ces petits tours de force anglais, sur lesquels j'ai écrit des mots pas trop pleins d'admiration.

Je trouve votre louange de Agatha Christie un peu difficile à engloutir. Sans principe sérieux, it est très mauvais goût de déprécier ses livres seulement parceque je les trouve sans intérêt pour moi, mais l'idée que Madame Christie dejoue ses lecteurs sans farce me parait presque impossible à croyer. N'est ce pas qu'elle fait ses surprises en détruisant le portrait d'une caractère ou d'un personnage de roman qu'elle a jusque qu'à ce moment peintu en couleurs complétement opposées au portrait fini? Tout cela est sans aucune vrai importance, sans doute, et les lecteurs qui a besoin d'être taquinés par cette espèce de mystère ne se donnent la peine d'être faché si le mystère existe seulement parceque ces autres sont trop paresseux de faire l'effort de penser.

Tout ce que j'ai écrit ici n'est guère autre chose qu'une manière de vous rendre mes égards. Rien de cela nous vous échappe—j'en suis bien sûr. L'écrivain de métier a du apprendre depuis longtemps que les jugements de l'écrivain-critique—souvent, sinon toujours tres justes—ne sont pas le témoignage décisif. C'est plutôt l'espace qu'une publication d'importance a donné au critique pour presenter ses idées au grand public.

Agréez, mon cher M. Campigny,
mes salutations les plus amicales.

Raymond Chandler[1]

1. Translation:

Dear Robert Campigny:
    The piece you wrote recently in the "Revue Critique," entitled "Raymond Chandler and the Detective Novel," reached me from the office of my London publisher, my longtime friend, Mr. Hamish Hamilton, and also from Mrs. Helga Greene, who is what is called in English "my literary agent." I am not quite sure of the correct word in French.

[472]

TO MAURICE GUINNESS

February 10th., 1958

Dear Maurice:

Your letter charmed me completely and I should not have been so slow in answering it, but I really have had a rather stringent life lately. Finally, mostly due to Helga, I finished a book, and mostly due to you I left Marlowe in a situation where he could be married—but it was not certain. I hope I picked the right woman. It seems to me, from my point of view as a writer, that there would be nothing in his marrying just a nice girl. But if he married, or almost married, a woman whose ideas about how to live were completely antagonistic to his, even though in shall we say, the boudoir, they met on very equal and satisfactory terms, there would be a struggle of personalities and ideas of life which would make a good sub-plot. I plan my next Marlowe story with a background of Palm Springs, *Poodle Springs* I call it, because every third elegant creature you see has at least one poodle. I have the very house in which Linda Loring might care to

---

It goes without saying that I took great pleasure in reading your work and I thank you very much indeed for the honor you have given me in writing with such care on a kind of literature which is often considered insignificant. Of course, I cannot write in French with your precision of style, but what I say is said by me alone.

It is scarcely probable nor even desirable that the novelist should always agree with the critic. The latter must create something that belongs to him alone, that has a unique value, and that possesses a true *raison d'être*. At the same time, I am forced to agree with you without much reservation that the American detective novel of the "hard-boiled" type can certainly become a stylistic cliché as boring as those little English *tours de force*, about which I have written unadmiringly.

I find your praise of Agatha Christie a little hard to swallow. Without serious consideration, it is in bad taste to denigrate her books simply because I find them without interest, but the idea that Mrs. Christie baffles her readers without trickery seems almost impossible for me to believe. Isn't it true that she creates her surprises by destroying the portrait of a character or of a person in a novel whom she has up to this point depicted in colors completely opposed to the finished portrait? All this is doubtlessly without great importance, and readers who need to be teased by this sort of mystery do not take the trouble to become angry if the mystery exists only because others are too lazy to make the effort to think.

All that I have written here is merely a way of sending you my regards. None of this will escape you, I am certain. The professional writer has had to learn early on that the judgments of the critic—often, if not always, correct—are not the definitive word: It is rather the space that an important publication grants a critic to present his ideas to the public.

Sincerely yours

[473]

live. The house is in La Jolla. It has the sort of offhand elegance and virtuosity which was once fairly usual in England among the upper classes. The people who live in it are clearly rich, but their enormous drawing room, or living room as we call it, escapes that air of having been done by an expensive decorator. It is full of things which I feel sure are priceless, but are treated in the most casual way. It has the largest oriental rug on the floor that I have ever seen. It has space and warmth. You sit in the room and you know that everything in it cost the earth, and you feel perfectly comfortable and at ease. I haven't known many genuine aristocrats in my life, naturally, but the real ones all have a certain way, not only of behaving with perfect ease in any situation, but of being able to impart this ease to others.

·   ·   ·

In most of the activities by which a man or woman makes money, there is a loser. I don't say this is wrong—living at all is a pretty competitive affair. But when a writer writes a book, he takes nothing from anyone. He adds to what exists, he does not deprive anyone for his own sake. There are writers, of course, and I have known them, who say to me: "Why do you help him? Are you creating competition for yourself?" I think this is a very narrow view. It is quite possible, of course, that if the *Saturday Evening Post* could publish four stories and yours or my story was the cause of their rejecting another, we might *appear* to be in competition with the other writer. But actually we are only in competition with a standard. If his story had been very good, instead of merely acceptable, the magazine would have taken it, and found a place for it. There is never enough good writing to go around.

·   ·   ·

You make light of your accident in rock-climbing, but it must have been rather awful just the same. And I do realise how depressing it must be to find oneself on retirement from a position of responsibility, importance, and affection. Retiring is a kind of dying. The best way to revive is certainly what you have in mind. Work like hell at something just a little creative. No man grows old as long as he can create. You may die in the midst of it—so may I, who am older than you are—but you don't die of lethargy. I hesitate even

[474]

to suggest that I might be of any help to you other than as a man who has faced the same problems and understands them, but if it should ever occur to you that I could be of help, surely you would not hesitate to allow me that honour.

.   .   .

Ray

TO LUCIANO LUCANIA[1]

21st March, 1958

Caro Signor Lucania,

I am an American author, not a journalist, not connected with any newspaper. I shall be in Naples shortly and should greatly appreciate the favour of an interview with you and the purpose of this interview would be solely the attempt one man to understand another and would be in no way under any circumstances to smear you.

I suppose we are both sinners in the sight of the Lord and it is quite possible that you have not been represented to the public in my country as you really are. I am aware that it is not what a man does, but what it is made to appear in court which decides.

I myself run a certain danger in this because a sympathetic interview with you might possibly make trouble for me, but I am willing to face this danger because the object of my life is to understand people, their motives, their origins, how they become what they are and not ever to judge them.

Some of my questions to you may be rather brutal, but if you decline to answer them, there will be no record that they have been asked. There will be nothing published by me which you do not say, but of course, I cannot be responsible for editorial comment.

I am sincere and I would like you to believe so, but I imagine

1. Lucania, known as "Lucky Luciano" was living in Naples, having been deported from the United States for criminal activities. Chandler interviewed Lucania and wrote a sympathetic article called "My Friend Luco" for the *Sunday Times* of London, but it was never published.

[475]

that it is now very difficult to believe that anyone would approach you sincerely.

If you are receptible to my request, would you kindly reply on this prepaid telegram, to the Ritz Hotel, since I do not yet know at which hotel in Naples I shall be staying.

Raymond Chandler

TO LUTHER NICHOLS

[September 1958]

Answers.[1]

1. Yes, I think the hardboiled dick is still the reigning hero, but there is getting to be rather too many of him. The principal challenger is, I think, the novel of pure suspense. The best of these seem to be written by women. There is an occasional very good detective story written almost in classic form, such as *Last Seen Wearing* by Hillary Waugh, but there are not enough of these to be a threat.

2. I wouldn't call any writer psychoneurotic. We're all crazy to some extent. It's a hard lonely life in which you are never sure of anything. Spillane is perhaps an extreme example of the sadistic writer, but I may be wrong. I can't read him.

3. My best offer [to explain its popularity] is that the detective story (I prefer the term mystery story myself—detective story suggests a type to me) is a completely integrated thing if it is any good; most novels are sloppy by comparison. It has the elements of tragedy without being tragic, and the elements of heroism without being heroic. It is a dream world which may be entered and left at will, and it leaves no scars.

4. No effect whatsoever [on actual crime] except that a man contemplating murder might pick up an idea of how to do it and escape afterwards. But the crime was already there.

1. Answers to questions from Nichols and written on form provided. Most of the questions are self-explanatory. The nature of others is indicated in brackets.

[476]

5. A decline of the hardboiled story on the basis of Gresham's law [is the trend]. They are too numerous, too violent, and too sexy in too blatant a way. Not one in fifty is written with any sense of style or economy. They are supposed to be what the reader wants. Good writers write what *they* want and make the reader like it. The hard-hitting story will not die completely but it will have to become more civilized. The mystery story in some form will never die in the foreseeable future.

6. I don't worry about reviewers. I've had it both ways, and that is how it should be. Some are stupid, even vicious, but so are some writers. My comment on mystery fiction in general is that I wish more people could write it as well as it can be written. It *can* be literature, you know. In Europe, especially in England, they recognize that.

TO HELGA GREENE

824 Prospect Street
La Jolla, California
October 1, 1958

Helga My Sweet One:

.   .   .

My short story, if you tell me to write it (I'll probably write it anyhow, because the problem is attractive) is about a man who tried to get out of the Syndicate organization, but he knew too much, and he got a tip that a couple of pros were being sent to wipe him out.[1] He has no one to turn to for help, so he goes to Marlowe. The problem is what can Marlowe do without getting in front of the guns himself. I have some ideas and I think the story would be fun to write. Needless to say, if the killers fail, others will take care of them. You don't fail the syndicate and go on living. The discipline is strict and severe, and mistakes are simply not tolerated. The only syndicate boss who was ever convicted of murder was Lepke

1. The story was called "The Pencil" and was actually written.

Buchhalter, at one time head of Murder Inc. in Brooklyn and head of a 'protection' racket in New York. I don't know how they got him, but he and one of his top men did finally go to the chair. They put [Frank] Costello in prison for a while and they may still be after him, but they won't get far, I should think. These boys all have good business fronts and very clever, although crooked, lawyers. Stop the lawyers and you stop the Syndicate, but the Bar Associations are simply not interested.

.   .   .

Ray

TO ROGER MACHELL

824 Prospect
La Jolla, California
October 14th. 1958

My Dear Roger:

.   .   .

My next book is to be laid in Palm Springs with Marlowe having a rather tough time getting along with his wife's ideas of how to live. He loves her and they are beautifully matched in bed, but there is trouble looming. She won't like it that he insists on sticking to his own business and modest way of life, and she fills an overdecorated and rather chi-chi house with freeloaders, even if the damn house (of which I have a detailed description) is only rented for the Palm Springs winter season. I don't know whether the marriage will last or whether he will walk out of it or get bounced. Of course I have to have a murder and some violence and some trouble with the cops. Marlowe wouldn't be Marlowe, if he could really get along with policemen.

.   .   .

Love,

Ray

[478]

TO WILBUR SMITH

824 Prospect
La Jolla
October 16th. 1958

Dear Mr. Smith:

You are quite wrong. Marriage will not be the end of
Marlowe, but will in fact provide a sub-plot.[1] It will be a running
fight interspersed with amorous interludes. Marlowe, a poor but
sincere man, in spite of his tendency to crack wise, will hate Linda's
style of living, he will hate the house she has rented for the season in
Palm Springs, an over-decorated job of which I have an exact
description. He will detest the bunch of freeloaders who are about all
you can find for party guests. She on her side will never understand
why he insists on sticking to a dangerous and poorly-paid profession.
I think they will only completely agree in bed.

I haven't the main, or murder, plot yet. *Playback* was fifth on
the bestseller list in England, the last I heard—it's probably off by
now, but I doubt that it will make any best seller lists in this country.

Yours sincerely,

Raymond Chandler

TO FRANK NORMAN

824 Prospect
La Jolla, California
October 16th. 1958

Dear Frank:

.   .   .

I haven't finished *Bang To Rights*[1] yet, but it stands up

1. Chandler envisioned Marlowe as being married to Linda Loring, a character from *The
Long Goodbye*.

1. Norman's book was about prison life in England and was derived from the author's
own experience.

well. . . . A real life story may easily lack the dramatic climax one has to contrive in fiction. The quality called suspense has to be in all fiction, although it may be got in various ways. The reader has to be made to want to know what is going to happen next. Life doesn't always give you this.

Helga has written to me that you had a story in *Vogue* and an article on slang somewhere. I am so glad to hear about it. How is the book going—what are the sales, as far as you know? Don't hesitate to demand the information from the publishers, since it is vitally important to you. I think your description of the attitude of a man in prison, forbidden to be himself, deprived of his own personality on the surface and condemned to a continuous false facade—I think you do all this very well, and it is remarkable that you kept a sense of humour. Very much to be admired. There is good sound sense about the effect or non-effect of prisons in the book too.

I'll write to you again after a while. Please let me know how things go with you. I know Helga is very anxious to help you in any way she can. No one who knows you would think of you as a natural wrongo, but a man can be driven to desperate things by persecution or hopelessness.

Yours always,

Ray

TO HELGA GREENE

October 22nd. 1958

Helga My Darling:

.　　　.　　　.

Don't mess around with writers as clients who don't sell anything to make it worth your while. I've always had a sneaking idea that a professional failure was always a moral failure. There are writers who look the situation squarely in the face and decide that they are willing to be poor if they can write well enough to satisfy their souls. I respect them, but a lack of appreciation is narrowing. Henry James felt it. It tends to make a writer exaggerate the very things that keep the public away from him. I am not a mercenary writer, but I do feel that in this tangled generation a writer who cannot face the rather cynical realities of his trade is lacking in more than popularity.

As for your Angry Young Men, it's natural in every generation to have them. But if they don't grow out of it they are immature. Shaw said, as you will remember, "If a man is not a Socialist at twenty, he is lacking in heart. If he is one after thirty, he is lacking in brains." Rather extreme, like so many of his statements, but it has a point.

.   .   .

Ray

TO CATHERINE BARTH[1]

524 Prospect St.
La Jolla, California
February 7, 1959

Dear Miss Barth:
I spoke to you on the telephone to thank you for the great honor the Mystery Writers of America have done me; but that does not seem quite enough—especially as the real work has to be done by the Executive Vice-President, Herbert Brean, and the Executive Committee, who seem to do all the work and get none of the praise.

I am sure you realize that I take this honor as a token of a long career, and that I do not take it very personally. I wish it could mean more to the Mystery Writers of America. I feel very humble about this, but I suppose there must be reasons why I have been chosen, even if these reasons are obscure to me. After all, most of my life has been spent in trying to make something out of the mystery

1.   Barth was Executive Secretary of the Mystery Writers of America; Chandler was elected President of the organization.

[481]

story—perhaps a little more than it was intended to be—but I am not at all sure that I have succeeded.

I am enclosing a couple of pieces which might possibly be of interest to you; if they are not, I shall not be in the least hurt if you deposit them in the wastepaper basket. I do not feel that we have made enough progress in promoting the dignity of the mystery story. I am sure every effort has been made, but somehow it seems always to end in frustration. This may be due to the fact that the organization does not have enough money at its disposal. My experiences in Hollywood proved to me that you have to be very tough to get anywhere, that this toughness may be resented at first, but that in the end it will be accepted if it is backed up by a logical attitude.

Now of course we face television, which is sometimes good but always poisoned by bad commercials. Therefore, I feel that as the titular head of an incomparable organization, I should make some effort to make our mutual endeavor seem as important as it really is. How to go about this requires assistance of other brains than mine. Mine, such as they are, are always at your disposal; but mine alone are not enough.

I have reached a stage in my career where I have nothing to fear. Probably I shall get worse; possibly I shall get better. I have a feeling that hard-cover publication has become in this country rather silly; that you give too much away, and that the question of prestige is no longer important, since one already has it.

I feel that any sort of discussion on these subjects would be something in which I should be vitally interested, and in which I should if possible desire to be of assistance.

Yours cordially,

TO MAURICE GUINNESS[1]

Feb. 21, 1959

.   .   .

I think I may have misunderstood your desire that Marlowe

1. Reprinted from a transcript.

should get married. I think I may have picked the wrong girl. But as a matter of fact, a fellow of Marlowe's type shouldn't get married, because he is a lonely man, a poor man, a dangerous man, and yet a sympathetic man, and somehow none of this goes with marriage.
I think he will always have a fairly shabby office, a lonely house, a number of affairs, but no permanent connection. I think he will always be awakened at some inconvenient hour by some inconvenient person to do some inconvenient job. It seems to me that that is his destiny—possibly not the best destiny in the world, but it belongs to him. No one will ever beat him, because by his nature he is unbeatable. No one will ever make him rich, because he is destined to be poor. But somehow, I think he would not have it otherwise, and therefore I feel that your idea that he should be married, even to a very nice girl, is quite out of character. I see him always in a lonely street, in lonely rooms, puzzled but never quite defeated.

Index

Chandler, Raymond (*continued*)
Messick, Juanita; writing for *Black Mask*, 64, 127, 459; denies Marlowe is himself, 66; royalties, 72, 74, 415, 461; refused to write introduction for Shaw's anthology, 74; on *New Yorker*, 77, 366; as screenwriter, 77–78, 89, 90, 94, 95, 97, 101–2, 121, 138, 179, 222–24, 231, 233–34, 237, 295, 298, 344–45, 435, 442–43; advice/help to writers, 83, 88, 166, 258–59, 278–79, 306–7, 432–33, 458–59, 474, as screen writer: suspended, 62–63; on Marquand, 84, 157; on writers, 88, 123, 148, 164, 220, 261, 289, 292–93, 370, 476, 480–81; on first drafts, 87–88; on tragedy, 89; reading public of, 90; on Sandburg, 91; on Bible, 93; on detectives, 93–94; on films, 93–94, 97–99, 110, 139–40, 148, 168–69, 276, 311–12; on book clubs, 94; on reprint and subsidiary rights, 94; radio program, 95, 117, 127, 132–33, 144, 153, 155, 175–76, 188, 337, 362; on critical magazines, 96; on cleverness, 96, 234–35; on criticism of his works, 97; on Barzun, 99; personal characteristics, 103, 238, 324; on manners, 103–4, 418; on O'Neill, 106; on Orwell, 106; on Committee on Un-American Activities, 106–8; on Doyle, 110, 159; does not want to write short stories, 111–12; prestige, 112; writing ambitions, 112; on translations, 119–20, 192, 341–42; on plots, 122, 246–47; changes publishers, 123–24, 343; depression, fatigue, 125, 146, 292, 300, 315, 319, 325, 345–46, 348, 350–51, 394, 405, 408–9, 411, 457; on plagiarism, 125–27, 332–34, 352; on World War II, 131–32; on U.S. justice and financial systems, 140–41; on Cozzens, 142; projected trips to Europe, 143, 144–45, 146, 206–7, 293, 375, 380–81, 382–83, 387; personal life and problems, 146–47, 291–92, 299–300, 359–60; on mystery story as literature, 149, 181, 386–87; on War Crime Trials, 149, 307–8; on mystery writers, 152, 224, 238, 364; method of learning to work, working, 154–55, 459; dislikes publicity, 155, 214; rejects Mystery

Guild offer, 169, 172–74; on Sayers, 169–70; value in his works not as mysteries, 169–70; something in his literary life repels him, 171–72; financial and tax matters, 173, 233–34, 281–84, 292, 345, 348, 350, 416, 433, 460; use of the mystery medium, 173–74; ethics, 177–78; refuses Mystery Book Club offer, 178–79; book promotion, 179, 198, 257–58; loses ambition and ideas, 180–81; rejects screenplay offer, 182; on homosexuality, 184–85, 420–21; on English politics, 185–86, 189–90, 307; literary reputation, 186, 254, 318, 320, 355, 359, 388–89, 415–16; on his short stories, 187; on Greek language, 192–93; on Communists, 193; on mystery story, 194, 196, 204, 277, 290, 314–15, 472, 473n1; on writing mystery story, 194–95; *Newsweek* cover story project, 198, 359; on successful books, 199; on British reviewing, 201; reaction to invitation to join P.E.N., 202; on playwriting, 203–4; on Maugham, 205; receives inscribed copy of *Ashenden*, 208–9; on *Saturday Review of Literature*, 212–13; on unsolved crimes, 221; on A. Freeman, 225–26; on reviewers, reviewing, 226–28; on his slowing down with age, 228–30; on television, 232, 240–41, 256, 433–34; is asked to write article by *Flair*, 234–35; on Fitzgerald, 239; on radio, 240–41; screen credits, 243, 246, 247, 345; on amateur detective character, 246–47; entertains Priestley in California, 259–60, 262, 303; on Priestley, 265–66; on Adelaide Bartlett case, 262–64; on socialism, 265–66; on Kefauver committee hearings, 266–67; should write straight novel, 277, 353; diary entries on works in progress, 281–84; on schools, 287, 351–52; at dude ranch, 287–88; never feels important as a writer, 292; on character of fictional detective, 297; on style, 300–1; on alcoholism, 302, 393–94; drinking, sober, 303, 392–94, 396n2, 400–1, 408, 409; on length of books, 306–7; rejects request to do film publicity, 313; on his cooking, 313–14; self-doubt, 315–16;

112–14, 134–35, 202–3, 292, 472, 473n*1*; English, 90, 160, 381, 460; *see also* Reviews
Crofts, Freeman Wills, 109, 225, 226
Cronin, A. J., 123
Crossman, Richard, 190
"Curtain, The" (RC), 281

Daily Express (London), 34; letter to editor of, 449–50
Daily Sketch (newspaper), 375, 388
Dain Curse, The (Hammett), 5n*3*
Dannay, Frederic: letter to, 284–85
Dark Crusade (Fox), 356n*1*
Davis, Norbert, 68, 167
Day, Clarence, 153
Dear Brutus, 57
Dear Ruth, 57
Death in the Family, A (Agee), 462n*2*
"Decline and Fall of the Detective Story, The" (Maugham), 211n*1*, 255n*1*
de Havilland, Olivia, 312n*3*
Delacroix, Eugene, 327, 341–42
Delay in the Sun (Thorne), 355
De Leon, Jean: letters to, 419–22, 438–40
DeMille, Cecil B., 134, 277–78
Dennis, Nigel, 195
De Pachmann, Vladimir, 360
Detective(s): character, 93–94, 195, 246–47, 272, 297; real-life, 294
Detective story, 5–6, 26–27, 29, 70, 99–100, 109–10, 190, 260–61, 322–23, 327, 476; "tough guy" school of, 13n*3*; honesty in, 16–17, 225–26; technique in, 19; hard-boiled, 67–68, 125–26, 285, 472 (473n*1*), 476, 477; as literature, 69–70, 285, 459; sales of, 74; *see also* Mystery story
DeVoto, Bernard, 36, 59, 92, 114
Dial magazine, 96
Dickens, Charles, 9, 69, 122, 150
Dime Detective Magazine, 68n*4*
Dinner at Antoine's (Keyes), 199
Disenchanted, The (Schulberg), 239n*1*
Divine, Father, 439
Dixon, Campbell, 328
Doctors, 424–27
Dostoevski, Fëdor M., 293
Double Indemnity (film), 28, 126, 237
Double Take (Huggins), 125, 126

Douglas, Lord Alfred, 34, 171, 249
Doyle, Sir Arthur Conan, 110, 159, 225, 415
Dozier, William, 176
Dreiser, Theodore, 311n*1*
Dryer, B. V., 173n*3*
Duhamel, Marcel, 401
Dulwich College, 15, 36n*2*, 49, 138, 168, 235, 251, 307n*1*, 351n*1*, 458
Dumas, Alexandre *père*, 9, 47, 69
Dust jackets, 51–52, 279–80, 412–13
Dyson (clergyman), 262–64

Edge of Doom (Brady), 182
Eisenhower, Dwight D., 131
Eliot, T. S., 40, 261, 305, 337
Ellery Queen magazine, 254n*1*
Ellis, Ruth, 391, 407
Enemies of Promise (Connolly), 184
England, 12, 143, 400; RC's projected trip to, 143, 144–45, 146; politics, 185–86, 189–90, 307; *see also* London
"English Summer, An" (RC), 445–46, 449n*1*, 451
Engstead, John, 49n*1*
Esquire, 3, 234–35, 459
Essay writing, 347
Etter, William K., Jr., 1n*1*
Euripides, 261
Evans, Bergen: letter to, 468–70
Evening Standard: letter to editor, 388, 391

Fadiman, Clifton, 69
Fair, A. A., *see* Gardner, Erle Stanley
Famous American Trials, 128
Fantastic stories, 296, 372, 401
"Farewell, My Hollywood" (RC), 148n*1*
Farewell, My Lovely, 10n*1*, 18n*1*, 22, 80–81, 89, 156, 165, 166, 192, 281, 282, 366; sales, 47
Farnol, Jeffrey, 34, 171n*3*
Farrell, James T., 56n*2*
Faulkner, William, 12, 30, 201, 293
Fearing, Kenneth, 152n*2*
Festival (Priestley), 307
Fiction, 59, 60, 72, 84–85, 290, 480; *see also* Detective story; Mystery story
Fields, Gracie, 267–68
Films, filmmaking, 139–40, 148, 168–69, 223–24, 276, 311–12; ethics in, 63–64; mystery, 126

Filmwriters, *see* Screenwriters
"Finger Man" (RC), 187
First draft(s), 87–88
Fisher, Steve, 55n5, 78
Fitt, Ernest, 33, 41
Fitt, Harry, 46
Fitzgerald, F. Scott, 239
Flair magazine, 234
Flaubert, Gustave, 204n3, 293
Fleming, Ian: letters to, 396, 397–98
Fletcher, J. S., 13
Flynn, Errol, 114
Fontaine, Joan, 176
Fontemara (Silone), 201
Ford, Ford Madox, 356n2, 373n2
Ford, Henry, 309, 456
Forester, C. S., 288–89
Forster, Peter, 339
Fortnightly Intruder: letter to editor, 1–3
Fox, James M.: letter to, 356–58
Foy, Brian, 168n2
Francis, Frank, *see* Francis, J.
Francis, J., 327, 382; letter to, 322–23
Freak Show (Sanders), 363
Freeman, R. Austin, 99n3, 100, 109, 225–26, 285, 357
Fry, Christopher, 261
Full of Valor (Jackson), 184
Fuller, Maj. Gen. John Frederick Charles, 131–32

Galsworthy, John, 123, 205
Gardiner, Dorothy: letter to, 362–63
Gardner, Erle Stanley, 13, 32, 84, 165, 236, 432, 434, 459; letters to, 8–9, 19, 67–70, 73–74, 95, 100–1; RC on, 47, 68–70, 152, 161–62, 194, 453
Gartrell, Deirdre: letters to, 423–24, 429–31, 440–41, 446–47, 455
Gaskell, Philip: letter to, 344–45
Gaudy Night (Sayers), 291
Gault, William: letters to, 386–87, 411–12, 433–36
Gentleman's Agreement (film), 140
Gentry (Mr.), 267
Gertrude Stein (Sutherland), 305n1
Getting Married, 57
Gibbs, Wolcott, 57, 77
Gibbud, Mike: letter to, 141–42
Gielgud, Val, 328

Gilbert, Michael: letters to, 410–11, 417–18, 431–32
Ginsberg, Henry, 63
Gladwin, Peter, 366n1
Glyn, Elinor, 34
Go-Between, The, 367
Goetz, Bill, 176–77
Goldwyn, Samuel, 77, 78, 182
Graham, Billy, 439
Grant, Cary, 270
Grattan, C. Hartley, 33n1
Graves, Robert, 202n1
Great Humpty-Dumpty, The (Chaucer), *see New Humpty-Dumpty*
Greek language, 192–93
Green, Gerald, 456n1
Greene, Graham, 122n1, 124, 128
Greene, Helga, 392, 400, 435–36, 449, 458n2, 465, 471, 473, 480; letters to, 394, 398–99, 400–2, 406–7, 414, 418–19, 428–29, 438, 441–46, 451, 454, 456–57, 462–63, 465–68, 477–78, 480–81; compatibility with RC, 464; effect of, on RC, 470–71
Gropius (Mr.), 251
Groussard, Serge, 366n1
Guard of Honor (Cozzens), 142, 152, 157
Guinness, Maurice: letter to, 473–75, 482–83

Hack writers, 224
Haight, George, 138
Haines, William Wister, 84n1
Haldane, J. B. S., 92
Halsey, Margaret, 12
Hamilton, Hamish (Jamie), 119, 158, 160, 208, 253, 315, 316, 338, 356, 381, 382, 383–84, 412, 413, 468, 471; letters to, 44–45, 48–49, 60–62, 75–76, 80–81, 121–22, 124–25, 137, 144–45, 151–52, 155–56, 161–63, 170–72, 177–78, 180–81, 182–84, 194–95, 199, 201, 202–4, 204–5, 206–8, 216–18, 219–20, 222–24, 230–31, 254, 277–78, 287–90, 303–4, 341–42, 387–88, 399–400, 413; letters to: specially bound copies RC works, 202, 354–55; biographical information, 235–38, 248–51; letter to: Taki, 256–57; letters to: Priestley, 259–60, 265–66, 267–68; letters to:

[492]

194, 198; screen rights, 207; Italian
translation, 252–53
Lives of a Bengal Lancer (film), 168
Living Novel, The (Pritchett), 134
London, 320, 324, 326, 327, 330–31
Long, Huey, 186
Long Beat Home, The (Gladwin), 366
Long Goodbye, The (RC), 129–30,
295–96, 314–16, 318–19, 320, 325,
342n*1*, 344n*1*, 354, 359, 366, 370, 412,
464, 479n*1*
Loring, Linda (character, RC), 473–74,
479n*1*
Los Angeles, Calif., 215, 268, 354, 405.
See also Hollywood
Los Angeles Times, 4, 449
Lost Weekend, The (Jackson), 184n*3*
Love Is Eternity (Stone), 381
Lovell (Mr.): letter to, 355–56
Loves of Edwy (O'Neill), 356
Lucania, Luciano (Lucky Luciano): letter
to, 475–76

M., 57
MacArthur, Gen. Douglas, 131, 277
Macbeth, 89, 135
McBride, Mary Margaret, 181
MacCarthy, Desmond, 45, 90
McCarthy, Joseph, 360
McCarthy, Mary, 112, 113
McClung, Paul: letter to, 301–2
MacColl, Rene, 449–50, 453
McDermid, Finlay: letter to, 232–34
Macdonald, Dwight, 462
Macdonald, John D., 163n*1*
MacDonald, John Ross; *see* Millar,
Kenneth
Macdonald, Ross; *see* Millar, Kenneth
Machell, Roger, 329–30, 371, 400, 447;
letters to, 338–39, 343–44, 361–62,
364–66, 380–81, 382–86, 412–13, 478
McInness, Helen, 269
McNulty, John, 40
MacPherson, Aimee Semple, 439
Madame Bovary (Flaubert), 203, 204n*3*, 249
Madame de Pompadour (Mitford), 366, 367
Magazine, 111
Magazines, 7; slicks, 45, 86–87, 370–71,
460–61
Maltese Falcon, The (Hammett), 5n*3*, 54,
58, 80; film, 37, 93, 126

"Man Against Crime" (television
program), 242
"Mandarin's Jade" (RC), 281
Mannix, Edgar J., 138
Manstein, Erich von, 307
"Man Who Liked Dogs, The" (RC), 281
Marlowe, Philip (character, RC), 25–26,
30, 32, 41, 43–44, 61–62, 64, 66, 71,
75–76, 80, 90, 122, 153, 165, 166, 242,
322, 327, 353, 427, 449, 457, 460, 477;
radio series, 95, 117, 127, 132–33, 144,
153, 155, 175–76, 188, 337, 362;
character of, 197, 294, 452, 478, 483;
RC gives "facts" about, 270–74; change
in character of, 315, 317, 318;
adaptation for television, 452–53;
marriage (proposed), 464–65, 473, 478,
479, 483
Marquand, John P., 59, 84n*2*, 123, 157n*1*,
181, 195, 199, 205, 292, 461
Marsh, Ngaio, 174, 246
Marshall, Raymond. *See* Raymond, Rene
Marx, Groucho, 395
Mason, Perry (character, Gardner), 69,
70, 84, 101, 162
Massingham, H. J., 328
Masters, John, 404n*1*
Maugham, Somerset, 33, 203, 204n*3*, 232,
322, 327, 355, 367; RC on, 205; letters
to, 208–9, 210–11, 255–56, 276–77
Mauretania (ship), 320, 323, 325, 327–28,
381, 382, 387
Mayerling, 57
Mealand, Richard, 63
Memoirs of Hecate County (Wilson), 79, 238
Men and Brethren (Cozzens), 170
Men of Good Will (Romains), 57n*3*
Mercury, see American Mercury, The
Merimée, Prosper, 203, 209
Merrick, Leonard, 438
Messick, Juanita: letters to, 274–75,
299–301, 339–40, 345–50
MGM, 53, 54–55, 61, 138, 139n*1*, 233
Middleton, Richard, 249–50
Mildred Pierce (Cain), 28
Mill House Murder (Fletcher), 13n*2*
Millar, Kenneth, 163, 173n*2*, 343n*1*
Miller, Max, 13
Miller, Seton, 139
Mind of the Maker, The (Sayers), 336–37
Mischief (Armstrong), 284
Mitford, Nancy, 292, 366n*1*

[495]